The Black Utopians

The Black Utopians

Searching for Paradise and the Promised Land in America

AARON ROBERTSON

Farrar, Straus and Giroux
New York

Farrar, Straus and Giroux
120 Broadway, New York 10271

Printed in the United States of America
First edition, 2024

Portions of this book previously appeared, in slightly different form, in *The Point*.

Owing to limitations of space, all acknowledgments for permission to reprint previously published
and unpublished material can be found on page 383.

Illustration credits can be found on page 385.

Library of Congress Control Number: 2024008342
ISBN: 978-0-374-60498-1

Designed by Patrice Sheridan

Our books may be purchased in bulk for promotional, educational, or business use. Please contact
your local bookseller or the Macmillan Corporate and Premium Sales Department at
1-800-221-7945, extension 5442, or by email at MacmillanSpecialMarkets@macmillan.com.

www.fsgbooks.com
Follow us on social media at @fsgbooks

10 9 8 7 6 5 4 3 2 1

This is dedicated to the founders of Promise Land, Tennessee,
the founders of the Shrine of the Black Madonna,
and those who carry on their work

Contents

III.   The Land of Corn and Wine

AS A BOY IN CHURCH, I OFTEN SAT BESIDE MY MOTHER'S PARENTS. My grandfather was an organist and deacon. My grandmother was a choir singer and interpreter for the deaf. They were perfect models of restraint, and they taught me the fundamentals of worship. During service, I did not need to stand up to prove my love for the Most High, raise my hands, or lift my voice. So I didn't. My loyalty to God remained muted. On Sunday mornings, in song-filled sanctuaries, I began to harden myself against the music—hymns whose names I don't remember now. The spirit of my grandparents' religion has faded in me, and I am left to tell a handful of stories about doubt, lasting hope, and black people's attempts to find new frameworks for our lives after old ones have crumbled.

Again and again, I have fantasized about starting my life over. I have wanted to take on the qualities of people who seem sure of their convictions. This includes my father. We are alike in some ways, both pained by our distance from Promise Land, our ancestral home in middle Tennessee. For decades after Emancipation, this village was a safe harbor for black families. Many of the descendants moved north. My father and I never lived in Promise Land—we came from Detroit—but we both held it sacred. The site of this former freedom colony feels like a memorial now.

In my own family, migrations never seemed to stop. There have always been movements toward and away from one another. My father, once incarcerated, has been trying to restore the sense of cohesion that defined our extended family during both of our childhoods. He wants to mend what I have mostly chosen to mourn—fraying connections with the land, religion, and people who made us who we are. Why did some of us take an optimistic stance toward the future while others, shaped by similar forces, chose to reject it? When I began to write this book, I asked my father for a favor—to replace the letters he wrote me from prison. I had lost them. Would he send me new ones? Would he tell me who he could have been if he could start his life again, and who he was now that he couldn't?

The utopian imagines a bridge that spans the gap between lives. These lives may be easily differentiated—my father's, my own—or found within oneself, across time: the people we thought we might have been and the people we became. Here, in the mirror of my father's life and the lives of many others that, in some ways, resembled mine, I sought variations on a theme. Who were the dreamers who always wanted more than they had? How did the disillusioned, the betrayed, the confined, the forgotten, and the persecuted not merely hold on to life but expand its possibilities and preserve its beauty?

What does utopia look like in black?

The Black Utopians

LETTER I: LOVE, DOE

◇◇◇◇◇◇

I love you, son. I can probably spend two hours per day writing about my experiences in life and I hope that my words are a valuable contribution to your book.

We are in a time of tragedy in the world. I don't know how you are framing your story, but the world seems to be heading toward obvious tyranny of government. No matter what happens, I want you to know that you were born from God. God in Heaven is the only one who could have created you.

Over the past two years, I have studied virtually under a

pastor by the name of Stephen Darby of Destined Ministries on YouTube. He is a follower of Christ who has studied, prayed, battled wickedness in the spirit realm, and who is by all accounts full of the Holy Spirit. You may find some value by learning about him and looking at two or more of his messages on Negroland, and messages such as "Who Are We?" This pastor spoke about how only before the time of the coming of Christ, during tribulation, would a lost people find out who they are.

The Confederate church used to have celebrations of the lynching of dark people, yet they called themselves Christian.

—Dorian Robertson, June 2020

Introduction: Utopia in Black

◇◇◇◇◇◇

I'll decorate the deprivations.

—MARGO JEFFERSON

My father tends to imagine the future by first returning to the past. He tells me how he should have lived his life, how his children might have loved him more had he done this or that differently, married my mother, taken more trips as a child to be with his parents' families in Tennessee, or "gone right" instead of purchasing a gun twenty years ago and robbing a two-star hotel's front desk with it. After ten years of imprisonment, Dorian Robertson is a free man again, in search of renewal and community. He is tormented by hypotheticals—what beautiful things could have been, what reckonings may lie in wait. He and I have similar worries. Would it have been easier had we followed the well-trodden roads that had been laid out for us, leading to the double doors of a Baptist church?

Dorian and I often wonder about the cause of separations—between us, between individuals and groups, between people's ideals and whichever realities their lives afford them. We dream, too, of unity. How much can be repaired in the aftermath of damage? What if all our spiritual, emotional, and physical injuries were mended, our familial land and relationships restored? What if time's rifts could be sewn back together? Above all, what would it mean to live as though all of this were possible even if we suspect it is not?

By the early summer of 2020, I had been thinking about the meaning of utopia in African American history for more than a year. My father and I spoke on the phone about the allure of life abroad, a substitute, perhaps, for the radically different world we desired in the United States. Who in our family had passports in case we were no longer able to imagine a livable future here, my father asked. Would we be willing and ready to leave, to take our chances in Europe or in a country like Ghana? (We knew nothing about life there, but Ghana's Year of Return campaign in 2019 invited African Americans "home" to "resettle" and invest in its economy four hundred years after the first enslaved West Africans landed in Virginia.)

I had long since moved away from home in Michigan, but I'd temporarily returned from New York City at the onset of the pandemic to be closer to family. My father was living in Texas, near Dallas, with his fiancée. With little else to do besides sit in a camping chair in my mother's backyard, unable to guess what the coming days and months might bring, I had been calling family to ask about their hopes for the world to come as it was taking shape.

Dorian and I broached the subject of police and prison abolition.

He did not think that abolishing cops or prisons was wise. He wanted reformers to address racial disparities in sentencing guidelines. End-time chaos was coming, he believed, and the social fabric of the United States would continue to fray. The country didn't need abolitionists to hasten the process. "This period in history, it is said, is going to be like the Dark Ages," my father warned. "These are the last days of this society."

Whereas I once would have dismissed his worries as conspiratorial, I didn't have the evidence or will to argue against him. Something in me wanted my father's prophecies to be true. For the first time in my life, the near future was something I couldn't vividly imagine. The presumption that I would always recognize the world I lived in began to erode. There was a blankness where tomorrow should have been. George Floyd was dead, and I was certain that others would suffer his fate even in the new world everyone said was on its way. This has proven true repeatedly. I couldn't imagine a reality in which people like Floyd, Breonna Taylor, and Ahmaud Arbery wouldn't be killed, even as—amid so much death—there was talk of reparations, universal basic income, universal childcare, quieter cities, the return of nature, the resurgence of organized labor, the elimination of student debt, the reduction of child poverty, and a Green New Deal. The world, no matter how beautiful, would have certain brutal constants.

◇◇◇◇◇◇◇

If tomorrow brought with it the possibility of death, as I too often expected, my conception of the future needed to be transformed. The apparent persistence of abysmal realities for black people, and the certainty that there exists much more besides, is the soil from which black utopianism emerges. This tradition has encouraged black people to decide for ourselves how our inner resources can best be used to transform the outer world. It is an unceasing orientation toward the possibilities inherent in black social life.

Once the usual horizons we depend on to orient our daily lives blur, the utopian impulse to create new forms of living arises. Unfamiliarity and disruption are the point. Utopia points to the ways our attempted solutions to large-scale crises might bend further away from the worlds that produced these problems. In the utopia that is black, constant striving for wholesale societal transformation is imperative, not optional. The creative expressions of black utopianism aspire to a world in which the social, economic, and political restrictions that have historically been imposed on black people will not define their futures.

The urge to act out alternatives to the constrictive rhythms of our days lies at the heart of utopia. It is not necessarily a place, but an expression of faith that is sustained by the innumerable ways we could have led our lives and could still. Those who believe in utopia's power refuse to live as though any path has been foreclosed. It is an ongoing exchange between people, and so it is never achieved, attained, or finished. It is only rehearsed. Utopia always describes a crossroads, a perpetual opening.

◇◇◇◇◇◇

Years ago, when I first learned about the concept of utopia, I didn't think of heaven like any good Christian boy should. I thought of my paternal grandparents' ten-acre plot of land in the middle of Tennessee, in a historic all-black town called Promise Land. (I have always liked that it was not the more common *Promised* Land.) As a child who made pilgrimages there for many summers, I never thought of Promise Land as a perfect place. I complained about the August heat, the chattering cicadas, the ticks hiding in underbrush, the creep of lethargy, and the town's distance from a big city like Detroit, where I was born. Two weeks spent visiting extended family and wearing myself out from playing outside were usually enough for me.

I did not compare Promise Land, a ghost town for as long as I have known it, to a paradise like the Garden of Eden that I learned about in church. And yet as I grew older, it became clear to me that Promise

Land was the only comparable place I'd known. Before I could articulate why, I had the sense that *utopia* was the most satisfying word I could use to describe the hamlet where my family's recorded history in the United States began. Whenever I would describe Promise Land to others as a small, unincorporated town in the middle of nowhere, I said this with pride. Promise Land was negative space on most maps, a largely unknown haven that had been providing sustenance for black families, including my own, for 150 years.

It was founded five years after the Civil War ended, in 1870, when some of the earliest experiments in black self-rule were beginning. Its founding and longevity were unlikely. It could so easily have been forgotten had just one vigilante burned it down or had its early chroniclers kept the secret of its existence to themselves. As generations of Promise Land's caretakers came and went, so too did its meaning transform. A place that should not have survived according to the deadly racial logic of this country yielded many fruits. Promise Land carried the dreams of each person who had lived, played, communed, and retreated there. It usurped the role I was told heaven ought to play by offering refuge during a dark season of my childhood and, more recently, orienting my family toward the common goal of sustaining it.

Paradise has been a useful idea with many real-world consequences for black Americans. So has the trope of the Promised Land, a terrestrial place that may be within our reach. Few people have the same vision of what constitutes either Paradise or the Promised Land. The attempt to respect individual interpretations of what makes the beautiful life and discover together where they intersect is the project of utopia.

Inspired by my memories of Promise Land, I decided to write a broader narrative of black utopia. How has the meaning of utopia evolved since the creation of Promise Land and the hundreds of black-towns like it that were, for a time, some of the most tangible proofs of black survival and prosperity? I wanted to trace an emotional lineage that linked various displays of black dreaming—from freedom colonies and the flight of fugitives to hopes for a separate land and the creation of iconoclastic art.

◇◇◇◇◇◇◇

I didn't need to travel far to begin. Early in 2019, I was reading about the radical activism of African American Catholics during the Black Power period. I picked up *Black Priest, White Church* (1970), a critique of racism in the Catholic Church by the Harlem-based priest Lawrence Lucas. Lucas praised the example of a Detroit pastor named Albert Cleage, Jr. I hadn't heard of him. I thought I already knew the names of the city's historically black parish churches, but I had apparently overlooked Cleage's curious-sounding Shrine of the Black Madonna. I soon learned that the Shrine was not part of the Catholic Church at all, but rather the United Church of Christ, a Protestant denomination. It turned out that many "Movement" people and leftists in the 1960s knew of and admired Rev. Cleage. The Shrine also happened to be ten minutes away from where my father's parents once lived on Detroit's west side.

Under a different name, the Shrine began as a church in the 1950s that catered mostly to middle-class black Detroiters. It found a permanent home in an area of the city where black residents moved as Detroit was undergoing the nation's first major urban renewal program. The resulting dispossession of black Detroiters on the city's east side pushed many to the neighborhoods around the Shrine. This would eventually place the church at the geographical and ideological center of the 1967 summer uprising in the city.

Albert Cleage, Jr.'s leadership during and after the Detroit Rebellion—one of the most destructive urban uprisings of the 1960s—elevated his profile. He became one of the most famous representatives of black nationalism in the United States, and the Shrine was thereafter regarded as a black countercultural mecca. For decades to come, its members and collaborators would include mold-breaking black artists, historians, and politicians; territorial separatists who wanted to create an independent black republic within the borders of the United States; Black Hebrew Israelites who searched for new Zions abroad;

New Age theosophists; and many others who challenged familiar structures of authority.

For nearly thirty years, Cleage would lead a group of dedicated Pan-Africanists who established Shrines throughout the country, three of which survive today, in Detroit, Atlanta, and Houston. Among the Shrine's members were small cadres that traveled across America and raised millions of dollars to support the mission of their movement, which Cleage called Black Christian Nationalism (BCN). He envisioned Black Christian Nationalists as a prophetic vanguard that would secure the psychological liberation and material well-being of black people. First they would need to separate themselves from white society by establishing other communes and Shrines in cities around the world. They planned to recruit millions of black people to sustain their movement.

◇◇◇◇◇◇◇

Cleage was one of the most consequential figures associated with the twentieth century's black freedom movements and, for a time in the late 1960s, the best-known black nationalist pastor in the United States. He and the members of his church attempted to merge heaven and earth—Paradise and the Promised Land—for black people everywhere by invoking the dreamworlds of social visionaries from the past and present. Although Cleage disliked the word *utopian*—he preferred to be called a *black realist*—he was well-versed in many of the thinkers, groups, and movements that are now regularly identified as part of a broader utopian tradition. Black Christian Nationalists learned about the histories of ancient Jewish monastic communities, the spiritual practices of gurus and mystics, the rebellions of Haitian slaves and maroons who lived in the swamplands of the American South, experiments in socialism and communism, and much more.

Drawing on his brief experience as a social worker in Detroit, Cleage followed developments in the fields of psychology, sociology, education, and even physics to keep his movement in touch with the times. He used the black church as a base for his movement because, for centuries, it had given many African Americans the support they needed to survive, but he wasn't convinced that Christianity was the only lens through which to understand the world. White slave masters and fundamentalist politicians had long weaponized religion to protect their claims to authority. BCN was an approach to spiritual and civic life that rejected all methods of domination that sought to erode the willpower and self-regard of black people.

Cleage believed that religion could encourage the pursuit of moral ideals. He was also a notorious firebrand and provocateur who thought that black people should destroy inherited idols—starting with the white Christ and his mother—and replace them with models in their own image. The Shrine would officially become known as the Pan-African Orthodox Christian Church in 1976, taking a cue from Marcus Garvey's earlier Pan-African Orthodox Church and signaling the church's support of the African independence movements unfolding in the latter half of that decade. Cleage described Black Christian Nationalism as an apocalyptic movement; he vaguely outlined a coming "Pan-African revolt," which, if successful, could bring about universal justice on earth. Justice was understood as a power balance between whites and blacks that would allow black people to build and sustain their own parallel institutions, belief systems, and iconography without the threat of destruction from white people.

◇◇◇◇◇◇◇

One countercultural experiment in the Shrine caught my attention early on. In 2016, a Black Christian Nationalist bishop wrote an essay about an institution in the church called Mtoto House. Members also called it the Children's Community. It was a "communal child-rearing structure" that lasted from the early 1980s until the late 2000s. The only other information I could find about this model of communal living was a book by the woman who first led the Detroit Mtoto House, a former elementary school principal named Shelley McIntosh.

McIntosh wrote that Mtoto House was influenced by socialist preschools in the Soviet Union, rural literacy campaigns in Cuba, traditional family structures in West Africa, and, most directly, child-rearing customs in the kibbutzim of Israel. This last detail fascinated me. The kibbutzim, communally owned agricultural settlements, were the most ambitious efforts before the creation of Israel to establish a Zionist Promised Land on earth. As predecessors to the Jewish state, they were arguably the best-known, most influential, and longest-lasting manifestations of a small-scale, collective utopian project in the twentieth century.

Like the kibbutzniks, Black Christian Nationalists set out to acquire land of their own to sustain their people. In 1999, with money earned through years of donations and fundraisers, the Black Christian Nationalists purchased one of the largest black-owned rural tracts in the United States, a nearly 4,000-acre property in South Carolina that Cleage named Beulah Land. After Cleage's death, the Shrine members who survived him were soon stranded on either side of generational and ideological divides as the role of the black church in social movements and the usefulness of black separatism were increasingly called into question. To this day, Beulah Land remains the most ambitious of the Shrine's attempts to create an earthly paradise for black people. It is not yet the productive farm that Cleage hoped it would become, but its story is not over.

◇◇◇◇◇◇◇

Before coming across the Shrine's story, not once had I heard about a black nationalist commune in the heart of my native city. Detroit is a place whose name has become a shorthand for American dystopia, black despair, and the dead end of progress. The common assumption is that utopia and the people who seek it cannot thrive there. Images of empty homes and the remnants of car factories, schools, and churches draw more attention than black Detroiters' attempts to rewrite these stories and insist that wherever they live is perfectible, the shining center of the world.

Learning about Mtoto House spurred my attempt to understand why and how black Americans have searched for utopia, just as my family did in Promise Land a century and a half ago. Many of the individuals who I write about in this book lived through the revolutionary shifts of the 1960s and '70s. I wanted to speak to people who launched an ambitious social project that centered black people during those years, and who also lived to witness the Black Lives Matter movement.

The aging revolutionaries of the Black Christian Nationalist movement once considered themselves outside the mainstream of American culture, initially not by their own choice but because segregation and enforced alienation were the preferred tools of social control in this country, as they still are. I wanted to hear from the perennial optimists as well as the disenchanted who felt that the black revolutions of the late twentieth century failed. I spoke to their children and grandchildren—people whose ages roughly aligned with those of my parents and me—to get a glimpse of the lives my own family did not live, the alternative paths that were always there, but which for our own reasons we did not follow.

◇◇◇◇◇◇

When I set out to tell this story, I thought I might be like one of those inconspicuous narrators of old travelers' tales who are shipwrecked upon the shores of an impossible island, or who awaken to discover a strange world of which they can never fully be a part. There would always be some degree of safety in playing the curious outsider who becomes a chronicler, recording the origins, beliefs, and practices of an unfamiliar people—in this case, a self-identified, black "nation-within-a-nation." I told myself that I could enter and leave this world whenever I pleased. But the utopian tale is a ghostly reflection. It points to our own doppelgängers whose features are slightly askew yet always, at least faintly, recognizable.

Book I tells one of many possible stories about black utopian impulses from the period directly following the Civil War through the end of one black countercultural phase in the 1960s. This narrative is told mostly through the lives of two men: Albert Cleage, Jr., and the painter of his church's famed Black Madonna mural, Glanton

Dowdell. Cleage and Dowdell seemed to represent stark opposites—privileged and poor, meticulous and chaotic, an obsession with the needs of the spirit and a concern for those of the body—but their utopian aims and approaches were not incompatible, which became evident when they finally came together in the Shrine. Book II moves on to later developments in black utopian history, as Black Christian Nationalists helped keep its spirit alive throughout new phases of the counterculture, in the closing decades of the millennium. The first two books are intruded upon by the present, by my father's letters. Book III moves toward my own reckoning with what black utopians have lost and attained here on earth.

Echoes are everywhere. The historical drama of the Shrine finds resonance in my family's story, a minor chord that resounds throughout the book. My father's letters run in spiritual parallel to the life of Glanton Dowdell, himself a formerly incarcerated man who would find an unlikely sort of freedom far from home. Likewise, the fates of the thousands of acres that constitute Beulah Land and the few that my family still owns in Promise Land have not yet been written. What happens to these places, and thus the dreams they represent, may determine whether a church and a family remain intact.

I   The Furnace and the Forge

In this locality shortly after the Civil War, freed slaves established Promise Land, the first African American community of Dickson County. Early settlers were Nathan Bowen, Washington Vanleer, and two brothers, John and Arch Nesbitt. In time, the community encompassed about 1,000 acres, included 50 homes, several stores, two churches and a school. Although only the St. John Church and the schoolhouse remain, heirs of the original African American landowners still own much of the land.

—TENNESSEE HISTORICAL COMMISSION MARKER ON
PROMISE LAND ROAD

Better an errant path than the known world.

—SAIDIYA HARTMAN, *WAYWARD LIVES, BEAUTIFUL*
EXPERIMENTS

Promise Land

◇◇◇◇◇◇◇

I didn't go back to Promise Land for more than ten years after my paternal grandfather's death. I had convinced myself that there was nothing left for me there but memories too sweet to taste without him and perhaps a rushed moment of tribute beside a gravestone. I regretted missing the family Christmas in 2018—I don't remember my reasoning—and when I finally decided to return for one of our infrequent reunions, in 2019, sickness incapacitated me the day before my flight from New York, in a hot August. I had been in love and was so fearful I was falling out of it that I could barely expel urine from my body. I phoned my grandmother to weep and apologize. What I called self-sabotage she called the devil. She prayed, crying quietly along with me, and shared a scripture, Psalms 34:19: "Many are the afflictions of the righteous: but the LORD delivereth him out of them all." The pandemic would delay my homecoming for another three years.

A prodigal son's return is usually a celebratory affair, but I arrived alone in front of the old chalk-white schoolhouse and the St. John Church on Promise Land Road. Little seemed to have changed. There was the lonely tree beside St. John's, closed for needed renovations and still dealing with its rust-red, slowly deteriorating roof; the covered stage between the church and school with a couple of picnic tables on it; and beside the road, a tall pole with a wind-whipped American flag. Other additions I didn't recognize. When had the concrete sidewalk connecting the church and school been laid? I had never seen the trailer behind the school that now served as the town's community center.

I was waiting for Serina Gilbert, the seventy-seven-year-old board chair of the Promise Land Heritage Association and the woman who would give me a private tour of the community center and school, which now functioned as Promise Land's museum. I was glad for the tour even as my pride made me bristle at the need for it. I had seen a picture somewhere of Serina, whom I had always known as Cousin Kay, giving a presentation on Promise Land's history to white members of a motorcycle club. The image of rapt, leather-clad riders sitting on tiny benches in the schoolhouse's original central bay—the very seats that black kids once occupied seventy years prior—was both amusing and touching. I feared I would get the same rundown on the origins and changing fortunes of Promise Land. I would assure Kay that *yes, yes, I knew that already. I haven't forgotten.*

Kay was my late grandfather Ruffus's cousin. They grew up together and attended the Promise Land School in the 1940s and '50s, many decades before its kitchen and dining wing became a gift shop that sold T-shirts and colorful jewelry, home decor and other trinkets. In the 1980s, when Kay was a medical social worker at Howard University's Center for Sickle Cell Disease, she had studied the behavior of medical staff toward black men with the illness. When the Human Genome Project began in the 1990s, allowing researchers to map the genes that cause sickle cell anemia, Kay developed an interest in genealogy and her family's heritage. "You become who you are based on what you've gone through," she told me over the phone, months before my visit. Kay retired the year that her mother, Essie Vanleer, decided she would no longer leave Tennessee to visit her daughter in Maryland. She would miss Kay, but her church and friends were in Promise Land. Who knew how much time she had left? Kay surprised herself by selling her house and moving back to Promise Land to be with Essie, at the urging of the Holy Spirit.

For more than thirty years, Essie and Kay, descendants of some of Promise Land's original founders, did more than anyone else to preserve the town's history and establish its reputation as one of the oldest known settlements founded by formerly enslaved people in the country. As the longtime executive director of the Promise Land Heritage Association, from 2006 until 2019, Kay brought Promise Land to the attention of state universities, government agencies, and cultural institutes, as well as national museums. She helped get the Promise Land School (originally built in the 1880s) into the National Register of Historic Places. She is trying to do the same for the St. John Church.

As I photographed my surroundings, Kay pulled up in her van. I waited while she maneuvered her motorized wheelchair out the side. Her youthful eyes and serious gaze looked much as I remembered. Because her high voice had never lost its vigor, the only surprise was the grayness of her thinning hair. I had always interpreted her smiles upon seeing me as tentative blessings, each one an invitation to fully assume the role of my grandfather's heir and take a proper interest in our common inheritance—this land and its manifold meanings.

The generation of people who founded the Promise Land Community Club in the late 1980s and, later, the Heritage Association were aging and dying. Kay, not only the town's greatest advocate but also its most important historian, could not continue this work forever. She planned to write a memoir with the help of a professor at Tennessee

State University. In the meantime, she encouraged younger people with familial ties to Promise Land to keep the place alive. In a later email to me, she wondered if her daughter, an L.A.-based musician, and I would consider "exploring the development of a rural colony/retreat for artists/writers/musicians/performers," citing the example of the Woodstock Byrdcliffe Guild in New York, an Arts and Crafts utopian community founded in 1902. I liked the idea, but to this day I have deferred its execution.

◇◇◇◇◇◇

Two months before my return, a nonprofit called Next Leadership Development launched the Black Towns & Settlements: Foundation for the Future project, which included an interactive digital map of historic blacktowns in the United States and Canada. It was a noble effort, but not at all comprehensive, featuring around eighty communities. The project's creators estimated that there may have once been anywhere between 200 and 1,200 blacktowns and settlements that existed throughout North America. These places were usually founded by former slaves who had escaped plantations, purchased their own freedom, or fought for it during the Civil War.

The only entry for Tennessee was a place called Free Hill, a town 150 miles northeast of Promise Land, near the Kentucky border. Founded in 1816, Free Hill was an unincorporated community like Promise Land, and its original inhabitants were the ex-slaves of a North Carolina planter's daughter. Perhaps Free Hill made the cut because it still had a small number of residents. One could barely call Promise Land a "town" in good faith since only two of its buildings still stood—neither the school nor the church served their original purpose now—and no one lived there anymore. These days, most visitors to Promise Land come for its annual summer festival or sporadic family reunions.

After visiting the community center, which still had displays up from a 2020 traveling Smithsonian exhibition on changes in rural

America, Kay and I ended our short tour at the schoolhouse-museum. Assorted display cases contained pictures of long-dead Promise Land residents, including descendants of the Nesbitt brothers, the founding fathers John and Arch. Shelves carried items that would have typically been found in the homes of Promise Land's early settlers: stoneware pitchers, crocks, whiskey jugs, a kerosene lantern, an enamel coffeepot, a cast-iron pot and flatiron, washboards, a metal coal scuttle. When I realized they were only replicas, I felt somehow duped.

When we finished, Kay asked whether I'd read a book by the sociologist Elizabeth Rauh Bethel called *Promiseland: A Century of Life in a Negro Community* (1981). I had. It was the second time in two weeks that someone had mentioned it to me. The last instance was during my trip to South Carolina the week before, when I visited Beulah Land, the Shrine of the Black Madonna's farm. My research trips had taken an unorthodox route, ending where perhaps they should have begun, with my own family. I told myself at the time that this was intentional. How fitting it would be to enact my grandfather's favorite biblical parable, the Prodigal Son, by coming back to a place that never really belonged to me but which many relatives said would always be my birthright. I avoided confronting one of my fears at the time—that after years of reflection on black people's attempts to imagine greater worlds, I might arrive in Promise Land to find a place exhausted of potential.

With Bethel's book I thought I had found a rare historical account of my Promise Land. It focused instead on a blacktown in the South Carolina Piedmont called *Promised* Land. It was also established in 1870, the same year that Washington Vanleer, one of Kay's ancestors, made the first land purchase in Promise Land—14 acres for $10 apiece. Like the Tennessee hamlet, the South Carolina blacktown had a general store, a church, and a school that closed when the county it was in integrated following the decision in *Brown v. Board of Education*.

These kinds of places, Bethel wrote, "forged a settlement based on economic security, held together by pressures from the world beyond [their] boundaries as well as ties within the community." Promised

Land, SC, and Promise Land, TN, were "microcosm[s] of the many Negro communities where people have devised unique strategies for coping with their racially defined subordinate status." Each was "a case study of alternatives to self-hatred, retreat, and accommodation." What had Promise Land been? What would become of it?

◇◇◇◇◇◇◇

During my childhood summers in the early 2000s, my grandparents and I would drive from Detroit down through central Kentucky, somewhere in the Outer Bluegrass, on our way down home. Promise Land lies an hour west of Nashville in a hilly region where the earth is scalloped with ridges and impressed with river valleys. In sunlight, the sheer limestone bluffs that loom over middle Tennessee's highways look glossy and brittle enough for lotto players to scratch their dust off with dimes. My papa always drove, Granny prayed for our safe passage, and I drifted in and out of sleep, trying to draw our destination closer. Once we hit Louisville, I would often wake, yawn, and slump over again until my head was beneath the opposite window. I had stopped counting the hours behind us—*seven, eight*—to focus on the hours left—*three, two*.

Interstate 65 leads from Louisville to one of the northern boundaries of the massive Cumberland River Basin, where Kentucky meets Tennessee. Starting at its headwaters on a far flank of the Appalachians, the jagged, 700-mile-long river feints in and out of either state. Throughout the basin, water eroded the underlying rock over millennia to create photogenic accidents: networks of limestone caves and quarries, waterfalls and natural bridges, sinkholes and sinking streams.

Dickson County is forty miles west of Nashville. From Dickson proper, the city of fewer than 16,000 where my granny was born, we would cross into Charlotte, a town of fewer than 2,000. And to travel the three miles between Charlotte and Promise Land, we eased off State Highway 48 toward Promise Land Road. Granny and Papa— Bettie and Ruffus Robertson—had known each other for most of their lives. Granny was the eighth of eight children. Her father was a janitor at the movie theater in Dickson and ran the projector for 4 p.m. dime Western matinees. Granny's mother cleaned the theater with him and, while they worked, little Bettie sold wire coat hangers for pennies to the local dry cleaners.

She and Ruffus attended the same high school in Dickson. Ruffus was known as a handsome, charismatic athlete on the field and court. He was the kind of boy that girls like Bettie were supposed to notice, my grandmother told me. (Although Papa had a soft smile and sharp cheekbones that would travel down the family line for generations, Granny had eyes for some of his cousins before she ever had eyes for him.) They were married at the Charlotte courthouse on Christmas Eve 1960. It would be eight years before they moved with their two young daughters from Dickson to Detroit, at the tail end of the Great Migration, the day after Richard Nixon was elected. Openings in the auto industry were more attractive than the low-paying jobs my grandfather took in Nashville, where he had worked as a porter and a night-shift employee at a department store. In Detroit, Papa cut glass for Ford Motor Company. Granny worked as a telephone operator.

Although my grandparents would live in Detroit for more than forty years, the city initially struck Granny as a cold place where the rosebushes of her childhood did not bloom. Papa loved the city much more than his wife and daughters did, but everyone was happiest when a trip to Promise Land was approaching. I would not begin to understand how restorative these returns were for my grandparents until I was an adult. In my elementary school years, I was too preoccupied with escaping my mother's husband, a Christian deacon who said he received supernatural visions attesting to my evil. He vowed to stamp it out and did not, as Proverbs 13:24 says, "spareth the rod."

I fled south almost every summer for years, accepting any offer to join my grandparents for their two- or three-week trips. I savored the air and played with time, stretching it out by roasting in the sun, shooting plastic arrows at the sky and treetops, and watching *The Red Skelton Show* well past the hour when I should have gone to sleep. I did not mind attending Sunday services at St. John's either, where people living in the county would sometimes gather for worship. The god of Promise Land seemed to bear no relation to my stepfather's.

◇◇◇◇◇◇◇

Each time we neared my grandparents' forest-encircled homestead, a few minutes away from the church and school, I thought of the covered trampoline and basketball hoop I would find there. We stopped at a swinging gate on Promise Land Road that would have been easy to miss, blending as it did into a wall of trees, were it not for the prominent mailbox. Papa would get out to unlock the gate, retrieve months' worth of mail, and then drive us the rest of the way down a long and steep gravel incline. This dip brought us into an unchanging world. The drop opened onto a vista of Granny and Papa's simple white modular home in the distance, on a low hill. Dozens of giant trees and squat bushes were sparsely distributed across the wide property, which my grandfather had inherited from his late uncle.

While I was lost in my own reveries, Papa may have been imagining the faded running paths of his childhood. He and his little sister used to forge trails through the woods as they pretended to pluck blackberries for their mama's jam. When Papa was born in 1942, Dickson's newspaper was calling Promise Land "Charlotte's 'little Harlem.'" But Charlotte had many little Harlems, not least of which was the area "up on the hill," inside its own boundaries. This was a part of town where the Robertsons and many other black families gathered for the annual Charlotte Picnic. There was also Celeste Heights, east of Highway 48, and the Coaling on Old Metal Road, where an iron forge had been built and worked by slaves before the Civil War. One of the country's great basketball players, Oscar Robertson, was born in Daniel Town, off Highway 49 and Collier Bend Road.

The history of Promise Land is tied more immediately to mines and metals than cotton. The iron age of the Cumberland River Basin began during the final years of the eighteenth century, when the first white frontiersmen who settled west of the Appalachian Mountains needed tools. In 1788, North Carolina's Act to Encourage the Building of Iron Works incentivized the development of iron factories throughout the Southwest Territory, fueling the purchase of slaves to work them. When the Scots-Irish explorer James Robertson discovered extensive iron ore banks in middle Tennessee while surveying land claims for Revolutionary War veterans, there was no confusion about who most of the miners and smelters would be.

Robertson, an original settler of the river fort that would become Nashville, is known as the "father of Tennessee." The name of my earliest-known ancestor appeared in 1870, when the census began providing detailed information on African Americans. His name was Charlie Redden. He was my Papa's great-grandfather. The Robertson name didn't become part of the family until Papa's mother, Hattie Redden, married her husband Hersey. It is presumed that one of Hersey Robertson's ancestors was owned by one of James's lineal descendants.

James Robertson built the coal-fired Cumberland Furnace a few miles north of present-day Dickson in 1793. Ownership of the furnace changed twice over the next thirty years, and by 1840, at the peak of production in Tennessee's iron age, one quarter of slaves in Dickson County worked on one of the region's many iron plantations. The months it took to yield whole tons of high-grade iron were grueling. Slaves uncovered ore-rich veins that were sometimes hundreds of acres wide and dozens of feet deep, spread out under ridge crests or near weathered limestone beds. The enslaved blasted quarries with amadou and rifle powder. Some lived at coaling grounds in the woods as part of groups that chopped hemlock, wormwood, and willow trees. They tended charcoal kilns that resembled bishop miters and likely hoped for windless weather so that the charcoal would burn at the proper speed.

While some of Promise Land's families, like my own, took the surnames of ironmasters whose descendants owned their ancestors, others bore the names of the work their people did. Cumberland slaves were masons, boulder hewers, barrowers, waterwheel menders, tilt hammer tenders, and draymen who put out wagon fires when charcoal ignited in them. They were guttermen who prepared sand beds for molten metal, ringers who tapped congealed clinkers from the bottom of crucibles, and foundrymen like my forebear Charlie. In 1857, a financial panic led to inflated slave prices, hastening the decline of southern ironworks as plantation owners hired fewer enslaved people to work them. After early Union victories during the Civil War, some furnaces in the Cumberland Region were destroyed. Many blacks, finally freed, dispersed throughout the area.

A Church and a One-Room School

In 1870, the freedman Washington Vanleer made the earliest purchase in Promise Land. Nathan Bowen purchased ten acres in 1875. In 1880, the brothers John and Arch Nesbitt bought more than eighty acres with their war pensions. As a result of the Nesbitt brothers' purchases, the presence of iron mines that continued to employ poor blacks after Emancipation, and a nearby highway that made it easy for Promise Landers to take crops to market in Clarksville twenty-five miles away, greater numbers of black people began flowing into Promise Land starting in the 1880s. The land was more promising than anything the federal government would ever set aside. This is how some elders in my family believe Promise Land got its name.

The Nesbitt brothers had been born into bondage and were liberated by Union soldiers during the war. They were two of the estimated hundreds of thousands of blacks who had been freed, in defiance of the Fugitive Slave Act, and deemed "contraband of war" by the federal government. The term *contraband* described their unprecedented legal status as neither legally free nor in fact enslaved. The so-called contraband often joined one of the many Union encampments that sprouted throughout the punctured Confederacy, from the Freedmen's Colony of Roanoke Island, off the North Carolina coast, to Camp Nelson in Kentucky.

Not all the black-inhabited zones inside Union camps had names, but many did: Uniontown, Corinth, Grantville, Camp Ethiopia, New Africa. Other refugees fled into crowded and not always livable towns— places consisting of little else besides shoddy barracks and conical tents. Sometimes these shantytowns and bottomlands fell to ruin. Or they survived and became model "darky towns" in regions scarred by war or on the peripheries of cities. In Tennessee, Promise Land became one of these communities, a spacious refuge for black people in the countryside. Such places have been called blacktowns or settlements, Negro or freedom colonies, and freedmen's villages. They are rarely identified as utopias. Many are remembered as merely transitional spaces—precarious stopgaps that provided the basics of life until they were dismantled or more tempting opportunities arose elsewhere: better housing, better jobs, more avenues for political and social involvement.

There is another way of looking at the history of these blacktowns, however. A black utopian perspective places the seemingly provisional, expedient, and rudimentary at the center of any vision to create a better world. It is an outlook that clings to what tends to be discarded. It assumes the "darky town" that survived for generations with limited resources, which was created to provide for people who weren't allowed to thrive elsewhere, presents some kind of blueprint for a desirable future.

◇◇◇◇◇◇

Papa was born in a section of Promise Land known as Gilbert Town (named after Cousin Kay's great-grandfather, a respected landowner in the village). He and his six siblings lived in a cabin with their mother and stepdaddy, a perpetually suited, traveling Sanctified evangelist who could pursue a wasp through a church and smash it as he delivered the Word. Their outhouse was mercifully set apart from the drinking well out back. Potbellied stoves fed on wood in most rooms. My aunts remember visiting their grandmother as little girls and enjoying the white cotton bedspreads and handspun curtains. One described the cabin to me as if it had been a palace. She recalled its stove and sink, a roller-board washer and a rocking chair, the sweltering attic under a tin roof, and bed pallets for visiting children.

The cabin is no longer there. It was torn down in the 1970s, two decades before I was born. At the start of the twentieth century, there were some fifty black-owned homes in Promise Land. More than five hundred residents left between its boom time in the first third of the century and the mid-1970s, at which point no more than a dozen people remained. The families of Promise Land had once owned more than one thousand acres of farm and timberland among them. By 1976, fewer than one hundred acres were left among the four families still living in the area and various absentee owners. Nearly everyone else had moved to the Midwest to find work or join family, spread mainly across Ohio, Indiana, and Michigan.

Promise Land's peak, in the 1910s and '20s, was something to behold. It seemed to be a place of dustproof shoes and dustproof cars. Having no dolls to play with, young girls canned apples and pears right off the trees, plaited tall grass bunches as though they were hair, and Hula-Hooped Saturn rings around their hips. Those girls whose fathers were sharecroppers and whose mothers worked in white people's homes during the day sometimes joined the boys in fields of dark tobacco to remove suckers from the leaves and prepare the plants for the fire cure. Children sauntered along Highway 48, rolling fat tires down hills. Under the moon, they screamed and ran from ghosts that chased them home.

The adults knew how to celebrate. By the eve of the Second World War, Charlotte's Annual Negro Picnic was an established tradition on the third Friday in August. It was "an almost national affair with the colored race," the *Clarksville Leaf-Chronicle* reported. Cars bore license plates from North Carolina to New York. Just to savor one of a dozen barbecued hogs that were sold out by midafternoon, visitors arrived in Cadillacs, on horseback or in pickup beds, by foot, in mink or collarless long-sleeved shirts. The floral dresses, hair ribbons, and white gloves of young women deemed too northern were ridiculed by jealous appraisers. Pipes and unlit cigars bobbed from crooked, immaculate, and gold-plated teeth.

The people of Promise Land built everything. The handsome, spectacled carpenter Theo Edmondson put up one of the general stores, Papa's childhood cabin, other homes, and barns. Theo and the young women who made up the Promise Land Singers crooned that every day would be Sunday on the other side of the Jordan River and soon lambs would be fiercer than bears. Theo often sang to himself by cupping one hand over his mouth and another behind his ear, creating an echo chamber to magnify the sound. His voice earned praise and drew blacks and whites (who perhaps heard him and the girl singers on the radio) to stand outside St. John's, shut their eyes, and listen. *As I step on board I'll be leaving,* went a favorite of the Promise Land Singers, *all my heartaches and sorrows behind. I'll be safe with Jesus the Captain, sailing out on the old ship of Zion.*

Promise Landers built the school benches and the chimneys. They created everything but the tattered books and newspapers that came to the schoolhouse from Charlotte when white children or their parents no longer needed them. They built the school's elevated stage, on which Papa performed James Weldon Johnson's poems from *God's Trombones* as a child. This included the one in which the heavenly Father admits to feeling lonely and finds joy in a new activity: "I'll make me a world." God sees deep darkness and rolls light in his hands like dough. He ornaments the black with sun and stars. He spits the seas out, awakens fowl and fish, and on a riverbank, he kneels in red dust to shape clay. He leaves an opening in the clay and blows soul into it, creating an image that looks and behaves like Him. This black God molds a creature that participates in His own divinity. Both God and humankind experience the undying urge to keep on making.

Many of those who were not landowners in Promise Land worked on the farms or in the homes of whites that lived in the surrounding areas. Some of the children who grew up in the town at midcentury, like my grandfather, did not feel constrained by this outer ring of white-owned property. The trees were not strict color lines. The forests where children played hide-and-seek were not disputed territories. Promise Land's surviving elders attest that blacks and whites mostly kept to themselves beyond the formalities of housework and the crop-lien. Memories of interracial contact convey a miraculous sense of peace or, usually in the recollections of men, a subtly enforced truce. Once, when some white boys challenged the black boys to a footrace, they refused. Why poke at peace as it slept? Any tussles took place away from the girls. Some elders spoke with a slow drawl when telling me about racial enmity in Promise Land. It was as though I was asking them to recall a fantasy. They themselves had only heard about cross burnings and lynchings happening in other places.

Until the day the Promise Land School closed in the late 1950s, every teacher who had passed through the town had been black. When Papa, Kay, and their siblings went to school, the stalwart Ollie Hud-dleston, Promise Land's last teacher and the only one Papa knew for the first fourteen years of his life, hobbled around the room teaching the three Rs—reading, 'riting, 'rithmetic—and leading the 4-H pro-gram that taught agricultural, domestic, and vocational skills. If the Dickson County school system hadn't integrated in 1957, I wonder how long the Promise Land School would have stayed open, how long it would have been until Papa stepped out of that little one-room and saw how large some worlds were, how small others.

Whether or not Promise Land's immunity from white teachers felt like a miracle, it did not begin that way. This arrangement owed something to the steady rollback of Reconstruction-era legislation. In 1869, Tennessee Democrats repealed a common school law that had standardized public education for whites and blacks across the state. Thus, individual school districts and counties—including Dickson County, to which the Promise Land School's half-acre lot was deeded in 1899—were compelled to manage their own education systems. Promise Landers made the best of a situation intended to undermine them, which was true of so many other residents of postbellum freedom colonies like theirs. These communities often developed in response to limitations imposed by the Jim Crow system, which encompassed

segregationist laws, terror campaigns, and behavioral norms that reinforced the separate status of black people.

Having been denied equitable institutional support in all areas
of life because of their race, black utopians were those who sought to
address such neglect with counterinstitutions and protected spaces of
their own. Most crucially, black utopians believed that worldly depri-
vation was not the only possible fate awaiting them. Not all agreed on
whether they could fully change the world into something better. They
did agree, however, that the worst could, to some extent, be resisted
or delayed.

Cousin Kay told me that the aura of total harmony which surrounds memories of Promise Land may have been projected, at least
in part. Her father used to go into Charlotte to purchase the family's clothes. The children and their mother stayed behind. When they
needed new shoes, Kay's daddy put their feet on pieces of cardboard
and traced the shapes. He took the cardboard with him to the store
and matched the outlines with the shoes. This was common enough in
the South. What happened on the road between his departure and return was his secret. The children did not think to ask. Had they tried,
Kay's father likely would have told them what Granny used to say to
me every time I rifled through her jewelry box in her master bedroom
in Detroit, searching for coins and candies: "Quit meddling."

◇◇◇◇◇◇◇

As Promise Land declined in the last decades of the twentieth century,
much of the remaining acreage owned by black people was heirs' property. The original owners had died without producing a will, leaving no
instructions for their descendants or next of kin about what to do with
their estate. Legally, equal shares of this land were then automatically
split among surviving heirs, even if they were not aware of the fact. This
created an unstable situation in which black-owned land was perenni-
ally in danger of being seized by courts and sold at public auction due
to unpaid taxes. (How could a person pay taxes on land they did not
know they now legally owned?) It was also possible for heirs' property

to be forced out of a family because one or more of the tenants in common, aware of their fractional share, decided to sell the land's title to an outside party. Legally, one tenant alone with a tiny share could initiate the sale of an entire property. Often the third party they sold it to was a white landowner or developer.

The problems posed by heirs' property, which represents somewhere between one third and one half of all land owned by black people in the United States today, are legion. This legal arrangement has been one of the major contributors to black land loss over the last hundred years. As subsequent generations of tenants have children and die without writing wills, the number of heirs who may own equal shares of a single parcel increases. This often leaves people with a false sense that land which has been in their families or communities for generations will always be there, shared among the collective. But land that should, in theory, be the source of intergenerational wealth and dignity tends instead to become the fulcrum of bitter disputes.

Dreams need a place to roost, yet many forces have been marshaled against black-occupied spaces: not only the developers who initiate partition sales of heirs' property but also discriminatory banks, tax assessors, and administrators of the United States Department of Agriculture. Historically, lynch mobs and other agents of state-sanctioned violence posed obvious threats to the land and the people who lived on it. Struggles to acquire and preserve an earthly inheritance for black communities are often as spiritual as they are legal. The maintenance of communal property can be a conscious act of resistance against forces that threaten to tear some families apart.

What animates every story that follows is my interest in the ways black people have tried to stave off loneliness and alienation by finding common causes in the world or carving out private inner sanctums. How have black people, together and alone, created good places from the various nowheres to which they have been consigned for centuries—the darky town, the ghetto, the reform school, the itinerant camp, the segregated church, the former plantation site, the riot-scarred street, and, as in my father's case, the prison?

LETTER II: GENESIS

I came from a respectable family with no criminals in it. My father was a Detroit firefighter and an entrepreneur who originally began working at Ford. My mother worked her entire career for BellSouth, then Michigan Bell, then whoever bought them out.

I had no place in prison. I had been at the Mound Road Correctional Facility for five years. As I sat alone at a steel table in the dining hall, with steel seats bolted to the concrete floor, I prayed that God would separate me from trouble. I wasn't what you would call a very flavorful person. I didn't tell jokes. All I did was read legal books, type, do push-ups, work out, and exist. So, no one sitting with me made sense. I'd never been anyone's favorite, but that day it was pronounced.

I'd asked my son's mother to come and visit me, but she wouldn't. She didn't respond to me. It was the result of me not treating her correctly. In the first two years of knowing Cindy, the tone for our future was set. I should have married her. We had a hard beginning, but I took all the blame for that. That was what I carried daily—missing the family that I was supposed to have. Decisions that went the opposite of where they should have gone led to an empty, painful, shallow life. We could have had a family, been complete, raised Aaron together, and had four other children like we had planned. I'd been carrying that pain, masking it. Even after all these years, nothing has healed.

When I met Cindy, I didn't know the value of courting a woman, saving money for marriage, choosing to only love that one woman for eternity and, most importantly, building love without wounding her. Instead, I went ahead with lust. She was beautiful and I was an unskilled thinker. If I had gotten to know Cindy, we would have established the basis for a family.

In 2002, my journey to prison began. I had lost my job. For several years, Cindy struggled to keep a distance between us while collecting child support. Our relationship had no hope of healing. There were no conversations between us, no matter how many times I tried. The stress of constant negativity grew into something that would take freedom away from me.

Life has events and it also has atmosphere. It wasn't the events that set me on a path of destruction as much as it was the atmosphere. I had the constant feeling that nothing could be made right. Everyone in my life seemed to have become someone who didn't like me. My entire life became about the conflict between Cindy and me. In the years after my son was born, in 1994, it became clear that no healing was going to happen between us. I managed to keep living. I went on dates. I eventually married a woman named Kelly.

I began looking for a way out of misery. I was sitting in my apartment at Wayne State University, reading a sales paper from a grocery store. I said something to my wife about what was in the paper and then decided that we should eat dinner. It was our habit to eat unhealthy, so our options were either the White Castle on Michigan Avenue or the Ram's Horn out in Warren, a suburb of Detroit. It's odd how choices are made, but that day

I wanted to eat healthy. When we got to the corner of our street, I took a left to Ram's Horn. Taking that left would initiate a series of similar events. My wife would soon be left, my son would be left, my daughter would be left. My life may have been very different had I gone right, off Hancock.

I pulled into the lot and parked the van right outside the kitchen in the back. I told my wife to wait in the van since it would only take a moment. When I got to the front door, I told the hostess I was there to pick up my food. As I spoke to her, I looked behind me into the parking lot. I saw an assault. Three white boys chased a Middle Eastern guy and were attempting to catch and assault him. The Middle Eastern guy was dodging them around a car.

I'm not a journalist, so I will interject my feelings as I tell you about my journey. I hate bitch-made people who don't fight one-on-one. I've never respected people who think the mob mentality is all right.

I turned my attention back to the hostess. As if the fight in the parking lot wasn't distasteful enough, the Middle Eastern guy was chased into the restaurant by the three hicks. The white guys stood at the door and held the entire crowd in the restaurant hostage. What I want the world to see is that I had never experienced any of this in my twenty-eight years in Detroit. Only in the suburbs have I ever witnessed racial hatred. A small white guy got tired of the disturbing scene after about three or four minutes. He got up and said, "This is ridiculous, I'm leaving." The guy was walking towards the door and one of the terrorists punched him in his nose. Blood began to fall. White-on-white crime, and yet the media tries to convince us that terrorism is limited to Middle Easterners, when in fact terrorism comes from those who appear to be evangelicals.

After the bloodshed, I stared at the hostess and asked why she had not called the police instead of standing there. In the moment, I had not thought to walk through the kitchen to my van. I would not have been stopped since everyone was apparently a coward. I do remember thinking to myself, I don't have a gun on me. The next day, I drove to the Gibraltar Trade Center and got stainless-steel knuckle knives. The blades were heavy and razor-sharp. They slid right onto my hand.

Over the next few weeks, I went to Dunham's sporting store, or maybe it was Dick's or MC Sports, and I bought a semi-automatic assault rifle with a banana clip and a .40-caliber Taurus. I had clearly gone overboard. I had these lethal weapons lying around the apartment. The assault gun had no bullets in it, but the handgun did. It was in its box, but those weapons should never have made it into my home with my wife.

The sad part is that I knew nothing about the law. I was supposed to learn about guns and gun safety. I did have a permit for my handgun, but no real education. My wife should not have been exposed to heavy steel. We also had a new daughter who was seven months old. My son was living with his mom in a nearby city. Life had become too heavy for me. Something was not right. There was a bad spirit in me. There was a bad spirit over me.

The Promised Land That Wasn't

◇◇◇◇◇◇◇

There is no single narrative about black utopia, which is why I could just as easily have begun this story in the Sea Islands of South Carolina, where the Union Army enabled thousands of blacks to organize their own free labor communities on former plantations during the Civil War; in the émigré settlements of Kansas and the Oklahoma Territory; or among the free colored communities of New Orleans. It is a story told from the many margins around a mythical center, a story of those who must leave their place of origin and those who have no choice but to stay. My own family's arc and, in a sense, that of the Shrine of the Black Madonna, began in Tennessee, making it as convenient a starting point as any.

Albert Cleage, Sr., the father of the Shrine's pastor, grew up two hundred miles east of Promise Land, near Knoxville. Born in 1883, six years after Reconstruction ended with the final withdrawal of federal troops from the South, the highly educated Cleage Sr. would leave Tennessee for the Midwest as white supremacist violence ravaged the apartheid South. This nadir was also the dawn of the modern era. Industrial capitalism and rapid urbanization were altering the nation's economy and the composition of cities. Developments in technology and the social sciences transformed people's relationships to work, one another, and their conceptions of a desirable collective future.

In few places was this more evident than in Detroit and its suburbs, where Henry Ford's factories were experimenting with assembly lines for the first time and attracting thousands of laborers to work them. At the beginning of a new century, Albert Cleage, Sr., did what most Promise Landers would not do until a few decades later: he went north for once-unimaginable opportunities, to a city that became a beacon of hope for black Americans everywhere, even as its churning factories and east-side slums threatened to consume many of them. Cleage Sr. became a model race man and one of the most prominent black professionals in Detroit at the very moment it became the center of the world's auto industry.

The diverse dreams, migrations, and collective social experiments of African Americans during and immediately after Reconstruction—as Promise Land was taking shape—often emanated from shared concerns. Visions of the future beyond a state of bondage began as refusals to accept any condition that threatened black people's claims to personhood, economic self-determination, unregulated mobility, and unsupervised time. The textures of black utopian visions varied widely across the South, but there were recurring themes and commonly held aspirations. Many were explicitly laid out and discussed at the hundreds of state and national colored people's conventions that took place between the 1830s and 1890s.

In Tennessee, after the Civil War, these Colored Conventions bemoaned the terror campaigns of white "pale riders"; this was the state where the Ku Klux Klan was born in 1866. (Tennessee was also where the formerly enslaved Benjamin "Pap" Singleton helped mobilize the Kansas-bound Exoduster movement in the 1870s, which marked the first mass relocation of African Americans after the Civil War.) Echoing pleas from black leaders in other states, Colored Convention delegates in Tennessee called for a nationalized education system for black children, the recognition of black men as free laborers, fair representation on juries, and, in 1876, even the creation of an all-black state that would have incorporated Tennessee, Kentucky, and Mississippi. Delegates praised the Colored People Cooperative Land and Emigrant Association in Clarksville, a couple dozen miles north of Promise Land, and encouraged freedpersons to learn German, the language of the Romantics, those idealists who had contemplated the beauty of abstract notions like Freedom and the Nation.

What was the place of the freedperson and the freeborn who yearned for the future but did not have many real models for what it might look like? Could they create something from what seemed like nothing? No matter what, the future would not resemble the past. It could not be allowed to.

◇◇◇◇◇◇◇

In the summer of 1910, Albert Buford Cleage, the dark-skinned son of ex-slaves, listened to the complaints of other young black men on a four-decker excursion boat, the *Eastern States*. The Detroit & Cleveland Navigation Company boasted that its steamer fleet represented the finest "honeymoon palaces" anywhere on the Great Lakes. The *Eastern States* often took bridal parties between Detroit and Buffalo. Its colored quarters had thirty-two beds, many triple-bunked. The boat's black workers, Albert among them, slept in steerage. Albert thought the Lake Erie route romantic if tiring. The other boys, however, never stopped thinking the water might change its mind about them. Distraught porters fastened on life jackets should the worst happen.

For the summer, Albert was an evening waiter among blacks whose ranks included Oberlin, Wilberforce, Howard, Indiana, and Michigan men. Two of them were Albert's friends from medical school. During the rest of the year back home in Indianapolis, the twenty-seven-year-old was studying to become a doctor. Now he was awaiting the results of his final exam. Far away from home and his betrothed, a choir singer named Pearl Reed, Albert's thoughts were troubled. Pearl was the product of one of the rare interracial marriages in Indianapolis. Her father was a white doctor of English descent, a man who had once rejected two of his own mixed-race sons' pleas for financial help because, he told them, "I know nothing about you people." He was nonetheless a person of means. As a sign of devotion to his daughter, Albert had even made the doctor's first name, Buford, part of his own.

Although Albert was an educated man, Pearl's mother regarded him as an unsuitable match for her daughter. He was born the youngest of five in the small east Tennessee town of Hackberry. His complexion was dark—perhaps too dark for Pearl's mother—but he was unfailingly elegant. In one photograph from the period, he looks svelte in a long waistcoat and striped vest. A sharp part cuts through his finely combed hair, and a fist hangs from his pocket by a thumb. He was so well proportioned that one could forgive his slight hunch.

Albert frequently prayed for Pearl's well-being and asked after her health. He spared her an engagement ring so as not to entangle her in the web of local gossips. While traveling with the navigation company, he sent Pearl sheet music of the songs he loved, and she mailed him pressed flowers in return. When Pearl visited her sisters in Benton Harbor, Michigan, Albert urged her to forget him, at least for a short while, so that her leisure would not be "marred by anxious thoughts of him who has brought naught but sorrow and discontent into your home and hardships into your life."

As much as Pearl's mother protested, no one could deny Albert's uncommon achievements. He had trained at Henderson Normal and

Industrial School in North Carolina before excelling at Knoxville College, where he was a decorated member of the literary society and a respected football captain. Knoxville College was one of the religiously affiliated postbellum schools that promised literary, classical, and scientific education for black people. In a book that the sociologist W. E. B. Du Bois published a decade before Albert graduated from the Indiana School of Medicine, *The College-Bred Negro American*, he observed that most southern black graduates were more interested in preaching and teaching than in practicing medicine or law.

Education was the fastest-growing profession for black Tennesseans after the Civil War, and by 1910, there were almost two thousand of them employed in state educational institutions. Nearly half had no high school training. Du Bois was a Fisk graduate and had been a teacher himself for two summers at the Wheeler School in Wilson County, east of Nashville. In Du Bois's estimation, he and someone like Albert Cleage were seers. They had perceived "the Veil that hung between us and Opportunity," outside the tiny, "half-awakened" hill communities that were so easy to mistake for the world.

There is no reason to believe Du Bois would have known about Promise Land, but I imagine he might have viewed it as one of those half-awakened towns that had less in common with Plato's ideal Republic than with his cave—an insular place where black people could hardly imagine a more perfect reality, and which prevented them from seeing that alternatives to what they'd always known did exist. When he visited the Wheeler School again decades after teaching there, Du Bois saw most of his former pupils humbled by their life circumstances. Most had never left home. For the fortunate few who had escaped, and who were closer in age to Albert Cleage than to Du Bois, "War, Hell, and Slavery were but childhood tales." The parents and grandparents of people like Albert were psychologically ruined, in Du Bois's assessment, by their memories of chattel slavery. This experience had irreparably cleaved one generation from the next. Who was left to imitate? Borrowers of other people's names? Refugees who had

THE PROMISED LAND THAT WASN'T   45

known too many states and homes? Women and men whose backs were patchworks of scars?

Albert was determined to be something new. Before his stint aboard the *Eastern States*, he had written to Pearl in May 1910: "This is a time you know where the most important material questions of my life must be met and settled and when I realize that to a very large degree my success in life depends upon the wisdom of my choice it makes me over anxious and perhaps a bit worried—the great question is:—where shall I locate and where does the greatest success await me?"

When Albert graduated from medical school later that summer, he did so with the second-highest score among test takers, which included whites, and secured an appointment with the Indianapolis dispensary as a house doctor and ambulance surgeon. He wrote to Pearl with the good news in August 1910: "Tomorrow I shall become a gentleman of title & hereafter shall be considered by the world—doctor—but to you I hope to always remain—just Albert." One month later, on September 29, the marriage of Dr. Albert Buford Cleage to Ms. Pearl Reed was noted in the *Indianapolis Star*. A reverend wed them in the presence of their families.

For their honeymoon, the couple embarked on a grand tour of the South, beginning at the Appalachian Exposition in Knoxville's sprawling Chilhowee Park. Inspired by previous world's fairs, the Appalachian Expo of 1910 suggested that the prospects for "New Negroes" like Albert and Pearl were improving in the modern era. The moral disorder that had defined the Civil War years could not be allowed to take root again. At the expo, conservationists called for trees, soils, and streams to be protected. Reformers argued that child labor should finally be abolished. Medical professionals predicted that the spread of diseases such as cancer and tuberculosis would be staunched. The expo gave many people their first sightings of airplanes and zeppelins, technological marvels that demonstrated a world coming of age.

If the world was going to be a better place for white men and women to live in, perhaps the same would be true for black folk as well. It was not only the white people of Appalachia who were on the cusp of new conceptions of themselves, but also the blacks on the edge of Chilhowee Park who congregated around their solitary building. Though the Cleages likely missed the expo's Colored People's Day—filled as it was with speeches from ministers and suffragists and long parades of fraternal and sororal orders—they would have visited the Negro Building. It was two stories of stucco on a hill north of the lake in Chilhowee Park, from which Albert and Pearl would have seen the timbered crests of the Smoky Mountains.

The spirit of Booker T. Washington's emphasis on vocational work was evident in the Negro Building, where exhibitions highlighted advancements in blacksmithing, dressmaking, printing, agriculture, masonry, horticulture, and literature. Albert and Pearl, climbing a double stairway to the mezzanine, would have overlooked the exhibition space and two hospital rooms furnished by doctors from Knoxville College, Albert's alma mater, who were there to provide medical services for anyone who needed them.

The influence of Knoxville College's successful black graduates was so obvious in the contained world of the Negro Building that Albert could hardly have missed the implication: wherever he settled, it would be his job to advance the general welfare of his people. He was a southern highlander about to turn his gaze north, the hybrid heir of Du Bois's idealism and Booker T. Washington's pragmatic embrace of self-help. In the Negro Building, Albert was as a prince visiting his principality. If we imagine that the official history of the Appalachian Exposition had devoted more than one paragraph to the presence of black people there, and if we could prune away everything but that lone building on the lakefront, we might say that fair was made for someone just like him.

◇◇◇◇◇◇

The following July, while traveling in Detroit, Albert Sr. dashed off a fawning note to one "Master A.B. Cleage, Jr.," who loved ones would call Toddy: "Did not forget you were 4 weeks old yesterday and tomorrow you will be one month. My, but you are getting old fast." Albert Cleage, Jr., the first child of an eventual seven, was born on June 13, 1911, at the family's home in Indianapolis. By the time his son turned one, Albert Sr. was still writing letters home to Indiana as he traveled elsewhere in the Midwest. Then a fortuitous bit of news came from Kalamazoo, Michigan. There was an opening for a town doctor. It wasn't so strange for the notice to make its way to Indianapolis. Many black people who had moved to Kalamazoo around the time of the Civil War had come from this part of the Ohio Valley.

Kalamazoo had a small black population and had been receptive to abolitionist sentiment—all reasons, perhaps, for its reputedly peaceful character. The Cleages relocated to Kalamazoo in 1912, where Albert Sr. opened his first private practice. He quickly became one of Kalamazoo's most prominent black professionals. He was made honorary vice president of the local Freedmen's Progress Commission by 1915, a Jubilee year that marked five decades since Emancipation. It was a year of plenty. A family friend, a dentist, encouraged the Cleages to take up where there were greater opportunities for black people of their stature, at the spinning heart of the modern world.

And so the Cleages arrived in Detroit the year before its Urban League opened in 1916. The city was about to undergo an enormous population boom that culminated in Detroit becoming one of the country's top manufacturing centers. Henry Ford's River Rouge complex, which opened west of downtown in 1917, was not the city's only architectural marvel. Some of its theaters, shopping centers, banks, and hotels, as well as its towering central train station, were hailed as world wonders. The Cleages hadn't been in the city four years before Albert Sr. and twenty-nine other black doctors bought a three-story house on the east side that they converted into Detroit's first black hospital, Dunbar Memorial.

Overextended and prone to heart flurries as he was, Albert Sr. belonged to the emergent class of black leaders who chartered institutions to secure housing, job training, and other services for newly arrived migrants from the South. The essential work of black professionals would make many of them, including Albert Sr., mainstays in the *Detroit Tribune*'s Society & Woman's page. They constituted the rarefied group that dined at fine restaurants such as Le Plaisir et Culture, played bridge at the Frogs' Club, and threw sumptuous dinners in one another's honor. Like many black leaders of his economic and social standing, Albert Sr. was a practitioner of race work, an approach to social welfare that promoted the virtues of self-help and mutual aid within black communities (many progressive settlement houses, welfare agencies, and social work training institutes barred blacks from entry).

What did it matter in this new age that a co-founder of a hospital was the son of slaves? With the proper education and moral upbringing, any child of former bondspersons could now earn their keep and drink from delicate glassware. The Cleages' spacious home on Detroit's west side looked like a watchtower. It was in the Tireman neighborhood, where members of the black middle class were starting to find much better housing than what was available on the east side, where poor blacks, European Jews, and other immigrants lived in inhospitable conditions. Pearl worried over her husband's demanding schedule. Albert Jr. sometimes joined him on assorted house calls. His father liked to prod him about political subjects, hoping to spark debate. When this happened, Pearl, along with Albert Jr.'s younger siblings— Louis, Henry, Hugh, Barbara, Gladys, and tiniest Anna—listened raptly or disappeared into the house.

◇◇◇◇◇◇◇

Albert Jr. was a serious-minded lover of art, music, and books, with his mother's light complexion. He wore white blouses and trousers. When he opened his mouth, he tended to speak at length. The mama's boy adopted Pearl's sense of piety. He took great pride in his family and would later defend his father against accusations from some corners of the black community that he was a typical race man, hardworking but overly comfortable. Some were disturbed by Albert Sr.'s affiliation with Charles Bowles, who briefly served as Detroit's mayor in 1930 and had once received political support from the Ku Klux Klan.

Bowles had offered Albert Sr. the position of police surgeon, but white resistance compelled the mayor to assign him the role of city physician instead. Albert Sr.'s appointment as Detroit's first black city doctor was a minor scandal. Recently fired white garbage workers accused the mayor and his public works commissioner of trying to replace white city workers with blacks. It was not personal, Bowles assured them, but most of the city's welfare cases were colored. Who better to serve in a public health role than a black man who had proven his ability to point other members of his race to jobs?

The position gave Albert Sr. a handsome salary and a car just as the Great Depression was beginning. It also cemented the Cleages' status as socialites. The Cleages would be flattered by a series of white mayors. Pearl and Albert Sr. appeared at Sigma Gamma Rho debutante balls and Iota Boule events. They were renowned hosts, especially of Albert Sr.'s friends from Knoxville College, itself representative of the New Negro ethos that had been shaping black middle-class notions of success since the Reconstruction period. It was not unusual to spot a visitor's Studebaker outside the Cleage residence. At meetings of the West Side Human Relations Council, a civic club, Albert Sr. and Pearl lectured on the importance of good home environments. They spoke in support of nurseries for black children and gave speeches on the problem of juvenile delinquency.

This was life for Albert Jr., who was raised knowing how to smile and dress like other monied black people. The Cleage children were taught to be mannered. Hugh was the same deep chestnut as Albert Sr., and Louis was the spectacled aesthete. Gladys, with her ruddy cheeks and prominent chin, was the clear compromise between her mother's and father's traits. Barbara's elongated face was a stage for her smart brows. Henry's and Anna's sharply relieved features made them the most classically beautiful of the brood. Albert Jr.'s drowsy eyes contained some of the inexhaustible humor that made his brashness more tolerable.

From 1915 on, one could often find high-society blacks like the Cleages vacationing in Idlewild—Michigan's "Black Eden"—one of the largest resorts for black people in the country before the heydays of Oak Bluffs and Aquinnah on Martha's Vineyard or Sag Harbor in Long Island. Albert Jr. had been going since he was a boy. His family was beautiful in Idlewild's light. They broke the surface of Lake Idlewild with oars that frightened the minnows and baby bass. Horses grazed near stables owned by a blind veteran of the Spanish-American War. Rowboats and cottages had names, and in the winter, one could ski over the frozen lake or trek to the peaks of nearby Caberfae. The Cleages rented a cottage here until the Second World War, at which point one of Albert Jr.'s brothers purchased a lot and built a house.

Albert Jr. could enjoy his family's scenic Idlewild get-togethers only to a point. Years before the sociologist E. Franklin Frazier wrote about the "black bourgeoisie" in his 1957 book of the same name—a text that would become a touchstone for Albert Jr.—Cleage *fils* had expressed wariness about his own upbringing. He did not ignore the blatant tension between his privileged life and the misfortunes that many other blacks in Detroit faced. In this way, Albert Jr. took after his spiritual leader at the family church, Plymouth Congregational.

Reverend Horace White, who became Plymouth's pastor in 1938, was an Oberlin graduate and member of the National Negro Congress (NNC), a workers' organization founded during the Depression by leaders who had progressive, Socialist, and Communist leanings. The NNC was one of the few militant organizations of the period that advocated for organized labor movements among the black working class, along with the civil liberties that groups such as the NAACP and Urban League were calling for. The NNC arose in part to compensate for the shortcomings of New Deal policies whose advantages did not always reach the most vulnerable black populations.

In his sermons, White drew on the headlines of the day and books other than the Bible, including novels such as Richard Wright's *Native Son*. In the 1930s, he became known for criticizing Henry Ford's relationship with some of Detroit's black pastors in the pages of the liberal magazine *Christian Century*. According to Ford's patronage system, those pastors who wanted their parishioners to obtain decent jobs at

Ford Motor Co. would need to limit their criticisms of the industrial-ist. White blamed these pastors for letting themselves become tools in the hands of "King Ford." He accused Ford of owning Detroit's black churches as surely as he owned any factory, diluting whatever salvific power they had left in an age marked by corporate greed, economic devastation, and the chronic suffering of the poor and oppressed.

In later years, White's tenure as a Michigan state representative and head of the Detroit NAACP's housing commission gave Albert Jr. one of his early models of a leader in the Social Gospel tradition. He was no Sundays-only Christian who offloaded the worldly concerns of his parishioners onto a higher power. What clear-eyed man of God in industrial Detroit could truly believe that progress was inevitable? One only had to look to the Black Bottom neighborhood on the east side for proof to the contrary.

Depression-era Detroit did not resemble the City on a Hill that its architects wanted it to be as much as it did a Promised Land that had failed to live up to its potential. By virtue of his father's station, Albert Jr. had been insulated from the east-side ghettoes for most of his life. After studying sociology at Fisk University in Nashville and then at Detroit City College, he was exposed to the living conditions of im-poverished blacks as a caseworker. In July 1938, Albert Jr. passed a civil service exam for a position in Detroit's overburdened welfare depart-ment. Firehouses were serving as supplementary welfare stations since the city's eight benefits offices couldn't handle everything on their own.

When Albert Jr. joined the department, there were almost 12,000 black people on the city's welfare rolls. Most of them were laid-off autoworkers. The welfare department had been disgraced because of accusations that the police were given illegal access to confidential client records. There were also reports of dole chiselers defrauding the department of its dwindling money. The director of the Works Prog-ress Administration and Welfare Department of the UAW-CIO pre-dicted that further reductions in funding would lead to an acute crisis for the poor in Detroit.

Albert Jr. soon quit his job. It became clear that piecemeal reforms would not ultimately bring about the kingdom of God on earth. He was more likely to accomplish something as president of Plymouth Congregational's Junior League, then one of Detroit's most socially active church youth organizations. Under Albert Jr.'s supervision, young men and women learned about the realities of unemployment and the rising tide of fascism in Europe. They heard their mentor call for the city's blacks to support unionization efforts at Ford Motor Co.

In another life, had he not seen it with his own eyes, perhaps Albert Jr. would have believed what white progressive reformers said about Detroit's black- and immigrant-inhabited east side: that it was a godless Land of Nod, full of brothels and licentiousness. But from the vantage of his social class, he saw how easily such elitist narratives had enabled the black bourgeoisie (a good many of them churchgoing) to turn away from the suffering of their downtrodden brethren. Albert Jr. saw his own face in the mirror of the high-society colored papers. Who was worse off? The poor in their ghetto enclaves or the spiritually dead black ghosts arrayed in tassels and silk, pursuing their own individual fortunes? The lines between these groups were thin, the boundaries more porous than perhaps they first appeared. As dapper as he was, Albert Jr. was still the grandson of slaves.

Years later, during the early years of his pastorate, Albert Jr. would ask himself in the margins of a scrap of paper whether he and all black people should be called *aliens* or *the lost and the damned* or *snakes in the garden of Eden*. He would wonder whether black people were *alienable* at all, which would assume they were not already at the far edges of social life. He considered himself an *alienist*—one who studies the lives of those who felt themselves apart. If the United States was in some ways an unfriendly foreign country for blacks who had been forced to engineer their own institutions and folkways to survive, was it more accurate to call them American *strangers*, *dwellers*, or merely *inhabitants*?

Black Bottom

◇◇◇◇◇◇

The central tenet of what would come to be known in the 1960s as black liberation theology—the decades-long enactment of which would be Albert Cleage, Jr.'s lasting contribution to the American utopian tradition—is that holiness starts from below, in the experiences and aspirations of the disinherited. Those whom white society has deemed little more than dirt are, in truth, the rich loam of the garden, in which God's emancipatory promises will bear fruit. By embracing the notion that their visions of an ideal life were worth pursuing, the disinherited could find not only freedom outside of Egypt but great abundance as well. Cleage Jr.'s theology would have more to say than "black is beautiful." Its radical purpose was to convince all black people, religious or not, that they already possessed the means for their own transcendence, though it would necessitate constant struggle to cultivate and maintain them.

For black Americans to rise above their current condition, they first needed to become iconoclasts. They needed to realize that the gods and values they had inherited from white society were false idols. Black people had to become heretics in the eyes of their oppressors, taking control of the institutions and images that had for so long been deemed holy by a white majority and inverting them. Profaning the hallowed beliefs of the dominant society would perhaps loosen their hold on black people's imaginations, enabling their own self-regard, mutual recognition, and a redefinition of the sacred.

When Albert Cleage, Jr., became a social worker in Detroit, he was thirty years out from making the controversial claim for which he is best remembered—that the historical Christ was a black man—but already he was developing an idea for himself of what the divine was not. If the God of Israel was one that would always protect the meek and usher them to freedom out of slavery, then surely that god did not sympathize with the industrial-capitalist class that exerted such power over Detroit's black communities. In the modern age, where else would God reside but in the most overlooked of places, the slumlands?

◇◇◇◇◇◇◇

Detroit's poor, overcrowded Black Bottom neighborhood, which in the early 1950s would become one of the country's first casualties of urban development, was a place where liberal dreams of gradual progress languished and died. It was here that the artist Glanton Dowdell was born in 1923 to parents who came up from Georgia during the first wave of the Great Migration. Today, outside of the Shrine of the Black Madonna, Glanton is remembered mainly by a small number of historians, art collectors, and surviving family members, along with a dwindling pool of black nationalists who knew him in the 1960s and '70s and an indeterminate number of people in Sweden, where he fled into exile in 1969 and lived until his death in 2000. In Europe, he became an international symbol of the black American revolution and a testament to the unceasing fight against fascism, imperialism, and capitalism around the world.

Like many other figures associated with the Shrine, Glanton Dowdell is largely absent from histories of America's countercultural and black liberation movements. His brief association with Albert Cleage, Jr., in the waning years of the 1960s shaped black nationalist activity in Detroit when the city was a focus of national attention following the 1967 rebellion. When Glanton painted the Detroit Shrine's chancel mural of a Black Madonna and Child earlier that year, he created one of the most galvanizing images to come out of the black counterculture. The painting became the symbol of Cleage's Black Christian Nationalist movement, giving generations of black people a visual point of reference for a new conception of themselves.

Glanton was not a God-fearing member of the Shrine, but he used the church as a springboard for finding his place in the wider world. When he realized that the black revolutions in his own country were foundering, he chose to go elsewhere. The utopian's dilemma has always been whether to fall in line for the sake of the group or to prioritize the sanctity of one's own needs. Glanton became the archetypal fugitive who saw, or forced himself to believe, that many paths were available even when fortune did not seem to favor him.

As I tried to piece together Glanton's story from the traces he left behind—an unfinished memoir, his many portraits of black life, his family and friends in Europe and the United States, and a mural that expanded the meaning of the sacred for scores of black people—I found that his biography at times defied conventional notions of truth and fiction. He told lies to hide himself. He was determined to stay off any kind of map I could easily read. In Black Bottom, where Glanton was raised by his mother and grandmother, Ruby and Annie, he had to choose whether to stay or to leave. When he chose to run, he was not racing toward something better, just something different than what he had known.

◇◇◇◇◇◇◇

◇◇◇◇◇◇◇

In one of Glanton's earliest memories, a white doctor who employed his mother, Ruby, parked a Cadillac in front of their tenement on St. Antoine and Palmer with a dead black bear splayed across the hood. Without delay, Grandmamma Annie ordered Ruby's boyfriend and another tenant to bring it up three flights of stairs. Children followed, squealing and prodding the beast. Other men puffed on cigarettes as they watched. By the time Annie's helpers brought the bear through a narrow hall onto a back porch, she had already laid down sheaves of newspapers. Glanton sat silently atop a box out of the way as the men hung the bear from its hind legs while his grandmother and a bevy of women tied their hair and aprons. Annie removed a set of knives from flannel wrap. The women sliced between the animal's hide and flesh. Its innards plunked onto the covered floor. All parts but the head and paws were boiled in massive black pots, jarred, and distributed to neighbors. Glanton and the other kids played outside in the meantime, caping themselves with the bloody bear hide and riling the dogs.

Glanton would remember the smells of kerosene, camphorated oil, and burning coal in his childhood home, as well as the scratching of the mean rat hordes that pulsed behind walls and under floorboards. Lovett Dowdell, Glanton's father, had come to Detroit from Americus, Georgia, to work in a car factory. Long before the stock market crash, Lovett enjoyed one of the best jobs a black man could have at the time before he received a notice of dismissal. Smallpox killed him in 1924, nine months after Glanton was born.

Annie had come up from Okefenokee in southern Georgia to watch the baby as his mother toiled in other people's homes. She quickly made their white frame house into a waystation for migrants from small Georgia towns who were looking for work, food, or lodging in one of the Midwest's industrial cities when there was little of any of that for black folk. Family from Cordele, Americus, and St. Petersburg sent up the crated hogs and citrus that turned their home into a soup kitchen, along with the hundred-pound sacks of cornmeal, flour, and beans that Ruby's boyfriend retrieved from who knew where.

Although it was not true, the boy thought his grandmother was old enough to have witnessed the Jubilee celebrations of the newly emancipated. She was a midwife who sheltered battered wives and a healer who took in survivors of botched abortions. Eventually, the family sent for Annie's elder sister, Sarah, bringing her up from Okefenokee as her mind declined. Sarah shouted questions in one room and shuffled into another to answer them. Lodgers watched without knowing how to help or what to say as Annie wrung out her fouled bedsheets, set a bath, and scrubbed her down under the glow of a lamp like she would also do for the boy.

The stories Annie told Glanton about Okefenokee sometimes made the town sound like heaven on earth, but also pointed to what he later described in his memoir as "the ever present horror just beyond the borders of our peaceful and vulnerable we-group." When Glanton was small, Annie often held him on her hip, which would one day make him think of Auguste Rodin's powerful sculptures. She poked ashes around in the early morning to rekindle fires, sewed buttons on the boy's clothes, snapped beans, plucked chickens, and in a darkened room smoked tobacco that she had somehow scavenged during the daytime when Glanton could have sworn she was doing other chores.

In these years of lack, Ruby would powder her face and put on lipstick and mascara for the rent parties she went to with her man Sam. Draped in a black floral kimono or a hand-me-down dress from one of her employers, she looked forward to dancing the Charleston and the Mess Around. Rhinestones framed her wrists, amber hung from her ears, and when Glanton told his mother how pretty she was, she looked at him hard before her coolness warmed. Ruby's beauty and Annie's ability to multiply fishes and loaves blinded Glanton to the fears of adults who huddled around stoves outside and stared at nothing.

The boy was known to ride the trolley past Hastings Street's shopfronts. As a seven-year-old, he had memorized the faces of prostitutes and turned over in his mind the still life of a dead man on the sidewalk. The thought of getting home too late—walking past neighbors who shouted, "What he need is a killin'!"—made his backside sting in anticipation of a plaited clothesline. Most of Glanton's days were spent trying to avoid the wrath of someone who loved him too much to let him rip and roar without consequence. He made games out of slipping away from Annie's near-omniscient gaze, Ruby's concerned rages, and the hard scrub brush and P&G soap used to wash away the dirt from his skin. For a while, he did not think about leaving Black Bottom. The neighborhood had given him so much. It was "this wondrous, geographical ribbon [that] shielded me, nourished me." Where was there to go? For now, all he knew were the aromas of hoecakes and moonshine tonic, the sight of mattresses swollen with urine and chinches.

In the alleys, men whom Glanton called "shadow people" played craps. The boy had a vague sense that the things these men talked about—*pink slips, layoffs, breadlines, evictions*—were what had made them shadows in the first place. He was hearing these words frequently around the winter of 1931, when diphtheria, scarlet fever, and consumption galloped through the neighborhood. Before he was ten years old, Glanton knew how to maneuver small coffins as a pallbearer for children struck down by polio and spinal meningitis. There were kids all over the place who limped as they played and raced even though they were fitted with braces. Annie made Glanton wear an asafetida necklace. When he became deliriously ill with pneumonia, he was treated with potions, alcohol baths, and the laying on of hands by people his family helped feed. Black Bottom lost some of its communal mother wit when the Depression came. People sank into lonely foxholes. Booze was "twisting and contorting an almost unbearable reality into something not quite as severe, not quite so final," Glanton remembered, keeping the illusion of a horizon alive by blurring everything else, including the road one had to follow to get there.

That distant horizon did not guarantee a better tomorrow. It wasn't so much a destination as a thing "abstract and awful [which] was hovering menacingly overhead and approaching." By 1933, Glanton had learned from listening to adults talk in barbershops, in front of pool halls, on the corners, and around the kitchen table that the loss of one's livelihood caused a contagious grief in the "we-group" of Black Bottom. Glanton was ten years old, but he had no more time for clipping out Lucky Bucks from the Sunday kiddie comics. To earn real money, he sold bottles, copper wire, rags, aluminum, and brass to junk dealers. He and the other black boys watched the hustlers at Eastern Market ply their trade and became their informal apprentices. They carried grocery bags, cleaned around the stands, loaded produce, and scrapped with immigrant boys over turf. Glanton brought home as much as seven dollars on weekends.

The money from hustling was more of a constant in these years than some of the people who came into the boy's life. He met a solitary, twenty-one-year-old factory worker named Virgil, who moved into his family's building. Virgil kept his flat clean. His wavy hair was parted to the side in a way that made him look like Joe Louis. He played the blues on his guitar for Glanton, singing "Balling the Jack" and "My Blue Heaven."

There was a black cop—a "coon killa"—who stalked the tenements after white men gave him a badge. The cop had heard that Virgil was handing out union literature in front of the River Rouge factory and came by telling him to publicly burn the pamphlets. With Glanton watching in the room with him, Virgil refused. He tried to run. Two shots in the back from the cop's revolver sent him the rest of the way down the tenement stairs. During the funeral service at Bethel AME, Glanton asked himself what kind of man Virgil must have been for white autoworkers and their wives to come weep beside blacks. What did those pamphlets say?

An aura of foreboding enveloped Glanton. He wondered aloud to Annie whether he was a soothsayer. "I get a feelin' somethin' gon' happen 'fore it happens," he told her. "Honest." His prophecies spoke to a limited set of outcomes that were more obvious to those with limited choices. It was a dubious gift. The boy reached an age when Annie felt she needed to remind him that suffering was not his unique cross to carry. She told him about the white men back in Georgia who had mutilated the genitals of her second husband for refusing to give away their beloved mule. This miserable image haunted Glanton. It was all he could think about for a time. He was eleven years old. He needed a new way of measuring the worth of a life beyond the fact of mere survival.

◇◇◇◇◇◇

There was once a time when Glanton believed in God. He remembered kneeling as a boy, clasping his hands together, reciting the Lord's Prayer, and arguing with an invisible presence. One Sanctified Right Reverend in Black Bottom, a small bald man who was always chewing on the food stuck between his gold teeth, heard that the boy could paint. His family had encouraged this skill in him. Even Ruby's boy-friend brought him paper and pads for him to draw his favorite movie characters—Popeye, Felix the Cat, and the cowboys played by the actor Tom Mix. A half dozen neighbors would crowd into Ruby's bedroom to admire his artistry.

The Right Reverend asked if the boy could paint a crucified Christ above his altar. For sixty bucks, Glanton figured he could. The sour face the reverend made at the thought of paying the boy a commission gave him his model for Christ's agony. The Right Reverend was a jackleg who almost succeeded in scamming Glanton out of his money, until Ruby's boyfriend intervened.

Someone would need to prime the wall with white paint first and bring him brushes, linseed oil, cans of paint, turpentine, and scaffolding. He worked a week of school nights, drawing, scaling, and enjoying the time alone. When the Crucifixion was done, one woman hung a veil over the mural until the next Sunday morning, when the covering came down with a rush of amens and tambourine jangles. It isn't clear whether Glanton made his own Christ black. How many of the congregants knew about the mural Marcus Garvey had enshrined during a canonization ceremony at Harlem's Liberty Hall a year after the boy was born, in 1924? That image showed a black Christ and Virgin Mary, giving weight to a claim that the AME bishop and black nationalist Henry McNeal Turner made in a 1898 sermon: "Every race of people who have attempted to describe their God by words, or by paintings, or by carvings, or any other form or figure, have conveyed the idea that the God who made them and shaped their destinies was symbolized in themselves, and why should not the Negro believe that he resembles God?"

Glanton's work on the mural brought neighbors to his home with pictures of their newborns and their dead, seeking portraits of their own. One middle-aged man whose daughter died suddenly at eighteen invited Glanton to accompany him to the mortuary for a session. The boy would have to use the only picture the father had of her as a reference, taken when she was nine, to imagine her light brown eyes.

Glanton was only a child. He wanted to help the man and was not afraid of the dead, but he grew uneasy at the thought of using a corpse as his model. Almost more nauseating was the prospect of telling the father no, when a cardinal rule of his upbringing had been, he wrote, "to do any and everything within reason to ease the suffering of those in mourning." It was decided that a photographer would capture the daughter's face in her casket, giving him a model to work from. An image was nothing if not a bridge, a transitional stage between the imagination and lived reality.

No One Starved in California

One of Glanton's downstairs neighbors, a fifteen-year-old girl, was surrounded one day by a dozen mourners after her two-month-old daughter was discovered dead in her crib. The bite marks and discolored bloating were the horrid work of rats. Neither Black Bottom's slumlords nor Detroit's board of public health were going to do anything about the rodents, so the community organized the Great Rat Hunt in vengeance.

The boys reveled in blood sport, pushing nails into broomsticks after church one Sunday and goring the rats for two cents apiece. Or they held them over small fires so that the fetid roasting stench brought the other rats screaming out of the houses into an open trap. Dogs lunged. The boys speared and clubbed. The girls watched in contentment and most of the adults, though shaking their heads, did not protest.

A circle of neighborhood women cornered the shop owner who was paying the boys to deliver dead rats into a wooden barrel behind the barbershop. They demanded that he stop encouraging Glanton, one of the most zealous exterminators. Glanton did not forgive the women for taking away his livelihood. From the rat hunt's proceeds, he had been able to buy himself a BB gun, silk stockings for Ruby, a new pipe for Annie, and a cigarette lighter for Sam.

Ruby thought her son, with his bony body, ashy knees, and possum claws, was becoming half-rabid. She knew he scrounged through garbage and sold coal that the boys stole from freight cars, tossing as many pounds as they could into gunnysacks. His grades in school were suffering, but he had many skills—an acrobat's agility, an artist's attentiveness. None of them, his teacher said, were especially useful.

◇◇◇◇◇◇

Tales like "The Ballad of Casey Jones" and *The Adventures of Huckleberry Finn* lost their mystique for Glanton as he began embarking on his own journeys. He caught rides for fun on freight cars going to the glass factory on the Detroit River. The formula was easy: ride, jump off when it felt right, walk back home. One day the train started moving too fast. Glanton could not leap down, so he stayed on top as the locomotive left familiar places behind and rattled past "vast industrial complexes that spewed smoke and fire."

The speed of the journey peeled the ghetto from Glanton's eyes and replaced clapboard houses with a landscape of farms and tree-studded fields. Daylight submitted to the dark. The train stopped hours later in Chicago's Central Yard. Uncertain of how to get home, he tried another train only to push deeper south into Illinois, to East St. Louis. Blacks in the train yard's tent city, the Jungle, advised him not to go to the police unless he was willing to risk the workhouse.

The Jungle was the only place many of its inhabitants were allowed to live without being harassed by the authorities. The encampment had its share of troubadours, vaudevillian comics, and jig dancers. Glanton's no-hands backward flips were celebrated here much like his drawings were back home. He overheard some blacks and whites in the Jungle speak reverently of one place—the "new world" of California—where "lodging was provided, and even if not, the weather was warm and sunny all year round with grapes and citrus fruit growing up by the side of the road." Those who could make it past railroad detectives, vigilantes, and the police could find themselves under the protection of the Associated Farmers of California. Their pamphlets of smiling field workers promised work for every able-bodied person.

No one starved in California, the boy thought, not heeding the warnings of travelers who passed through the Jungle on their way east. They said California was "a land of slavery and betrayed hope" where the Associated Farmers—nothing like the union that Virgil had advertised outside River Rouge—made women and children into widows and orphans. Glanton did not think about how many people were trying to reach Detroit as hard as he was now trying to leave it behind. He had not wanted much until he left Black Bottom, and he hadn't meant to leave.

"If there were riches to be got in California, and my folks were as poor as they said," Glanton later wrote, "I'd be less than a man-child not to pull my weight." A man-child was someone who left home with good intentions and didn't know the way back. A concerned young mother in the Jungle promised Glanton that she would send Ruby the letter he wrote for her: *Mother, the people here say there is a lot of money to be made in California. I know we need money so I am going out there to make some.* The woman tried telling him, "California ain't goin' nowhere, and you got plenty time to grow up and get there," but he and many others in the camp were too far gone in their reveries. Glanton had been there only a few days.

Jungle children from Tennessee, West Virginia, and Pennsylvania whose fathers died from black lung, consumption, and mine explosions were, like the adults, riveted by "visions of the Garden of Eden to be found in California." Communing with dispossessed farmers and industrial laborers, Glanton adopted their fantasies as his own. "This crackling enthusiasm was a self administered placebo against the onslaught of hopelessness. Instead, I became infected with the dream and drawn into a not very wise commitment."

A man named Zeke, who volunteered to accompany Glanton as he also went west for a job he didn't yet have, hoped that the journey would show the child something. "You will soon learn, boy, not too late, I hope, that everything that's said isn't necessarily so."

From a rail yard, Zeke and Glanton spotted their freight train as it bore out of the east, blowing black smoke into a purple sky. Once

Zeke helped Glanton into an empty boxcar, the boy had to square the exhilaration of independence with pangs of homesickness. They shared a car with a white boy around Glanton's age who had fled an orphanage in Delaware after he had been beaten and sterilized. Was this what bred amity between the races? Union literature and universal misery that always seemed to be running away from itself? Glanton and the boy mused about where they were going and imagined "unlimited opportunities in a state that needed bodies." They watched the plains and mountains go by. Eventually, Glanton cradled his head between his knees and slept.

◇◇◇◇◇◇◇

He suddenly felt the warmth of floodlights. Another train yard. Men charged the tracks with clubs, axe handles, and shotguns. Glanton scrambled out of the freight car to hide beneath a truck. Where were Zeke and the white boy? A flashlight on his face and a round of kicks to his side convinced Glanton that this was not a dream. First there was a paddy wagon and then, in a strange building, Glanton was sprinkled with white powder. It had something to do with the spreading of lice.

He sought an explanation from the kind but distant nursing staff. Had he made it to California? Yes, though not exactly the land of his dreams. He was in Los Angeles, in a holding center for vagabond children. Those whose families could not be found would be placed in foster homes. Fortunately, Glanton knew his address by heart, even if he did not know the route home. There was nothing to do except send him back east. Now he was like one of the travelers who had warned the Jungle's dreamers. On the four-day bus ride home, one of the drivers referred to Glanton as a runaway. Glanton didn't believe this was true. Runaways fled hell. He was racing toward paradise.

When he returned to Detroit, dozens of Glanton's neighbors met him at the bus station. There was no shouting, only relieved tears. Glanton was surprised to learn that a letter to Ruby from the young mother he had met in the Jungle was sufficient insurance against his family's wrath. The letter explained everything the boy was trying to do for his loved ones. They now asked one thing of him: to accept the Lord as his personal savior so that, should he ever decide to do something so stupid again, he would at least be in God's hands. That Sunday, the pastor preached a sermon on the Prodigal Son, impressing upon the once-lost child that "just as the family is a collection of single souls, so is our community a collection of single families." Annie put it in more vivid terms during the service. She told Glanton that the finger which is cut off from the hand will rot even as the hand heals.

"I just wish to say to you all that the truth is right at the end of your arms," the pastor cried. "When vanity, greed and folly tempt you to leave the circle of family, church and community—to leave the hallowed circle of loved ones, look to your hand and remember the profound words of Sister Annie."

Glanton quit vagabonding. He fell in with some of the older kids who stole meat from the delivery trucks outside butcher shops. They

◇◇◇◇◇◇

had seen Glanton's little scrawny self run and knew nobody could catch him. Could he distract a driver long enough for the others to strip the truck of its contents? Sure. Over time, the boys stole hundreds of dollars' worth of prime beef. The Russell Street Gang met in the attic of a yellow frame house where they smoked and played dominoes. Hanging around the older boys yielded luxuries Glanton had never known: salami loaves, smoked hocks, cans of corned beef. Bullies at school stopped teasing and then avoided him altogether. Most children did, in fact, including Glanton's friends. Their families barred them from spending any more time with a boy who must have been up to no good with that thieving ragtag.

In 1938, the same year Albert Cleage, Jr., accepted that social work would never fundamentally improve conditions in Detroit's ghettoes, Glanton was fifteen and growing fiercer. When a white man raped an eleven-year-old neighborhood girl, Glanton found him and stabbed him with an ice pick. There was enough blood to scare the boy into thinking he had killed a grown man. The scene reminded him of the Great Rat Hunt. Ruby wiped the white man's blood from Glanton's face and neck with a wet towel at the kitchen table. Given the seriousness of what he'd done, she was being uncharacteristically tender.

◇◇◇◇◇◇◇

Glanton stopped thinking of his robberies as criminal. "By now I instinctively knew that the game rules known as laws were conceived to provide me and mine with a crippling handicap. Maneuvering through, around and over these restrictions entailed risks, but risks, for me, were a fact of life." He was sitting on an unusable war chest of more than one thousand dollars, money that may as well have been Lucky Bucks since no one in his household would have knowingly let him spend the ill-gotten cash on them.

In his barbershop, Glanton heard about the National Negro Congress, which the Socialist labor advocate A. Philip Randolph of the Brotherhood of Sleeping Car Porters was leading. One brother in the barbershop shared NNC literature with Glanton and brought him to a local chapter meeting where, to the boy's surprise, young white immigrants from Europe were in attendance alongside blacks. The reading material Glanton had been given had the same magical effect as Virgil's union pamphlets.

Did the boy's Communist sympathies begin here? Communist Party members made up a small part of the NNC. A. Philip Randolph criticized Party leaders as opportunists who were often insensitive to the racialized struggles of black Americans, and he would leave the organization in 1940 over concerns that Communist ideology was incompatible with the organic growth of black mass movements. Initially, however, he wanted the NNC to be a popular front for blacks of many political persuasions, including Communists, so long as the pursuit of black civil and economic rights was their priority.

Did Glanton hear one of the trade unionist brothers call for robust unemployed councils, the passage of a federal anti-lynching bill, collective bargaining rights, or a shift in the tax burden from the poor to the rich? Would he have learned that his neighbors dreamed about the creation of a Farmer-Labor Party, consumer cooperatives where people could "buy black," a declaration of rights for black Americans, or an interracial coalition against the creep of fascism?

For at least the last ten years, ever since the black Bolshevik Harry Haywood called for global black self-determination at the Sixth Congress of the Communist International in Moscow, some black Americans from the Cotton Belt to the Manufacturing Belt started to see themselves as members of an oppressed and functionally separate nation within the United States. The competing appeals of Communists and Garveyites for solidarity across ethnic, geographic, and class lines captured their imaginations. One day, Glanton would embrace the belief that a workers' revolution led by an enlightened avant-garde could eliminate fascism around the world.

He would not fully appreciate what the National Negro Congress was fighting, though, until 1939, when he was sent to the Boys' Vocational School in Lansing, Michigan. After robbing the reception desk of a theater, Glanton had attempted to make a getaway. An old acquaintance from elementary school spotted him the moment he hailed a taxi. With time running out before he was discovered, Glanton hurried the boy into the taxi, impulsively stole the driver's money at gunpoint, and left the cabbie fearing for his life in an alley. He then took the car with his friend still in it and dropped him off at home with half the take. When officers found and violently interrogated Glanton the following day, he rightly suspected the other boy of snitching.

The Boys' Vocational School, Glanton wrote later, "might easily have passed for an idyllic university. Beautifully ivy-covered landscaped grounds, dotted with clean, red brick buildings did not resemble a place of incarceration. That is what it was, however." Before being assigned a cottage, each of which housed forty-two boys, the young people of the Boys' Vocational School spent two weeks in quarantine and silence. Among the boys were white supremacists who supported the American Nazi Party, the German American Bund, and the Black Legion. They attacked black children and were especially brutal toward young Jews. Glanton had never seen this before. Poles, Hungarians, and Italians were beating up Jewish kids more than those from his own we-group.

Glanton was made to read Carl von Clausewitz's *On War* and he excelled at a rigorous battery of military drills. Their instructors denounced the pagan ways of antichrist races. The school's moral lectures were given by evangelical temperance groups that condemned drink, perversion, and masturbation. To emphasize their point, they showed the boys pictures of rotting penises.

Glanton internalized the words of Sergeant Duncan, an American Legionnaire whom the school's director invited to shape the boys into fighting men: "Can you imagine what a sweet privilege it is for those who, on the spur of the moment, in the prime of life, are able to give their life for something they believe in, for something they love, for the good of those they leave behind?"

Sergeant Duncan railed against the Huns. He was advising Glanton to be wary of Germans, but to the boy, "the Hun" was just another term for the buckra, the white man. The sergeant told Glanton that against a "good American fighting man," the Hun would not last long.

"Remember that!" the sergeant said.

I did, Glanton wrote.

Little else is known of his time at the Vocational School except that he left it prematurely. One day, all that stood between him and freedom was an unsecured window. He leapt from it and soon thereafter began a new voyage south, to Florida. This time, he knew exactly where he was going.

The Kingdoms of God

From either side of an economic and social divide, Albert Cleage, Jr., and Glanton Dowdell witnessed the stark contradictions of modernity that would propel a variety of utopian experiments in the era of Jim Crow. Many of the most successful to include black people in the interwar period, when Albert and Glanton were coming of age, were multiracial in nature—workers' institutes and folk schools, rural and urban pacifist cells, socialist cooperative farms and sharecropper unions in the South, integrated churches. They arose in response to many factors, including the invigorated labor movements around the country, the far-reaching devastation of the First World War and the Great Depression, and the Great Migration, which brought blacks and whites into unprecedented proximity to one another. Out of many of these experiments emerged future civil rights leaders. In the spirit of the Social Gospel and early utopian communities found throughout the country in the nineteenth century, participants in these experiments often included Christians, socialists, and those who identified as both. The framework of Christian socialism would end up guiding Albert Cleage, Jr.'s own career.

It was not until Albert met Reverend Horace White that he began to care much for his mother's religion. White was the first minister Albert heard who insisted that Christianity ought to have "some kind of relationship with the world." Disenchanted with social work but emboldened by Rev. White's activism, Albert decided to cast his lot with the ministry. In 1938, he enrolled in the Graduate School of Theology at Oberlin College, where White had also been a student. He would split his time between Michigan and Ohio, directing the youth program at Plymouth Congregational back home in Detroit and serving as a student pastor at another Congregational church in Painesville, Ohio.

For more than one hundred years, Oberlin College had enjoyed a reputation as a liberal bastion with abolitionist roots. It was one of the first American institutions of higher learning to integrate, accepting black and white students as early as 1835. But by the time Albert became a student, leaders of the school and town of Oberlin had long since strayed from their earlier commitments to racial egalitarianism, thanks in no small part to the separate but equal doctrine that had been codified in the *Plessy v. Ferguson* decision in 1896.

White Oberlinians' fear of social equality and interracial mingling was pronounced. Albert joined the institution one year after a scandal involving a white woman and a black man dancing at a recreational college event. A small group of supportive white students published a circular intended to remind the school of its founding mission to promote co-educational, interracial education, but to no avail. The school's president refused to make any commitment to social equality on campus, going so far as to write, in the year Albert arrived, "[e]quality for the Negro in Oberlin is not a thing settled by the Trustees . . . but a long, slow, gradual growth, in which the main factor has been and must be the proof given by Negro students themselves of their inner equality in ability and character."

Black students in Oberlin largely lived, dined, and relaxed in separate establishments. Perhaps the only reason the Graduate School of Theology had a higher representation of minorities than other divisions of the college was because, in the early years of the Great Migration, the training of black and immigrant ministers to accommodate the rapid growth of their communities in the North was made a priority. Albert's professors did not directly apply their understanding of scripture to the everyday lives of black Americans. Still, he was attracted to the work of prominent liberal pastors, theologians, philosophers, and historians who wrote about the historical development of religion, modern crises of spiritual disillusionment and doubt, and the need for ideals capable of guiding human action.

Like Ralph Waldo Emerson, Henry David Thoreau, and the other New England Transcendentalists of the previous century, many of whom believed that the meaning of biblical scripture was open to interpretation, Cleage prized his own intuition when it came to deciding what was true and false, what was beautiful and holy in humanity and what was sinful. No books, professors, or institutions could teach what the soul innately knew. Cleage was trying to see a way past the many forces that would have estranged black women and men from their own sense of worth.

At Oberlin, Albert was exposed to the Christian socialist Harry Ward's writing on the threats that industrial society and capitalist greed posed to the imagination. The Quaker mystic Rufus Jones celebrated the direct access every person has to the divine (in one book, Albert underlined Jones's assertion that God "fringes the inner margins of ourselves"). The humanist Eustace Haydon argued that the longest-lasting gods in human history were those believed to have served the material needs of the living rather than the eternal demands of the dead. Haydon and others whose work strongly resonated with Albert, from the theologians Paul Tillich and H. Richard Niebuhr to liberal ministers such as Harry Emerson Fosdick and Ernest Fremont Tittle, emphasized a point that would remain at the heart of Albert's own thought: God was inseparable from human history and human nature. The very identity of the sacred could be discerned only in the world we were given, not the one to come.

These were the kinds of lessons that led Albert to scrawl, in the margins of one of his books on contemporary religious thought, statements such as "The *meaning* of the gods is down in the thick brew of people—not in the thin air of abstract thought"; "God *is* in history"; and "God is the functional idea—important thing is what God *means*.

God is personified reality. Ask: Not is it literally true—but is it dynamically and *meaningfully true.*"

The influence of pragmatic theologians left a large mark on Albert's understanding of the relationship between private spirituality and public life. One of these theologians, Reinhold Niebuhr, would become a major influence on black utopians in the first half of the century, from Cleage to Martin Luther King, Jr., despite his own arguably dour stances on human nature. Niebuhr's view of a transcendent god that existed separately from human action and institutions did not align with Albert's belief in an active god of history. But Niebuhr's beliefs about power appealed to his sense of religious pragmatism. According to Niebuhr, personal beliefs, no matter how noble, would need to confront the harsh realities of a world in which power struggles were always taking place. The life of Christ was a perfectly fine thing to want to emulate, but in reality, few people could become like him. Sometimes, other models might be required to help one live a life that honored the collective good.

With these insights in mind, Christian realists would navigate life knowing that the pursuit of self-interest among the ruling classes was a pervasive problem that demanded creative solutions. A "pragmatic realist," as Albert later described himself, had to believe that there were, in fact, truths that transcended the present, and that there were many unexpected ways to discover them. It did not matter in the end if you were a Christian or not. The fight against white supremacy and the degradation of black souls might well require alliances between whoever was willing to join the struggle: scientists and the faithful, black Christians and black Muslims, communists and socialists, pacifists and armed self-defense groups, and everyone in between.

◇◇◇◇◇◇

After graduating from Oberlin, Albert was ordained as a pastor by Reverend Horace White at Plymouth Congregational on February 4, 1943. He had also recently fallen in love. Albert had known his wife-to-be, Doris Graham, since she was a child. Doris, twelve years younger than

Albert, was no less connected than any of the Cleages. As teenaged members of the Social Sixteen Club, which threw dances and house parties that were lauded in the black press, both Doris and Albert's sister Barbara had been known to dress as stylishly as their parents. Doris's father, a man erroneously listed as white in one census, had been a treasurer and founding trustee of Plymouth Congregational. A cousin of hers published the *Detroit Tribune*, one of the city's leading black papers.

In November 1943, days after Rev. White united the Cleages in marriage, Albert took the helm as pastor at Chandler Memorial Congregational in Lexington, Kentucky. Within two months, the newly-weds were fed up with the state. When the *Tribune* got word that they were returning to Detroit, the paper informed readers that the "young couple found the South's dyed in the wool policy of segregation and oppression of Negroes most distasteful." For one, Albert's attempt to get an NAACP chapter running in Lexington had died on the vine. Dixie turned out to be nothing but a land where "the fog is too heavy or something," Albert later wrote.

One of Albert's former sociology teachers turned the Cleages on to the idea of the Golden West. A white liberal Presbyterian, Alfred Fisk, had an opening for an interim black co-pastor at a new church in San Francisco's Fillmore District. Recently migrated blacks, many of them shipyard workers, were filling homes in this area once occupied by Japanese Americans and Japanese immigrants who were detained in wartime internment camps. Journalists originally described Fisk's Church for the Fellowship of All Peoples as the "Inter-racial Church." His permanent co-pastor, the man for whom Albert would substitute until he was free of his obligations at Howard University's Rankin Chapel, was Howard Thurman, the Quaker-inspired theologian and Christian socialist. Thurman's visit to India and his meeting with Mahatma Gandhi in 1936 solidified his reputation as the nation's most prominent black mystic. He appeared at forums on world peace and universal harmony, and he once chaired the Fellowship of Reconciliation, a pacifist organization that counted social reformers, clergy, socialists, communists, and labor activists among its founders.

Born out of a commitment to Gandhian pacifism and racial egalitarianism, San Francisco's Fellowship Church popularized the interracial church movement that started during the Second World War, when fascism was spreading abroad and racial terror festered on the home front. It was to be a model for "something new in American Christianity," Thurman wrote, and strike a blow against the hypocrisy of most churches, segregated institutions that were somehow expected to model heavenly communities centered on unconditional love and justice. Albert had come highly recommended to Fisk and Thurman, and before Thurman knew whether he would be able to commit to the job, he had mentioned to Fisk the possibility of Albert staying on full-time.

San Francisco promised the Cleages a paycheck, and they needed it, though financial help from Albert's family back in Detroit was only a letter or two away. Because their parsonage was not yet ready when Doris and Albert arrived in February 1944, Fisk opened his home to them. The church had been organized only weeks earlier and had fewer than forty members. In less than six months, Albert soured on the church, and Fisk soured on him. Complaining in a letter to Thurman, Fisk described "the divinity student who is associated with me now" (Albert was no longer in seminary) as "in many ways quite immature." He blamed Albert for neglecting his duties to the congregation and accused him of embracing the defeatist spirit of "nationalism," which at the time meant segregationism.

Albert, for his part, thought Fisk was docile and stubborn. He could not support a church that did not seem to recognize its own weaknesses. Few churches in the country had attracted as much initial excitement, curiosity, and skepticism as did All Peoples. Albert's issue with the place was that it was explicitly designed to be a "neighborhood church" that broke down racial barriers through moral suasion instead of social outreach. Thurman feared that if the church got involved with community work in the Fillmore District, where many poor blacks lived, it would be misunderstood as a charity arm. Albert later recalled that by limiting the "total world in which they live" to a handful of city blocks, Christians without a social program would be stuck "making pleasant and ineffective gestures in restricted and isolated areas of living."

Albert believed that members of the congregation and Fisk himself had narrowed their gazes to a pinhole. The "Negro problem," Albert wrote, would never be properly addressed if people made no effort to undo "the socio-economic framework out of which it has grown and upon which it depends." The best kind of church had to be "more than a place where Negroes and whites can worship God together, or it will inevitably become less." The disagreements between Fisk and Albert came to a head in May 1944 when Albert organized a forum at the church on the American Federation of Labor's discriminatory union practices in Bay Area shipyards. Most of the speakers Albert invited were associated with the Communist-leaning unions of the Congress of Industrial Organizations. It was clear that Albert and the disgruntled flock of the Fellowship Church were at a dead end. Albert's contract expired in June, and he left San Francisco days before Thurman arrived.

<><><><><><>

Los Angeles beckoned. Albert, who had a great love for photography and hoped to use film as part of a future ministry for young people, had enrolled in the film and religious studies programs at the University of Southern California. He had turned down an opportunity to lead another interracial church in Berkeley, one of the first of its kind in the Bay Area, and although schools in the South had vacancies for a religion professor and pastor, the pay was pitiful. At USC, Albert supplemented his income by taking a part-time preaching post at a nearby Congregational church.

In Los Angeles, the Cleages sometimes chose to forget their light pocketbooks and dined with other black folk at the Faun, a favorite restaurant of their neighborhood's nouveau riche. Apart from the kitchenette without a stove or sink, Albert didn't mind their new setup in a bachelor's apartment on South Hobart, its wall-to-wall blue carpeting, white woodwork, Venetian blinds, and wine-colored drapes right out of *House & Garden*. The living room fold-out bed was a nice touch. Their home "on the hill," outside of which trees stood sentry along the curb, reminded Albert of Detroit's North End neighborhood, where black life was vibrant.

Albert wrote to his family often to ask how things were getting on back in the "hinterland." Life on the Pacific coast made Michigan feel like the backcountry. Still, "I seem to be headin' for Detroit both consciously and unconsciously," he speculated in one letter. Albert wanted to organize a church that was not gagged by oversight committees, and which actively engaged in social struggle instead of simply offering paeans to racial harmony.

Rev. White kept Albert apprised of churches where positions might soon be available, including at St. John's Congregational, a historically black church in Springfield, Massachusetts. St. John's pastor was set to resign in February 1945. Albert had no expectation that "one of the old New England Elite outfits" would want to hire him, though, and that spring, he wrote to Howard Thurman to request a reference letter for a position at Detroit's new Church of All Peoples, which was inspired by the San Francisco example. The two men had never met. Albert must have recognized the awkwardness of his request, but this did not stop him from confessing that he was "sincerely interested in the inter-racial church idea, and [felt] that its extension during these critical days is a most significant contribution to the building of a more Christian world."

Albert was not yet a black nationalist. He did not abhor integration outright, but he also did not believe that it was a worthwhile end unto itself. Interracial churches would need to do more than simply bring people together. Thurman wrote a restrained letter of support for Albert, describing him as a "deeply religious man with a full social problem orientation." Albert did not get the job. No matter. On August 28, 1945, weeks after the Hiroshima and Nagasaki bombings and days before the war ended, Albert was chosen as St. John's next pastor. He started in October.

St. John's looked like any wood-shingled English country church. Its façade was taken up mostly by stained-glass windows dedicated to bygone church members and abolitionists such as John Brown, a former congregant of St. John's. The church Albert inherited was no longer the shining exemplar it had been before the Depression, when it was a major provider of social services for Springfield's black population. Albert would spend the next six years attempting to restore St. John's to its former glory.

He had been there for only one month when he wrote to family in Detroit of his plans: "I'm trying to gradually get everybody *doing* something." He mentioned putting together "activity groups" led by lay leaders. He established a youth program that included Girl and Boy Scouts, sports, and community service. He became a public-housing advocate and a vocal critic of abuses by the police. Staying true to his convictions that the meaning of religious life and the purpose of the church varied depending on the historical moment, Albert tried to distinguish St. John's from the slavery-era plantation churches that he believed served mainly to offer spiritual comfort to black people instead of true autonomy. But by working to improve the lives of black people wherever his vocation took him, Albert had unintentionally sown discord at every church he'd passed through. His unapologetic activism sometimes provoked suspicions of Communist influence, an accusation that was becoming increasingly charged in the postwar years.

◇◇◇◇◇◇

By 1951, Albert and Doris had two young daughters, Kristin and Pearl, born in 1946 and 1948. Albert, no longer a young man, longed for the familiarity of home. Albert Sr. was one of the organizers of St. Mark's United Presbyterian Church in Detroit. Facing a shortage of suitable pastors, church leaders sent for the doctor's son. Albert Jr. answered their call, moving his family into a parsonage down the street from where his parents lived.

St. Mark's turned out to be a place perfectly suited for those wanting an insular church experience. There the colored folk sang in Latin. Renditions of the Te Deum and Gloria Patri frequently resounded in a church that had been abandoned by white Lutherans and restored by black housewives' leagues. Despite St. Mark's conservatism, membership increased more than threefold during Albert's tenure, surging above three hundred congregants. He especially appealed to young people who wished to perform good works in the world beyond the church.

It did not take long for St. Mark's older traditionalists to grow wary of the younger Cleage. He started inviting controversial speakers such as Paul Robeson, who had urged American reconciliation with the USSR, advocated for state socialism, and received the Stalin Prize in 1952. After only two years, St. Mark's trustees voted the doctor's son out in March 1953. One of Albert Jr.'s own uncles sided with the turncoats. The betrayal at St. Mark's enraged Albert as much as it wounded him. These were not strangers. He had come back to the city for them. It took this treachery for Albert to see how little these staid, well-dressed black folk wanted an actual church. He delivered his last oration the Sunday after he learned his fate.

It had otherwise been a promising spring for the reverend. He was about to chair the Detroit NAACP's membership drive, one of the largest in the country. In late March, after the ousting, the *Tribune* still referred to Albert as St. Mark's pastor. Apparently, the paper hadn't gotten wind of the revolt. Albert spoke optimistically of his plan to use neighborhood workers to recruit thousands of new NAACP members. He did not reveal that at the end of his last sermon, he had walked out of St. Mark's not knowing where or what was next for him. He did not share that there had been many people—his supporters—who stood up from the pews and, seeing nothing for them at St. Mark's anymore, followed him out.

Two days before Albert spoke to the *Tribune*, 143 of the separatists who left St. Mark's in solidarity with their outcast pastor met in the auditorium of a recreational center. One hundred fifty-six more joined their ranks by Easter. They pointedly called themselves the St. Mark's Community Church. They would need a pulpit stand, chairs, and a place to worship. A high school where Albert had spoken one month prior opened its auditorium for their use. The schismatics thus began their search for a new world, in which the needs of the spirit would never again negate those of the flesh.

Southeast Corner of My Cell

◇◇◇◇◇◇◇

Working under a false name, the artist who was barely more than a child took jobs that others did not want. In Florida, he painted water towers. When that gig came and went, he washed dishes in a restaurant. Life was unremarkable, which meant it was going well, until he ended up in a street brawl and had to disappear quickly. If he was tired of running away, he did not act like it. In Jacksonville, he caught a boat to Cuba. For four months he lived there, never ceasing with his painting. He cobbled money together as a freelancer, an artist-for-hire. What had started as a hobby became the key to his survival.

It is unclear why Glanton returned to Detroit when he did, although it may have had something to do with his mother, Ruby. He had escaped the juvenile detention center in Lansing, but the boy still had an armed robbery charge looming over him. Ruby knew what to do. She raised five hundred dollars by drawing from her savings and borrowing from others so that she could pay a broker to whisper in the ears of Detroit's corrupt cops and city officials. She made her son clean in the eyes of the law.

The odd jobs didn't stop when Glanton came home. Most of them were worse than the ones he'd had in Florida. When he wasn't on the clock cleaning barrels for Chrysler, he painted portraits, which helped him cover most of his family's household expenses. His unabashed embrace of communism took him, for a while, off the shop floors. He was eighteen years old, it was 1941, and the National Negro Congress hadn't lost its appeal for the boy despite the heightened dangers of being identified as a Red after 1939, when the Soviet Union signed a nonaggression pact with Nazi Germany. Weeks after the death of his grandmother Annie that fall, he was passing out Party pamphlets one day when he was arrested with a gun in his pocket.

Glanton was sentenced to two years' probation and fired from Chrysler. Every time he attempted to find peace in the world, the world seemed to reject him. He tried on various hats that fit him poorly—gardener, babysitter, a worker at a crane repair company. The last straw was his realization that the National Negro Congress was a moribund organization. He suspected that black union leaders in the NNC "weren't real Communists" anymore, but "just a middle-class gang." And at this point, what reason did they have to be otherwise? Political sentiments in the country were changing rapidly. The same nationwide trade union movement that the NNC helped activate during the Depression was now turning against it as an emerging black middle class saw little use anymore for talk of class revolt. This was especially true in Detroit, where the United Auto Workers had become one of the most powerful labor unions in the country. It appeared that the more money blacks acquired, the more likely they were to oppose communism and side with those who dismissed an interracial movement for economic self-determination, social inclusiveness, and civil rights as "subversive."

Foreseeing the end of a once-promising road toward black liberation, Glanton became a "drifting man" and bohemian, traveling around the United States. He went as far away as Alaska, staying at artist colonies and painting portraits of just about anyone who asked for one. Using the money he made as a portraitist, Glanton enrolled at the Art Institute of Chicago in the late 1940s—it was then one of the few art academies to accept blacks—and, after that, the Society of Arts and Crafts in Detroit. It was not until his midtwenties that Glanton decided to formalize his study of art. He would never identify with any specific school, scorning the label of "realist" in favor of, he said later, "my own little battle striving for originality." The academies taught him the visual languages of European portraiture that he never saw any reason to emulate, and which he would continue to undermine in ways both spectacular and mundane.

⬦⬦⬦⬦⬦⬦⬦

There would be conflicting accounts of what happened in the spring and summer of 1948, omissions and revisions in news articles and Glanton's own retellings that made it hard to know the truth. The papers said that in May 1948, Glanton was involved in a holdup in front of a Detroit apartment complex that ended with him shooting a local bar owner, who later died in the hospital. Glanton's coat, sunglasses, and two .38 revolvers were discovered in a basement near the murder scene. The FBI got involved when he was believed to have fled the state. Glanton would tell a very different story decades later. He explained that he had gone to the home of a family in Detroit that had commissioned a painting. The husband, a mafia drug lord, showed up with two accomplices who grew hostile toward Glanton and pounced. The artist claimed he didn't know why the situation turned, but he grabbed hold of one of their pistols and shot at the boss, killing him. The mafia boss was never given a name in these stories, but the bar owner, Alphonso Smith, was most certainly dead.

Glanton left the state on suspicion of murder and checked into a cheap hotel in Baltimore under the pseudonym "John Singleton." He was apprehended by the Baltimore police in early August after he and another man got into an altercation with a soldier at a bus depot. The mysterious person who the *Evening Sun* described as an "itinerant colored sketch artist" was found guilty of armed assault and robbery. His sentence—two years in the Maryland penitentiary—was suspended so that he could face second-degree murder charges in Detroit. In 1949, he was found guilty. Glanton faced between thirty and forty years in the State Prison of Southern Michigan.

Years later, Glanton would tell one of the journalists who came to visit him in prison that "the creative process is largely a matter of painting between and around restrictions." Only the truly "creative person can benefit from any experience he survives," he went on, and "even deep misfortune can have its rewards." Glanton's time in prison was brutal. He never forgot the abuse by guards or the sixty-two days he spent in an isolation cell: "pitch dark, no windows, a wooden bed with a thin cover, thin long johns your only clothes." He had to wrap himself tightly in his cover so that he would not freeze to death. He developed ugly scars on his hips from sleeping on hard surfaces.

The prison's Department of Individual Treatment, hailed as a progressive reform measure in an otherwise inhumane environment, instituted an art mentorship program that put Glanton in touch with the black artist Robert Stacey. Stacey had been a scholar of Latin and Greek and a teaching assistant at the University of Michigan until he was convicted of arson. With Stacey's guidance, and through correspondence courses at the University of Chicago, Glanton picked up some Greek and Russian. Other inmates called people like Glanton a *dog*, which meant anyone who was trying not only to survive in prison but to improve themselves there. "If you don't watch yourself, you become intellectually calloused," Glanton told a journalist. "Death loses its meaning. I'm chiefly a rebel. That's why I paint as I do. Sometimes I get very depressed, and I sketch to overcome my depression."

Six years into his sentence, Glanton painted *Southeast Corner of My Cell*, a grim self-portrait. In it, the artist has hung his light blue jacket over a mirror that is screwed onto a dark mass of steel. The image is tightly focused. Glanton is shirtless, his expression flat, and the viewer can only see above his neck and shoulders. The mirror's glass is cracked, and it appears that the top half of the artist's head has been severed from the bottom. The painting won Glanton an honorable mention in a 1955 exhibition at the Detroit Institute of Arts. Not long after, he had an agent. Over the next few years, Glanton's work received more praise. One painting that also showed at the DIA, *Observation Ward*, depicts four inmates he had seen being corralled into the prison's psychiatric wing. He was unable to attend his one-man shows in Detroit and New York City but turned over whatever profit he made from selling his art to his mother (this was after Ruby had sent him money so that he could buy materials for his craft).

At one point, for more than twelve hours a day, six days a week, his job was to teach art students in the prison's vocational school. From an improvised studio—a small corner of a classroom, perhaps, or the middle of his cell—Glanton showed these men how to create something that was entirely their own. He told them they could pick up stones from the prison yard, paint them, and create something novel. They did not even need a canvas. By the winter of 1958, nine years after he went in, Glanton was dividing his time between studying, painting, and patrolling as a cellblock clerk. His work brought favorable press to the state prison ("sob stories," he called these articles). Few reporters failed to notice that he was a somber, scholarly sort, remarkably careful in choosing his words. He was liable to give a short lecture on any subject at all, from his own mortality to the evils of the wretched institution in which he experienced what was then his greatest success.

"The artist as a mutation on the social body has no will," he wrote to one of his art dealers. "His function is to absorb, synthesize and eject. The compulsion to place within the range of perception the heretofore unperceived is almost libidinal in nature—the ultimate purpose of which is to further the evolutionary process." This was hyperbole. Glanton was not the kind to sit around waiting for the muse. He told a reporter that he wished one day to paint a large mosaic mural depicting the life of the Negro in America. Incarceration would not obstruct the development of his art but only send it flowing through unexpected channels.

LETTER III:
BAD SPIRIT MULTIPLYING

All things are spiritual, and the decisions that I make have got to be morally correct. Time after time, I had not done the correct thing. This came from me wanting freedom in life after always feeling limited, restricted, held back. College was my way of escaping my environment. I always searched for a better life, but my socialization problem made me feel that college was my place of refuge. After Cindy and I reached a point of no return, everything became unreal.

My parents had become too involved in my relationship with Cindy. They felt as if I was the bad guy and favored Cindy over me. I remember that things were so bad, and I was so shut out of my parents' hearts, that when I asked my mother what school Aaron attended, she refused to tell me. They were like a clique, and I was the shunned outsider. I took responsibility for creating this environment, in a way, but the lack of love was confusing for me. There were very logical reasons why Cindy and I did not become a family. No one took note of how there was fault on both sides, but that was no longer important to me. I felt as if I were gasping for air.

I recall a Christmas party at my parents' house. My son was there and my mother had assumed the role of caregiver because my parents wanted to be there for him. My parents' help prevented Cindy and me from having to deal with our would-be family. I was circumvented, passed by. My parents acted as if I were not present when I was. I thought that perhaps they would relent and realize that Cindy and I had created Aaron, but that never happened. When Cindy showed up to pick up my son, Aaron began crying, saying that he didn't want to go because he didn't like his mom's boyfriend. I went to ask Aaron what he meant, and Cindy stepped in front of me and said, "Oh, he's just tired." Both my mom and Cindy said that Aaron was just tired.

I knew how foolish I could be. At that moment, I considered violence. I was fed up with Cindy's disrespect and my parents' disrespect and thought that I should physically move them out of the way since they felt the need to keep me from hearing my son's testimony. I knew that they would probably call the police or find some reason for saying that I was wrong. I was outraged that their malice for me would make them cut Aaron off from telling me why he was so upset.

The bad spirit in me grew. I drove past Cindy's apartment that night, where she stayed with her boyfriend. I wanted to see what was going on. I could see Cindy washing dishes. I had an uneasy feeling. The troubling part was that Cindy blocked me from hearing Aaron out. Why?

I eventually went to prison for armed robbery. I used the excuse of losing my job to misuse my firearm. After being in Michigan prisons for four or five years, I finally felt peace in my soul. Prison was much better than the disdain that had grown for me in my family.

I had a friend by the name of Ali. Ali was African American

*like me. He had a different religious practice. He was Muslim.
He didn't claim Sunni or Shia Islam and believed that there
should be no factions in the Islamic religion, just as there should
be no factions in Christianity. Why are there Catholics and
Protestants, Baptists and Episcopalians, the Church of God and
the Church of God in Christ?*

*Ali and I were both at Mound Correctional Facility. I never
had any biological brothers, so my friendships with men my age
were always important to me. Brotherhood is a gift. Ali was truly
my brother in my heart. He called me by my family nickname,
Doe. I had met Ali when we were at Macomb Regional Facility
in New Haven, Michigan. We were from the same way. His
family raised him near Grand River, and I was raised off
Puritan.*

*About a month before we were transferred to Mound
Correctional, we were at a prison in Coldwater, Michigan. When
incarcerated, you are shipped off to different prison camps to keep
people from becoming too cemented at a single place when things
are not peaceful. The idea is that gangs and allegiances and fights
are broken up by sending immature and troublesome people to
different locations. I had grown aggravated by everything, so I
did not value any level of correction.*

*When we were in Coldwater, I caused a stir because I refused
to go to my designated area of housing. I was being denied
diabetic medication. I, in turn, decided that I no longer needed
to follow directions about where I should sit, stand, or sleep.
My refusal to go lie down in my bunk caused me to be locked
in the hole for two weeks. It's called segregation. You're shut in
a room for days on end without a shower or human contact. I
would watch the sun come up and go down. I stared at the moon
throughout the night.*

*Before I went to segregation, Ali and I had spent a lot of time
walking the yard and talking. Ali was in prison because he used
to make and sell illegal substances and he injured someone during*

an argument. They later died from the injury. During our time walking together, he found out that one of his ex-girlfriends was a childhood friend of mine. I learned that his godsister had tried to trick me into thinking that her daughter was my daughter. We knew the same people. We got a kick out of that. We joked and laughed, and Ali even told me why he didn't like Christians. He said the crazy thing about Black Christians is that we know Southern Baptists and Catholics hate us, yet we still believe in Christ.

Just because what is good gets misrepresented does not mean that it is bad. My belief is that God is an entity that can be reached personally. I don't have to accept an interpretation of God from any source that does not prove to be true, logical, or reliable. Not all Christians are fake and hateful people. Some people who claim to believe in Christ have good hearts. I was one of them.

Ali was the head of security for the Islamic group within our prison. His Muslim brothers questioned my faith. They thought that because of the way I carried myself I must have been Islamic. Ali and I walked on the yard and worked out together. There was no beef between us. He worshipped in his way and I praised God in mine. We both truly loved our Creator. He praised Allah and told me that ours was the same God. Ali and I were both better than the place we had put ourselves in and the things we had done to our lives. The last time I saw him, we were laughing. I know I should have written to him and kept in touch after I got out. I am ashamed that I did not keep such people in my life.

Imperium in Imperio

◇◇◇◇◇◇◇

In 1957, from his new church on Linwood Street, Albert Cleage, Jr., heard the uproar of brass and shout bands half a mile away. Bishop Charles Manuel Grace—known as "Sweet Daddy," Holy Prophet of the Last Days—was holding midsummer services that were so loud they were deemed a public nuisance. The practiced voice of Sweet Daddy Grace crackled from loudspeakers mounted on sound trucks. The Cape Verdean preacher had received a direct mandate from heaven as a child mystic. The guardsmen at his United House of Prayer wore powder-blue garments, and plumes jutted from their militaristic helmets. They wet their lips before blowing the dust off Sweet Daddy's black cloak, which was lined with crimson silk. His billowy, permed gray hair looked much younger than his face. He clumped his curls under a sombrero.

Outside his church, musicians would clap and play cornets, trombones, bugles, and tambourines past midnight. The outdoor baptisms that Sweet Daddy was known for compelled observers to bring parasols or, if they lived nearby, to latch their windows. Candidates for baptism, dressed in white garments and shower caps, pranced in the streets as Sweet Daddy or one of his elders sprayed a fire hose like it was a howitzer, deluging the roads.

The black residents of the Dexter-Linwood neighborhood were tired of these false prophets descending on their blocks. Sweet Daddy and others like him tended to follow the scents of desperation and credulity. They loved this part of the city more than any other. They extended jewel-encrusted hands to the deaf, the blind, and the sick. The left hand accepted donations and gifts purchased on credit. The right sold hair products, cold creams, toothpaste, amulets, and images of the crucified Christ, on the back of which were scrawled three digits for playing the numbers.

The various prophets of Linwood were jealous and competitive gods. They either ignored one another or, when one of them ran afoul of the law and was forced to sell their properties, bought some other disgraced prophet's old buildings and started their own congregations. In his reach, Sweet Daddy Grace was no Father Divine, the wealthy spiritual leader known for his Depression-era, interracial cooperative movement, the International Peace Mission. At the peak of Father Divine's influence in the mid-1930s, there were perhaps tens of thousands of Americans, white and black, who believed he was God on earth, as he claimed to be. His free Sunday banquets and job clinics, charisma, evangelical fervor, and pacifism brought him scores of followers. Second only to Marcus Garvey's Universal Negro Improvement Association, the Peace Mission of Father Divine was considered one of the largest black utopian movements of its time.

As the country recovered from the Depression, the need for Father

Divine's food pantries and communes (he called them his "heavens") declined. Sweet Daddy would eventually buy Father Divine's heavens in Harlem, where the Peace Mission once had its greatest influence. Meanwhile, Father Divine languished at his mansion in Pennsylvania after facing legal troubles of his own. When Sweet Daddy came to Detroit, he moved into a château that another Linwood Street preacher, Prophet Jones, had vacated after creditors started hounding him for missed payments. In 1959, one other growing religious movement that began in Depression-era Detroit, the Nation of Islam (NOI), would move its original Temple No. 1 from another part of the city to a small building on Linwood, a few minutes' drive from Albert's church. The NOI had gained notoriety in Detroit twenty years prior after one of its members stabbed another man to death in his home as a supposed sacrifice to Allah. Following what the mainstream press denounced as a ritual murder, the NOI was popularly viewed as a cult of "Islamism" or "voodooism," a preview of the stigmas that would follow the organization for decades.

There was good reason for so many religious leaders like Albert, Sweet Daddy Grace, and others to make their spiritual homes on Linwood Street. In 1946, Detroit began implementing a redevelopment project that would, over the next twenty years, price tens of thousands of black people out of their homes. Slum clearance policies and highway construction slowly destroyed the neighborhoods of Black Bottom, where Glanton Dowdell was born, and Paradise Valley, its adjacent commercial center. The city's relocation office could not track precisely how many people were displaced or where everyone went. Thousands were pushed into projects, and some crossed over into the west side's Twelfth Street corridor. Linwood Street was one of its main appendages. Although this area had once been largely blue-collar and white, depreciating home values and the proximity of established black neighborhoods drove most white residents away and transformed Dexter-Linwood into a center of black life in Detroit. Linwood Street's poorer, vulnerable pickings were ripe for the divinely inspired.

Father Divine may have been something of a conman, but for

Albert Jr. what mattered was that his ministry had been oriented toward mass social action and economic uplift. He dismissed charismatics like Sweet Daddy Grace as "Candy Men" who "mesmerized the Ghetto" with sweet nothings. Their followers who believed that positive thinking alone would secure their well-being were sick in mind and spirit, Albert believed. The Candy Men were afflicted by a kind of invisibility. Albert was not thinking about Ralph Ellison's *man of substance, of flesh and bone, fiber and liquids*. Rather, these prophets resembled the Invisible Man of H. G. Wells. "He must wrap himself in something like a mummy if he is to be seen by other people," Albert wrote. The only thing that seemed to make these people real in the world were objects of the flesh—nice clothes that could be draped over an absence, beautiful gems that could fill a hole. Albert was frustrated by the black bourgeoisie as a class—his own—and the self-serving black person who obsessively "wraps himself with the 'right people' and a house on the 'right street.'"

Albert would later equate his task to that of Hosea, the Old Testament prophet to Israel's apostates, who worshipped false gods and indulged in hedonism. He pointed to Hosea 13, which admonished the nation of Israel to reject idolatry. Black social climbers, Albert believed, were like ghosts who did not know they were dead, moving through the world and having no lasting effect upon it. They were the same people who either complained about displaced blacks moving uptown or took advantage of them. Albert described Detroit as "a place of contrasts . . . a city of lights and shadows." The holy men and women who should have been spreading the light were merely basking in it.

◇◇◇◇◇◇◇

Albert finally bought a car, the easier to get to his church at 7625 Linwood. Reverend Horace White and the Congregational Association of Detroit helped Albert find a new location for his church in 1957, after years of holding services in a school gym and a sixteen-room parsonage where the Cleage family lived until Albert and Doris divorced amicably in 1954. For St. Mark's Community Church to be accepted into the

Congregational communion, Albert had to drop the name *St. Mark's*. It might otherwise be mistaken for the church he'd left. In a nod to Rev. White's hope that his church would become a cultural and spiritual center for black Detroiters, Albert renamed it Central Congregational.

The Linwood church was built early in the century in homage to New England's classical columnar porticos and stark bell towers. It looked like a colonial courthouse. For thirty years, the building was home to a white congregation named in honor of William Brewster, leader of the first English colony in New England, and the other Pilgrims who had come over on the *Mayflower*. The round-arched, stained-glass window behind the altar showed the Puritan governor William Bradford disembarking at Plymouth Rock and holding a Bible. The image honored one of the nation's foundational myths— and one of the first white utopian communities in North America. The building had carpeted lounge and bridal rooms, a gymnasium, an industrial kitchen, and a dining hall with a terrazzo floor. Cylindrical pendant lights hung over the sanctuary's broad balcony section. Troubles with a slowly crumbling roof would eat away at the church's coffers for years, but Central Congregational was ready to be filled.

In the late 1950s, attracting new members to Central went as well as anyone could have hoped. The church's Boy Scouts canvassed door-to-door. Newspaper ads, mailing campaigns, and sound cars brought more visitors out. Youth groups spent weekends washing cars, raking leaves, cleaning basements, and holding bake sales. The young people of Central were so unusually organized for religious youth groups at the time, with their solemn statements of purpose and rules of conduct, that the church's reputation grew partly out of their work in the community. When a recession struck the country in 1958, drying up some of the usual tithes, Central's high school and college students supported an effort to raise thousands of dollars for building upkeep.

At the same time, some adults in the church broke their fundraising commitments and went on vacation. Albert feared that too many people lacked enthusiasm at a critical stage in Central's growth. He came up with a slogan for Central to honor: *Mobilization for Christian*

Action. By 1960, obligation trumped as-your-heart-moves-you as a matter of church policy. This would be a place for people who wanted to be active in the world at large. "It was felt that we must seriously consider a conscious effort to change our church's 'image' in the community if we are to effectively minister to our immediate one-mile area," Albert wrote. Within a year, the radius of what he called Central's "total community" extended to the three miles surrounding it. Like a torch lighting the decade ahead, Central's 1960 calendar laid out a vision that would sound familiar to champions of that decade's burgeoning countercultures: "We do not pretend to a hypocritical piety which would isolate us from the main streams of contemporary life. We do not believe that Jesus calls us 'out of the world,' but rather that He has commissioned us to confront the world and transform it by His spirit and in His name."

◇◇◇◇◇◇

Albert would not allow his flock to drop out of society and pick daisies in the woods. The cautious optimism that black people around the world were feeling at the start of the new decade, and the keen awareness that social and economic disparities in the United States persisted despite the legal defeat of the "separate but equal" doctrine, made this impossible. There were clear reasons for black Americans to feel hopeful, especially those who looked elsewhere in the world for inspiration. The year 1960 belonged, in part, to Africa, where nearly twenty nations had recently been freed from the colonial rule of the French, the Italians, the British, and the Belgians. The planetary tumult was unprecedented, reminding many observers of history's great black uprisings, from Haiti to the battlefields of Adwa in Ethiopia. "We feel a sense of panic at the passing of the familiar, the understood, the stable," Albert wrote in 1961, reflecting on the first eight years of his church. "We wonder in the face of an unknown future . . . There is so much to be done, and even with a rapidly growing membership, we are still so few."

The previous year, at the Democratic National Convention, Senator John F. Kennedy articulated his own vision of what the decade could be. The 1960s represented a New Frontier of "unknown opportunities and perils, the frontier of unfilled hopes and unfilled threats." He looked to the stars and bade Americans to revive the expansionist spirit of the pioneers. He asked them to join the "race for mastery of the sky and the rain, the ocean and the tides, the far side of space, and the inside of men's minds."

In 1961, an election year in Detroit, Kennedy's optimism was felt deeply among Democrats. A thirty-three-year-old lawyer and political newcomer named Jerome Cavanagh defeated the Republican incumbent mayor. It was an astounding upset. The election results didn't surprise Albert. He joked that Cavanagh's win had nothing to do with his youthful looks. The black Detroiters who helped put Cavanagh in office weren't voting for a man, Albert believed. They were voting against more of the same. The televised Freedom Rides and sit-ins in the South that year had turned simmering grievances to a boil. Why was it, then, that the local press kept describing the deliberate mobilization of black voters as some kind of spontaneous protest?

Albert and his siblings had been preparing for the moment Detroit's black populace shifted the balance of power in the city, as had innumerable social and block clubs, trade unions, citizens committees, churches, and individuals connected to no organization at all. Hugh and Henry Cleage had been running a lithographic printing shop, Cleage Printers, since the late 1950s with financial support from their brother Louis and a family friend, the attorney Milton Henry. Their little sister Barbara joined them. Money flowed in from printing handbills for nearby businesses. The Cleage brothers also made flyers, newsletters, and magazines for local artists and the Socialist Workers Party.

Never missing an opportunity to expand his public platform as Central grew, Albert joined the family endeavor. On leftover pink paper used for making handbills, the Cleage siblings began printing *The Illustrated News* in 1961. Henry and Barbara were editors. Hugh Cleage and Milton Henry's brother, Richard, were on the editorial board. Louis Cleage would write a humor column. Albert came on as a contributing editor. Like so many other black-run circulars since the nineteenth century, *The Illustrated News* carried op-eds, satirical cartoons, and commentaries on issues that affected black communities. Thousands of copies started appearing in barbershops, church lobbies, and other places throughout the city where black people gathered.

◇◇◇◇◇◇

In November 1961, Albert and the Henry brothers, Milton and Richard, discussed what to do about a spate of violence against blacks in the city. The county prosecutor had refused to issue arrest warrants for assailants in three recent attacks, two of which were fatal. Why weren't the NAACP and the Urban League making more noise? The Henry brothers wouldn't stand for it. Richard, a journalist for the black-run *Michigan Chronicle*, had first met the Cleage family while partnering with Henry and Hugh in the mid-1950s to publish a weekly paper of their own. And Milton, a lawyer in the city of Pontiac, had earned a reputation as a vehement defender of black people who had been subpoenaed by the House Un-American Activities Committee. In Albert, the most outspoken of the Cleage siblings, the Henry brothers found a kindred spirit. As the three of them saw it, the negligence of the major civil rights groups left a leadership vacuum in the city. Detroit had been made into a moral wasteland of empty philanthropy, empty promises from Uncle Toms, and empty liberal visions urging patience and recourse to the law. The freedom struggle, Albert wrote, was a "headless revolution."

Within a week of Cavanagh's mayoral victory, *The Illustrated News* announced the creation of the Group on Advanced Leadership (GOAL), an alternative to the mainstream civil rights groups. Albert and the Henry brothers would co-lead. At the same time, the *News* was inviting guest columnists to write. Many were black teachers who complained of terrible conditions at their schools. Now on the last pages of almost every issue of the *News,* the number of churches subscribing to the paper grew. Albert received invitations to speak before lawyers' guilds, fraternal lodges, churches, and other groups in the city.

Whatever the term *New Negro* had meant during the Harlem

Renaissance, Albert grasped its implications for Detroit and other large cities whose demographics were changing rapidly in the early 1960s. The New Negroes were pushing out white politicians who mistakenly thought their jobs were safe. They were teasing the Uncle Toms who cried when Eleanor Roosevelt died in 1962 or rejoiced when the Republican governor George Romney took office in Michigan in 1963; Albert regarded these two events as the symbolic conclusions to an era of liberal optimism. Albert and the other New Negroes of Detroit took Romney's win as further confirmation that the Democratic Party was, at every level, a "dead carcass." Albert had been thinking JFK was full of hot air anyways. He'd gone silent on the violence in Birmingham, Alabama, and Albany, Georgia, as well as the James Meredith integration scandal at the University of Mississippi.

Albert's profile was growing outside of his church thanks to his articles for *The Illustrated News* and the *Michigan Chronicle*, as well as his many public appearances. He had not yet disavowed the nonviolent tactics that had worked in the South. He believed that sit-ins and bus boycotts angered white people, who then spilled the blood of blacks, demonstrating that the latter possessed, Albert wrote, "a moral and spiritual superiority which is invincible." This was the kind of statement that alarmed Albert's critics. Perhaps it wouldn't have been so concerning if Albert was a Sundays-only preacher. But since the late 1950s, he had been popping up everywhere, shaming administrators at school board meetings, endorsing black political candidates at tea and garden parties, and addressing ministers' wives during breakfast hour at the YWCA. He told anyone who would listen to vote for blacks, buy from blacks, and to prepare themselves for the "Second Industrial Revolution," the era of automation that was already putting black factory workers out of a job.

By 1963, Albert was becoming a problem for the city's public officials. The issues of overflowing classrooms, school days so short that some places were in danger of losing accreditation, biased history textbooks and hiring practices, and irresponsible educational leaders were talking points during his almost two-year-long campaign against school millage increases. At almost 250 events throughout the city in 1962 and 1963, Albert urged civil disobedience, telling black audiences to "vote no." His view that black people should not have to pay more property taxes to fund a school system that neglected their children drew loud outcries. Some said that Albert was a dangerous extremist who was sabotaging the futures of black youth. It is impossible to say how much Albert's campaign affected the outcome, but the tax increase did not pass.

◇◇◇◇◇◇◇

The national freedom movement had other concerns. The Southern Christian Leadership Conference (SCLC) was leading demonstrations in Birmingham, and in May 1963, the city's public safety commissioner Bull Connor turned fire hoses and dogs on protestors. Fury crawled north. In Detroit, the events in Birmingham prompted Clarence La-Vaughn Franklin, the famous pastor of the New Bethel Baptist Church, which had recently relocated to Linwood Street, to organize a march that would raise money for the SCLC. With the encouragement of Harry Belafonte and Mahalia Jackson, Martin Luther King, Jr., agreed to lead the Detroit march. Albert was not officially on the planning committee, but he convinced Franklin to widen the march's purview and call attention to the inadequate state of housing, education, and employment for blacks in the North as well.

The date of the Walk to Freedom was set for Sunday, June 23, 1963. More than one hundred organizations throughout Michigan called event headquarters to commit marchers in the dozens or hundreds. Thousands of bumper stickers and handbills advertising the march were distributed. It was now time for the New Negroes of the North—those who had been waiting, as Albert wrote, for a "palace revolution"—to rise.

"Dr. Luther King's strength lies with the masses of Negro people," Albert wrote in *The Illustrated News* two weeks before the march. "The entire southern protest movement is a mass movement. The Detroit NAACP is a class organization. The reason for the success of one and the failure of the other is obvious." Albert was speaking of a bubbling revolution from below, in which blacks of all backgrounds, not only middle-class gatekeepers, could take part. He felt that the day of the march would either be a disaster or signal a changing of the guard. Detroit's police commissioner suggested that the police band lead marchers down to the Cobo Hall convention center, where Dr. King and others would speak. In a city that was now one-third black, one wrong move could set the dry earth aflame.

When June 23 came, it could have been mistaken for a feast day. Albert would recall how the Walk to Freedom that afternoon looked like "much more of a triumphant thing than Jesus had in Jerusalem." The press estimated the number of marchers at 125,000. Others, including the police commissioner himself, placed the number as high as a quarter million. Albert later ridiculed the police officers stationed along the twenty-block route who knew that the mostly black crowd "could have walked them into the asphalt of the street without even striking a blow." King had been rushed from his hotel suite to reach the procession. He walked arm-in-arm with C. L. Franklin some distance from the front. Albert was nearby, marching behind them. Some of Albert's family were in the audience of twenty thousand that made it into Cobo Hall while excess crowds milled outside on the lawns, listening to loudspeakers.

Before King delivered his address, an early version of the speech he would refine for the March on Washington that August, Albert issued a fiery call for a picket of local grocery stores that were reluctant to hire black workers and sell products from black business owners. His microphone was cut off. It didn't matter. He was said to have delivered a speech as electrifying as King's, depending on what kind of message one wanted to hear that day. The Detroit march was downplayed by the national press, but King and others described the Walk to Freedom as the largest civil rights demonstration in the country's history to that point.

Albert thought the event's afterglow would last for years, but it faded within weeks. In early July, there was news about a philanthropic fund that would support major civil rights groups such as the SCLC, the Congress of Racial Equality (CORE), and the Student Nonviolent Coordinating Committee (SNCC) ahead of the March on Washington. This sounded very much like a muzzle—white capitalists buying the cooperation of black groups before they received the national spotlight—and a death knell for whatever radical spirit of direct action remained. Albert had hoped that, for King, the expression *freedom now!* meant something like traffic blockages shutting D.C. down for a week and sit-ins inside both chambers of Congress. But with cities screening participants before sending them on trains and buses to the nation's capital, with preapproved signs and songs, the March on Washington was shaping up to be more like a Sunday school picnic than a protest. The defiant King who had sat in a Birmingham jail in June 1963 was the last version of the man Albert could get behind. The King who stood in the National Mall two months later was a poor imitation, an integrationist who believed too strongly that the word of *Brown v. Board of Education* was inviolable.

◇◇◇◇◇◇

On the day of the Washington march, brochures were passed out in Detroit and its suburbs announcing the formation of a political party that saw no future for black people in either the Democratic or Republican camps. William Worthy, a journalist for the *Baltimore Afro-American* and a close friend of Malcolm X, was on a national speaking tour for his Freedom Now Party. Its emphasis on ideological independence was influenced by political groups abroad like Ghana's Convention People's Party and Algeria's National Liberation Front. Worthy admired Albert, and a week after the March on Washington, *The Illustrated News* reprinted one of Worthy's speeches. "To get anywhere," he wrote, "we must make a clean break with the cold-war liberals, white or black."

The Freedom Now Party was based in New York City, but its most active chapter was in Detroit. In October 1963, Albert hosted the party's Michigan organizing drive at Central. Hundreds of people listened as "an all-black slate and a platform for liberation" were proposed for the 1964 elections. Among other points, the platform called for an end to police brutality, better schools for black children, and solutions to people's everyday needs that were not stymied by "the economic theories of this society." Albert was one of the organizers for the party's Michigan branch, as were the Henry brothers and Wilfred X. Wilfred was Malcolm X's older brother and the minister at Temple No. 1. Albert received a standing ovation as he compared the Freedom Now Party to an emerging African nation. Wilfred X enjoyed rousing applause of his own when he outlined a separatist plan for an all-black nation that literalized Albert's analogy.

C. L. Franklin was starting to distance himself from Albert, who served with him on the Detroit Council of Human Rights (DCHR). Albert had predicted that Franklin would, like King, become one of the out-of-touch Negroes who "spoke loftily of the disciplines of 'non-violence' and the power of 'redemptive love,' not realizing that neither meant anything to the people they were 'leading.'" Franklin had been planning a fall summit in Detroit to create a northern counterpart to the SCLC, which he was calling the Northern Negro Leadership Conference. Soon after Albert suggested that William Worthy join a DCHR exploratory committee for the summit, Franklin cut Albert out of the planning process. He feared that an endorsement from the Freedom Now Party would make him look like some unpalatable Marcus Garvey type. As far as Albert was concerned, the DCHR was dead. In his resignation letter, he wrote that, "in renouncing the independent black political action represented by the Freedom Now Party, and the new Negro image which is called 'black nationalism,' the DCHR has renounced any reason for its existence."

Albert, the Henry brothers, Wilfred X, and the other Freedom Now organizers were suddenly untethered from the "respectable" black groups. The once-radical promises of the SCLC, SNCC, and CORE had been co-opted. No Republican or Democrat was worth taking seriously at the national level. The New Negroes who were now referring to themselves as black nationalists called up Malcolm X. Would he headline an alternative event that they were planning, to take place on the same day C. L. Franklin was hosting his? Malcolm X had watched the feel-good Walk to Freedom on television. It was a display, he said, "with clowns leading it, white clowns and black clowns." It would be his honor to speak at an event that promised something more. Malcolm requested Elijah Muhammad's permission to speak at the Northern Negro Grassroots Leadership Conference in November. The Messenger assented.

On November 10, 1963, Malcolm entered Detroit's King Solomon Baptist Church. The Art Deco structure had plenty of room to accommodate the three thousand visitors who came to hear the Nation of Islam's deputy speak. Many of the attendees were factory workers, teachers, and students. Conference delegates pledged support to the Freedom Now Party. In his address, Malcolm told the rapt audience that they should not mindlessly agree to being called provincial *Negroes* when the struggle they ought to participate in was borderless and *black*.

"Whoever heard of a revolution where they lock arms, as Reverend Cleage was pointing out beautifully?" Malcolm asked.

Black revolutionaries wanted land for a country of their own, Malcolm said. *Negroes* were incapable of revolt and slithered back to the plantation. Malcolm's message to the grassroots conference was a totem to which the city's revolutionaries would return in years to come. A couple of weeks after the event, reflecting on the limitations of suffering in the name of redemption, Albert thought of Christ's crucifixion. Too many Negroes closed the Bible at the part in the story where Christ dies on the cross. Had they flipped a few more pages, they might have seen that he had awoken from his brief sleep and made his way out of the tomb.

LETTER IV:
JUST A PRISONER

Sometimes criminal behavior has no logic. I was not a person of low means. I had options in life and most of them were positive. Though I was Baptist, I went to Catholic school from first to eighth grade. My classmates' parents were writers, directors, lawyers, and judges. I played youth football and was in the Cub Scouts, from Webelos to well beyond Tiger Cub. My parents had a brand-new Honda, a BMW, and a Volvo. I was given the best life.

What happened in my mind and heart that would lead me to put myself in prison? Even with the dysfunction of my parents' household, I was not supposed to be there. I was lying on my hard, freshly made, cotton-stuffed mattress, covered with a sheet and two wool blankets. The upside of segregation was that I was alone and able to pray. Prayer was my only peace. I truly believed that God allowed for situations that made me react in ways that sent me to segregation. Segregation gave me the only time I could talk to God alone. In prison, it was imperative that I pray.

Prayer kept trouble away from me. God does not lead men into terrible situations, but when I led myself into a terrible thing, He did not leave my side.

Segregation is often in a setting where steel and finished cinder block make up the walls of a room. These rooms usually surround a command center for corrections officers. In Coldwater, the room was set up like a motel. I lay and prayed. I did this day and night with no other human interaction for about eighteen days. These eighteen days in segregation were brutal. I had never truly been without any human contact in my life. Day after day, the only sign that another person knew I existed was when a food tray slid through the slot at the bottom of the steel door for three meals each day.

I spoke to no one except God. There was nothing else to do. I had a window in my room that was purposely high on the wall, out of reach. I could only see the moon during the night if I stood on my bed, but otherwise I saw nothing else except sky. I asked God if He could help me. One officer brought me some Better Homes & Gardens *magazines. The only way for me to get water was to save the milk carton from breakfast and rinse it out, then drink from the bathroom tap.*

Being in prison meant that a certain amount of hope was gone. Each day was a reminder of being lost. Lost in that we were not living normal and productive lives. We were not raising our children. We were not loving our wives. We were not invested in careers, neighborhoods, or society. We were lost there. The only way to be found was to build our minds.

Each day in prison we wore the same outfit. It was a midnight-blue button-down shirt, usually short-sleeved. Short-sleeved shirts meant that you couldn't hide a knife or contraband on your arm. People who go to prison often mask the shame of their choices by acting as if it's a badge of power, experience, or honor. It is none of these. Prison is the result of going the wrong way in life. It's not fashionable.

I want to begin the real story. The story that aligns with you—in freedom. The real story starts when I was released from my long yet temporary imprisonment. Freedom is when I am next to you.

A Strategy of Chaos

The few members of Central who felt ill at ease with their pastor's activism in the early 1960s thought he had lost his spiritual way. For these conservatives, Albert's involvement with the nationalist Freedom Now Party and the pro-black *Illustrated News*, which in some weeks circulated 50,000 copies, made him a bigot no better than the Alabama governor George Wallace. Unable to tolerate more, this group left the church in the first half of the 1960s. By the start of 1964, Albert was calling for all-black economic and political organizations to be built.

Discussions about neighborhood integration were lively in Detroit because of ongoing fair housing debates, which would determine where non-whites would be allowed to live in the city. In 1963, Governor Romney called a "free and open housing market" a public responsibility and said that housing discrimination was the most serious civil rights issue in the state. A fair housing bill that his administration supported died in the state legislature. Albert followed these events closely. "You would have thought [the bill] was an ordinance designed to put a black rattlesnake into every white home in the city of Detroit," he said in a speech supporting the Freedom Now Party. In one of his most popular articles for the *News*, Albert wrote that whether black people received open occupancy privileges or not, there was going to come a time when it would be "desirable that the great majority of black men choose to live together in separate Negro communities."

Albert believed that *Brown v. Board of Education* had been a red herring for integrationists. With few exceptions, white people had proven time and again that most of them did not want black neighbors. This was useful information. It reinforced Albert's certainty that true integration would never happen and that racial conflict would never end. He admired the work of the German philosopher Friedrich Nietzsche, who had written in *Beyond Good and Evil* (1886) about humanity's unquenchable will to power and the necessity of conflict. In *The Illustrated News*, Albert had written that the "'will to power' of the group becomes the sum total of the collective drives for personal recognition of its component members. The group, then, cannot cease and desist in its struggle for power, without destroying the sense of self-regard of its members and at the same time destroying its reason for being." When Albert spoke about the need for black people to attain power, he was talking about the importance of being able to see one another clearly, without the distorting effects of self-hate.

Albert invited his black readers "to evolve a strategy of chaos." He was asking them to accept the reality of "inevitable, inescapable, interminable conflict." He was also adapting a concept from the Martinican psychiatrist Frantz Fanon's book *The Wretched of the Earth*, which had been published a few years earlier. Fanon's book, a sacred text for anticolonial movements around the world, spoke of decolonization as "a program of complete disorder." Freeing oneself from the shackles of a white-dominated world required a hard-fought balance of method and unruliness, a firmness of intention and an openness to the future's random swerves. The script that would dismantle the familiar world was unwritten.

Seen from the proper angle, these realizations led to the opposite of despair and pessimism; they enabled acceptance and preparation. There was no guaranteed success. Making peace with the fact that the freedom fight was unpredictable and potentially fractious would allow black people to "devise a strategy of conflict for all time to come," Albert wrote, "not for a brief period of bitter struggle to be followed by a millennium when the lion and the lamb will lie down together and every man will sit in peace and contentment." Violence in self-defense would always be one of conflict's possible expressions, but this was not Albert's primary concern. He was more worried about what it would take for black people to combat white society's favorite power plays: gerrymandering, redlining, blockbusting, scaremongering, and urban renewing among them.

Between blacks and whites, Albert believed, the arc of history was either headed toward a tenuous balance of power or one side's destruction. The will to live had always begotten black nations-within-a-nation. And for blacks in Detroit, one of many "nations" emerging, the combination of newfound political power and pronounced racial inequalities would spark the creation of what Albert termed "a Black brotherhood of necessity." It was Albert's utopian belief that "the Negro must seek to develop a separate racial economy and social existence within the established framework of American life."

Dreams of revolutionary class warfare or a multiracial beloved community were impractical and less likely to succeed than a black liberation movement based on long-established principles of cooperation and mutual aid. "When the Negro has realistically re-stated his goals in objective terms," Cleage wrote, "and no longer seeks to [lose] his physical identity through 'Assimilation,' nor his psycho-social identity through either Christian brotherhood or revolutionary marxian economics, only then will he be in a position to TAKE THE NEXT STEP by undertaking a comprehensive program of independent black political action and independent black co-operative economic action."

◇◇◇◇◇◇

Freedom Now was a national party with only one notable arm, in Michigan. After receiving enough signatures across the state to make it onto the 1964 ballot, Albert, the party chairman, was optimistic about the future of independent black politics and the party's slate of twenty-five candidates. He had accepted his nomination to run for governor on the Freedom Now Party ticket. A vote for Freedom Now was not a throwaway. If enough people got behind the party, Albert reasoned, it might force concessions from Democrats who took black support for granted. But when November came, Freedom Now was put out to pasture. Back in July, when thousands of people in Harlem rebelled for six nights after a cop killed a black teenager, party leadership thought 100,000 votes in their favor was a modest estimate. They waited for results on election night and rejoiced when they learned they were getting votes in the tens of thousands. The celebration was short-lived. An election official told them it was a technical error. They had received a few thousand votes. The Freedom Now Party's nationalistic platform proved too extreme for the average voter. The party dissolved shortly thereafter and *The Illustrated News* went with it.

Over the next two years, Albert made three more attempts at political office, having accepted that the Democratic Party was, for pragmatic purposes, the most feasible way for black people to have a hand in government. He lost a city council race in 1965 and, in 1966, his simultaneous campaigns for Detroit's board of education and a congressional seat were defeated. Albert wasn't trying to make a rhetorical point with these successive failures. He wanted to win. It would be impractical for black people to withdraw from politics entirely when the struggle for power was still so uneven. The uncomfortable truth was that compromises were part of realizing any utopian vision in the world. The question of which compromises were acceptable would later be at the heart of Albert's disagreements with other black revolutionaries. But politics was only one prong in the "total program" of black liberation that Albert was thinking about. He was a minister, after all. There were matters of the heart and soul to consider. His ideas were falling into place, and now what he needed was people, the ensemble that would help him enact them.

◇◇◇◇◇◇◇

Edward Vaughn, an Alabama native and deacon at Central who had provided logistical support for GOAL, the Freedom Now Party, and *The Illustrated News*, had come to Detroit looking for work in 1955, when he was twenty-one. He got a job as a Woolworth's busboy before joining the Army, which stationed him in Germany for two years beginning in 1957. When he returned to Detroit, he became a postal worker.

In 1962, the Jewish American journalist Ralph Ginzburg published *100 Years of Lynchings*, a compilation of newspaper accounts that laid bare the history of racial violence in the United States. It was an immediate touchstone for black readers at a point when interest in such history was growing. Dissatisfaction with the way black history was taught and censored in the media and in schools was compounded by the dearth of black-owned bookstores, which were almost nonexistent even in major American cities. Detroit did not have one. Vaughn eventually obtained a copy of Ginzburg's book, and other black postal workers were soon asking to borrow it. They requested more books, at which point Vaughn began ordering and selling them from the trunk of his car. Demand never died, and with his aunt and co-owner Polly Rawls, he opened Vaughn's Book Store in December 1964 on Dexter Avenue. It was a five-minute drive from Central.

Vaughn's was Detroit's first black-owned bookstore. In addition to books and plays, the store sold art, teaching guides, periodicals like *The Illustrated News*, records, prints, and more. Many of the prints featured the work of the Detroit portraitist Jon Onye Lockard, whose art had drawn Albert's attention. Two of the best-selling Lockard prints were his *Black Christ* and *Interruption*, a depiction of an African mother breastfeeding her baby boy. On Sundays, Vaughn sold books at Central. Another churchgoer suggested that he hold forums at the bookstore on topics of interest to the black community. He took that advice, and the weekly Thursday discussions at his store formed the basis of a program he called Forum '66. Because of Vaughn's connections to Detroit's most outspoken black nationalists and the uniqueness of his enterprise, Forum '66 became a major nexus for the city's black intellectuals, artists, and inquisitive young people in the wake of Malcolm X's assassination in February 1965.

In Vaughn, Albert saw an ideal partner. Using their respective bookshop and church as interlinked bases, Vaughn and Albert decided to invite local and nationally known black thinkers together. These vibrant exchanges would help forge artistic and political coalitions among young revolutionaries. The first major event Vaughn and Albert partnered on was a remarkable proof of concept. Vaughn's Forum '66 committee and the men's club at Central were the main sponsors of the first Black Arts Conference and Workshop, which was scheduled to take place at Albert's church in June 1966. The event would be held in honor of Marcus Garvey, whom Albert had designated as Central's patron saint. No other person that century had done more than Garvey to inspire a global utopian movement for black autonomy, in body and spirit. His example planted the seeds in Albert's mind for a new movement that could launch in Detroit and spread to every corner of the black world.

The young organizer who had replaced John Lewis as SNCC chairman in May of that year, Stokely Carmichael, was originally slated to deliver the opening keynote for the Black Arts Conference. An injury he sustained at a demonstration thwarted those plans. A correspondent for the Nation of Islam's paper, *Muhammad Speaks*, read a message at the conference on Carmichael's behalf. Hundreds of people from around the country attended programs that lasted for three days. Panels were held on black creativity and the arts—from the international Négritude movement to the need for more black-focused publishing houses and theaters. Speakers called for a reframing of history, religion, and educational practices through the lens of black nationalism. Malcolm X's widow, Betty Shabazz, was in attendance, among many other luminaries: activists such as the actor Ossie Davis and the jazz drummer Max Roach; Max Stanford, a founder of the Revolutionary Action Movement (RAM), a pioneering organization that sought to create an independent black socialist republic through guerrilla warfare and protest in cities; leaders of the young Black Arts Movement including the poet and dramatist LeRoi Jones and the art critic Larry Neal; and artists and writers such as the exiled South African poet Keorapetse Kgositsile, the sculptor Oliver LaGrone, and the novelist John Oliver Killens.

The first Black Arts Conference was a watershed event that made

Detroit—and Albert's church, in particular—one of the capitals of the black nationalist turn in the 1960s. Although he missed the conference, Stokely Carmichael managed to visit the city for a July 30, 1966, rally in support of Albert's candidacy for the U.S. House of Representatives. Carmichael came back to Detroit that September and received his due welcome at Central. Listeners crowded doorways and stood atop tables in the balcony section to see him. How long had it been since the Holy Spirit flowed through someone so young, a twenty-five-year-old like this? Carmichael addressed the audience with the excoriating love of a preacher. He took digs at the women and men in the crowd with wigs and straight or processed hair. The jokes received raucous approval.

"We have been running so long, but now we're out of breath," he said. "My great-grandfather took it, my grandmother took it, my father and mother took it, but it's time for all of us now to stop and look this thing over real good, and then do what we gotta do." He made the invocation people wanted to hear—"Black Power! Black Power!"—and they said it back.

"Tell it like it is, baby!" someone shouted.

Carmichael said that black people needed co-ops and stores, credit unions, and real estate that couldn't be taken away. If Detroit raised property taxes, he said, it would hardly affect blacks in the city because most of them had no property to speak of. Carmichael's call for black cooperative movements spoke to something that was already under way at Central. During Albert's 1965 city council campaign, his brother Henry had lighted upon the idea of a jointly owned cooperative. A study group soon came together, and in December 1965, the group incorporated the Black Star Co-operative. It was named after Marcus Garvey's steamship line that was meant to take black Americans to the African continent.

Ed Vaughn was appointed chairman of the co-op, which was based at his bookstore. Members needed five dollars to join—the same amount that stock certificates for Garvey's Black Star Line and Negro

Factories Corporation had gone for. Shares would start at $25 apiece. The first plan the co-op announced was a supermarket to be located right next to Central. Its top priority, however, was the creation of a "cooperative housing corporation designed to bring us together in one place so that we may support one another in our endeavors and free a larger portion of our resources for the task at hand."

◇◇◇◇◇◇◇

Late in 1966, after the Black Arts Conference and Carmichael's speech at Central, Albert made Vaughn chair of Central's cultural committee. The committee would be responsible for revising the church's conventional Christian rituals and songbooks, recording and distributing Albert's sermons, and replacing its most glaring concession to the dominant imagery of the past—this was the first thing most people saw when entering the sanctuary, the stained-glass depiction of a white Pilgrim arriving on America's eastern shores. Albert put Vaughn in charge of coming up with an alternative, though he thought Jon Onye Lockard's painting of a black Christ was a clear winner. Vaughn disagreed because Lockard's Jesus—afro-wearing, with dark skin reflecting the light of burning crosses behind him—had long, glassy tears dripping from baby-blue eyes. His blue eyes were the sort that people like Elijah Muhammad imputed to the devil.

The Detroit writer Harold Lawrence had published a poem in *Negro Digest* a few years earlier that Vaughn never forgot. The title, "Black Madonna," was mentioned only in the back of the issue:

DaVinci, and Angelo, wiped you white,
Released floods of forgotten nights;
But you remained beautiful still

Vaughn didn't yet know how popular black Madonna imagery was in other parts of the world, but a colored mother Mary was an enticing and provocative idea. Her image would do more than replace the white

Pilgrim—it would inject new life into black Christianity itself. When the new year arrived—1967—Vaughn wrote that the cultural committee's "first project is a Black Madonna painting for the sanctuary."

Among the Black Arts Conference's more understated panelists was the quiet painter and Forum '66 committee member Glanton Dowdell. In 1962, after thirteen years in prison, he was freed on parole. The next year, an artist friend that Glanton had met before his incarceration introduced him to Leslie Bell, a single mother of two boys. Leslie was irreverent, decisive, and firm in her opinions, as Glanton found out the night they met for a double date with the artist friend and his wife. While driving Leslie home, Glanton's friends asked him about some other woman. Why, Leslie wondered, had they brought her here to dilly-dally with a womanizer? Her night was ruined. Come to find out, the woman in question was Glanton's guitar. Leslie and Glanton married not long after.

Ed Vaughn learned about the artist and his acclaimed work after his release. It was through Vaughn that Glanton and Leslie were introduced to Detroit's black radicals. The couple entered the stream of nation-building activity with natural grace. Glanton's most important "organization," he joked, was his new family, which expanded as he and Leslie had three children together—Lance, Stacy, and Lindiwe—in addition to the two boys from Leslie's previous marriage, Gary and Keith. By 1967, Glanton, Leslie, their children, and Glanton's mother were living together. By then, Glanton owned his own art gallery not far from Central, and early that year, the church's cultural committee commissioned him to paint a Black Madonna mural large enough to cover the tall window depicting the Pilgrim.

"You Were Beautiful
When Your Apparition Formed"

◇◇◇◇◇◇

In 1959, at sixteen, Rose Percita Brooks had two choices: the Navy or the nunnery. The way her grandmother Rosie beat her for kissing a boy on a couch in her home made the girl want to run into a convent. At least there she would be far from the old woman's wrath. Whatever inspired Rosie's cruel beatings may have been a holdover from an ancestor's pain during slavery times, some ghost haunting the old woman. Rosie was not yet born when slavery existed in Memphis, but she would always moan joyfully in church as though she had witnessed the first Juneteenth. It was clear when the spirit possessed her. She grunted more loudly than anyone else. *Oh, that's grandma*, Rose thought. *She's happy now. She's got the Holy Spirit.*

It was Rose's grandfather who told his wife that the girl was in the living room with a stranger. They had flirted from opposite ends of the sofa until Rose accepted the boy's slow departing kiss. That same evening, Rosie surprised the girl when she was changing for bed. As she recoiled from her grandmother's blows, Rose thought of herself as an abused housewife, so wholly bound to her captor that she started to feel indistinguishable from Rosie. Would she ever escape her grandmother's orbit? Rose bathed the woman, laid out her church clothes, and had nearly the same damn name.

"What are you doing with that man?" Rosie demanded. The worst thing the girl could do was lift her arms to protect her face. Rosie's force increased each time the girl tried to shield herself from the blows.

The old woman's rage pushed Rose Percita away. Her dreams of Howard University and Tennessee State receded. In Nashville, the Navy recruited Rose before the sisterhood could. She gave them her loyalty and hoped they would be gentler than the Marine Corps or Air Force. Boot camp and a nearly fatal swimming test were her first obstacles. She was posted at a naval station in Arlington, Virginia, as a stringer photographer for a Navy paper. Over the next four years, few aspects of life on the base escaped her notice. She and her sole colleague, a white man from North Carolina, ran the publishing operation, "a cute little thing up on a hill," Rose would later call it, a world of their own. The delight of developing film and watching outlines take form on the photo paper kept Rose's mind active.

Clubs for noncommissioned officers and enlisted men adjoined the photo lab. One captain, a surgeon at Walter Reed Hospital, charmed Rose. He would not let the usual rites of courtship stand in his way, however, and so he tied her up and "took it." It was her first time. Rose could not hide her "little watermelon" for long. Her honorable discharge in 1963 stranded her again as a twenty-year-old. She was an expecting mother with no income and no roof. One of Rosie's daughters, the girl's aunt, lived in Detroit and agreed to take her in. The aunt was just as mean as Rosie. Rose forgave it but could not live with it and she fled to the home of her uncle. She then met and married a kind man, naming her son after him: Bernard Waldon, Jr. They called the baby boy "Barney."

◇◇◇◇◇◇◇

By 1967, Rose Waldon had been in Detroit for a few years, but she still could not afford to buy herself a washing machine and dryer. She would often take her three-year-old son to the laundromat with her. A man approached them one day by the laundromat entrance as they were walking in. Was he some kook? What did he want? The man introduced himself as the assistant at an artist's gallery. He made a claim that Rose would start to hear more often in the North: he told her that she had a memorable face.

It was true. Her jawline was sharp and her cheeks reflected varied gradations of light. Each of her dimples was a shallow depression. The assistant asked Rose if she would like to model for a mural of a Black Madonna and Child at Central Church. She did not know what the church was or why this man would think a mother with her child at a laundromat would accept his invitation, but when he explained what the church was about, she said, "Why yes, I would be honored to try that."

Rose and Glanton developed an easy rapport during the first interview at his studio. He was quite handsome with that beard, those wide eyes, and the baby-faced pucker to his lips.

He asked her where she lived.

Not far from the gallery.

Had she done any modeling previously?

She had not.

Well, she might consider it.

Glanton had her sit in the back of the studio as he drew a portrait study in charcoal. The oils came later. Rose was asked to find a beautiful outfit. She had a designer weave a pretty caftan that made it appear as though she moved like water over rocks. Some of their evening sessions were brief, with not much accomplished, Rose thought. But on Glanton's canvas, she took on new form. Her face was looking like the sculpted clay busts of modernist black artists—William Artis's *Head of an African American Woman* (1939) or Sargent Claude Johnson's *Chester* (1931). The collaboration between the artist and his subject took one month. In the final image, Glanton captured not only some semblance of Rose, but also his earliest memories of growing up in Black Bottom, where the first sights he remembered were the brown legs, worn shoes, and swishing skirts of the women in his household. Those women had "hummed, chattered, and laughed," alchemizing Glanton's hunger and want into something more bearable.

Glanton's Black Madonna was too stocky to be a replica of Rose alone, and when she later walked into the church to view this woman who was herself and not-herself, she would observe her dark face on a woman with a "happy" body. It was hard to say who the original woman was or where the artist's influence began, as if there were a single source. Was the shawl over the Madonna's head what Glanton described as his own grandmother Annie's "thick iron gray hair . . . over a deep, brown face"? Were her lips drawn tight because of Annie's "awesome quietness" and her aversion to idle chatter? If Annie was in the painting, too, it was because the stories she had told Glanton when he was a child were, the artist wrote, "meant to define me to myself."

Was Rose looking at herself, or the mother figure that the women in her own family wished they could have been? Was this what she would look like in her thirties or forties, or was this the person she must try to become? When Rose first saw the Black Madonna, she began to cry, the first time of many throughout that day. She understood at once the pride that the Muslims of Elijah Muhammad's Nation must have felt when they grew their own food, as they were known to do in states across the South and Midwest, including Michigan. The mural brought to Rose's mind the landscape of a farm. The portrait had the power to sustain.

Rose could not see the future, but if she had, she would have seen how the hard-jawed Madonna exhumed black people's memories of their mothers, grandmothers, and other ancestral spirits. She would make people feel that they had seen someone like her before. The Black Madonna had the difficult task ahead of her of reminding black people that they could be united in a single image or purpose that reflected many conflicting selves. She was a divine archetype and an individual unlike anyone else. For all her poise and stillness, the Black Madonna was not static. She looked out, and in her eyes were glints of recognition.

◇◇◇◇◇◇

Throughout history, Black Madonnas from Europe to Asia have usually been understood as alternatives to the norm. In Poland, an ancient Black Madonna icon housed at a monastery in Częstochowa became a beloved symbol of national independence and resistance against invaders. The original icon of Our Lady of Kazan in western Russia was a foot-tall wood painting adorned by admirers with precious stones and said to have inspired miracles and armies. Before the Crusades, the Black Madonnas of the Byzantine Empire were revered outside of the Roman church. The materials that Black Madonna statues were made from—meteoric stone, the wood of oaks, cedars, and fruit trees—were as diverse as the guises she was thought to have taken in various mythic traditions: Isis, Demeter, St. Mary of Egypt, the Queen of Sheba, the bride in the Song of Songs.

The mystery of the Black Madonna's color had perplexed historians and priests for centuries. Had she been blackened by candle soot? Was it aged wood or paint? Was she darkened by the solar radiance of her love? Stained by soil after a burial, to hide her from Muslims during the Crusades? Few seemed to believe that her blackness made sense, despite her popularity in many parts of the world and the tendency of people to create art in their own image.

Years after Glanton painted his mural, some New Age astrologers, spiritually minded feminists, and psychoanalysts inspired by the theories of Carl Jung would regard the Black Madonna as the archetype that best embodied the Aquarian age (though none of these people seemed to know about Glanton's painting). The Age of Aquarius would be defined by the destruction of dangerous ideologies that threatened the Black Madonna, who for some became the symbol of a fertile, healthy earth. For different utopian thinkers from the 1960s on, the Black Madonna was understood as an enemy of capitalism, militarism, nuclearism, environmental degradation, white Christianity, and white supremacy. Her emergence from the black collective unconscious, when Glanton Dowdell awakened her from a long dormancy with his brush, sounded the bells of *kairos*—the appointed time for what Jung in *The Undiscovered Self* (1958) called a "metamorphosis of the gods."

◇◇◇◇◇◇

As Glanton's work on the Black Madonna proceeded apace, the first two months of 1967 looked bad for Albert, who again found himself leading an ill-fated organizing effort. When Congress stripped New York's Rep. Adam Clayton Powell, Jr., of a House committee chairmanship for misconduct, Albert and other activists tried to plan a national one-day boycott in February. They asked black supporters to stay home from work and school in protest. The "general strike" was a humiliating failure. The organizers were either ignored or castigated in the press. Some journalists described Albert as a race chauvinist who may have finally received his comeuppance. One critic suggested that he had "the backing of only a minority of his own people."

Albert was not deterred. In the two weeks leading up to Easter Sunday, he preached at Central on "the black messiah's call to discipleship" and the "betrayal of the black messiah." If the Madonna could be black, what of her son? In preaching about a black Christ, Albert was continuing a provocative, centuries-long tradition. It harked back, in part, to Albert's Oberlin days, when he studied the work of liberal Christians who believed that the Bible was open to interpretation and that God was active in history, embodied by flesh-and-blood individuals. The theologians who, in the nineteenth century, began to analyze the historical and linguistic context of the Bible also inaugurated a quest to find evidence for the life of Jesus.

The search for the historical Jesus coincided with the rise of scientific racism, which found its greatest champions among white Christians. Many believed that black people were descendants of Ham, son of the biblical Noah. After seeing his father naked, Ham's son Canaan is cursed and destined to be "a servant of servants," a slave. Black people had every incentive to contend with white enslavers over the true meaning of Ham's story and of any biblical tale at all. If white supremacists wanted to play a bad-faith interpretive game that shored up their power, then black freedom seekers could frustrate the game's premise, complicate its rules, and find their own use for sacred texts.

In 1901, the black writer W. L. Hunter published *Jesus Christ Had Negro Blood in His Veins*. The black Christ appeared later in the writings of Harlem Renaissance authors such as Countee Cullen and Langston Hughes, as well as the work of W. E. B. Du Bois. Albert was developing his own argument that the historical Jesus was a black man who, before his untimely death, led a revolutionary movement against his white Roman oppressors. In describing Jesus as black, Albert was applying a bit of irony to his earnest belief that Christ descended from Israelites who had, for generations, been mixing with Egyptians—often conceived of as colored Africans by Afrocentric thinkers—and ethnic groups in the southern Levant. If this were true, then Jesus was, in contemporary terms, a mixed-race Middle Easterner who would not have passed the "one-drop rule" that had once been legally enshrined in parts of the American South.

"By American law," Albert later wrote, "God is black." If the son of God had been unfortunate enough to live in the United States, he would only recently have been afforded his civil liberties. The idea that Jesus was akin to a zealous black nationalist, albeit a martyred one, showed the members of Albert's church that they had it within themselves to carry on a long-standing historical struggle. Inevitably, as the story goes, the Black Messiah rises from the dead.

◇◇◇◇◇◇◇◇

The Black Messiah's resurrection was the subject of Albert's sermon on March 26, 1967. The many years of spiritual bondage that black people had endured needed to end. Black nationalists, in Detroit and elsewhere, were demanding revolutions in politics, economics, and the arts that would transform the meaning of Christ's kingdom on earth. Albert would show that the revolution could extend even to the black church, which Elijah Muhammad and Malcolm X had so loudly decried as useless and dead.

Albert agreed that the black church was littered with hypocrites and selfish leaders, but by no means was it dead. He believed it was still the epicenter of black American life and would need to play an essential role in whatever mass movements were to come. The day of the resurrection sermon was memorable not only for the official unveiling of the Black Madonna and the absence of its creator—Glanton was scheduled to appear in court for his involvement in a disturbance that nearly escalated into a riot the summer before—but also for Albert's declaration that the next stage of the pursuit for Black Power was about to begin. He called it the Black Christian Nationalism movement.

This was news to many in the church, and nothing had prepared them for the sight of an eighteen-foot-tall, nine-foot-wide black woman. She stood on a pile of rocks with a horizon of spires and shacks behind her. Wearing a lavender tunic and sky-blue throw, the implacable Black Madonna stared at her viewers from the center of a triangle of light and cradled her swaddled son. A journalist who had seen Glanton's Madonna two days before the reveal described her as a "weary earth mother, protecting a young child in her arms."

Albert's slow delivery that day betrayed his awe. "We really don't need a sermon this morning. We'll just sit here and look at the Black Madonna and marvel that we've come so far, that we can conceive of the possibility of the son of God being born by a black woman. That's a long way for us because it wasn't so long ago when that would've been an impossible conception . . . We didn't believe that even God could use us for His purpose because we were so low, so despised. Because we despised ourselves."

Betty Shabazz would speak at Albert's church on Mother's Day a couple months later. "I don't know much about what Mr. Cleage is doing," she said, "but anyone who has such a beautiful picture of a black woman in his church must be a great man. Anyone with such a painting that is so beautiful and has such a spiritual quality, I think what he would do would be for the good of black people."

Shabazz's comments were prescient. Albert's Messiah and Glanton's Madonna were instruments to show black people that the most sacred struggles took place in the flesh. They had the power to insert themselves in history, to rewrite and therefore create it. Each person had to make a choice. "Was he going to be a part of the Nation," Albert asked in his resurrection sermon, "or was he going to stay outside the Nation?" Not everyone could make it in. And among those who did, not everyone would last. It was hard to find people who could commit to sustaining a revolution and sacrificing old notions of what their lives would become.

"When we march," Albert would write the year after the Black Madonna's unveiling, "when we take it to the streets in open conflict, we must understand that in the stamping feet and the thunder of violence we can hear the voice of God."

A New Faith

On the morning of Sunday, July 23, 1967, Albert received a series of phone calls from parishioners and journalists. The first group wanted to know if service was still happening that day, and they advised Albert of the safest routes to church. The latter asked Albert whether he intended to go on the radio and call for peace after fighting had broken out on Twelfth Street, about a five-minute drive from Central. Early that morning, police had raided a speakeasy where a party was thrown to celebrate the return of two GIs from their service in Vietnam. More than eighty people were arrested. Thousands were now out on the streets.

It was too early to tell if this would be a short-lived riot or the start of a longer uprising, but Albert made it clear in his sermon that morning that he was going to support the insurgents. At the time of the Watts Rebellion in 1965, Albert had preached on the biblical figure of Samson, one of the hotheaded judges of Israel who defended his nation from the Philistines. The spirit of that hero was being revived today. "We are fighting for little boys who don't dress nicely, who don't know how to talk, who don't know what manners are," Albert said of the Samson-like discontents who were upturning the world that day. "Little boys who are nasty, who steal, who are darting around in the slums, learning the hard way, who don't have any opportunity."

Over the next four days, what unfolded would variously be referred to as a riot, an insurrection, a revolution, and, from the viewpoints of many who would later join Albert Cleage's church, a rebellion. Most of the violence and destruction occurred between the start of the raid and the following Tuesday. Fires spread rapidly from where the rebellion began on the city's west side, consuming homes, tenements, and businesses across city blocks. Many of the businesses were white-owned. Looters, black and white alike, took from stores, in groups or on their own. Disbelieving spectators watched from their lawns, their homes, and their cars. Firefighters who attempted to douse the flames and mediators who tried to pacify the rebels were pelted with stones and bottles.

Sympathetic observers of the chaos would later differentiate this uprising from a riot that tore through the city in 1943, which was mainly motivated by racial antipathy and resulted in thirty-four deaths. Whatever was going on now may have been a broader outcry, an unprecedented protest against decades of economic inequality, housing shortages, poor living conditions, and police brutality. It was unclear what a new and better world might look like after this, but even the blurriest vision revealed a reality much more desirable than the one they had. The future Detroit mayor Coleman Young recalled in his autobiography that while "the city was pillaged and burned, it became graphically evident that the black citizens were hell-bent on destroying the artifacts of their own haunted fate."

In the immediate aftermath of the Twelfth Street outbreak, Louis Lomax, the journalist who had brought national attention to Malcolm X and the Nation of Islam as a producer of the documentary *The Hate That Hate Produced* (1959), blamed what was happening in Detroit on an unfounded conspiracy between a small group of revolutionaries. Among the names he mentioned were Albert Cleage, Jr., Edward Vaughn, and Milton and Richard Henry. All four were generally acknowledged as the most outspoken leaders of black political struggle in Detroit.

Local and state police, as well as National Guardsmen, had fanned out across Detroit well before President Lyndon Johnson authorized nearly 5,000 federal troops from the 82nd and 101st Airborne divisions to enter the city late on Monday night. By 3 a.m. the following morning—the day that tanks equipped with .50-caliber guns arrived in the city—the paratroopers had moved into the city's east side. Most police and National Guardsmen were patrolling the west side, where many accounts of intimidation and brutality by law enforcement emerged. Authorities shot out streetlights to navigate stealthily at night, which only exacerbated the situation. Police cruisers stalked dark alleyways with their windows rolled down and shotgun barrels aimed at shadows. According to many witnesses, the National Guardsmen were the most feared and despised perpetrators of violence. Many of them were young white men who lived in other parts of Michigan and had come to the city with frayed nerves and trigger-happy impulses.

When Ed Vaughn returned to Detroit from a Black Power conference in Newark, he saw that his bookstore had been raided by the police. They had firebombed the building, torn down images of Stokely Carmichael, Malcolm X, and the black Christ, then flooded the shop. Police later claimed they were investigating reports that firearms were being stored inside, though Vaughn denied there were any weapons. Glanton Dowdell's art gallery, the Easel, suffered even worse damage at the hands of law enforcement. The police roughed Dowdell up and arrested him on a curfew violation charge that was later dropped. The citywide strife ended with 7,300 arrests, some 1,600 fires set, 1,200 people injured, more than 400 buildings destroyed, and 43 people dead, 30 of them at the hands of law enforcement.

The youngest of those killed was a four-year-old girl, Tanya Blanding. After a Guardsman armed with a machine gun mistook a man's cigarette in an apartment unit for a sniper's sight, he fired and accidentally caught Blanding in her lung as she hid under her dining room table. Blanding's funeral, which took place at Central, drew hundreds of mourners who viewed the little girl in her yellow silk dress and small white coffin. One man gently positioned a doll under her arm. Albert gave her eulogy. "Look at this child—innocent, young, powerless,

unlimited beyond all possibility—here in this box. She is a symbol of
the end of a period we won't tolerate anymore."

◇◇◇◇◇◇

After the rebellion, the local department store magnate J. L. Hudson,
Jr., brought together a group of mostly white businessmen, philanthropists, and civic leaders in an initiative called New Detroit. It began
within days of the final troop withdrawals. The almost total absence of
black leaders in New Detroit was laughable to the city's black nationalists, as was Hudson's confidence that he could mend social relations
in Detroit without the help of the people who lived and worked in the
Twelfth Street corridor that he vowed to rebuild.

Hundreds of blacks representing moderate and militant activist
groups gathered for an August rally and demanded that half of the
New Detroit committee be made up of black people. Sensitive to the
delicate situation he was now in, Hudson agreed to work primarily with
a new group called the Citywide Citizens Action Committee (CCAC).
The CCAC had elected Albert and Glanton Dowdell as co-chairs and
was, as one journalist wrote, "the rallying point of [Detroit's] militant
separatists—a mix of angry Negroes whose desires shade from self-
determination in their own community and a voice in what happens
there to all-out war if necessary and a separate Negro state."

Albert's record as the spokesman for various Detroit groups over
the last dozen years made him the clear choice to be the face of a black
nationalist coalition backed by some of the most powerful white leaders in the country, including the UAW president Walter Reuther and
the Ford Motor Co. CEO Henry Ford II. As unlikely as this partner-
ship was, the unprecedented scale of the destruction in Detroit led
to a temporary truce. The Detroit rebellion capped four successive
summers of urban conflicts around the country. Few such uprisings in
the nation's history had been so explosive, so captivating to watch on
television, and so consequential for the relationships black and white
Americans had with cities and with one another.

Although it came at a tremendous cost, one of Albert's long-held wishes had been granted: Detroit was at the center of the black American revolution. It was the subject of international fascination and federal concern. There was never a single united front that spoke for all the city's black militants, but Albert had no qualms with the way Detroit's black and white leaders, the media, and many of his own peers viewed him. Rev. Cleage was the ringleader of the most-feared militants in a city many people said was going to hell and not coming back.

"If we can't have justice in Detroit," Albert said during these busy months after the rebellion, "we can't live in Detroit." It was the kind of statement that people cited to malign Albert as a hopeless separatist. But Albert was not an emigrationist seeking the western shores of Africa. The white proprietors who ruled housing markets, fled their own homes when black people moved in next to them, or developed the land around black people's houses before pricing those residents out were, in effect, perpetuating the conditions which showed Albert that American blacks were already living on separate islands, in unintentional communities of their own.

In December 1967, it appeared that New Detroit was going to give money to support the funding arm of the CCAC. After a more moderate group of black community leaders threatened to boycott white-owned businesses if they did not receive support, the New Detroit committee wavered. Hudson and his people proposed a compromise: New Detroit would offer a little more money, but it would be split between Albert's organization and the moderates. New Detroit would appoint an overseer for the two groups, neither could use the money for political purposes, and auditors would have open access to their financial records.

Albert was ready to accept money from white people, but he rejected their undisguised bids for control. In January 1968, Albert turned the money down, severed ties between his organization and New Detroit, and hinted that the inability of wealthy whites to cede power to the black community might lead to a repeat of summer '67 in summer '68. Those who didn't know Albert well couldn't fathom the drastic move. A flustered Mayor Cavanagh asked for Albert's rationale in a private meeting. What was the reverend angling for if not money to fund the social and economic programs he had been talking about for years? Floyd McKissick, national director of CORE, flew to Detroit to support Albert at what felt like a critical moment in the city's history, the opening of an irreparable rift between its independence-seeking black nationalists and the paternal liberal order. "What happened in Detroit may well set a pattern for the entire country," McKissick said. "It is more important than anything that has happened in New York, Chicago, or anywhere else."

◇◇◇◇◇◇

From the outside, it may have been easy to forget that Albert Cleage was first and foremost a pastor, not a politician. But as black nationalists around the country clamored for revolution, Albert was paving the way for a new utopian movement. The first gathering of the National Committee of Negro Churchmen took place in Dallas in November 1967. The NCNC was a group of some three hundred ministers who had published a full-page statement in *The New York Times* supporting calls for Black Power in 1966, though many of its members rejected the label of "separatist." At the Dallas conference, Albert presented a paper "developing a new theology for the black church based upon the historic truth that Jesus was the Black Messiah." A week later, he gave a similar talk in Chicago.

Ever since Albert had taken the lead in the CCAC, new members had been streaming into his church. At a meeting in late November 1967, Central's executive board discussed plans to draft a new constitution for the "Mother Church" of an imminent confederation. Albert was preparing a book of discipline for his Black Christian Nationalist movement, an "international brotherhood" that was to start in Detroit and then extend far beyond it.

Albert's church, renamed the Shrine of the Black Madonna, received a small grant from the racial justice commission of the United

Church of Christ, the denomination to which it belonged. In a grateful reply, Albert promised that the money would contribute to "the development of an experimental ministry involving the establishment of satellite preaching-in-action centers related to Central Church and located in various parts of metropolitan Detroit and surrounding communities. We expect these centers to be self-supporting once they [have] actually established competent leadership."

Albert was spreading the word of his black theology when a disturbance rocked Robichaud High, an integrated school in Inkster, a small city fifteen miles outside of Detroit. When the son of a black school board member got in a fight with a white gym teacher, more than one hundred students spilled into the halls and fought until some tumbled out into the streets. A dozen patrol cars showed up, tear gas was thrown, and within an hour, some forty black students were arrested for reportedly hurling stones. A planned meeting at the high school to discuss the "student riots" two days later was canceled because of a bomb threat.

In response, the inaugural meeting of Albert's first "action center" took place at the Inkster home of one Shrine member days after the bomb threat. The group's goal was to set up a parent-student action committee to intervene at Robichaud High. Two weeks later, the action center opened its own location in Inkster. Albert gave the opening sermon, accompanied by nearly one hundred members from the Mother Church on Linwood—Shrine No. 1. As dozens of curious visitors to the Inkster location joined the Shrine in the following weeks, Albert gave its lead minister several congregants from No. 1 to assist him. "It is our hope with your help to become a scale model of Central Church 'Shrine of the Black Madonna,'" the minister wrote to church leaders.

For too long, churches had been allowed to mislead black men and women with unrealistic hopes, Albert thought. The Shrine of the Black Madonna was to be more than a church. It would be a laboratory for social experiments, open to all who supported black liberation, starting in a maligned, dream-filled city. While many other black nation-building movements were disappearing at the end of the 1960s, Rev. Cleage assured his people that their work was only beginning. The black revolution was not only about tearing things down, or building things up, or letting their hair fly free. It carried within it the wisdom of the divine spirit that moved through each of them, convincing them that they were holy because they were common, earthbound.

II | Counterculture

The Kingdom of God has come!
We are in the Kingdom.
The Kingdom is within us
And we wait patiently for its coming.

—JARAMOGI ABEBE AGYEMAN, "THE BAPTISM OF FIRE"

New Afrika

Within a year of the Black Madonna's unveiling in March 1967, the birth of two movements to create autonomous black nations inside the bounds of the United States would be announced at the Shrine: the New Afrikan Independence Movement, whose plans to liberate territory in the South for a provisional government faltered spectacularly, and Albert Cleage's own Black Christian Nationalism movement, which he would lead for more than thirty years, into the twenty-first century. Both movements began in Detroit but hoped to expand beyond the borders of a single city.

Late in March 1968, Albert loaned the Shrine to his former collaborators Milton and Richard Henry. They had renamed themselves Gaidi and Imari Obadele and were proposing the creation of a nation-state in the Black Belt of the South. The region was plentiful in natural resources and black communities, they said, and perhaps poor enough that white people could be convinced to leave en masse. Albert let the Obadele brothers use his church for the sessions of their National Black Government Conference, where delegates announced plans to create the Republic of New Afrika.

Albert was clear that, though he was happy to give other people in the black liberation movement space for their event, he did not stand behind the ideological approach of the RNA. He respected the nation-building ethos of Malcolm X just as much as the Obadele brothers did, but they went a few steps too far by taking literally the fallen leader's proposition that "a revolutionary wants land so he can set up his own nation, an independent nation." Cleage thought the New Afrikans' geographical interpretation of black separatism predisposed them to failure. At what point in history had the federal government given land freely to blacks on the basis of reasoned argument? New Afrikans, Black Panthers, black Maoists, and other urban guerrillas exhibited the theatrical signs of what Albert called "heroic death syndrome."

The dream of an actual black country in the American South owed much to the New Orleans native Audley Moore, who was almost seventy years old when she attended the National Black Government Conference. A former Garveyite and branch secretary for the Communist Party USA, Moore's ideas about black nationhood were notably influenced by the Communist Harry Haywood. In the late 1920s, Haywood argued that black Americans in the South were living in feudal-like conditions, making them an oppressed nation within a larger, colonizing nation. These people had the right to seek autonomous status. Moore had become an advisor to Elijah Muhammad and Malcolm X when the Nation of Islam came to national prominence. She gave shape to Muhammad's desire for land, suggesting five contiguous states in the Black Belt—Louisiana, Mississippi, Alabama, Georgia, and South Carolina—as potential homelands for internal exiles of the United States. These states would comprise the RNA's planned colony.

In their 1969 Declaration of Independence, the New Afrikans committed "to build a New Society that is better than what we now know and as perfect as man can make it." Imari Obadele wanted a New Society in the South to be a place of "brotherhood and justice, free of organized crime, free of exploitation of man by man, and functioning in a way to make possible for everyone the realization of his finest potentialities." The first step would be for the United Nations to call a plebiscite supporting the black Republic. The New Afrikans sought paths to legal and international recognition, citing the U.S. Constitution and the Geneva Conventions to claim legitimacy.

Using reparations payments from the U.S. government, the RNA wanted to create thousands of "New Communities" for ten million southerners in black-majority counties. Food, housing, clothing, education, armed defense, and social services would be provided. Economic surplus from a national bank funded by land certificates, property taxes paid by citizens, and donations would be distributed as personal income. In addition to freeing American blacks from subjugation to the country's punishing legal systems, New Afrika would provide refuge from the draft lottery, the devastation of urban renewal programs, and weapons of "chemical warfare"—the meth and heroin that were becoming problems in black neighborhoods.

After the National Black Government Conference, Detroit became a major base of the RNA's consulates, which were set up in almost a dozen states to advertise and fundraise for a Black Belt–bound exodus. The Shrine was one of many places spread across Detroit's mostly black, low-income areas that the RNA used to mobilize. Although the New Afrikans were not the first to create maps imagining what a black territory within the United States could look like, they revived the visual concept in the era of Black Power.

New Afrikans displayed maps of the RNA's national territory and its Kush District—the stretch of counties along the lower Mississippi that would be the core of the New Communities—which were often accompanied by calls to *Free the Land!* These maps were among the reasons the RNA started making headlines across the country in papers such as *The New York Times* and *The Boston Globe*. The New Afrikans' highly publicized attempts to negotiate a peaceful transfer of power from the U.S. government to the RNA were ridiculed as presumptuous by most people, and possibly as seditious as the Confederacy.

◇◇◇◇◇◇

On August 18, 1971, the FBI and local police showed up at an RNA safe house in Jackson, Mississippi, armed with shotguns, revolvers, tear-gas rockets, and an armored tank. The confrontation ended with a shootout. One police lieutenant died, another cop and an FBI agent were wounded. The arrest of eleven RNA members that day led to various charges, including one based on a pre–Civil War statute: the levying of war against the state of Mississippi. In the months after the Jackson raids, New Afrikans across the country, including some in Detroit, were systematically targeted and arrested. The length of their prison sentences varied. The New Afrikan Independence Movement would survive in later years under different guises, but the dream of an autonomous territory in the South met its end.

A couple of months after the shootout, Brother Imari, a self-proclaimed prisoner of war, wrote to Albert from the Hinds County jail in Jackson, Mississippi. "Greetings from the land of the Beast—soon-to-be-ours!" The joviality was for show. The RNA president did not confide to the reverend that for the last couple of months he had been getting by on candy bars and cookies that supporters sent so he wouldn't have to stomach the jail's bug-infested food. The New Afrikans were no longer asking the reverend to use his church for New Community fundraising benefits (church leaders denied one such request earlier that spring even though some New Afrikans were also in the Shrine). Instead, they needed money to fund the legal defense for the jailed RNA-11. Would the reverend please see what he could do?

It was a humble position for Brother Imari to be in considering that the days of unity between Albert and the Obadele brothers were long gone. The men had been openly criticizing one another in the wake of the Rebellion as their responses to black abjection diverged. In his book *Prophet of the Black Nation* (1969), Albert's biographer Hiley Ward asked Gaidi Obadele about the RNA's separatist philosophy. Gaidi took a dig at Albert. "He doesn't see that God requires physical separation sometimes." Albert retorted that if a "black extremist" wants "to get so far out with absolutes, which is his greatest danger, he leaves the total black community which is not ready to die for absolutes."

Given the similarities between New Afrikans and Black Christian Nationalists, the falling out between Albert and the Obadele brothers was a remarkable measure of which way the wind was blowing for black nation-building projects in the late 1960s and early 1970s. Both Albert and the Obadeles had open-minded approaches to religion.

They believed in the importance of the *internal revolution* that precedes action, and they felt that American blacks already comprised subjugated nations within northern cities and the Black Belt. They had written down their own communitarian covenants based in part on the seven principles of Nguzo Saba (with special emphasis on *Ujima*, "collective work," *Ujamaa*, "cooperative economics," and *Kujichagulia*, "self-determination"). And though they did not necessarily mean to replace the Holy Bible, two publications in 1968—Brother Imari's pamphlet *War in America: The Malcolm X Doctrine* and Cleage's *The Black Messiah*, a compilation of twenty of his most popular sermons from 1967 and 1968—would be treated as such by some black nationalists throughout the country and elsewhere in the world.

Albert took a few stances the Obadeles could not abide, however, including his "counter-revolutionary" support for Eugene McCarthy's presidential bid in 1968 (New Afrikans had an official policy of noninterference in the internal affairs of foreign nations, including the United States). They did not respect Albert's support for one of the century's most ambitious calls for reparations, the SNCC co-founder James Forman's 1969 Black Manifesto, which looked to white churches and synagogues for hundreds of millions of dollars in payments (the Obadeles thought this money should come from the federal government instead).

The brothers' loudest objection to Albert was what they saw as his concessions to the black capitalist mindset. The Obadeles accused any black person who would rely on financial support from white investors of deserting the black revolution and succumbing to bourgeois temptations. Albert may as well have just gone ahead and accepted the strings-attached money the white capitalists of the New Detroit committee had offered him after the Rebellion. What, the Obadeles might have wondered, was to be expected from the high-yellow son of a high-society doctor anyways?

LETTER V:
CONNECTING THE DOTS

In 2014, I sat in an empty prison visiting room. It felt as if death, life, sadness, and newness sat with me on the early morning of my release from prison. My heart had died twenty years earlier when I began to spiral into the abyss of bad domestic relations. I spent ten years not knowing how to manage my life, failing as a father, and failing as a man until I finally found myself in prison. Then I spent ten years being healed and saved by God. I made it. After ten years of being locked in cells for days, weeks, nights, mornings, ten hours at a time, twenty-three hours at a time, growing from age twenty-eight to thirty-eight in a prison—I made it.

That was the visiting room where I saw Aaron for the first time in prison, nine years earlier. Nine years earlier in that very room, I stood as I saw my father and mother and Aaron walk through the door. Aaron saw me as I stood and ran with all the excitement of heaven straight to me.

I was in that dark room, only lit by the early morning sun coming through a locked door that led to a play area where small children sat with their imprisoned fathers. I was waiting

LETTER V: CONNECTING THE DOTS

for my sister and brother-in-law to pick me up. After an hour and a half, a corrections officer brought me some clothes and said that my brother brought them for me. I took the clothes, the belt, and the shoes, all with sales tags still attached to them, into the bathroom. I was putting on the clothes of a free person for the first time in ten years. The shoes were black, low-top New Balance sneakers with a gray metallic "N" on the sides.

I was free.

Walking out of prison was, in a way, like walking up a staircase. I felt as if I was walking out of a dark basement up a brightly lit stairwell. I was ascending into value. My life had been a series of hallways, fields, and staircases. What kind of building was I constructing with my life? Was I walking up staircases, falling off cliffs, and never ascending past the second floor in life? Would I be a person who aged but never accomplished, morphed but never developed? Prison for me was a circular journey, but thank God in the highest heaven that it was a half-circle, mentally and spiritually. The true change in me was evidenced by the fact that I couldn't relate to who I used to be, or the thoughts that used to be in my mind.

My sister got out of the passenger side and hugged me tightly. I was redeemed. I smelled new winter air. There is a difference between the air of freedom for an heir of freedom, and the air of imprisonment for an heir of imprisonment. My brother-in-law drove away from the prison, and I was talking for the sake of conversing. The freedom was captivating. Looking at the land as we passed it, I was speechless. We were making the five-hour drive home. I breathed into my soul each field of grass, corn, cows, horses, barns, each stretching mile of trees. Thank God for the open road.

My family had always made me feel as if I was a king. I had two sisters who adored me, and every person in my family had been supportive during my senseless imprisonment. My family did *not turn their backs on me. I knew that God moved on them to support me. Even people in my family who didn't like me before I was incarcerated supported me with love, cards, and words of encouragement.*

To my surprise, we pulled into the parking lot of a nice hotel. As we got out of the car, I felt like I had won a big prize from The Price Is Right. *My brother-in-law walked me straight to the hotel's breakfast area. A full breakfast. This was in stark contrast to the last five years. There had been times when I was locked in a cell that was about 100 degrees for twelve hours of the day, and the only air-conditioning came through a straw out of the ceiling. I remembered cooking in a cell for over two weeks as I stood under the straw that dispensed cold air. I would often stand completely still for almost four hours as the prison guards tortured me, knowing that the heat was deadly in my cell.*

Prison guards take joy in torturing dark people. This is why Muhammad Ali, Marcus Garvey, and Malcolm X so vehemently demanded separation of African Americans from Caucasians. Yet I was there in the hotel, eating waffles and sausage and yogurt in a perfectly shaded breakfast area of a very exclusive-looking hotel.

Politisk Asyl åt Glanton Dowdell!

◇◇◇◇◇◇◇

As midnight approached one Monday evening in December 1967, months after the uprising in Detroit, Glanton Dowdell was working at his restored art gallery with a friend. His friend asked where some art materials were located and Glanton rose from his drawing board to help him search. As he passed the bathroom near the rear of the gallery, the first of four shotgun blasts exploded, shattering the bathroom window.

Glanton dove to the floor. Pellets lodged in the wall above him and plaster coated his head. Uninjured, Glanton and his friend ran outside as soon as the gunfire stopped. They watched a light-colored vehicle speed away with two white men inside. Glanton later told a journalist that he did not know anyone who would want to kill him, but the subtext of the article that ran about the assassination attempt was clear enough: as one of the leaders of the Citywide Citizens Action Committee, and as "one of the most eloquent spokesmen of [Detroit's] new-breed black militants," Glanton almost certainly had a target on his back.

A few months later, in March 1968, a couple of white men visited Glanton's gallery and claimed to represent "influential actors" in the world of illegal gambling. Although Glanton never got a good look at his would-be assassins, these men didn't seem to be connected to the December incident. When Glanton asked for more information about their employers, however, they didn't give names. All they said was that they wanted to give money to the black liberation movement.

"We were open to contributions from anywhere," Glanton would say a few years later, "as long as they didn't come from groups that were at odds with our struggle." The central committee of an organization that Glanton was involved with, most likely the CCAC, balked when Glanton told them about the two men's proposal, calling bullshit. It was obviously a trap. These men were trying to gain leverage over Glanton's organization or get them in trouble for tax fraud. The committee instructed Glanton to reject the money and find out where it came from. Drug syndicates? Army spies? Detroit police? The mafia? It was sometimes hard to distinguish among them.

When Glanton went to meet the two white men at an associate's home, he brought a bodyguard for protection. One of the men revealed himself as the vice chairman of a bank that was going to give Detroit's black radicals a financial boost. A shoebox on the kitchen table contained bonds made out to "James Valente." They asked Glanton to look inside. He thumbed through what he thought were millions of dollars in bonds. Which one of these white boys was James Valente? No one by that name was in the kitchen. When the white men asked

Glanton to come with them to the bank so that they could cash the bonds and give him the money, an argument ensued before Glanton and his bodyguard rushed out.

It was a trap. The next day, the associate who had hosted the rendezvous at his home was arrested for apparently trying to cash tens of thousands of dollars in stolen savings bonds by using forged signatures. Glanton learned that the two white men had been caught only by watching the evening news. Glanton's organization sent him to follow their hearings at federal court a few days later. One of the men noticed Glanton and pointed him out to the police, saying that he'd been at the scene of the crime. During his interrogation, Glanton figured out that the white men had framed him for conspiring to sell stolen savings bonds. He had touched the papers, after all. He was put in jail but got out the same day on bail.

In the end, one of the white men was sentenced to prison. Glanton's associate was put on probation. The indictment against the other white man, however—the "vice chairman"—was dropped after the prosecutor cited insufficient evidence. Glanton later learned that the man was a federal agent known for entrapping militant organizers.

◇◇◇◇◇◇◇

It had always been dangerous to be a revolutionary black nationalist, but the situation in Detroit was becoming untenable. Since the Rebellion, Ed Vaughn, also a member of the CCAC, had been noticing that, as part of Glanton's effort to bring everyday black folk into the liberation movement, he made appeals to "street workers"—the lumpenproletariat, society's rejects. The people Glanton was surrounding himself with hardly knew what they were doing, Vaughn thought. They were part of an underground contingent that counted criminals among its ranks. Some of them were violent. But they also made up the muscle that Glanton needed to combat the heroin problem that was starting to devastate black communities. The epidemic of drug addiction took Glanton back to the Depression days of hard-hit shadow people in

Black Bottom walking around in glazed stupors. Now he watched as preadolescent girls and boys dealt drugs, stole, and got caught up in exploitative sex work. In his eyes, streets without substances would make for a better world. "Drugs, whatever their shape or form," he once said, "create social, physical, and psychological misery . . . [Their] social acceptance represents a cultural regression."

Under Glanton's direction, some of his recruits seized drugs and money from dope houses. He was concerned that these men were starting to step out of line, however—becoming too aggressive—and in spring 1968, a handful did. Three of Glanton's men kidnapped a payday lender who targeted Ford autoworkers and took him to the Collingwood Apartments complex a couple miles from the Shrine. According to Vaughn, Glanton confided in him about what happened next. The three men started torturing the lender to get money out of him. The owner of the apartment, an associate who had lent his home to the three men and learned of what was happening, alerted Glanton. In his fury, Glanton went to the apartment with his bodyguard. It is unclear why Glanton would have gone to such extremes, but he demanded that all three men get on their knees and then he gave his bodyguard the order to kill the trio. They were shot in the back of the head and their bodies were strewn throughout the apartment: one in the dining room, two in a bedroom.

The rationale for the murders is still a matter of speculation. Vaughn believed Glanton had intended to send a message to his most disorderly street workers: no more disobedience. Lack of discipline within the black liberation effort threatened everyone involved. Decades later, while writing his memoir, Glanton would allude to the way his indecisiveness as an adolescent had thrown his life off course and landed him in a school for delinquents. When he robbed that taxi with his school friend as a witness, some part of him was aware that the other boy was a liability. But he had been too hesitant to kill him, perhaps not hardened enough by his experiences. "I knew that I had not responded correctly to that shift in the situation," Glanton wrote.

"It came too quickly. [The boy] was a loose end [. . .] When what I should have done popped into my head, I shuddered. I was not yet ready for that."

Now as a man, Glanton had found a horrible new resolve. His actions were in line with something he had written for a prison weekly in 1960, near the end of his sentence, on the occasional necessity of making unexpected decisions to save oneself: "Too many of my comrades here know only too poignantly how irreversable [sic] a situation may seem. Too many of them know the experience of being backed against the wall—of having their fate sealed with inexorable finality . . . And yet, somewhere in the maze of each man's situation there is a win—if he will but develop and use his creative ingenuity." Glanton, once again at a crossroads, took the desperate route. There was no victory in sight. A story in the *New Pittsburgh Courier* asked whether the "gangland" execution of the three black nationalists at the Collingwood Apartments was "the work of the underworld or the underground." The FBI interviewed Glanton about the murders. He claimed no involvement and declined an offer of protection from the authorities.

Glanton continued assessing local drug-trafficking operations into the fall of 1968. He interviewed elementary school teachers, addicted teenagers, social scientists, and others to better understand how drugs were affecting the city. Over the last two years, Glanton had by some miracle made it through setups, an attempt on his life, and general insubordination by his men. But the Collingwood executions and the bond forgery case had left Glanton's underground operations in shambles. Vultures were circling above his head, lower to the ground than usual.

◇◇◇◇◇◇

In the summer of 1967, Tryggve Hedtjärn, a Swedish medical student based in Stockholm, dated a woman visiting from Detroit whose mother mailed her newspaper clippings about the uprising. She ended up going back home to the United States. Tryggve planned to visit her the next summer, but the relationship ended before he could go. He decided to visit Detroit anyway, where he would write about the aftermath of the Rebellion for a Swedish audience. He was the editor of a leftist student publication known for supporting international solidarity efforts.

Around Easter 1968, the Swedish filmmaker Ingrid Dahlberg aired a television program on the Rebellion that featured conversations with city leaders. The broadcast mentioned the Shrine of the Black Madonna and showed an interview with Glanton Dowdell. Tryggve called Dahlberg, asked to meet, and she gave him material on Detroit that she no longer needed. The city's unusually influential black nationalists set something alight in the Swede.

Once in Detroit, Tryggve contacted Albert Cleage and visited the Shrine. Church leaders were still relatively amenable to white journalists asking questions, in the presence of security, but when Tryggve asked about Glanton, Albert became suspicious. He could've been a spy. The Swede was out of luck until he got a lead from a social worker who was friends with Glanton. A few weeks passed before the social worker invited Tryggve to join him on a trip to Sault Sainte Marie in Michigan's Upper Peninsula, at the Canadian border, where Glanton was leading an arts camp for teenagers.

When Glanton saw Tryggve, the first thing he asked was, "Can you help me get political asylum in Sweden?" It had become clear to the artist that the federal government was on his tail for his suspected role in the bond forgery case. Tryggve had contacts in Sweden's recently formed American Deserters Committee, which was trying to recruit those who fled from the conflict in Vietnam to speak out against the war. Many of the soldiers who found refuge in Sweden were black. Glanton was no war deserter, but perhaps the white leftists in Europe could help him. Tryggve promised Glanton that he would try.

◇◇◇◇◇◇

In the late 1960s, Sweden was home to one of the largest Vietnam War deserter colonies outside of North America, and in the process of building one of the most comprehensive state welfare systems in the world. Young people in Sweden were not afraid to side with parties to the left of the powerful Social Democrats, including the Communists and Maoists, if they did not do more to address the war. As a result, the Social Democrats helped fund a lobbying group, the Swedish Committee for Vietnam. Sweden became the first Western nation to diplomatically recognize the Democratic Republic of Vietnam. Government officials in Washington, D.C., regarded Sweden under Prime Minister Olof Palme's leadership as the most caustic Western opponent of the war.

At the height of the American Deserters Committee's influence in Sweden, the challenges that black deserters and other minorities in the country faced were generally overlooked. "[I]s there any good reason to believe that Scandinavia should be a utopia for blacks?" one historian asked in 1972. It was an open question for black war resisters and defectors, fugitives, artists, and other dissidents who relocated to Sweden or else found political support there. Sweden was one of the few countries to give refugee status, work permits, and welfare benefits to Vietnam War deserters. Many of them were blacks who chose to live in cities such as Stockholm and Malmö. At the same time, groups in countries throughout Scandinavia, including Sweden, were creating solidarity committees to support Black Panthers whose politics Swedish leftists saw as complementing their own.

Relations on the ground were sometimes strained. The American Deserters Committee had a hard time convincing the people they helped to take an active role in politics. The political inaction of most American deserters upset Committee members and caused many to lose interest in their plight. A string of highly publicized criminal cases against deserters, mostly black ex-soldiers who were charged with narcotics distribution, alienated the Swedish public even further. Some black deserters detested these quid pro quo arrangements. When the press asked one of them how it felt to receive support from Social Democratic politicians and exuberant leftists, he compared it to being back in the United States and receiving an invitation to a cocktail party so that liberal whites could bask in their own generosity. It was like eating hors d'oeuvres on an auction block.

◇◇◇◇◇◇◇

When Glanton landed at the Arlanda International Airport in Stockholm on June 14, 1969, Tryggve was there to meet him. Glanton had brought his sketchbook and his portraits of Paul Robeson, black workers, women and their children, and bitter images like that of a black man hanging from gallows. Only a few people had known that Glanton was coming to Sweden. In phone communications, the Swedes had been using the name "Willie Jackson" to refer to him. Tryggve gave him money to start off and drove him directly to the countryside home of a sympathetic civil servant. For the next few months, Glanton stayed in Forsmark, a southern suburb of Stockholm.

That October, Glanton called Tryggve saying that something was about to happen and he would need his help securing asylum status. The U.S. government would soon demand his extradition. The American embassy in Stockholm monitored the activities of various fugitives who opted to stay in Sweden, and the United States suspected the Soviets of fomenting dissent among American ex-servicemen, which put agencies such as the FBI and CIA on alert. Glanton hadn't left a war, but he did leave the country while he was the suspect of a criminal investigation, making him a fugitive from the law. The White House had already selected a prosecutor in Detroit to arrange a unit that would bring Glanton back to the United States.

Tryggve consulted with the staff of the leftist journal he edited, and together they formed a group to support Glanton's bid for asylum. His lawyer would be Hans Göran Franck. Franck had been elected president of the Swedish chapter of Amnesty International in 1964, and he was one of the world's leading advocates for the global abolition of the death penalty. Glanton made clear to his supporters and, increasingly, the Swedish press that sending him back to the United States would be like sentencing him to die. He feared that another imprisonment would be his best-case scenario. At worst, the authorities would find some way to kill him, as they'd done to Fred Hampton. One Swedish journalist for *Dagens Nyheter* concurred, writing of Glanton: "If he is allowed to stay, here as in prison, he will just need to survive. And if he cannot stay in Sweden? Well, then he knows his fate."

Glanton was not forgotten back home. He was in touch with his family, as well as friends from the League of Revolutionary Black Workers. Both he and Leslie had become part of the League, a Marxist-Leninist labor coalition founded in 1969. The League organized within and outside of Detroit's auto plants, offering a broad political education to black factory workers, students, and community members through mass media, classes, and other means. It emphasized autoworker militancy and youth education in a time of growing economic uncertainty.

Before fleeing to Sweden, Glanton had generated much of the League's grassroots support. He led its intelligence and security operations and became known as a strict disciplinarian. As a result, some thought of him as the invisible glue that kept the League together. Still, the Dowdell family had been facing hard times. Leslie was making $90 a week as a pharmacy technician and using almost half of that to enroll her two youngest children in daycare. She and Glanton had trouble paying for their asthmatic daughter Lindiwe's hospital bills, and Ruby struggled to pay her property taxes. With occasional support from other League members, the family was living paycheck-to-paycheck.

When it became clear that Glanton's situation was dire, the Dowdells in the United States had to decide what to do, whether to leave or stay. Sweden gave Glanton work and residency permits by the summer of 1970, but his long-term fate wasn't clear. His participation that fall in Amnesty International's Week for Political Prisoners showed exactly how precarious he felt his situation was. Nearly two years after arriving in Sweden, Glanton's landlord informed him that two police officers were asking for him. The United States had officially requested his extradition. He turned himself in, and in March 1971, his case was passed on to the Swedish Prosecution Authority.

◇◇◇◇◇◇◇

Glanton's case was a cause célèbre. The demonstrations in Stockholm began immediately. In Sergel's Square, on an overcast day in late March, fluttering red banners and signs in Swedish read *Political Asylum for Glanton Dowdell!*, *Full Freedom for the Labor Leader*, *Reject US Government Pressure*. Glanton's advocacy committee, composed of dozens of groups, was throwing its full support behind a man who reminded Swedish radicals of their own Joe Hill, the immigrant to America who wrote ditties for the Industrial Workers of the World, rode the rail lines between itinerant jungles, and was ultimately condemned to death by the state. It was not only the American Deserters Committee that showed up. Glanton had the backing of the Black Panther Solidarity Committee, communist and socialist leagues, Social Democratic student groups, workers' communes, a painters' union, and a temperance society as well. The request for Glanton's extradition even inspired a protest in Finland led by African American expats there.

"The emigrant's condition is riddled with problems," Glanton told his audience in the square, "and it's difficult to know what can be realized when you've been robbed of the task you had in your own country."

In Sweden it seemed possible, Glanton said, that he would experience the fairest trial a black American worker had ever been given. He also warned his listeners that they should not expect him to provide "some sophisticated intellectual revolutionary rhetoric" to explain how it was, exactly, that he had survived the hunger, desperation, and death that had defined his own childhood and the adult lives of many others. "A system where this question, the question of surviving day by day, is the black people's problem leaves no room to master revolutionary terminology."

"Are they hoping to prove that for those who oppose the tyranny of the United States there is no refuge anywhere in the world," Glanton asked of his pursuers, "thereby extinguishing the hopes of my people?" He was obliged to report to the Swedish police once a week. No more running away. The only thing for him to do now was show Swedish authorities why they should take an interest in his case when the promise of so many other black American defectors had been wasted. Glanton made them a vow in Sergel's Square: "I will strive to be an asset, not a burden, for Swedish society, if given the chance."

The deportations in fall 1970 of American war deserters who had been convicted of selling narcotics in Sweden gave Glanton an opportunity to set himself apart from the disgraced GIs. Conservative Swedish politicians and journalists had chastised liberals for failing to protect Swedish youth from drug-dealing washups, as they described the expelled black GIs, who depended on welfare without contributing to the social good.

Appealing to Sweden's zero-tolerance policy toward drug use, Glanton became a spokesperson for the country's temperance movement. The prospect of becoming a propaganda tool for Sweden's government didn't seem to bother Glanton. Wasn't that what the Underground Railroad had been all about? He would be the Frederick Douglass to these Swedish William Garrisons. If Glanton had ever read the book by the brother Ernest Dunbar, *The Black Expatriates: A Study of American Negroes in Exile* (1968), he might have chuckled, seeing a description of someone like himself: "Like other reactions to symbols, the emotional response of the Scandinavian to the black expatriate as an escaped lynchee makes it difficult for a Negro to explain the subtleties and convolutions of the very condition—the American Negro's—that the foreigner seeks to understand."

From Stockholm to Brickebacken, Glanton lectured on the virtues of sobriety at school and youth club meetings. "The culture of distraction and passivity created through drugs, and which has its source in increased alcohol consumption," he said, "can only have a disintegrating and dissolving effect on society's morals and cultures." Knowing how much this work could help his case, Glanton's political asylum committee printed a letter by a seventeen-year-old student to the Swedish government in pamphlets they were selling for one krona apiece: "Let Glanton Dowdell stay, don't extradite him to the United States! He saved me from drugs." The head of Sweden's health and welfare board eventually added his name to the growing list of public figures who supported Glanton's cause.

◇◇◇◇◇◇

Where did the needs of Scandinavia's supposed socialist utopia meet those of an American black man who had been climbing up out of a fathomless bottom for decades, all the while spurning European ideals in his art?

"I have spoken with the workers here," Glanton said in his Sergel's Square speech, "with the employees and your youth, from Kristianstad to Kiruna. I have stayed with you in your cabins and I have walked with you in your mountains. And I am not afraid." He was the guest of honor during a crowded event at Blue Hall, the immense, brick-walled banquet site in Stockholm where it was usually the Nobel Prize dinner that brought out so many Swedish functionaries. Top-billed Swedish musicians appeared alongside MPs. A folk musician led the audience in a rendition of "The Internationale" and hundreds of hands rose to sway with the music. One former MP shared his experiences in Nazi Germany, where he had seen how an aggrieved ruling class responds with terrorism. "It should make us proud that an American union leader is seeking safety here," the MP said. "May we not fail him!"

In his remarks, the communist journalist Anders Ehnmark said that Glanton's extradition case was "not just about the individual, Glanton Dowdell," but about all black American workers who opposed fascist and imperial regimes. Glanton's example was useful in showing Swedes "ideals [that] appear impossible to bring about in capitalist society." To attack Glanton, added one union representative, was to also spit on the Swedish labor movement, the very "principle that the working class should be entitled to be in control of its own destiny and labor power." The fight against U.S. imperialism was the fight for

Swedish socialism, and Glanton was a would-be martyr in the ongoing struggle.

Glanton's own Blue Hall speech was a confession and a pledge. He promised to fight not only for black Americans but also for the liberation "of the Mexican American workers in the United States, of the poor in the Appalachians, and the most destitute of mine workers in South Africa." He told them of Black Bottom and the age "when the industrial tycoons housed their labor power in disease-stricken ghettoes situated in close proximity to the ill health of the industrial neighborhoods."

If the people of Europe wanted to understand what created men like him, the flames that ignited their own moral light, they would need to understand what it was like for Glanton to have seen a black baby girl chewed to death by rats. He was the ideal of what a Swedish Social Democrat should strive to be: a union-loving, drug-hating socialist whose work inspired the lowliest to set themselves free.

◇◇◇◇◇◇◇

While Glanton's asylum committee published open letters, posted flyers, held informational meetings with unions, started petitions in workplaces and schools, and led protests in cities such as Lund, Gothenburg, Örebro, and Visby, Glanton's coming trial stirred his friends and family in Detroit. His story made news in some corners of the black and radical press. Calls were issued in Detroit and other cities to write letters in support of Glanton to Sweden's prime minister and anyone else who might have a sympathetic ear. The League gave Glanton a ceremonial new title: International Representative in Scandinavia.

An organization in Detroit planned a fundraising concert and banquet in April 1971 to help pay for Glanton's legal fees and allow Leslie and their five kids to go over and join him. The event was a hit. Less than two months after the Detroit fundraiser, Sweden's prosecutor-general denied the extradition request for Glanton, citing insufficient evidence for the charges against him. The rest of the Dowdells had made it over to Europe by the time Glanton was granted asylum. They stayed with him in a row house south of Stockholm. Glanton's aging mother stayed in Detroit.

Leslie quickly enrolled in a Swedish-language school and found work as a nurse's aide, though she did not plan on renouncing her American citizenship. The kids had a much easier time picking up the language, particularly the girls. Stacy and Lindiwe spoke fluently within three months even as Leslie hoped they would stick to English in the home. They did not. Glanton understood Swedish well enough by then and could get his gist across haltingly, but the new arrivals put him to shame.

Was this what he could focus on now? Playful competition with his children to see whose pronunciation was best? Wasn't that the first question asked upon reaching the New World? *How do you say—?* For the first time in a long while, Glanton had much of what he needed for peace: his family, if not a home. By accepting asylum in Sweden, he ensured that he would never again set foot on his native soil. "I will only return to the U.S. once it's a free country," he told a journalist. "That will not happen anytime soon. The United States is becoming an increasingly harsh fascist state."

◇◇◇◇◇◇

From America, Glanton's friends in the League and other black nationalists who knew him stayed in touch after his trial. Leslie, however, was done with him by 1974, after three years in Sweden. Glanton was an emotionally unavailable husband. He had politics and other women on his mind. He would go on to father two more children with a Swedish woman, though he never married again. He was a loving but often absent dad. The American-born kids saw him more. Glanton's Swedish daughter, Anna Simoni, who shared his memoir with me, remembers seeing him on occasion throughout her life. In one picture, in which Anna is four years old, she and her father stare bemusedly into the camera, surrounded by books and sketching material.

Glanton thought Swedes were mostly kind, but he saw the effects of racism, too. Perhaps the hardest thing about living in Sweden, he told a magazine, was that it was "so difficult for you to show your feelings, to yell, to laugh, to cry." Although Glanton had once praised the Swedish school system, his American-born children were mercilessly bullied for being black. Gary and Keith, teenagers when they arrived in Sweden, refused to be pushed around by their harassers and obeyed their father's command to fight back when provoked. Stacy, who was six years old when the family moved, and her brother Lance had such a hard time dealing with the racist slurs and emotional abuse from adults and children that they were temporarily enrolled in a school for the children of foreign diplomats. Lindiwe started school last and got by with fewer problems than her siblings.

After his divorce, Glanton settled down in a third-floor apartment unit just outside of a forest in Tumba, a suburb of Stockholm. The building had no elevator, so the stairs kept his joints oiled. His apartment had a central hallway that branched off into a guest room arrayed with his art, two little bathrooms, a small master bedroom, a makeshift studio with a huge architectural desk, a balcony, and a table pushed against the kitchen window with three chairs around it. There was always enough room for Lance and the girls. Glanton opened his salon-like apartment to what the girls later called their "communist" "aunties" and "uncles," most of them white. They discussed politics with Glanton while the children sat around, hearing everything.

Glanton took a job at an arts-and-crafts center where he taught photography, painting, and carpentry. He liked to bake cookies with his daughters, listen to the *Dreamgirls* cast album with them on repeat, and fashion little guitars out of cardboard and paper. A few times when the girls were young, Glanton vacationed with them and some of his friends on a Finnish island for a week each year. Though banned from returning to the United States, which he would always see as the only true arena for his political struggles, Glanton continued exploring far beyond it.

He did not stop moving. He became an avid photographer, and

during the Soviet-Afghan War took pictures for a communist news-paper, traveling between Russia and Afghanistan. He, Stacy, and Lindiwe strolled through the Tumba forest, walking the hour to a lake he loved or camping for the night. He would vanish for a month or two in the summers, alone, often to the Scandinavian Mountains.

◇◇◇◇◇◇◇

◇◇◇◇◇◇◇

"It was a split world, in a way," Lindiwe told me of the years in Sweden with her father. Like every other member of the Dowdell family except for Lance, who died as a young man, Lindiwe eventually returned to the United States. "We knew of injustice, we knew of the difficulties, and of course there was prejudice in Sweden, too. Just not the same way as here."

For most of his life, Glanton had been taking advantage of a right that was eventually recognized in Sweden's constitution in 1994: *al-*

lemansrätten, "the everyman's right" or "freedom to roam." It means, Stacy explained to me, "that no matter what forest it is, who owns it, everyone has a right to be in it. You go in there and pick blueberries, mushrooms, and you play in the forest. It's not like forests in the States. You could actually move around in it."

Stacy did not know whether her father's love of solitude and nature was connected to his past imprisonment. The girls caught glimpses of his longing to return home when he tried and failed to figure out how to smuggle himself back in for his mother's funeral in 1989, or when he talked about wanting to send some of his art to Detroit to stage a show. The show never materialized. Glanton's own unfinished creations, those things that, like him, were in a permanent state of suspension, bothered him. In the last years of his life, Glanton did not seem happy with his artwork. There was always something to be done, some revision to make, even when he could not seem to do it.

Before writing his memoir and reading parts of it aloud to Stacy and Lindiwe, Glanton did not speak extensively to them about his years in Detroit. When he was almost eighty years old, having lived in Sweden for the last thirty years, his lupus worsened. He had learned of his condition decades before and enjoyed reasonably good health for almost twenty years. His life had lasted much longer than he would have predicted as a young man. The new millennium was approaching and, as he reflected on his life, he could feel his own end coming. "I've always comforted myself that death for me would come quickly," he wrote for his children, "a [bullet], a knife, or some sort of summary execution, with no margin for anxiety. Men like me usually die."

To have escaped all the dismal ends he could have met during his Black Bottom days felt like a gift. It was bittersweet that his own body betrayed him now. His joints and organs were inflamed. His legs would need to be amputated soon before he died, but he wasn't going to wither in hospice and he refused to take tranquilizers for the pain. Death would wait for its cue. When Glanton was ready to let go, that is just what he would do. Leslie would scatter his ashes in Stockholm.

But before then, he would do his best to fulfill a promise he had made to his children. He wanted to describe for them "the delicate, interpersonal things" that made his time on earth what it was, the "roaring, swishing turbulence of that life [which] left little opportunity for retrospection." His self-portrait would always be incomplete. For every patch of light that revealed an aspect of his spirit, there were many disturbing voids, gaps which may have made him out to be a better man than he was. Glanton was a chimeric fugitive, a man who wove himself into myths. He often lived between disappearance and reappearance. Remembering his exploits on Hastings Street in Detroit, he wrote, "I ran. I ran. Oh, God, I ran with the wind roaring in my ears and voices brimmed with love and care, and laughter, saying as I whooshed by, 'Lawd, that boy!'"

LETTER VI:
FROM EIGHT MILE
TO THE INFINITE SOUTH

In 1979, when I was three, I sat in the back seat of my dad's Lincoln Mercury. My parents and I would take several trips to Tennessee every year. I stared out the rear passenger-side window at the beautiful landscapes we passed as my father drove. I remember the beauty of Ohio's farmlands off Interstate 75.

On the road, Dad lightly hummed along to any song that he liked and moved his head back and forth to the beat, every now and then murmuring the words. If it got real good, he sang aloud for a second or two. He was shy about singing. I didn't know that yet, but Mom would tell me about it thirty years later. Back then, I noticed only the good things and had no concept of time.

What I loved about those trips to Tennessee was that I got to see my parents' families. I was the only child in Michigan in my entire extended family. I had no cousins, uncles, or aunts where I lived. After my sisters moved away, there was only my father, my mother, and me. Traveling from Detroit to Nashville where the family was took an entire day. I would be content with the weeklong vacation at Uncle Joe and Aunt Opal's house, my perfect place of peace. It was a ranch-style house on a country corner. There were no sidewalks. It was grass then road.

When I was in Detroit, I went into a cocoon. Even though I was born in Michigan, I needed Tennessee. My soul grew only when I went there. I tried to survive for eleven months each year. I was alive for about a month. Even my parents seemed to heal when we went to their home state. Whenever we would pass into Tennessee, I could tell we were close to seeing family because the hills right off the interstate that looked like mountains and huge precious gems had this beautiful swirling rock. I had all these cousins that I got to see twice, maybe three times a year. Daryl was the cousin I looked up to the most. He was thin and well-groomed. When we pulled up to my aunt and uncle's house, I knew there was going to be a party. Many of the partygoers were my cousins. They were all around eighteen. There were about fourteen of them by the time everyone got there. With me being the only kid, it felt to me like the party of the year.

Being happy in Tennessee made me realize that I hated Detroit. Whenever we left to return north, I would enter my first stage of depression. The depression would deepen in Kentucky. By the time we were in Toledo, Ohio, I was bracing for the disappointments of my daily life. The hatred I had for life because I could not be around my cousins was one of my first emotional problems. Until the age of twenty-eight, when I went to prison, I would return to Tennessee only fourteen times. I wanted so much to be a part of my relatives' lives, but they didn't know me. I was a visitor. Our connection would last for a few days. The place that I loved, the place that brought so much senseless joy, hurt.

As I was growing up, my mother said that I should write. She was the glue of my life. She was everything to me because we spent so much time together. She said that I was a good writer, but when I was twelve years old, I sat down to write and nothing would come out. I'd always felt that I had nothing to write about, no life experience concerning anything. I could have written about the Pentecostal church that I attended seven days a week. I could have written about how my mother worked so hard and had to come home lonely and depressed while my father was out. I could have written about how I watched television to escape all the things I didn't have. I could have written about how my father was good, and angry, and afraid because of the things he had been through. However, in my culture, transparency brought shame and embarrassment for what you were not.

At home in Detroit, Dad would leave six out of seven days between 11:00 a.m. and 1:00 p.m. and he would come back at 2:30 in the morning. Every day I was in a constant state of loneliness and taking care of my mother. Dad was there sometimes, though. He tried. He wanted to be a great father to me. He did a great job at times. But for most of those first fifteen years I had to go it alone. Dad was a drinker, but he also became pack leader of my Cub Scout troop at the parochial school he and Mom put me in. He was also an assistant coach on my football team. My depression kept me from seeing that he was trying.

I would stay at home as a child when I was not forced to be at church. I wanted my mom to know that someone was there for her. Had I not been there, what semblance of family would we have had? The truth about life away from Tennessee was that my father was at the bar seven days a week, sitting in the dark. My mother was at the church seven days a week, sitting in the glaring light and praising the Lord, crying, swaying, and having only Elohim as her salvation.

The grace of place was what I needed, and that is what Tennessee gave me. Otherwise, I would sit in my parents' basement each day in Detroit. When I wasn't at school or church, I would listen to albums and tapes to get away. I was an abnormal child in an imperfect family. I did not know that we were in such an imperfect society.

The Valley of Dry Bones

◇◇◇◇◇◇

In April 1970, after decades of failed attempts to integrate Detroit's schools, the city's board of education voted to approve a controversial desegregation proposal. Detroit's superintendent called it a "plan of hope." Many conservative politicians in the state, black advocates of community-based control of schools, and angry white Detroiters saw it as an April fool's joke. It was a heavy-handed scheme of social engineering, some critics said, devised by people who obviously couldn't see that whites did not want to integrate, especially after the events of 1967. Michigan lawmakers and the new governor, William Milliken, tried to stop the plan. The national NAACP sued to let it proceed. A district court ruled that Detroit's schools were so segregated that the only way to integrate them was by rearranging the boundaries toward them. The black kids were taken by surprise. Some turned desks and chairs into makeshift defensive weapons. They were miles away from help, closer to the wealthy Grosse Pointes near the northeastern edge of Detroit than they were to the areas they knew well. The neighborhood around Osborn was a no-go zone for many of them. They wouldn't have been seen around there had they attended the majority-black Pershing High like they were supposed to before the "plan of hope" changed everything.

The unrest at Osborn spread quickly. In one classroom, a white boy pushed his way out a window and got caught by a loop in his belt. Another one laughed at the absurdity of the scene as black students ran through the halls, thumping on classroom doors to tell the other black boys and girls: *You better get to the gymnasium now.* Barricading themselves together in the gym would be safer than taking their chances outside the school. Individuals might be able to escape if they were fast, but they could also be isolated and overrun. How many of them would know where they were going?

The white kids thought the Negroes were finally coming for them. They had been warned that, ever since the riots a few summers ago, something like this could happen. Detroit's school district was integrating, but some of the white students did not feel that they were part of it anymore. They believed the city was being lost to the blacks. For years now, white families had been preparing for the worst. Worried mothers chartered citizens' clubs. In the months after the 1967 uprising, mock military drills in public parks were not unusual. Groups like the American Legion, the United War Veterans for Defense of the U.S. Constitution, and the Citizens Committee for the Civil Defense had contemplated the likelihood of another urban war with blacks in 1968.

The black students had to hurry. The ones fighting in the halls corralled those who did not know what was going on into the gym. Some wore stained football pads and helmets, clutching baseball bats and whatever else they could find. Later, when the black students finally escaped, they would learn how the story of what went down had been twisted. Someone would tell them that Martha Jean "the Queen"

Steinberg, the DJ on WJLB, one of their own, told her black listeners something like, "You better get your kids causing trouble at Osborn." It was all their parents needed to hear before they got in their cars. The stories that would go to print made it seem that when the tactical mobile unit officers arrived, they jumped out of their cars and shouted *go, go, go,* waving their arms like disaster workers, opening the gym doors so that the students could go free.

In fact, the police beat them with their billy clubs. Students were handcuffed. Law enforcement cordoned the area off to give themselves carte blanche. Black parents could not get past the barricades until the police were ready to let them through. Those whose parents couldn't pick them up were herded like oxen down Seven Mile in the middle of the street. They had to walk three miles to Pershing High, where they would have been students had the plan of hope never been approved, and where buses were waiting to take them home.

◇◇◇◇◇◇◇

A sophomore at Osborn, Demosthene Kimathi Nelson—his friends called him Donnie—was outside when the violence broke out. The morning quiet was shattered when white adults approached the school grounds carrying shovels, bats, and bricks. None of them knew they were walking toward a miracle child. Donnie had been his mother's first successful birth after her five previous tries. He knew he was in danger when the sticks and bottles started flying. Some of the black students were kicked by the adults. Among the assailants, Donnie thought, seemed to be supporters of the recently assassinated American Nazi Party founder George Lincoln Rockwell. Kids covered their heads on the ground. A few whites were stomping a girl younger than Donnie and he dove for her. He would not feel the pain from those blows to his arms and shoulders until later.

Donnie had seen this same cruelty toward black children in the nuns at Santa Maria Elementary when he was a boy. He began attending the Catholic school after a priest took note of the little boy riding his tricycle in the neighborhood, started talking to him, and

THE VALLEY OF DRY BONES 173

eventually recommended the school to his parents. Once during a solemn ceremony in honor of the Blessed Virgin, Donnie's little brother Samuel was chosen to place a crown of roses on a statue of the Virgin. Normally a middling student, Samuel had worked unusually hard to earn the honor, excelling in his classes. All of Santa Maria assembled in the gymnasium for the May Crowning. When it was time for Samuel to climb a step stool beside the statue and remove the floral crown from its pillow, he turned to the audience, spotted Donnie in the crowd, smiled, and winked. He tipped the crown on Mary's head to the side, making it look like some fascinator pulled drunkenly over her hair, and pimp-walked away. The sisters snapped and pulled the boy behind the stage curtains. Donnie hopped up and ran after him.

Santa Maria's parish disbanded when the Detroit archdiocese closed it and other inner-city parochial schools in 1968. The Church said money was tight that year. If they could not offer quality education for black children, they would not offer anything at all. The parish school closures may have been the Santa Maria nuns' only source of comfort that year, as there was a theological revolution under way that was transforming the Catholic Church from the inside out.

Almost half of the country's 150 black priests met in Detroit in April 1968, within weeks of Martin Luther King's assassination, to hold the first black Catholic clergy caucus. There black priests declared the Roman Church "primarily a white racist institution." And though a fine candidate to open the caucus would have been Father Donald Clark, Detroit's only black diocesan priest at the time, it was the Protestant pastor Albert Cleage who was invited to address the apostolate. In his speech, Cleage reminded the brother-priests that no matter how much they worked to redesign the interior of a white power institution, they had always been and would continue to be outsiders.

"We were separate in a very real sense, in every aspect of our lives," the reverend told the priests. "To realize suddenly that you are not an American, that you are an alien, you are in a strange land, that these people around you are not your friends, they are enemies, that they are your oppressors. This is a difficult thing for a people to go through

psychologically in a short period of time . . . Black people are beginning to build caucuses in every organization, in every church group
throughout America on a sense of unity that stems from a knowledge
that we are a separate people and live a separate kind of existence,
and that we have to utilize the separateness and come together in some
kind of unity which gives us power."

Later that year, Albert would publish *The Black Messiah*, which
catapulted him to a level of fame and notoriety that few other black nationalists would achieve. The book, published by a small, New York–
based press known mostly for its work with Catholic authors, was a
broad survey of the state of the black revolution after the deaths of
Malcolm X and Dr. King, a rallying cry for the creation of a black
spiritual nation organized around economic and housing cooperatives,
and a prophetic text that predicted the country had not seen the end of
tumultuous racial violence. The book was best known for elaborating
on the reverend's beliefs that Jesus Christ was a revolutionary black
Zealot who led Israel, a "black" nation, against the white oppressors of
Rome. No one, perhaps since Marcus Garvey in the 1920s, had stated
so boldly that true Christianity was an instrument for black revolution. Albert's message suggested to black people around the world that
the low, the forgotten, the dejected, and the poor were the constituent
elements of the future.

The Detroit rebellion had elevated the reverend's profile on a national scale. *The Black Messiah* would extend his reach abroad, from
Italy and France to Israel and South Africa. The book was an immediate sensation in the United States and a bestseller, receiving wide media
coverage on television and the radio, and in publications ranging from
The New York Times and *Negro Digest* to local dailies around the country. A reporter for the *Detroit Free Press* called the collection of sermons
"the most detailed formula for the institutionalization of black protest
yet to be printed in the rebellious 60s."

For every ardent admirer of the book, there seemed to be an indignant critic. One columnist in Gulfport, Mississippi, writing for
The Dixie Guide, complained that "[w]ith the integration of the public

schools, colored television, and a veritable flood of Black Power literature flooding the market, it was to be expected that the integration of
the Son of God would follow."

◇◇◇◇◇◇

That there were spaces for a *separate kind of existence* for black people
was no secret to young folk like Donnie. In Detroit, there were many:
Vaughn's Book Store, the Nation of Islam's Temple No. 1, the Black
People's Topographical Research Center, the Black Conscience Library,
the Tuesday-night consciousness-raising groups at Hartford Memorial
Baptist Church, the Shrine of the Black Madonna. Donnie knew that
the pastor of the Shrine appeared frequently on the radio and television, and that he wrote a column in the *Michigan Chronicle* (Donnie
was only eleven when *The Illustrated News* ended its run). The reverend
was at least part of the reason why Donnie's school syllabi had many
black-authored books on them.

He was introduced to the Shrine by his scoutmaster and neighbor,
Wallace Ribbron, who went by Jomo. When the beatings at Osborn
High were over and the black students were escorted home, Donnie
went to Jomo's basement library, where he liked to retreat for solace.
Jomo was one of three black chemists in Detroit's Food and Drug Administration lab. He was not known to be a churchgoing man, and so
his wife, Emma, would go to her Baptist church on her own. One of
Jomo's FDA colleagues told him about the Shrine, a church that was
not one of those old-timey, stuffy joints. He visited, he joined, and then
he became a deacon. Emma and their children went with him.

It was not long before Rev. Cleage put the Ribbrons to use. In
1969, Emma organized ice cream sales after Sunday services, a music program featuring slave songs, hymns, spirituals, and jazz, and a
church library with books that students could use on Saturday mornings at the Shrine's School of Black Studies (SBS). At the SBS, girls
learned to dance and boys learned karate. All children started learning
Swahili and were shown the "no-no chart" of things that harmed black
families: white dolls, white Jesus, heroin dens.

Jomo was the registrar for the SBS, which was described in a church newsletter as "an alternative to the miseducation of Black youngsters." His basement was an informal extension of the school. Here Donnie read books by black writers whose names were everywhere and others whose names were known mostly to specialists. He wanted to do something about what was going on at Osborn. Jomo advised Donnie and his friends to start organizing. Twice a week Jomo would lend his basement to the thirteen young men and one young woman who formed a group they called the Black Cultural and Social Brotherhood (with apologies to the lone sister).

Before the Brotherhood could return to Osborn, though, they needed to convince themselves that they could dress the part of people who deserved respect. They had been actors for their entire lives, in a sense—at home, at school, and in the wider world—reading ugly stories about themselves and wondering if there were missing pages. It was time for them to find a new look. In Detroit, the Afro-Mod boutique that the Shrine had recently opened on Livernois was the hottest place to go. A white donor had helped the Shrine purchase the three-story building that housed its art and furniture gallery, bookstore, beauty parlor, jewelry manufacturer, and cosmetics distribution company. It was called the Sudan Import and Specialty Shops before the church renamed it the Cultural Center and Bookstore.

Upon entering, Donnie and his friends smelled frankincense and saw glass cases stocked with earrings, bangles, and necklaces. On display all over the first floor were masks and human-size sculptures from Ghana, Senegal, and Nigeria. In the Black Star Clothing Factory on the lower level, where the Brotherhood was headed, two of Rev. Cleage's sisters, Barbara and Gladys, ran the sewing shop that ordered diverse fabrics by the yard. They used Dutch wax cloth and Kanga. They made felah hats, cashmere, mohair, and buba suits, and black dashikis with red and green pockets that the Brotherhood would go back to school wearing on casual day.

When Donnie and his friends walked into Osborn again looking the way they did, people's eyes popped. Some were in awe, and most looked concerned. It was not quite the effect the Brotherhood wanted, but now that they knew they were walking time bombs, they would make sure everyone saw them fiddling with the detonators.

◇◇◇◇◇◇◇

Donnie had first seen Rev. Cleage speak at an event for the pastor's friend Yosef Ben-Jochannan, the famous Egyptologist and frequent guest speaker at the Shrine. Dr. Ben had just come out with *Black Man of the Nile and His Family* (1972). Donnie and his boys shared that book among themselves to learn what Europe had gotten wrong about Alkebu-lan—Africa—the ambrosial Land of the Blacks and mother of all civilizations. The second floor of the Shrine's cultural center was used for readings and other events. Notable visitors made appearances all the time: the journalist Samuel Yette, whose book *The Choice* (1971) examined black America's sorry state despite the promises of the Great Society; the Pan-Africanist scholars John Henrik Clarke and Asa Hilliard III; Ron Karenga, the creator of Kwanzaa, whose seven communitarian principles of Nguzo Saba the reverend would soon apply within his own movement; the filmmaker Melvin Van Peebles, whose X-rated breakout *Sweet Sweetback's Baadasssss Song* (1971) premiered in Detroit; and the Black Arts Movement poets Sonia Sanchez and Nikki Giovanni.

For all the good Rev. Cleage had done for the community, Donnie's minor quibble with him was that his brusque demeanor offended the boy's own sense of decorum. Though he wouldn't have minded if the reverend softened his knock-me-down tone, Donnie knew there was no haven like the Shrine, where he and his friends went sometimes when they were hurting. It was where they turned after a hard Saturday night early in 1972 when the notorious Detroit police officers known as the Big Four accosted Donnie and his friends, drawing guns on them and dumping their belongings into the street. The boys weren't Shrine members, though they had been thinking of themselves as part of a broader fellowship, occasional drop-ins hungry for a comforting message. They drew up a shortlist of black nationalist organizations that were still around, one of which they promised to join together: the Nation of Islam, the Black People's Topographical Research Center, or the Shrine of the Black Madonna.

The storefront think tank that the boys briefly considered joining, the Black People's Topographical Research Center—the Top—was a national organization based in Chicago. The interior walls of the original building on the city's South Side were covered with color-coded maps of cities throughout the country showing how black communities had been gerrymandered, subjected to restrictive housing covenants and coercive settlement patterns, and slowly transformed into economically ravaged "ghetto reservations." Top centers offered tours of the cities where they were based, from Detroit to Boston, and formulated dire predictions about the mass incarceration of blacks and other genocidal scenarios that whites might carry out in places where blacks were clustered. The ghetto reservation tours had a radicalizing effect on many of the black youth who witnessed them. The Top's shocking visuals brought the unmapped into focus and gave clear answers to the question: *Where are the black folk on the maps of the world?*

Rev. Cleage did not always deliver the sermons anymore because of the demanding speaking schedule he had been keeping since 1968, following the publication of *The Black Messiah*. Cleage had deputies to fill in for him when needed, but on the day that Donnie and the other boys sat in on a service, he was at the Shrine to preach. He spoke about the prophet Ezekiel's vision of a valley floor littered with dry bones. *Son of man*, the Lord asks, *can these bones live?* The Lord breathes a great sigh of wind and the bones of the dead start rattling. They clacker like castanets until the flesh that fell off in stinking heaps from the bones slides back to encase them. Vultures go hungry again once the flesh no longer reeks. The Lord gives Ezekiel breath to blow new life into the undead, a vast, exiled army that is the whole house of Israel ready to return home.

Cleage's sermon brought the audience to their feet. One brother in the sanctuary was high on prednisone because of a fused spine, but it seemed as though the reverend's preaching filled him with the spirit.

The brother urged the four young men who had been coming around lately to stop watching the services like expectant stool flies and start helping build a black nation. Everyone knew they had weathered something at Osborn and that the Big Four, who rode around in their hulking Plymouth Gran Fury to terrorize blacks, had gotten to them. Many people who came around to the Shrine had a similar story to tell.

"What'd you think of the sermon, brothers?" the man asked. "You believe in what we're saying, right?"

The boys affirmed, *yeah!*

"You're committed to the struggle, right?"

They said they were, *yeah!*

"So what are you doing? Just sympathizing and coming by for a pick-me-up every now and then? When you goin' put the shoulder to the wheel?"

The brother's enthusiasm sent the boys down the aisle. They went upriver to the source, to Rev. Cleage at the altar. Amens and cheers erupted. When Donnie stepped outside the church to find a line of cars stretching the length of the block and around the corner, waiting to take all those who joined the Shrine that day to the orientation center, he knew he was about to enter a new home.

LETTER VII: THE ART SHOP

I had no idea that the Shrine of the Black Madonna was a church as well as a cultural center. When I was in the eighth grade, I was in my last year of school at Gesu Elementary. It was a Jesuit school where we wore sky-blue button-down shirts and midnight-blue pants as our uniform. I would hear guys talk about the Shrine. It was an odd-sounding place to me.

I instantly assumed that it was some strange art shop where artists would paint their pro-Black inner visions. It seemed as if a shrine that was devoted to anything African American and spiritual had to be a pastime for artists. I was so tuned out of culture. It's not that I was anti-me or anti—my race. It just seemed to me like my people were mostly interested in wearing beads and medallions and learning history. The pro-self was limited and aesthetic.

After I'd been at Gesu for several years, the Shrine of the Black Madonna did come up in conversation one day. My father, though progressive and culturally aware, never took me to the Shrine. It was clear that some of my classmates had ventured out to the "art shop," but that was the extent of the conversation. I could not tell you where it was located precisely. This is at a time when phone books and pay phones were all we had. That was my final conversation and thought about the Shrine until now.

Things were relatively good at Gesu. I was enrolled there when I was five years old. My parents didn't like the increases in tuition that they were charged annually, but I received a proper education. I was raised by nuns during the day and fellowshipped with people who looked like me when I was not in school.

Gesu was a school where the children of affluent people went—middle-class and upper-middle-class families, mostly Black. The parking lot would have Mercedes and other nice cars. The experience of going to school was enriching for me. However, there was a nun who was harsh and mean. One day in her frustration, the nun wanted to choose a child among us to do something.

She said, "Eenie meenie miney moe, catch a nigger by the toe."

Shock ran through the classroom. It was confirmation that this woman truly was who I thought she was. After class, Tamika Grimmett and I flew up the basement stairs of the school to rush to the office and report this. I had never been called a nigger or even heard the word in real life. Not from anyone. Detroit was predominantly my kind, in most areas. This was in 1988. I was twelve.

You know how you catch animals to use for game, food, skinning, killing? This was how whites saw me, according to what this nun said. She was notorious for being condescending and uptight. She showed us no love. For almost eight years, I had attended this Catholic school and I had always felt that she was bad. Her saying this was a gift. I would get to burn her ass. She had been rude to students and so, as we reported it to our assistant principal, she became troubled and nervous.

The nun would later be forced to resign. She quickly got a better job teaching even younger children within the archdiocese.

Time Rituals

◇◇◇◇◇◇

In the aftermath of the Detroit Rebellion, Rev. Cleage foresaw the creation of a New Black World. Could there be a place where evictions did not happen, where there were few worries, no social disorganization, no isolation, no abuse of women, no abandonment of children, no bad schools, no diseased spirits, no blood lost to white violence, no draft, no war, no dope or addiction, no welfare stigma, no Big Four, no infiltrators, no Uncle Toms, no white Jesus, no debt, no spoiled food, no unforgiving pessimism, and no predetermined sense of what the future could be? To achieve this, Shrine members would need to

transform their own ways of thinking, their most intimate relationships, and their city. The revolution would begin at home.

As was true for many other utopian cooperative movements
throughout the world since the nineteenth century, the inspiration
for what Cleage called his "mystic economic brotherhood" was the
example set by the Rochdale Equitable Pioneers' Society (est. 1844),
made up of poor English textile weavers and other workers who were
mad at the industrial system that bred so much inequality in Brit-
ain and put so many people out of work. The Rochdale Society had
opened their club to workers for a nominal fee and were determined to
create a system in which credit would never restrict someone's ability
to build a life, one vote would hold the same weight as any other in
making economic decisions, and basic needs would be met through
the creation of cooperative stores.

Within months of the Detroit uprising, the Shrine established two
nonprofits, the Ashanti and Black Star Co-operatives, with the purpose
of securing real estate for cooperative businesses, much like other black
utopian projects had done throughout the century—Garvey's UNIA,
Father Divine's International Peace Mission Movement, the Nation
of Islam, Depression-era black business leagues, and others. To fund
their co-ops, Shrine leaders solicited money from religious groups that
supported racial justice efforts, took up tithes, and canvassed throughout Detroit. While Albert Cleage and Glanton Dowdell commanded
attention in the city as leaders of the Citywide Citizens Action Committee, the Shrine supported its co-op efforts through street rallies and
leafletting motorcades. Ed Vaughn was chosen to lead the church's
cooperative enterprises and tasked with finding opportunities in retail,
manufacturing, and agriculture.

It was a natural part of the nation-building process to scrap
some plans, however. The strip malls the Shrine wanted to open in
ten cities around the country never took off. After the Rebellion and
King's murder, they never managed to establish their planned network of storehouses and survival centers stocked with first-aid kits and

nonperishable goods in case curfews were ever again imposed in the city. And because the city's housing commission seemed only to release the federal funds it received for luxury apartment complexes, it would take a while for Rev. Cleage and his collaborators to figure out how they could buy and rehabilitate residential properties for their developing black nation. They would need financing and technical expertise.

In Cleage's vision of a black cooperative movement, no area of life would be left untouched. If Shrine leaders couldn't find housing right away, they could at least build a cooperative store that promised healthy food. A bank loan allowed the Shrine to establish the Black Star Co-op Supermarket and the Black Star Gas Station right next to the church. They lasted for a few months, then failed. There weren't enough workers to keep the gas station going. At the store, prices were too high and there was competition from big supermarket chains that had long been household names. The store was always in debt, there wasn't enough money to keep full-time employees, subpar refrigerators let the food go to waste, and there was barely a place to park.

The Shrine could not afford to fall into such deep financial holes again. Endless debt and loan repayments would kill any grand vision of a black socialist commonwealth. There could be no more pleading to banks, no more relying on philanthropists or arguing about money because the black nation's businesses couldn't make enough of it. Shrine members had tried the way of black capitalism and the "buy black" ethos, and they failed. What they needed to form a true black counterculture were "counterstructures," independent institutions that would protect black people from a slave mentality.

◇◇◇◇◇◇

Cleage suspected that there were other, more mundane hurdles standing in the way, too. If workers at the Black Star supermarket, for instance, had suspected that the operation was failing, as indeed they had, why had they not called attention to its weaknesses sooner? Were they afraid that their brothers and sisters in the black nation would judge them for harboring doubts? No course of action would succeed if one's own house was not in order. This revelation was central to what Cleage called the "group process." It was the certainty that small, focused groups of people who were devoted to the same clearly defined cause and to one another would have a greater chance of succeeding than mass movements that were bound to fracture or admit dissenters.

Members of the Black Christian Nationalism movement, Cleage wrote, would need to disentangle themselves from the traps of white society—the "slave culture." This meant, chief of all, rejecting what Cleage called the slave culture's "time ritual." Time, Cleage wrote, was a value system. It was "the power to control the individual's total environmental experiences." Questions about the meaning of time had always come up within utopian movements that resented the way capitalism seemed to take control of it. How much time was wasted going to work for employers who cared only about the money you could make for them? How did this life of work shape the values of individuals and communities? Black utopians often wondered how much time had been stolen from them, going back to the age of plantations and extending to the age of prisons. In what other ways might this time have been used if the conditions that tired black people out, that killed them, were changed?

To begin answering these questions, black utopians would need to step outside of the slave culture's framework of time. Cleage thought that only once black people decided there was more for them than integration could they start thinking about who they really wanted to be. The utopians had to leap outside the bounds of the familiar, into the unknown, where nothing was aligned with the destructive values of the world they wanted to leave behind. There would be no more grooving to the predictable whir of the assembly lines.

The only tool black people had to work with was the earth, though, not heaven above. It was the great crime of white Christianity, and the black churches that shamelessly carried its mantle, to convince so many black people that they might one day be able to mortgage a house in the Celestial City. White people's wars against earthly black Promised Lands had been waged on multiple fronts in vastly different theaters, some violent, others ideological. For hundreds of years, centers of black social life and black homes had been bombed out, burned down, and razed.

Cleage's interpretation of black separatism was one that encouraged black people to use the ways they had been alienated to their advantage. If white Christians loved a God that upheld cruel hierarchies, black utopians would denounce that god and re-create it in their own image. If whites wanted to ensure that black people were crowded in dense cities, black utopians would use these places as their social laboratories.

As Cleage contemplated the most effective way for members of his cooperative movement to live together, he drew on the work of a few thinkers. One was the behavioral psychologist B. F. Skinner, whose novel *Walden Two* (1948) had become a sensation among idealists in the postwar period who, horrified by the brutalities of fascist utopias, were nonetheless interested in creating carefully designed intentional communities. Skinner elaborated the concept of *operant conditioning*, a phrase that Cleage would use constantly to describe the ways white society, through institutions like the church and media, had kept black people mentally enslaved by punishing any attempts to break free and rewarding acquiescence.

There were ways to reverse this psychological conditioning, but it would require immersion in an environment that protected black people's minds and souls from the slave culture. This process required full commitment. Cleage was deeply moved by another popular book of the postwar period that dealt with the consequences of totalitarianism and nationalism, and became a centerpiece of his own thought. This was the social philosopher Eric Hoffer's *The True Believer: Thoughts on the Nature of Mass Movements* (1951). The book was primarily wary of its titular subject. In the twentieth century, however, mass movements created both Hitler and Gandhi. Cleage read the book positively, as a call for those who believed in the black freedom movement to sacrifice all traces of selfish individualism. As Hoffer wrote, "Salvation is found by losing oneself in the holy oneness of the congregation."

Finally, Cleage took a cue from the sociologist Erving Goffman, who wrote about the subject of "total institutions." These were places—such as monasteries, orphanages, and asylums—that were "organized to protect the community against what are thought to be intentional dangers to it." As with Hoffer, Cleage read the book against the grain. Just as he saw the usefulness of group devotion for a black revolution, he also believed there were advantages to living in tailored spaces governed by norms and rules. Drawing on the work of behavioral and group psychologists, Cleage concluded that a person's environment, for better or worse, produced "the total pattern of life."

Cleage was an optimist about certain human impulses and forms of social organization that had the potential to spill over into zealotry. Commitment to the cause of black liberation could produce fanatics and crusaders, but Cleage hoped that the Black Christian Nationalism movement would be led by a group of commonsense folk who would avoid the pitfalls of a personality cult. Black utopia was found wherever sacred urges directed everyday life. For Cleage and the thousands of black people who joined his movement, this was the black ghetto. In the end, he made a promise to the people of his church that many of them have since said was kept: "[W]e are going to take the ghetto that the white man has despised, into which he has crowded us, and make it the most beautiful community in the world."

Formation

◇◇◇◇◇◇

The people of the Shrine wanted to remake the world, but first they had to recognize that they were lucky and that where they ended up on this earth had very little to do with them. Humility was the price of admission, and the generations of those who became Black Christian Nationalists in 1967 and beyond were well prepared to pay it.

The parents of the younger ones, those who joined as teenagers in the late 1960s, may have served in the war against fascism. Or, if their parents weren't participants in that struggle, they made their livings as nurses, homemakers, butchers, milkmen, furniture salesmen, and autoworkers. Their parents were themselves the children of Christian missionaries and of Garveyites from just down the road in Detroit or as far away as St. Thomas.

The Black Christian Nationalists were born in Detroit or, if not there, in Saginaw, Pontiac, Flint, or some other city farther south—Newton in Mississippi, Wakefield in Virginia. In Star City, Arkansas, one of them worked in cotton fields as a child and was baptized in a creek. Another, in Steele, Alabama, grew up in a family that built the structures on their property. They owned cows and hogs. Words like *mortgage* and *housing project* were foreign to them.

Their families grew and sold sweet potato or cotton, surrounded by stands of pecan trees and watermelon patches. Their hometowns had several churches and a one-room school. They were the only child or one of eleven. They were Baptists, Methodists, some unclear mix of different denominations, or they were unbelievers in a household of unbelievers. They went with Momma to Leland Baptist Church or stayed home with Daddy. They went with Daddy to Calvary AME Zion or stayed home to help Momma with the chores.

The first signs of their consciousness showed at different times. There was no onetime revival that swept all of them up at once. The slow great awakening that Rev. Cleage helped bring about, what he called the "Black Protestant Reformation," would not have happened if they hadn't walked out of Detroit's Northern High in 1966 to protest their poor education, or gotten bused to Osborn High, or demanded black history classes at any one of Detroit's other high schools. For some, the breakthrough came upon listening to a Western Michigan University professor named Donald Lester—later known in the Shrine as Sondai—teach on race and culture. Shrine members would call him the church's *son of thunder.*

Others watched the Freedom Riders on television. Some witnessed tanks rolling down their streets during the Detroit Rebellion, saw the uprising on their television screens, or played lookout for their family members as they joined the looters, stripping stores of their wares. They spotted flyers at Kalamazoo College advertising a performance by the BCN Players, the Shrine's theater troupe. They sat in front-row seats at talks by the Guyanese historian Walter Rodney or the Trinidadian historian C. L. R. James. They heard about the Christ statue that had been painted black in front of a Catholic seminary during the Rebellion, or they listened to Roberta Flack's melodious voice singing about little black angels in "Angelitos Negros."

◇◇◇◇◇◇◇

An in-law or a half-sibling brought them to their revolutionary-style church one day after saying all through the week, *you gotta come, you gotta see it.* They may have first heard Rev. Cleage on radio programs such as *Night Call* or *Voice of the Black Nation.* They saw pictures of the Black Madonna in *Ebony* or *The New York Times.* They read both of Cleage's books: *The Black Messiah,* of course, but also the one from 1972, *Black Christian Nationalism: New Directions for the Black Church.* The second book was meant both for insiders and those curious about the philosophy and program of Black Christian Nationalism. While writing it, the pastor considered the experiences he heard about from his people, the hard mornings and long nights that had brought them to his church, to formulate his own "theory of society."

He wrote, "We are all liars because we are permitted to see only through one pair of eyes in terms of one experience." It was imperative to remain open to the world as it came, to its various ideas and people, so long as these things contributed to the well-being of black folk. Christianity and the Bible were only where some people began their search for absolute freedom. Those who knew Rev. Cleage's life and work also knew that he was inspired by many different models: black Muslims and Garveyites, communists and Christian socialists, social scientists and preachers, paragons of reason and titans of faith.

The creativity and irony of Rev. Cleage's ideas were something many of his critics seemed to miss. Mainstream journalists and academic theologians, black and white, accused him of distorting history, making it quasi- and pseudo- by applying the one-drop rule to Christ. The reverend wasn't saying that Jesus was symbolically black because he sympathized with the oppressed, as the black theologian

James Cone argued in two groundbreaking books of his own, *Black Theology and Black Power* (1969) and *A Black Theology of Liberation* (1970). No, Cleage said that Jesus was just as black as Glanton Dowdell had painted him in his mother's arms.

Whether this was true did not matter greatly, in the end. For black Americans, Cleage believed, Christianity had been a plantation religion based on falsehoods that benefited enslavers. Who was to say what was and was not true? Didn't self-determination first begin in the mind?

◇◇◇◇◇◇

The cigar-loving James Dismuke—General Masai Balogun, the leader of the Shrine's security force, the Maccabees—heard that some of the boys who had recently joined the church were working at Saturday car washes to raise money. The boys' shirts were off, their muscled backs shone, and they were scrubbing windows as though the spirit of God resided in their hands.

Some days later, notes were slipped under the boys' doors, wherever they lived in the city, inviting them to become Maccabees. They would need to make it past the predawn training sessions. General Masai intended for the Maccabees to become a defense force on par with the Fruit of Islam of Elijah Muhammad's Nation, the Panthers, and the Republic of New Afrika's Black Legionnaires. They were to prepare for any possible threat to their people—infiltrators, hostile law enforcement, and other unforeseen dangers.

During that first 6 a.m. gym session in 1971, the trainees were instructed to sit in chairs that had been provided for them, feet flat on the floor, palms over their knees. They were told to straighten their backs and look forward. No matter what they heard or what happened around them, they were not to turn their heads. Major Sekou, a small, tender man with soft hands and a patch over his left eye, ran the length of the gym with a full set of barbells on his shoulders. He taught the trainees calisthenics and martial arts and said they were going to use parts of their body they didn't know they had. Some felt good after that first day, but their inability to move the next morning was a revelation. One of the boys who became a Maccabee felt like Gort from *The Day the Earth Stood Still*, a machine that would suppress any threat against the black nation, even if the danger came from those who created it.

While on post, Maccabees read Howard Fast's novel *My Glorious Brothers* (1948), published the year the state of Israel was founded. The book exalted the second-century Maccabean revolt, during which Jewish peasants rose up from the land in Judea and defeated an invading Hellenistic empire. When new members were inducted, the Maccabees sang one of the most beloved songs in the Shrine: *We are, we are, we are, we are, we are, we are, we are the Maccabees!*

◇◇◇◇◇◇◇

Before speaking to a clerk inside the Cultural Center and Bookstore, some of those who eventually joined the Shrine did not know that it was a church at all. Alone on a whim or with a dedicated group, young people uprooted the lives they knew in New York or Chicago or Philadelphia to take part in whatever was going on in Detroit. Others, after reading *The Black Messiah*, wrote to Rev. Cleage from their prison cells or seminaries asking if they were eligible to join his church.

Of the more than one hundred undergraduate and graduate students around the country who applied to participate in the Shrine's first ministerial training group in the summer of 1970, a couple dozen were accepted and asked to come to Detroit. These were the first novitiates to learn under the aegis of laymen Black Christian Nationalists and learned seminarians. They studied the BCN philosophy and witnessed the church's first ordinations. In 1971, the first training groups went out to find new members. Although it proved too ambitious a plan, the Shrine had hoped to recruit at least 6,000 members within a year.

Not everything could be easily achieved. Rev. Cleage told his listeners that white society had trained them to place too much value on individualism. Notices in the weekly church bulletins announced who in the Shrine was meeting their assigned fundraising goals and who was lagging. This strengthened the group process, moving the theory of "the emerging new Black Theology for the Black Church," into action. After the second ministerial training program in the summer of 1971, Rev. Cleage marveled at what the Black Christian Nationalists had already achieved. He wrote, "Learning to live with and love our Black Brothers and Sisters became a new priority and this was something that none of us ever dealt with seriously."

When the reverend wrote, alluding to the work his people were doing with him, that "We have merged the heaven process with the survival process and we are engaged in building a heaven on earth for all Black people everywhere," a "Black communal society which can protect the minds and bodies of Black men, women, and children," he meant that Christ and his mother in heaven could only survive by coming down to breathe the same air that they did.

◇◇◇◇◇◇

And so the Black Christian Nationalists patted their pockets for their wallets and hoped they had a spare five dollars left over from whatever the previous week had taken from them. This was their once-a-week starting pledge: three dollars to the church, a dollar toward co-op development, and a dollar to the Benevolent and Protective Order of the Black Madonna, the social services arm of the church that helped them find work if they did not know where to look and cared for the disabled and chronically sick.

To plan for the next thousand years on earth, as the reverend urged, his people imagined what the next ten years might look like. They would go one step at a time. Starting with a project called Operation '69, they began to view themselves as a real collective. They developed plans for a "technological industrial communal society," which would bring with it the elimination of debt, the creation of a farm and rehabilitation center in the American South that would send healthy food to black neighborhoods across the North, a "Kibbutz-like total care center for children," and revolutions in fitness and dieting.

Within ten years, they hoped that the Black Christian Nationalist philosophy and cooperative programs would extend around the world and reach hundreds of thousands, if not millions of people. Church leaders wanted to establish the movement's international headquarters in Kingston, Jamaica, where a democratic socialist became prime minister in 1972. They hoped to send cadres of Black Christian Nationalists to develop satellites of the Shrine in South America, the Caribbean, and Africa, where they could work with locals to build "church-centered Black Counter institutions."

They couldn't have known it when Operation '69 began, but the obstacles the Black Christian Nationalists would face in the coming decades were legion. Thieves broke into their properties at night because they knew the Shrine was amassing money. In front of the Shrine on Long Island, New York, which, like the one in Harlem, did not last long because there wasn't an active enough base of supporters, vandals would dump white phosphate on the steps. The criminals would splash white paint on the sides of the Shrine and draw *Blackie Go Home* in green crayon.

Gangs would target some of them, perhaps because they knew Black Christian Nationalists were good marks, people who meant something to somebody. Mayors and senators would visit the three Shrines that would last the longest—in Detroit, Atlanta, and Houston. Politicians would hire Black Christian Nationalists to work in their administrations or thank them for getting their communities behind them at the polls.

Bullies would throw stones at their children, and the Maccabees would escort them to school. The children would sometimes be misunderstood because they knew very well who they were and found it hard to comprehend the immaturity of kids outside their black nation, so damaged as they were by the slave culture or broken homes. Some parents in the church, wanting to protect their children from the slave culture, would help them co-raise one another. In the communes that they called Mtoto Houses, the children lived, ate, played, and studied in contained worlds that some of them, but not all, said were close to perfect. The housemothers and housefathers of Mtoto House oversaw these havens for the youth.

◇◇◇◇◇◇◇

By the mid-1970s, Black Christian Nationalists would speak of preparing for the Third Covenant, the glorious age of restoration during which they would build ramparts and palaces on earth. There were fraternal and sororal groups to help them get there. The Holy Order of Nehemiah, a group of carpenters, would take dilapidated places and convert them into Shrines. The women in the Holy Order of Nzinga were appointed Keepers of the Holy Spirit and Caretakers of the Children. The original names for the women's order did not stick—Daughters of Africa and then, in homage to the women's auxiliary of the UNIA, the Black Cross Nurses. The Order of Nzinga had much in common with the Muslim Girls' Training and General Civilizational Class that the Nation of Islam started in 1933.

Some Shrine women believed there was no such thing as patriarchy in the church, only equality between the sexes. Or they believed that obviously there was—how could there not be sexism in a Christian church?—and they promised to abolish it. Once, to prepare for their ordination, some of the candidates for the Order of Nzinga fasted until Rev. Cleage convinced them in their exhaustion to eat something. In red satin chemises and flowing, ankle-length skirts, holding lit candles, they walked in single file, chanting, "Nzinga, my Lord!" At every major Shrine, the orders were led by Mothers Superior.

Awaiting their initiation, Order draftees sat in a room where meditation music played, incense burned, and red lights were dimmed. In the interview room, one woman at a time was asked to search the contents of her mind and soul to excise a myth that had been promising to kill her since she was born: the *declaration of black inferiority*. The interviewer asked if she was willing to wipe herself clean and allow her sisters to remake her. Would she sublimate her ego into the will of the black nation? Could she break her old self down to become something bigger?

Yes.

During meditation hour, she and the other draftees arranged themselves in a seated triangle around a candle in the center of a room. The teacher led an invocational prayer and reminded the women to breathe. Their backs straightened into asana.

"She finds her labor well worthwhile," the teacher said. "Her lamp does not go out at night. She sets her hand to the distaff. Her fingers grasped the spindle."

The teacher shared with them the trials of Nzinga, an African woman, the Catholic queen-warrior and diplomat who drove out the Portuguese from the kingdoms of Ndongo and Matamba. The draftees knelt and received a mark of ashes on their foreheads.

"Nzinga strives to enable the black nation to live when we shall have passed on, and our children, and their children have passed."

Their response came from the seventh chapter of the Song of Songs: "We, like all others, are too mortal women. We were modeled in flesh within our mothers' wombs for nine months, taking shape of her blood, by means of virile seed and pleasure, sleep's companion."

"We, too, when we were born, drew in the common air," the teacher finished. "We fell on the same ground that bears us all. A wail our first sound, as for all the rest."

◇◇◇◇◇◇

Their project could not succeed without mutual recognition and love. They saw the emotional nakedness of their sisters and brothers in pull-up-a-chair group encounters, screaming matches, loving and listening sessions. Each one of them was the analyst and the analysand.

You've been selfish, brother.
Thank you for your dedication, sister.
Sister, you make it hard to be here.
Brother, where would I be without you?

At the Latin Quarter in Detroit, they disguised work as fun and play, holding fashion and cabaret extravaganzas to raise money for the Shrine's projects. Hundreds of people clamored to come in and see.

One Black Christian Nationalist who had moved to the city from New York arranged the balls to unquestionable success, asking for five dollars at the door. She convinced many people to model for the show. A local jeweler crafted steak bones, tin cans, bamboo fishing poles, and coconut shells into items they loved wearing.

They could hardly believe what they were accomplishing. At one of the shows, a DJ put on War's "Slippin' into Darkness" to cue the finale everyone was waiting for. One woman stepped out in a bathing suit by herself. She stopped and posed for a moment at the end of the catwalk. A shirtless, dark-skinned, Donnie Simpson–looking brother who was sparkling with baby oil knelt as she steadied herself on his shoulders and waited nervously for him to stand. When he did, she was the most exalted person in the room. A stranger just walking in might have thought the crowd spotted Aretha for as much as they screamed and clapped and laughed. The woman wondered for a moment whether *she* did that to them. It occurred to her then that every mirror she had ever looked in before coming to the Shrine was defective. She saw herself anew.

◇◇◇◇◇◇

On New Year's Day 1972, Operation Kodi began. Shrine members were asked to double their weekly contributions from five dollars to ten. One half went toward *kodi*, a voluntary Nation tax, and the other went to the church's expansion fund. It was a new year and many of them had been given new African names or found one for themselves. At Rev. Cleage's request, one of the elders in the church rechristened him. Albert Cleage, Jr., became Jaramogi Abebe Agyeman. It meant *Liberator of the People, Defender, Blessed Man.*

"Within ten years," Jaramogi wrote, "we must be established or just be prepared to go to the gas ovens." The economy was suffering, and he saw the consequences of a General Motors labor stoppage in Lordstown, Ohio. The possibility of permanent unemployment hovered over black workers who went on strike. Workplace unrest in the country had not been so bad since the year after the Second World

War ended. Predictions about the dismal prospects for unskilled workers were often made in the clinical language of job elimination, which Jaramogi translated into the more alarming language of black extermination. Whenever jobs were permanently lost, it meant that many black workers would no longer be required. It was all too easy for black laborers to become defunct pieces of industrial machinery.

In this year of labor unrest, Jaramogi also wrote about a final race war, the Pan-African Revolt he said was coming, which would ring in a period of black self-rule and peace. He never defined what this war might entail. Conflict in the cities would likely be a part of it, but it was not clear whether the main theater of war would be people's minds or the streets. The possibility of a racial apocalypse always seemed to rear its head around periods of economic stagnation. Even so, Jaramogi offered a vision of the future that would witness the destruction of the present slave society. Apocalypse and paradise, dystopia and utopia, were conjoined.

◇◇◇◇◇◇◇

Operation Kodi initiated the Shrine's search for a housing commune. Shrine leaders had considered multiple locations in earlier years, but it was not until 1972 that the church found the site of its National Training Center and Residence Hall (NTC). In 1926, the Prussian immigrant Albert Kahn, known for his work with Henry Ford, designed the Abington, a seven-floor, 130-unit apartment-hotel at 700 Seward Street in Detroit. Its dark red brick, crown moldings, and bay windows had a neoclassical elegance. Celebrities who visited Detroit, many of them stage actors, often stayed at the Abington, north of the city center. As whites left Detroit later in the century, occupancy at the Abington declined and the owners put it up for sale.

Aided by years of contributions from church members, and money from the Shrine's fundraisers, the Black Christian Nationalists purchased the building and established their first commune. That December, the church decided that those who wanted to help spread the Shrine's presence in other cities would need to move into the NTC and enroll as seminarians. The commune was to be, in part, a kind of monastery. One of the many advantages of designating the NTC as a seminary was that it allowed the Shrine, through its Committee to Aid Draft Objectors, to become a refuge for black religious folk who opposed the Vietnam War. Jaramogi wrote many letters in support of people who sought conscientious objector status.

Since the mid-1960s, Jaramogi had been one of the busiest black antiwar activists in the country. He had spoken at teach-ins alongside Quaker pacifists and leaders of the Students for a Democratic Society. He marched in New York City with organizers of the Spring Mobilization Committee to End the War in Vietnam. And, after news broke that he was being surveilled by federal authorities, he had agreed to be one of the few black antiwar activists to appear as a plaintiff in *Laird v. Tatum* (1972). The question at the heart of this Supreme Court case was whether it was constitutional for the military to monitor the lawful activities of civilian antiwar activists. The plaintiffs argued that their awareness of such surveillance had a chilling effect on their exercise of free speech. The case ended when the Supreme Court decided the plaintiffs did not have enough standing to sue. The Court concluded that because the plaintiffs did not suffer "direct and immediate" harm as a result of government surveillance, their case wasn't valid. The intimidating military apparatus of the United States was vindicated. Injustices like this had led Jaramogi to declare before his congregation, in 1967, that "we separate ourselves from the war in Vietnam and in this sense . . . identify with the enemies of the United States."

◇◇◇◇◇◇◇

Jaramogi was adamant that his form of black communalism was distinct from the white hippie communes that proliferated in the 1960s. "Secular socialism and youth communes in the Western world fail to grasp the fact that they have stumbled upon an ancient African spiritual truth," he wrote in *Black Christian Nationalism*. He specified what his vision of black communal living would entail: "We are not talking about a commune where hippies are hanging all around the place smoking pot . . . We are talking about a building in which each family has its own apartment, and the bottom floor is used in common with a nursery, a library, and a recreation room, etc., where people who are struggling together, can also live together."

Though the communes of other black utopian religious movements were guides for Jaramogi, the "African spiritual truth" he alluded to was to be found in the example of a mysterious Jewish sect called the Essenes. In the 1940s and '50s, the discovery of ancient religious texts in a network of caves near the Dead Sea brought attention to an isolated group of ascetics who may have lived during the lifetime of Jesus. There was evidence that this group, commonly identified as the Essenes, shared property in common, required total commitment from initiates, sought to distance themselves from corrupt religious leaders, denounced warfare, and rejected slavery.

Later in the 1970s, Jaramogi would call the Essenes a useful model for Black Christian Nationalists. These sectarians—whom Jaramogi considered African because of their origins on the continent—were "the holy people that lived out apart from the other people because they were trying to get close to God," he wrote. Likewise, those in the Shrine who would move into the NTC had chosen to flee the moral wilderness that surrounded them. Any Black Christian Nationalist, even those who did not want to be ministers, could take courses and move into the commune. Most were not professional scholars, but they learned about the history of Christianity and Judaism, communalism and counterinstitutions, socialist and capitalist economics, social and educational psychology, sociology, and ethics. "The whole community is the classroom," Jaramogi had written, "but the class is also a community."

◇◇◇◇◇◇◇

Some Black Christian Nationalists were barely twenty years old when they told their mothers and fathers, brothers and sisters, grandmothers and grandfathers, uncles and aunts, *As long as I'm with this church, you don't have to worry about me.* That was when their families knew their lives were no longer an affair for them to govern. The first wave of move-ins lasted for months. They hauled boxes and furniture into a lobby with cherrywood-paneled walls. Maccabees were assigned to protect the building and assist in whatever way necessary. Groups of women operated the switchboards around the clock.

It didn't matter how much they'd seen, how old they were, or how far they'd traveled to get there. Whether they sold their heirlooms, engagement rings, a second car, or withdrew from their savings to bring heaven that much closer to earth, for all of them, time seemed to flow differently in the Shrine. There was a joke that all those who joined became newborns again, starting life afresh. With the purchase of their first commune, they could begin to create the total institution that their pastor envisioned. It would be a place embedded in the social fabric of the city and in many ways divorced from mainstream values. It was the hoped-for crucible of a better future.

Messiahs

As Albert Cleage was devoting himself to building the Black Christian Nationalism movement in the early 1970s, the question for those who had known of his public activism in the previous decade was, *Where had he gone?* Was he still part of the greater black revolution, which seemed to be dying off, or had he abandoned it to focus on his increasingly inward-looking community? Outsiders wondered whether Cleage and his movement were relevant at all anymore. What good was a Christian church anyways? What place did the white man's religion have in a future supposed to be free of the white man's ideologies?

The most likely reasons Cleage and the Black Christian Nationalists tend to receive little notice today were apparent as early as the late 1960s. Even in Rev. Cleage's own lifetime, the radicalism of his separatist and theological beliefs placed him on the fringes of public approval. Although his work and ideas inspired many of his contemporary black nationalists, young agitators of the New Left, countless black educators, business owners, artists, Afrocentrics, and religious believers, the height of his popularity came after the Detroit uprising and the publication of *The Black Messiah*. When he chose to abandon the national speaking circuits and focus on expanding his church, Cleage fell out of mind as the years went on, even for some people in Detroit. He was not appearing on TV or on the radio as much anymore, and by the mid-1970s, one straw poll suggested that fewer people in the Detroit area recognized his name compared with the immediate period after the Rebellion.

As recently as 2021, Cleage received no substantive mention in Henry Louis Gates, Jr.'s popular book *The Black Church: This Is Our Story, This Is Our Song* or its accompanying miniseries on PBS, though both included images of Glanton Dowdell's Black Madonna mural. The book's discussion of black liberation theology was devoted almost exclusively to the influence of James Cone, the systematic theologian whose extensive writings on the subject established him as an intellectual force. Cone's ideas were partly influenced by Cleage's preaching around the time of the Detroit Rebellion, and he appeared as a guest speaker at the Mother Shrine in the late 1960s just as his own work was gaining attention. In addition to Cone's teaching appointment at Union Theological Seminary in New York City, which placed him at the center of progressive Christian thought for decades, he also adopted a more symbolic—and thus more palatable—view of God's relationship to blackness than did Cleage.

One explanation for Cleage's marginality comes from Raphael Warnock, the Georgia-born pastor who wrote a book about black liberation theology in 2013, nearly a decade before he became a U.S. senator. Warnock cited Cleage's unorthodox "theological conclusions coupled with the sectarian ecclesiology of the Shrine of the Black Madonna, centered exclusively around his leadership" as reasons that the church isn't more widely known today. Cleage's religious beliefs were too obscure, in other words, his practices too Afrocentric, his outlook more inclined toward conflict than peace, and his plan for worldwide black liberation too dependent on his singular vision.

Another historian suggested that Cleage had much in common with the sixteenth-century German preacher and mystic Thomas Müntzer. Müntzer is well-known among those who study the history of utopianism for his role in the German Peasants' War of 1525, which led to his execution. Comparing Cleage with this figurehead of the Radical Reformation was another way of saying that he struck some as a heretical revolutionary who tried to convince black people that they could usher in a new world by destroying the one right in front of them.

◇◇◇◇◇◇

In the 1970s, new religious movements—Black Christian Nationalism among them—were emerging in response to the many ways American society appeared to be failing its people. There was a thin line separating pragmatism from extremism. What some called spiritual havens, others decried as toxic cults. As I learned more about Black Christian Nationalism, becoming increasingly aware of the way its tenets challenged many of the bourgeois values that had defined my own youth, I began to see that the question of whether it ever constituted a cult would be the most sensitive one to raise. It is also one of the hardest to answer.

When I first asked my mother's parents what they knew of the Shrine of the Black Madonna, their mouths twisted. Ours was not a family of black nationalists (though one fun, free-spirited great-aunt had paid a visit to the Shrine sometime in the 1970s). My grandfather James was formed in the mold of his mother's much more famous church in Chicago. She had attended Mt. Olivet Baptist in the 1950s, during the halcyon days of Reverend Joseph Harris Jackson, one of Martin Luther King, Jr.'s most vocal black opponents and, later, a critic of liberation theology. Mt. Olivet was a church in the Booker T. Washington fashion—espousing thrift, racial uplift, self-improvement, and harmony within the bounds of the existing social order. Even as a child, I sensed that there was not much tolerance in my family for deviation from the norms of respectability. Albert Cleage, Jr., was, in my grandparents' eyes, the leader of a cult.

A 1996 *Cite* magazine feature about the Shrine titled "Ghetto Utopia," though mostly admiring of the church's longevity and "thoughtful, socially redemptive mission," echoed the most common concern about the institution—that it was an ideologically rigid place that revolved around the precepts of an all-powerful patriarch. If the Shrine was in some ways a black utopia, it was perhaps limited by the discouragement of public dissent or criticism from its members and Cleage's nearly unquestioned authority. *Cultish*, if not cultic, said the church's critics.

Within the broader history of black utopian movements, the word *cult* has a particular relationship to the notion of social power. In *Black Gods of the Metropolis* (1944), the anthropologist Arthur Huff Fauset wrote of "black cults" such as the Nation of Islam, the Black Jews, and the Peace Mission Movement of Father Divine. Fauset was sympathetic to black movements that had no desire to be understood by outsiders. His study of the new black religious movements of the pre-WWII era inspired the later work of one of the leading black religious historians of the 1960s and '70s, Joseph R. Washington, Jr. In his own book, *Black Sects and Cults* (1972), Washington defined cults as "islands of moral unity" and "variations of the search for power." These moral islands arose in rejection of an establishment institution or ideology. For those who inhabited these islands, it was better to be free and misunderstood than to be a debased slave. In the black cult, Washington wrote, "it is understood that the enemies of black people will be defeated, that black people will live in joyful abundance in a new world of their own creation."

Washington, writing in a new age of black utopian movements, did not share Fauset's sympathetic outlook. In his book, he called Cleage "a tragic figure." Washington believed he was a middle-class escapist who duped his people with "sheer utopias" represented by the pretty mural of a black woman holding a black baby Jesus. According to Washington, Cleage was "in love with his own cultic fantasy, rather than the black reality."

◇◇◇◇◇◇

On her wedding day in May 1969, Jewell Eralene Worley, a seventeen-year-old student, was one of three white brides standing at the altar of her church in Ukiah, a rural settlement in northern California. Each bride wore a long-sleeved dress of white satin and a veil that hung at her elbows. They were distinguished by the colors of their dress bows, which matched their carnation ribbons, the dresses of their attendants, and the frosting on their cakes. Jewell's color was blue. Her pastor's wife, Marceline, sang a solo over organ music, a Sondheim song about finding peace and quiet in some unknown place.

One month later, Jewell wrote a short letter to Albert Cleage at the prompting of her pastor: "Dear Rev. Albert B. Cleage Jr., I'm writting [sic] just to let you know that I think it's wonderful what you are doing for your people. I just want to praise you for the strong stand and the pride you have for your people. I'm a member of People's Temple pastor [sic] by Jim Jones, Although my pastor is white he has adoped [sic] black children and many other races. I was wondering if you would send me a picture of your black christ for my chruch [sic]?"

Another member of Peoples Temple, Jodi Jow, explained in her own letter to Cleage why he might find a like-minded spirit in her pastor. "[Pastor Jones] bases his teachings and his life on the practice of racial equality and love," she wrote. "We live in a predominantly white town, but nearly all of the Black people here belong to our church and we pride ourselves on this fact. We hope to have more joining our congregation . . ."

Jewell and Jodi both requested duplicates of Jon Onye Lockard's *Black Messiah*, which hung in the Shrine's lobby. From California's Redwood Valley, Jim Jones was, like Cleage, becoming popular for criticizing the social norms of American society and hypocrisy within mainstream Christianity. Since the 1950s, Jones, a white man, had been styling himself as a holy seer and faith healer in the mold of black religious leaders such as Father Divine and Sweet Daddy Grace. Jones was on the cusp of opening another branch of the Peoples Temple in San Francisco's Fillmore district, where Cleage once lived as black wartime workers came to the area in the early 1940s. After Cleage left San Francisco, black migration to the district continued for the next thirty years and peaked in the 1970s. By then, the Peoples Temple was at the height of its influence, commended by the local press and composed mostly of black members.

As early as 1969, Jones was starting to conflate blackness—the social status that he said society feared most—and godhood. "Black is a consciousness," he said during a service in 1973. "Black is a disposition. To act against evil. To do good." Jones's messages around this time were as reminiscent of Howard Thurman as of Father Divine. He insisted on equality between people by denying that race existed. He profaned race by profaning blackness, calling himself a "nigger," seeing his own face reflected in Cleage's invocations of the Black Messiah, and listening to his wife, Marceline, singing "Black Baby" for the Peoples Temple Choir—a promise that racial prejudice would one day leave the hearts of men.

Some of the bad press the Peoples Temple started to receive in the early 1970s spilled over to the Shrine. In October 1972, a month after the journalist Lester Kinsolving became one of the first people to expose abusive practices at the Peoples Temple in a series of articles for the *San Francisco Examiner*, he dismissed the Black Christian Nationalists as "Cleage's Black Jesus cult." He called Cleage himself a "white-hating minister." Kinsolving's conflation of Cleage and Jim Jones's efforts "to create a Utopian community along the lines of the early Christian church" was the kind of rhetoric that pushed the Shrine to the edges of a movement it still had every intention of helping lead: that of building enduring black nations within the nation.

Six years after Kinsolving's remarks, in 1978, Jim Jones ordered the deaths of hundreds of his followers on the Peoples Temple Agricultural Project compound in rural Guyana. More than nine hundred people died by murder or forced suicide, including Jones himself. Patty Parks and Judy Ijames, two of the other women from the Peoples Temple who had written letters to Cleage in 1969, died in Jonestown as well. The massacre reinforced the fear that groups which sought to separate themselves from mainstream society, no matter their stated goals, were likely to bend toward fanaticism and abuse. The hope that one man might truly be a prophet became the expectation that he was probably a crank.

◇◇◇◇◇◇◇

On the surface, the resonances between Jones and Cleage were profound. Both men were fluent in the evolving languages of black revolution. Each led militant social action churches that spanned the periods of civil rights and black nationalist agitation. Their churches provided social services—access to rehab programs and medical support, child and elder care, communal living arrangements—that were missing from most other churches around them. But though Cleage believed in the possibility of some kind of black apocalypse—a slow, mass death brought on by crises of joblessness and despair—Jones was sure that doomsday was inevitable and near. He feared the dropping of atomic bombs or ambushes by armed government forces. Unlike Jones, Cleage's response to the ruin he saw in black communities was to refuse the death wish. He wanted to send self-sufficient apostles into the world, where they knew some great change was afoot even if they could not name the hour.

Though it did not always succeed, the purpose of Cleage's ministry was to diffuse power rather than consolidate it in himself. He was one black man among many people, he assured his followers in the church, and he was vulnerable to the same diseases of the soul. Cleage had issued a warning in 1967 against "personality cults," writing that an organization "has to be more than a group of people who are attached to a personality and are ready to follow him." Still, he would never entirely escape the contradictions of his stated goals and his position as the patriarch of a Christian church that had its own strictly enforced hierarchies.

It is true that Cleage was sometimes skeptical of gifts from Shrine members and expenditures on his behalf. Offering him a new watch when he had one that worked fine made as much sense to him as printing his face on a T-shirt, a gesture that once infuriated him. It didn't seem that he wanted to be treated like an indispensable savior, but a minority of Black Christian Nationalists nevertheless referred to him as "my father," the "Master Teacher," one of God's great revelations, or the very sort of black Messiah he described in his book.

The notion that a prophet or an elect group possesses special insight into the nature of good and evil has always been an ingredient of and impediment to certain visions of utopia. Since the late 1960s, Cleage had been telling the members of his church that they were "God's chosen people," like the persecuted Israelites, who would never be fully cowed by their oppressors. With this declaration, Cleage intended to instill a sense of purpose in those who would listen. In theory, he was working toward his own obsolescence. He wanted to ensure his movement outlived him, and that when he died, Black Christian Nationalists would continue their fight for dignity and their search for a lasting Promised Land.

Cleage gave himself the great challenge of guiding a spiritual nation through the dark, away from an illuminated horizon that only seemed to light familiar trails. But although the BCN movement was unusually egalitarian in many ways—with its emphasis on communal work and shared resources, rotating leadership roles open to men and women, and semi-autonomous groups that led the Shrine's expansion into other cities—Cleage was always at the reins. His approach to leadership was fatefully entwined with the patriarchal nature of the Christian church. Like many utopian prophets, Cleage did not expect he would live to see his most dire predictions borne out or his most beautiful dreams come to full fruition. He felt it necessary, all the same, to lead his people until he could do it no more.

LETTER VIII:
FREE THOUGHTS

I am what is considered a "Black" man. This designation comes from Caucasian men who are obsessed with classification and separation, and who judge themselves against anything that is not of their own likeness.

I have been in America for my entire life. My forefathers were here going back at least five or six generations. In 2006, my father, his brother, and my sister did research that led the family back to 1870. I was told that we could have gone even further back to find out about my ancestry, but the information was disturbing to my family members because of the slave trade mentality. People were considered cattle.

At the age of seven, my parents told me that I was Black, and I told them I was not. I argued that black was a color, and I was clearly a human being. I have never spoken to aqua, sienna, or pink. I have never met blue. I understand that I have native countrymen, but don't classify me as a color.

I realized as a child that my parents were trying to instill in my mind a notion that someone before them had put in place for all of us. All people are told that they are part of a group, and though family pride has validity, this is where the problem begins for interactions in the world. People find illogical conflict in differences. It can be hard to maintain the discipline of tolerance. We should have stayed away from trying to build the tower of Babel.

I desperately loved my parents and wanted to help them understand that I was a person, a boy. My pride was in my beauty as an individual. Some would like to say that a person must first identify with their heritage and tribe, country and countrymen. It is sometimes good when people can stand together and have something in common, but pride in the flesh is often futile. I love how I look and am grateful that I was born with my heritage, but we live in times that push for the separation of people.

Would I allow myself to be a person obsessed with group conflicts, or would I be an individual who lived as the human being that I am, not allowing my heritage to determine everything that I say and think? Do I look at the beauty of my son, and my father, and where we come from as the basis of who I am?

Can a government or an education system convince you that your strength, identity, and legitimacy are in your heritage, or are you intelligent enough to know that your strength, identity, and legitimacy are in who you are as the singular person who was born to your mother? Will you waste your time on the irrelevant, or will you spend it looking beyond the body into the soul?

The constructs of country and tribe prevent a person from having free thoughts and free reign to be their individual selves. One day we'll only be loved for the love that we lived. Though each man should embrace his earthly circumstance, it is only an earthly circumstance. We expire once the heart stops and the brain goes dead. I don't think it's wise to boast the temporary over the eternal.

The Science of Becoming What You Already Are

◇◇◇◇◇◇

In 1961, an eleven-year-old girl named Shelley Elaine Miller walked through grounds decorated with trees and flowers to reach a baptistery's sacramental font. Her blue plaid dress, blue socks, and black patent leather shoes were spotless. The baptistery was a gaping hall without any chairs. The lighting was poor except for the pool's illuminated front. The water's shadows flickered against the wall.

Six five-year-old girls arrived with their parents and were shown to a room of stalls, then directed to change into white swimming caps and floor-length cotton gowns. Shelley had arranged for the baptism of these girls, who she had been teaching in Sunday school at her preacher father's church. Shelley's father, a Freemason and former Army sergeant named Rufus James, had come to Detroit from Florida in 1949 looking for work. Her mother, Ruth Lee Miller, had taught school briefly in the South before leaving that behind to care for her four children. Shelley was the second oldest of the bunch.

Shelley's parents maintained an orderly home with the standard trifecta of icons on the wall—JFK, MLK, and white Jesus. Rufus James's ban on dancing, drinking, and ungodly music did not stop Shelley or her siblings from grooving to Smokey Robinson or Martha and the Vandellas. Unbeknown to their father, they went on doing the Bop, the Jerk, the Twist, and the Hully Gully. The gender barrier around his pulpit was the only boundary his three daughters could not cross. And though there was not a single white person in Rufus James's church, the image of white Jesus would never come down. He conceded to Shelley that many of the figures in their Bible stories were black men and women, but, he said, "There was nothing I could do about it."

◇◇◇◇◇◇

Shelley started at Wayne State University in Detroit, in 1968, where she studied physical therapy until her interest waned. She left school and took a test that placed her in the new labor relations unit of the Detroit Police Department. She worked as a stenographer and secretary for her boss, a white man. Shelley, though typically a well-mannered person, became "completely revolutionary" in front of her employer. She began showing up late and wearing halter tops and hipster jeans in defiance of the strict dress code City Hall imposed on women.

Some fresh spirit of revolt had gotten into her ever since the winter of 1971. Her older sister Vernice came home one day with earrings, a silver bangle, and a copy of *The Black Messiah* from the Shrine of the Black Madonna's cultural center. Shelley borrowed and finished the book in three days. It confirmed the very truth her father had felt the need to deny. The old, unexamined ideas about the true nature of Christ, and the images of his supplicatory white face, were lies. Shelley, Vernice, and one of their friends caught the bus on a Sunday morning and transferred to the Linwood route. They entered the Shrine and Shelley stared at the visual affirmation of the truth that Jesus Christ was born to a black woman. The author of *The Black Messiah* himself was there, too, wearing a navy-blue suit, white shirt, and black bow tie. Dressed the way he was, he looked almost like one of the black Muslims.

The three young women took their seats as the church's music director brought the choir down from "Lift Every Voice and Sing." Another man stood to lead the congregation through the Prayer of the Black Messiah: "Almighty God who called together the Black Nation Israel, through Thy son the revolutionary Black Messiah, Jesus, hallowed be Thy name. May Thy Black Nation speedily come and Thy will be done on earth as we accept commitment to daily sacrifice and struggle. Give us this day our daily bread, and forgive us our trespasses as we forgive black brothers and sisters who trespass against us. Help us to resist temptation as we struggle against individualism and may the Black Nation Israel stand as a living witness to Thy power and Thy glory forever and ever. Amen."

Shelley was among the seventy people who joined the Shrine that day. At night after her city job, she began attending the church's mandatory orientations and group meetings. The same brother in the church who had given Rev. Cleage the name of Jaramogi rechristened Shelley as Monifa Dara Omowale, *the Lucky and Beautiful One, the Daughter Returned Home*. She fell in love with another young Shrine member, married him, and gave birth to a daughter in 1972, the year that Monifa was ordained as a minister.

With a baby girl, she had to decide what to do about Jaramogi's expectation that she leave her home on Wisconsin Street to move into the National Training Center. Jaramogi had promised every Black Christian Nationalist "security from the cradle to the grave," from mothers on down to their children. Without that promise, Monifa and other young parents in the church would not have given the idea another thought. Who were they building a nation for if not the next generation? Monifa left the police labor relations department and, for a while, the world of conventional work in total commitment to her faith.

Late in 1973, Monifa would become part of the Shrine's small full-time cadre whose members left behind their "slave jobs" for full-time missionary outreach (MOR) work, what Black Christian Nationalists called *reaching*. Soon after one Shrine member, inspired by groups like the Red Cross, successfully solicited donations for the church one day, Black Christian Nationalists hit the streets. They made some pedestrians, black and white, feel like good Samaritans. Others who donated were certain they had made a small contribution to the black revolution. The early reaching trips hit Detroit's suburbs, Michigan's Upper Peninsula, the greater Midwest, the Northeast, and sometimes even Canada. At the height of the church's expansion in the late 1970s, the Shrine would send hundreds of people across the country to collect thousands of dollars on the weekend. They reached most weekends for a generation. The money from these trips would help fund their most ambitious project years later, the purchase of thousands of acres of pastureland in South Carolina.

The Shrine's communal budget began in 1975, using money mostly from the reaching efforts and the paychecks that some working members of the church voluntarily turned over. Under this arrangement, the Shrine started practicing a version of what some early Christian communities had done. As described in Acts 2:44–45, the verses from the Bible that have inspired utopian communities around the world for centuries: "All that believed were together, and had all things in common; and sold their possessions and goods, and parted them to all men, as every man had need."

For many in the Shrine, the communal budget created a life virtually free of debt, in which they did not need to worry about paying bills, buying food, or slipping into economic ruin. When someone who relied entirely on the budget had something they wanted or needed—a new pair of blue jeans, an appointment at the dentist—a budget director evaluated the feasibility of the request before disbursing the funds. The role of budget director, like many other positions in the Shrine, was not filled by one person alone but changed depending on the church's needs and the individual's abilities.

Jaramogi lived and ate among the Black Christian Nationalists in the NTC, leaving his home in the Boston-Edison neighborhood to move into a two-bedroom apartment on the seventh floor. A smaller unit beside his apartment that came with a bed and bathroom served as his den. Monifa heard this man, the patriarch of his chosen family, ask the Black Christian Nationalists to give up things he had relinquished long ago. The pioneers were advised to put a moratorium on planning families as their nation opened new Shrines. Romantic love and children were beautiful things, but for now they would need to be subordinate to the true revolutionary mission. Jaramogi's own daughters were adults by now, leading their own lives. Any doubts or anguish about the time with his own family Jaramogi sacrificed to run his church were private concerns. Some young Shrine members would find Jaramogi's request too hard to follow. As a result, there were those who chose to leave the expansion cadres—select missionary groups tasked with developing new Shrines in different cities—or even the church itself.

In Jaramogi's radicalism, Monifa saw a man devoid of the hypocrisy and avarice that had come to define so many leaders in Christian churches. Her own responsibilities expanded as Jaramogi listened to her speak up in group meetings. She became a group leader and was chosen to be in the Order of Nzinga. By 1974, when Monifa was twenty-four, Jaramogi had made her administrator of Shrine No. 2, a smaller satellite church, on Mack and Burns. No. 2 was one of the various Shrine outposts that were founded throughout the wider Detroit area in the 1970s. A few were extensions of the Mother Shrine. Others, such as Shrines No. 7 and 8, were churches in Kalamazoo and Flint, run by Black Christian Nationalists who had moved to those cities.

Jaramogi had announced back in 1969 plans to open Shrines outside of Michigan, in cities throughout the Midwest and Northeast.

Most were never established or else did not last long. At its height in the first half of the 1970s, the Black Christian Nationalism movement may have had a few thousand formal members around the country, but it was no mass movement like the Nation of Islam. It was long, difficult work building bases of power in other cities while the core in Detroit was still figuring out life in the commune. Jaramogi did have a wish for the future churches of the Shrine, when and wherever they were founded: "If they accomplish nothing else than to get the idea of a Black Messiah across, they will be an influence," Jaramogi said. "This form will make other churches change."

◇◇◇◇◇◇◇

When Coleman Young, Detroit's first black mayor, won his election in 1973, he defeated a former police commissioner for the city. Young was a Tuskegee Airman, labor organizer, and state senator who had been celebrated in the postwar years for standing up to the House Un-American Activities Committee when the inquisitors came to Detroit. Charismatic and often unfiltered, he had been an occasional guest at the Shrine going back to 1962. By the end of the 1960s, Young was one of Jaramogi's occasional confidants, participating in discussions at the Shrine on the future of Detroit's schools. Young ran for mayor, in part, on a promise to reform the city's police department. A nonprofit that Cleage and other Black Christian Nationalists founded, the Black Slate, was one of the first black-led institutions to endorse Young's campaign. After his narrow win, he opened positions in the mayor's office to more blacks than any administration had before. Black Christian National-ists would work in Young's administration throughout the twenty years he served in office.

By the time Young spoke at the 1975 opening convention for Shrine No. 9 in Atlanta, he was one of the most well-known black mayors in the country. Atlanta's black mayor, Maynard Jackson, made an appearance at the event as well. The Black Christian Nationalists of Shrine No. 9 on Gordon Street, in Atlanta's West End, were based in one of the most diverse areas of the city. The West End was friendly to black Muslims, Rastafarians, and Black Hebrew Israelites. One of the Black Hebrews' famed Soul Vegetarian restaurants was just down the street from No. 9. The *Atlanta Constitution* would call No. 9 "a sort of nation-within-a-nation; a separate communal black state that will, as far as possible, be totally independent of the rest of American society." The year No. 9 opened, Mayor Jackson declared April 1 as "BCN Day" in Atlanta. Jaramogi's daughter Pearl, who was then working in the mayor's office, drew up the proclamation.

Despite the initial optimism around the likes of Young and Jackson, victories for liberal black politicians around the country and the growing black voting power in cities smoke-screened the devastation that had been wrought on the black liberation movement as Jaramogi had once known it. Besides the sectarian disputes and counterintelligence suppression campaigns that were tearing black nationalist groups apart, larger forces were weakening any semblance of a united front. In the Shrine, the effects of economic stagnation, the continued loss of manufacturing jobs in Detroit, and worsening social crises such as the War on Drugs compounded the sense that there was an ongoing siege against inner cities. "Our urban enclaves offer the only place where Black people can escape from the inner-loneliness, confusion, insecurity and feelings of inferiority that torment them daily," Jaramogi wrote. "Our URBAN ENCLAVES protect you from the relentless social forces now undermining the existence of Black ghettoes."

◇◇◇◇◇◇

In Detroit, Donnie Nelson—who went by his middle name, Kimathi—proved a reliable deputy when Jaramogi needed something done quietly and well. He had come to know the reverend while serving as the region's Maccabees commander and bishop. It was a rare distinction, as few people on the Shrine's security force also learned the intricacies of Jaramogi's theology. Ministers and Maccabees, respectively the sacred apprentices and Swiss Army knives of the church, sometimes clashed as they jockeyed for authority. With his loyalties to both groups, Kimathi mediated disputes.

Although his public prominence had declined, Jaramogi was not free from the occasional threat of violence. After one Shrine member overheard a conversation at a restaurant on Linwood Street about plans to kidnap Jaramogi and hold him for ransom—the financial success of the church's reaching expeditions was no secret—security arrangements were bolstered and Jaramogi never traveled without a Maccabee anymore, not even driving himself. As the dewy-faced colonel in charge of Detroit's Maccabees, Kimathi became Jaramogi's chauffeur, taking him wherever he needed to go, to doctor's appointments, to see movies and eat at restaurants. During their conversations, Jaramogi perked up. The hours Kimathi had spent in Jomo's basement library were showing.

"You're a learned Negro," Jaramogi told him.

"What do you mean?"

"You actually read books."

Jaramogi had found an intellectual sparring partner worthy of taking him around town. The young man's watchful gaze could also spot ruptures in the Shrine's still-expanding operation. When Kimathi rose within the Maccabees to become an officer, he was assigned to intelligence. He led a team that informed Jaramogi when church members were doing something illegal or otherwise dubious. He would gather and verify information before telling Jaramogi, who would then decide whether to hold some kind of probationary hearing for the offender. Kimathi's intelligence-gathering was one defense against further organizational decay, and part of the reason Jaramogi broke his own rule that prohibited Maccabees from leading Shrines.

As part of the church's expansion plans, Jaramogi had been investigating possible locations in the South. In 1976, a Houston city councilman informed him of an available 30-unit apartment complex in the city. Jaramogi toured the site and decided he had found the home of the Shrine's next urban enclave. Shrine No. 10 opened in Houston in 1976, in a 1,500-seat sanctuary. Its first few months were hampered by inept management. When Texas Rangers began snooping around the Houston church for no apparent reason and it became clear that church leaders weren't managing the situation well, Jaramogi transferred Kimathi to No. 10 to take over as senior bishop. He was twenty-four years old.

◇◇◇◇◇◇◇

In 1978, Jaramogi called for a churchwide synod in Houston. Black Christian Nationalists from Detroit and Atlanta streamed into Texas for the announcement that the Shrine of the Black Madonna was re-incorporating under a new name, to reflect a shift in the church's priorities: the Pan-African Orthodox Christian Church (PAOCC). Most people would still call it the Shrine. The church's renaming occurred shortly after African nations such as Mozambique, Angola, Guinea-Bissau, and others completed their transitions to independence. Their beacons blazed brightly for weary black nationalists on the American front. By this time, the church was still committed to planting Shrines "across the world" and setting up "theological Training Centers and Residence Halls for Clergy and theological students, non-profit housing for members and those in need, Bookstores and Cultural Centers, Farms, Camps, Retreats, Meditation Centers, Information Centers, Rehabilitation Centers, Social Service Bureaus, Schools [and] non-profit businesses." But after a global oil shock pushed the U.S. economy into the second major recession of the decade, Jaramogi confided to church leaders that the black revolution was basically dead.

The black revolution was a set of ideas, and many people had lost faith in those that held sway a decade before. Guerrilla war wasn't likely anymore. Black people commandeering the shop floors of auto plants felt more like a fantasy than ever as those jobs were slashed and companies relocated. What was needed now was a focus on the survival of Black Christian Nationalists, with an emphasis on their spiritual health. It was time for the Shrine to fulfill its practical purpose as a Christian community, offering itself as "a safe haven" and a locus of "transformation rather than revolution."

Jaramogi believed that a church was only as sustainable as its people. To live in a changing world as a Black Christian Nationalist meant that individuals would need to update their rituals and beliefs to keep up with the times. "We must find the ancient disciplines," Jaramogi would write in one of his poems, "used by Seekers in every generation." He was looking for new frameworks to help him think about the next step toward black liberation. In this new and uncertain age, what was working for other people who were attempting to change what it meant to live in the world?

◇◇◇◇◇◇◇

Monifa often returned to a memory from her first year of college. In a park with her boyfriend, a dark-skinned Air Force man, she lay down on a blanket. The couple stared into the sky until, at once, Monifa's boyfriend seemed to vanish like some kind of mirage. Unaware then of her physical body or its weight, Monifa was, she would later write, "immersed, embraced, and encompassed by the sky, the clouds, the birds, the trees." It felt like a high, a mystical, direct communion with everything. Her trance lasted for two hours. She told no one.

Early in her days at the Mother Shrine, Monifa attended yoga classes. The instructor was a woman who wore forest-green leotards and showed her students how to wade through a river of movements—Cobra, Bow, Spinal Twist, Forward Bend. Monifa balanced on her head and learned about the seven chakras. Her out-of-body experience in the park all those years ago prepared her for her first experience of *kundalini*. With further practice, the dormant coil of energy at the base of her spine, in the sacrum bone, unwound. Monifa's movement flow was an awakening. There was a *snap*. It was her cue to wake up from a hypnotic state.

Was this what it meant to possess insight? To recognize that movement constantly trumped stability and that the flexible lasted longer than the fixed? Hadn't Jaramogi been teaching believers to adapt their mindsets and real-world strategies for survival along these lines? The United States was a young country that thought it knew more than it did. The great, ancient civilizations of countries like Egypt and India had rich spiritual traditions and bodies of occult knowledge that had survived for eons. Perhaps they could be rediscovered and updated for a generation of black people who had seen and tried so many other strategies to try and free their minds. Every black American revolution was once new, but their deepest impulses were immemorial.

Monifa's asana movements seamlessly joined each pose to the ones before and after, in a great fluid unity. They rejuvenated her body and participated in that essential dynamism which discoveries in the field of physics were only now revealing to Western scientists. Jaramogi had read about the modeling of grand unified theories in the mid- and late 1970s. There existed different states of matter, and different energy levels were required to influence the relationships between them, but the basic components of life seemed to be connected. For people with a countercultural orientation like Jaramogi, the formulation of the standard model of particle physics and the discovery of elementary particles such as quarks confirmed that there was much more unknown about the universe than not, on every scale. White Western scientists did not possess all knowledge. Quantum field theory humbled them. No single person could be the gatekeeper of truth when there were still so many unknown variables. Perhaps openness to revelations from beyond the known world would prevail over hard-faced presumption. This position was taken in some of the most popular books of the time, such as the Austrian American physicist Fritjof Capra's *The Tao of Physics* (1975).

"In the beginning, nothing existed but the power and creative intelligence of God," Jaramogi would tell his congregation in a 1984 sermon. He was echoing the teachings of the famous Indian guru Maharishi Mahesh Yogi, who established what he called the Science of Creative Intelligence. Jaramogi had come across similar language as early as the 1940s, when he was a student at Oberlin reading the work of the progressive Presbyterian minister Henry Sloane Coffin. Coffin liberally interpreted God as "that creative Force, behind and in the universe, who manifests himself as energy, as life, as order, as beauty, as thought, as conscience."

"Out of a mystical explosion of divine energy," Jaramogi would say, "the cosmos and everything in it was created. This act of creation provided an orderly unification of the four fundamental forces of nature in a Unified Field controlling the functions and interactions of all things."

◇◇◇◇◇◇◇

Monifa was a voracious reader, devouring books like *Discover the Power Within You, Body-Mind, Creative Conflict,* and *Awareness.* She continued her yogic practices, taking over for her old instructor when she left her post. She taught yoga in the years when things were getting bad in beautiful cities and Jaramogi started speaking of God as "one constantly expanding unified cosmic energy field."

There could be no real knowledge of God while suffering alone. Fostering a sense of redemptive communalism was the purpose of what Cleage called the Transforming Community. In group encounters, Black Christian Nationalists would hold themselves to account. They called out one another's shortcomings and gave praise when it was merited, when the work was good. They were not afraid to cry. They tried exorcising their rage and self-hate by reaching an emotional fever pitch, leaping to a higher energy level. It was as though they were performing one of the sacred dances of the Greco-Armenian mystic George Ivanovitch Gurdjieff. Gurdjieff recognized that men and women consisted of pure movement. They sought emotional catharsis through frenzied but precise motions. (In Jaramogi's notes, he scrawled the names of Gurdjieff, the psychotherapist Sue Holland, and Rajneesh, the guru known for his Dynamic Meditation method. Above them he wrote "Human Potential Movement.")

Jaramogi named the syncretic belief system that would become the renewed heart of his black liberation theology KUA (in Swahili, *kua* means "growing"). It was a "sacred sacrament of rebirth," the "science of becoming what you already are." KUA's doctrine was one of communal healing and realignment. Every person was permeated by cosmic energy and contained "a spark of the transcendent divinity that is the ground of all reality." It was another, modern way of saying that God, the creative essence of the universe, was within every black person. As practitioners of KUA, Black Christian Nationalists spoke of a "chain of operant conditioning" that disturbed their minds and blocked their energy chakras. The buildup of unreleased cosmic power, obstructed by selfishness, greed, self-hatred, and other wicked habits learned from the slave society, was ruinous.

"We have lost the integration of mind, body and spirit with which we were born," Jaramogi said. "The church must have therapies that can liberate seekers from the socially derived imprisonments that isolate us from self, each other and from God, inhibiting us from becoming all God meant for us to be." Meditations, macrobiotic diets, breath work, tai chi, dance, yoga, positive affirmations, and sacramental rituals were all part of a "complete therapy for the 'Awakened Group.'" One lesson Jaramogi adapted from Gurdjieff was that a single person could not reach the highest energy level needed to open her inner channels by herself. But if she could reach that state, her disordered body would find harmony once more. The unhindered flow of pent-up cosmic energy would shatter old associations and learned habits. This was the experience of *Kugasana*. Confessional group encounters were the only way to understand one's own personal limitations and set the Holy Ghost free.

Cleage admitted that, with the development of KUA, practices in the Shrine were starting to resemble those of what he called the "self-realization" movement or the "consciousness revolution"—what might now be referred to as part of the New Age phenomenon of the 1970s and '80s. "The Pan-African Orthodox Christian Church uses all the techniques that the consciousness movement is trying to use separately and apart from the church," he said in a 1978 sermon. More and more people seemed to find fulfillment in bioenergetics and psychosynthesis therapies, Transcendental Meditation, and the weekend workshops of the popular Erhard Seminars Training movement, which emphasized personal responsibility as the most important factor in spiritual transformation.

"The consciousness revolution is going to only illustrate the fact that people have such a terrible need to fill the empty vacuum which is their life," Cleage said. If its purpose was to expand one's sense of what was possible in life and to create a sense of openness to other realities that complemented what was already known about the world, perhaps the consciousness revolution would become the secular religion that made Christianity obsolete. This was Cleage's fear. He saw the rise of the consciousness revolution as a reaction against Christian churches that failed to help people become aware of "themselves, their relationship with other people, of nature, [and] the relationship with the whole world in which they live." Still, he saw these movements as having limitations of their own. He criticized them for offering only "a temporary illusion of community" that did not require the same levels of commitment, accountability, and sacrifice as his own Pan-African movement. American society was experiencing acute crises of loneliness, faithlessness, and pessimism. It would be the responsibility of Black Christian Nationalists to bring the modern language and practices of the consciousness revolution into the church, where Cleage still believed they would have the broadest impact in black communities.

Black Kibbutzniks

In the right environment, no one was more capable of rising above the devastations of slave society than a child. "In order to find who you really are," Monifa remembered Jaramogi saying, "you must return to the womb." Black children who were part of the "awakened group" might yet find a way to escape a life of automatism and self-hate. Jaramogi knew something of the emotional lives and social needs of black children. In Detroit, his advocacy for better learning conditions in schools had been the reason many people first noticed him. In *The Illustrated News*, he had published screeds against "pensioners"—principals and superintendents who found it easier to dismiss black girls and boys as problem children rather than ask themselves why some schools were so overcrowded that students had to take classes at the local Y, sitting in folding chairs under poor lighting.

With help from Detroit public school teachers, Jaramogi opened a Freedom School at Central in 1964, in the spirit of the freedom schools then operating in Mississippi to support voter drives. In a publication for GOAL, his sister Barbara explained that Central's Freedom School was intended to help "free the child from the brainwashing American [*sic*] has given her black children through the almost complete omission of black America in its visual and historical life." For six weeks that summer, students read about African history, black revolutions, and black American literature. A few years later, conversations in the

Shrine turned toward reorganizing the church's Sunday school to emphasize cultural heritage. The School of Black Studies that the church ran in 1970 was the result. Like the church's 1964 Freedom School, the SBS rejected accreditation from the city of Detroit as a measure of legitimacy. It was an independent institution that received its authority from the people who ran it, whether they were formally trained teachers or not.

The Shrine's educational programs were far more than run-of-the-mill Sunday school classes. They brought to fruition Jaramogi's sensibilities as a social worker, spiritual leader, and black nationalist, as well as his broad knowledge of behavioral psychology. Shrine children were as likely to learn about the Haitian Revolution and advancements in group therapy techniques as they were to discuss the Old Testament. "Whatever we do," Jaramogi told a journalist in 1969, "its validity is in terms of the ability to translate it to youth. Youth change faster than the church . . . The effort now is to relate to the Black Revolution and to fit youth into a black action organization."

Ultimately, the Shrine gave a permanent structure to its educational initiatives, opening one more school within the church in 1972. The Alkebu-lan Academy began with thirty-five elementary and middle school students. Courses were offered on black history and theology, music and drama, journalism, and other subjects. A church report described Alkebu-lan Academy as working "to undo the educational damage which has been done to all Black students by the slave schools."

The Shrine's experiments in raising and educating black children were reactions to the poor slate of options available to parents in the church. There was another purpose, too. The parents of Shrine children were still in the process of disentangling themselves from the former world of slave comforts and habits. They didn't have the innocence of children. They couldn't restart their journeys toward liberation without the baggage of their emotional lives, their bouts of cynicism, and their ugly scars.

A "five-year-old has already begun to learn from his parents and to catch their psychological sickness," Jaramogi wrote in *Black Christian Nationalism*. The children of the sick needed a radically new environment in which to structure their days and think about their futures. They needed rituals that removed them as much as possible from the mainstream of slave time. The children deserved to discover their true selves and one another with minimal interference from their guardians. They would require not only an alternative form of schooling but new value systems as well. "If we cannot enter into the Promised Land," Jaramogi had declared in one of his sermons from *The Black Messiah*, "we can at least build the institutions that are necessary so that our children can enter in, with courage and knowledge. Our children will not be shepherds in the wilderness because of our faithlessness!"

◇◇◇◇◇◇

In 1978, Jaramogi sent Monifa from Detroit to join the Houston cadre at Shrine No. 10. She had set out on a dedicated path, so fervent in her commitment to the black nation that some people started calling her "Ms. Black Christian Nationalism." If any person in the Shrine could make someone believe they had more than two hands, it was her. Monifa's methodical work ethic and frankness drew the admiration and ire of peers. Jaramogi's unshaking commitment to the liberation of black people had pushed Monifa into a "whirlwind of making and doing."

Given her penchant for working with children, Jaramogi encouraged her to pursue an education degree at the University of Houston. While there, she read the work of progressive educators such as Lawrence Kohlberg and Jonathan Kozol. Kozol's book *Children of the Revolution* (1978), about the successful, youth-led Cuban literacy campaign of 1961, was an early inspiration for Monifa. During that campaign, legions of adolescent *brigadistas* were dispatched throughout the Cuban countryside to teach illiterate peasants how to read and write, in what Kozol called "a moment of political and moral transformation for large numbers of young people who had never before been outside of the circle of their homes."

Other examples of alternatives to youth education in the United

States were the preschools of the Soviet Union described in another book that Monifa read, *Lenin's Grandchildren* (1971) by Kitty Weaver. Weaver claimed inaccurately that Soviet preschools were required by law "to be built in every apartment-house complex." Monifa was attracted by the idea, questionable in its veracity, that young Soviets were treated like citizens with "most of the responsibilities that citizenship entails," as Weaver wrote. The Soviet system of *dezhurstvo* ("systematic work activity") looked very much like Saturday afternoon *kazi* in the Shrine, requiring young people to perform "socially useful labor for the good of the collective," anything from cleaning the premises to setting tables for communal meals. Americans would prove their opposition to anything that resembled the Russian approach the year after Weaver's book was published. A congressional bill that would have provided federally subsidized daycare centers was killed over concerns that the "Sovietization" of preschool education would threaten conservative family structures.

◇◇◇◇◇◇◇

The Austrian immigrant Bruno Bettelheim, one of the most controversial child psychologists in the United States and an inspiration to Jaramogi, also noticed the "Soviet experiments with raising children in institutions." For their admirers, Soviet schools were some of the many examples in the 1960s and '70s, along with Chinese communes, Cuban liberation schools, and Israeli kibbutzim, of reimagining how holistic models of education could produce generations of hardworking citizens dedicated to nation-building. For Bettelheim, whose ideas were influenced by the work of Sigmund Freud, one defining characteristic of modern society was that its people always seemed to be on the verge of a collective nervous breakdown. To avoid this fate, children would have to sever their psychological links with their parents, "abolish[ing] the . . . bridge between generations."

Bettelheim was known as the longtime director of the Sonia Shankman Orthogenic School, a residential treatment center in Chicago for youth with emotional and behavioral challenges. Although

Bettelheim referred to the school during his tenure as a "therapeutic" center, his many critics in the field of psychology and some of his former students characterized it as an unethical environment where care practices lacked scientific rigor, rules for the patients were irresponsibly lax, and physical punishment was common. Bettelheim developed a reputation as the enfant terrible of child psychology whose academic qualifications were dubious and whose ideas seemed to be based more on pop psychoanalysis than evidence-based science.

Despite this, Bettelheim's work appealed to parents and educators who were tired of conventional education methods and drawn to the idea that a child's emotional suffering could be remedied through careful changes in their environment. Jaramogi paid close attention to Bettelheim's work, especially his popular 1969 book on raising children in the kibbutzim, *Children of the Dream*. He asked Monifa to read it. Bettelheim argued that the black "slum child" who had reaped few benefits from America's educational systems was, like the young Shomer of the kibbutz, shaped by a "uniquely self-contained [world] . . . constituted by extremity."

Whether they were looking to escape American ghettoes or European shtetels, black children and young Jewish kibbutzniks strove to "forever do away with the very conditions that bred them," Bettelheim wrote. This meant getting as far away from the neuroses of their caretakers as possible. Even well-meaning parents could not restrain themselves from dominating their children's lives by hovering over them like tyrants. Jaramogi disagreed with Bettelheim's conclusion that "the kibbutz anima is too radically different from what prevails in our large urban centers [in the United States]." Instead, he ran with Bettelheim's point that black ghettoes were the places where "such child rearing methods might conceivably modify what is currently misnamed the 'culture' of poverty." Applying the communal ethos of the kibbutz in black communities "would best resolve the problem of our slums," as Bettelheim wrote, "and in short order."

The collective farms of Israel's kibbutzim, which at most had numbered nearly three hundred in total, had long been viewed as some of the twentieth century's most ambitious utopian projects. The example of group cohesion, democratic decision-making, and economic prosperity that these socialist enterprises set would inspire black American utopian visions and movements from the 1960s on. One of the earliest examples of a black utopian settlement inspired by the kibbutz model was the Orthodox Jewish community of Adat Beyt Mosheh (the Colored House of Moses), which established a commune in the New Jersey Pine Barrens in 1960. Led by the African American rabbi Abel Respes, the black Jewish communards of Adat Beyt Mosheh dreamed of settling in Israel, which they believed to be their spiritual homeland, though the community's membership declined after Respes died in 1986.

The influence of the kibbutzim on black utopian thought would become more apparent starting in the late 1960s, as Israel's government and Zionist advocacy groups in the United States sponsored kibbutz tours and cultural-exchange trips for black Americans. These were attempts to earn the sympathies of an influential minority group amid Israel's conflicts with Arab countries, particularly the Six-Day War in 1967. Organizations such as the Histadrut—Israel's largest labor group—the American Jewish Committee, and the Anti-Defamation League often invited civil rights leaders to visit the kibbutzim. James Farmer, the first president of CORE, visited Jewish farming communities in 1965. Andrew Young, as executive director of the SCLC, went on a similar kibbutz tour in 1966.

When a delegation of black journalists was invited to Israel in 1969 to write about the kibbutzim, one man writing for the *New York Amsterdam News* observed in wonder that, "[o]f all the the [sic] things we experienced in Israel the most dramatic and useful to blacks in America is this community way of living which we would do well to imitate [. . .] If the Israelis can make deserts bloom, it seems as if blacks with more fertile land and water, could follow the blueprints of the Kibbutzim and carve out the good life in America. All it takes is togetherness." The journalist added: "Kibbutz living would solve many of the ills now present in the economy of the poverty stricken in America. There is enough land available, along with the teeming poverty stricken masses, to make collective living a going thing."

◇◇◇◇◇◇◇

It was a rare thing for an outspoken Pan-Africanist like Jaramogi to embrace the model of the kibbutz so openly, and to make it central to his nation-building vision. By the late 1960s, many black nationalists, including Jaramogi, viewed Palestinians as allies in a global movement led by people of color against racism and imperialism. They tended to view the kibbutzim as inextricably tied to the ongoing saga of Arab displacement and Israeli brutality in Palestine. Many kibbutzim had, in fact, been built directly over the ruins of depopulated and razed Arab villages.

Weeks before the Detroit Rebellion, in a sermon about the Six-Day War, Jaramogi had expressed skepticism of black Christians who celebrated Israel's swift victory. Though he understood that many of them identified with stories of persecuted Jews in the Old Testament, he believed this blurred the bloody realities of the Arab-Israeli conflict. The modern nation of Israel, Jaramogi believed, was founded by white Jews with European ancestry who used "terrorism and violence" to suppress non-white peoples.

"In the present-day [crisis] in the Middle East," he said, "we cannot but define the struggle as one between black and white, with the Jews as white." Three years later, in 1970, Jaramogi would be one of nearly sixty signatories to an advertisement in *The New York Times* prepared by the Committee of Black Americans for Truth About the Middle East. The statement opposed U.S. economic aid to Israel and declared "Afro-American solidarity with the Palestinian people's struggle for national liberation and to regain all of their stolen land."

Despite Jaramogi's opposition to Israeli Zionism, his attraction to the kibbutz reflected a matter-of-fact approach to adapting other examples of nation-building for his own purposes. "We can't be on the side of Israel because they are on the white side," he said in his 1967 sermon, "but we can look at what they did, how they did it, and why they did it." For Jaramogi, who adopted reductive views of Israel's history and the ethnic composition of its people, the creation of the kibbutzim exemplified a nation's successful pursuit of power. It was a coolly utilitarian outlook that required Jaramogi and the Black Christian Nationalists to put aside reservations they may have had about the origins of these communities.

The interpersonal practices that kibbutz living encouraged mattered more to Jaramogi than the farms themselves. He hoped that his own movement would draw inspiration from the kibbutzniks' dedication to work, their shared budgets for clothes and health costs, communal dining habits, conflict resolution practices, and most important, their separate living arrangements for children. In 1980, Jaramogi summoned Monifa back to Detroit to institute a new educational program at the Mother Shrine. In Detroit, she would lead the first Mtoto House, which Black Christian Nationalists also referred to as "the kibbutz."

"I looked at how [Israeli Jews] were intent on building generations that would outlast themselves," Monifa would later say. "They were also very intentional about creating a generation of children that would be better than they were. Anything that occurred in terms of their lives, they tried to deal with that in the kibbutzim . . . It wasn't that it was all perfect, but they had a vision about how do you develop children to sustain Israel?"

◇◇◇◇◇◇◇

In the kibbutz, the black children were asleep in their bunk beds when a houseparent came in to relieve the night watch. A groggy watchman slipped out while the housemother or housefather lit candles on an altar. They put a meditation tape in the cassette player.

"Good morning. Rise and shine," the houseparent crooned.

Chimes rang for the first observance in the Children's Community. The children stirred and sat in a half-crescent formation around the altar, eased their shoulders if they were not already slack, relaxed their faces, turned their palms upward, and breathed in and out, slowly.

"We quiet our thoughts so that we can enter the Narrow Gate

where there is no thought," the houseparent said, "where there is no consciousness."

The children would return to be with their birth parents on Saturday after the communal lunch, but they were here during the week. Some did not understand why they could not see their mothers and fathers whenever they wished. Others bragged that life felt like a continuous sleepover with their brothers and sisters in the black nation. The houseparent asked one of them to set the day's guidelines for how they would show accountability to one another. If they bickered, how would the argument be resolved? If they erred, how would they find a more righteous course?

It was a school day. Their clothes had been ironed and laid out for them. There were not many options, not enough variety to stoke jealousy. After breakfast in the dining hall, they wiped the tables, picked up prepared brown sack lunches of sandwiches, fruits, and juice, and went to the bus stops and church vans that would take them into the slave world for inferior educations. These were only formalities, requirements imposed by the state. The Mtoto House kibbutzniks were not better than any other children, but they might have been more patient than most, less prone to outbursts. They were adept at ignoring the insults other children sometimes directed at their stunning uniformity. They were not the black Muslims for whom some people mistook them. Who, then, did they think they were?

On the seventh floor of the National Training Center, where Jaramogi had his apartment, were the children's rooms, a library, computer and typing labs, lounge space, and study halls. After school, the students changed into their Alkebu-lan Academy uniforms and gathered in a common area for prayer and discussion. Homework and recess went like clockwork. Alternative rituals presented the children with unusual ways of living in the world. They washed one another's feet. When it was time for the group showers, in the early days of Mtoto House, the girls on their periods were permitted to go ahead of the others. There was some snickering and shame before the children had seen enough of one another's bodies to mind them less.

They recited the seven affirmations. The most foreboding was the sixth, the Betrayal.

"In the Garden of Gethsemane," a young group leader called out, "Jesus was betrayed by all his disciples. We see how easily disciples betrayed Jesus when they lost faith and began to doubt."

The children avowed: "We will not betray this Sacred Community upon which we depend for both our salvation and our survival."

They lined up for the evening devotional. A ringing bell ended all chatter except for the incantation of "Wash Me Through and Through, O Lord," sung to open their inner channels. Some went to sleep during the night ceremony. The second ringing of the bell meant it was time for bed. Their bodies were washed. Their souls had been cleansed.

They would keep their promises to one another. Like the Israeli *chamulot*, the kinship clans of the kibbutzim, they would reunite for weddings, anniversaries, and funerals. Their lovers would become jealous. Who is that man you are always seeing? That woman you keep laughing with on the phone?

My family, they said.

When they became adults, those who grew up in the Shrine would struggle to explain what it was like to live in an urban kibbutz and why their relative seclusion had been necessary at all. Just how far they could take comparisons to the children of Israel, and to what end, was uncertain. The Shrine children's *hevruta*, their intimate community, sprouted with the promise of group salvation through labor in an unredeemed land. In Hebrew this was *hovat hagshama*, the duty of self-realization for the improvement of the collective.

◇◇◇◇◇◇◇

As I listened to the stories of Black Christian Nationalists who had been raised communally in the Shrine, I found myself envying many of them. Mourning the detachment from kinship networks that I have felt for much of my life, I wanted what the Shrine's kibbutzniks had been given. Nearly from the moment I learned of Mtoto House's existence, I had romanticized the upbringing of those children—now adults—who grew up as brothers and sisters, learning about mutual aid and self-love.

To idealize the lifestyles of the black kibbutzniks, I had to downplay the misgivings of those who ultimately left their community because they, too, felt limited by the lives they had. I longed for the sense of cohesion and direction that groups sometimes provide, and some of the Black Christian Nationalists yearned to strike out and explore new ways of living. There were those who simply wanted an opportunity to define themselves on their own terms and discover something beyond the communal ethic, which is the notion that the individual is most valuable as the instrument of a collective.

In the Shrine, renegade desires always flowered, if not on the surface then underneath it. Young lovers wanted romance or families the minute those urges called, against every injunction that they wait or withhold for the benefit of a social movement. Others needed space for themselves, apart from any commune. They wanted their children to be theirs alone, not raised by other people. Or they refused to watch their parents get lost in holy devotion to something deemed more important than family. The safeguarding of the individual was sacred and necessary, too. It was the individual who stood discretely on the riverbank, watching the baptism of others from afar. When separation from others was a freely made choice, it could be beautiful to stand alone. The yearning to live differently could not be dammed. It often required one to abandon a familiar church and replace rehearsed songs that for so long had soothed the ear without trying.

III   The Land of Corn and Wine

If a world is not known, how would anyone recognize its shape, even if they happened to catch a glimpse. Some people put faces on their gods or give their gods names and intelligible languages. I'm smart enough to know better, but ask my unanswerable question anyway. What surrounds me.

—JOHN EDGAR WIDEMAN, *AMERICAN HISTORIES*

LETTER IX:
PRODIGAL SON

I left Michigan after calling it home for many years. I moved to Ohio to be with my mother because Dad passed away by the time I was thirty-five years old, in 2011. Mom had moved to Ohio to be around family members in the afterlife of my father's passing. I wanted to believe that I was helping my mother. I had lived a very distinct and lonely existence up to that point, in a sense.

For most of his life, my father lived far from his brothers and sisters. Though he brought our family to the North for work and economic stability, the separation from family destroyed his heart in many ways. He battled depression like I did, and so did my mother.

I always assumed Dad didn't want to be home with me and my mother. For about eight years, starting when I was seventeen, I would drive through Detroit and see my father's gray Dakota truck parked outside of one particular place. I was twenty-five years old when I finally walked into the bar Dad had been frequenting for thirty years. I entered the dark bar called the Locker Room. I knew my father would be there that day because

I saw his pickup. When I walked in, the man was sitting there by himself, drinking silently. That was the first time I knew he was chronically depressed and had been for not only my entire life, but probably even before then. As soon as I saw him, my heart broke.

I walked up to him and said, "Hey, Dad." He instantly lit up. That smile let me know my dad loved me. It was all I needed. I needed to know it after all those years of me sitting in the basement, dancing by myself, reading album credits, and crying. It healed everything for me. I knew his soul in that moment. I learned who he was. He was a man driven and depressed by something. He was so broken that he would sit there for hours, every day of his life. He was so sincerely excited that I had come to see him. Oh, how that hurt me. He said to the bartender, "This is my boy." He repeated it to someone sitting two or three seats away. At that point, my dad would be with me for another eleven years. It hurts me very much that I did not see him for who he was.

Do not miss out on love. If you watch YouTube and the news shows, those videos and scripted reports are going to have you focused on the destruction of God's peoples and creations. The value of life is not found in interest rates, currencies, insurrections, or changes in government. Those things will expire just as human life does. What will not expire is the moment my dad smiled at me, the moment he came out of his depression because I showed up to visit him. This is why God breathed life into those of us who are good. Those of us who are houses of love create godly energy when we do things to make others smile. That godly energy is what moves Him to be continuously on Earth with us.

I was in a subpar Kroger when I was forty years old, wheeling down an aisle. My legs stopped. Grief grabbed me when I had nothing on my mind but taco seasoning and, out of nowhere, I realized that I missed my dad. He had been gone for five years.

He was thirty-three when I was born and he was sixty-nine the last time we sat and laughed together. He drove hours to see me that final time. We sat and talked while cancer was with him. After we spoke, he grabbed my waist because over the years I had grown taller than him. As we hugged, he pulled me closer than he ever had before. This signaled to me that it would be the last time I saw my dad alive.

In 2021, as I write this, the world is being pushed into chaos by intricate social engineering. It is no coincidence. It is not random. Self-preservation for evil people means the destruction of others. Why are people who look like me so hated, disenfranchised, and mistreated in every way? Perhaps that's a question for a heavier book, one with more chapters, slightly different than this. Life has a way of writing the story for us if we don't purposely contribute to every page of our lives.

There is a war between groups that has been stoked in the beautiful pastures of Tennessee and in every part of the United States of America. Despite my sheltered view of what life was like when I was a child, I and many generations of my family have been born into a land of evil and violence. This is part of the American journey.

No matter who the presidents, senators, representatives, parliamentarians, monarchs, or dictators are, no matter who is in power at whatever time and in whatever part of the world, the people in my family vote for God in heaven as king. This is how the generations of my family have survived. My prayers are the daily casting of a vote to give God room to establish and enforce grace for me. I have never cared about being superior to anyone else. I know that God has breathed life into me.

When I look at pictures of my ancestors, I see God in us. I know that to some this sounds arrogant, but in the picture of my great-grandfather, he stood there with his wife and all his children before most of them died. He looked very calm and blessed. You could see the grace and strength in his face. Then I saw pictures of my grandfather, tall and strong. Then my father and his brothers. I am here, strong and able, and then there is my incredible son. There are families all over the world that are like this.

I am not God, but what I am saying is that I see God in us. God is in me. God who creates also inhabits, especially if invited to reside. It is peculiar that men, women, and children were enslaved, mistreated, and tortured to come and work for free in the United States of America, but the peculiar can be unraveled.

The Prison Letters of Dorian Robertson Are Missing

◇◇◇◇◇◇

We have lived lives of quiet desperation,
Locked in a prison house
Of Loneliness
[. . .]
Deliberately
choosing emptiness
To avoid vulnerability to pain
We sought to anesthetize our emotions

So that we could feel neither love nor hate
[. . .]
We were closed away
In a shell of our own making.
Neither the sunshine nor the sunset
Could fill us with awe

—JARAMOGI ABEBE AGYEMAN, "TRANSFORMATION" (1984)

A smooth young minister flanked by several men entered the sanctuary. He was late. He was surrounded by deacons acting as personal guards. The preacher strolled slowly and looked like a brawny descendant of Prince, similarly short and light. I wasn't surprised to learn that he had accepted his calling early, as a child preacher. Those of us in the sanctuary pressed our faces against the glass of the preacher's aloofness.

I did not know, coming in, that this was a revival. I sat with my high school girlfriend and her mother at the far end of a pew. When my girlfriend's mother invited me to join them this evening, I had agreed to go out of a desire to charm her daughter. I knew early in our relationship that I was falling out of the faith as she grew confidently within it. She held piety and worldly participation in enviable balance, singing in choir, attending dances. The holiness of some people is such that the things they touch become holy as well. I hoped that the example of her devotion would refresh my memories of the god my grandparents loved, bringing me back onto that same consecrated ground.

The timbre of the young preacher's voice was surprising. He spoke as though plucking each consonant from a garden. I don't remember the content of his message or how long it took him to lead us to the brink. The weary stood and those who were still started to tremble. Hands lifted in surrender. Heads bowed. I realized then that I had made no effort to understand where I was. I didn't even know the name of this church, and now I was trapped. This preacher was going to crack us open. He growled and most people were on their feet. He told us to ignore our neighbors as we came right before God. We were to shut out the shouts and hollers and survey ourselves.

"Only you and the Lord know what needs addressing."

I did not expect to catch the same spirit as everyone else because I thought I had recently expelled it. I was flirting with the word *agnostic* because of situations like the one unfolding in this sanctuary. I was too pliable to claim atheism. I thought of my father as the preacher spoke. All he could do from prison was write. I had been letting his mother, my granny, take the calls from his various prisons in the years before she and Papa left Michigan to return South. They were in Tennessee again. Somehow, the letters my father had mailed me over the preceding decade, dozens of pages, were gone. I hadn't intentionally discarded them. But they were never securely stored. If they were in a box, I wouldn't have known how they ended up there. It was as though I had gathered the letters, gone outside to read them on a windy day, and set them down before going back inside and locking the door.

My girlfriend's mother accepted the preacher's invitation to the chancel rail by the altar. I didn't follow. It would put me too close to the preacher's gaze. The hands of other confessors would reach out to me if I went. Would they recognize a backslider? I had nowhere to go. My girlfriend stayed beside me. I couldn't tell what she was thinking. I wondered why her mother went up and why she remained behind. I didn't want her feeling obliged to keep me company. The pastor continued pushing us. *Amen. Amen!* A woman ran up and down one of the aisles and dropped like dead weight in the arms of sweating men who I assumed were deacons.

The preacher's bearing was steady. I could no longer keep myself separate from the theater. My choices were to either watch my co-stars dumbly from the wings or review my lines and enter the spirited swell. The revival's clamor masked its private nature. The preacher insisted that only God and I were in the room. *Don't mind anybody else. Let them worry about themselves.* I obeyed. I thought of my father's long days. In his cell, he held on to the faith that I denied. My face warped. My girlfriend saw me crying and pulled me to her. I was the wrong person to be in this church. I didn't want these people to think I belonged with them anymore, though they were paying me no mind. My father should have been the one in this pew. I couldn't keep whatever vows I was here to renew.

◇◇◇◇◇◇

I had known the smells of churches as a child—sweet and nauseating potpourri, colognes and perfumes, and Wednesday night Bible study chalkboards. Some of my past churches had names that sounded like flowers: *Bethany, Elim, Merriman*. A thousand mothers and fathers raised me. I grew under the shade of women's flower-studded derbies. I knew how light fell through tall windows onto the pews depending on the time of day.

Before I was born, my young mother—unmarried and under her parents' roof—submitted to the Lord's plan. She would have me. I would be a test and proof of my mother's faith, and a channel for her affections. In winter 1994, I brought our household to seven—my mother, her three siblings, their parents, and me. Though in theory I was the product of extramarital sin, I became a gift to the family in the flesh. My mother never took the Robertson name. The Staples family lived in a suburb of Detroit. The township of Canton, where we were, was not named after the cantons of Switzerland as its tremendous wealth and mostly white population would have suggested, but after the port city of Canton in China.

It didn't occur to me until I was older why my mother's father, James, moved his family so far from the city where Granny and Papa lived. The farther James's children were from young men like my father, the better. After serving as a medic at a naval hospital in Okinawa during the Vietnam War, James had done well as an electrical engineer for a spark plug company. He had once imagined that he would live a life like so many other black workers in Detroit: devoting one's career to cars for forty years only to drive a decent one. Instead, ten years after leaving the spark plug company, he would retire from a job where he created parts for DOD missile silos. He would drive not one nice Camaro, but two. Our home in Canton had a second-story foyer window that flaunted openness and chandelier light like the other houses in the Meadow Villages neighborhood. Rolling, fenceless backyards flowed into one another. There were no palisades or thuja trees to obstruct one neighbor's view of another. The residents of Meadow Villages loved to show what little need they had for fences.

◇◇◇◇◇◇

When I was six, my mother met the man who became my stepfather. I was the only witness at their courthouse wedding. In the beginning, he was gentle. He turned pancakes for me until the edges were crisp. We raced, and although he had once played football, I won on my own merits or else he let me win. He was a bulky Yale man and a spiritual seer, a Christian. Because he was legally blind, he would enhance biblical scriptures under the scope of a low-vision Merlin magnifier to read. His readings would slowly reveal to him truths about my mother, my absent father, and myself that he said we ourselves could not see. Quiet spirits told him when I was being deceitful and when my mother was being steered by demonic influence.

I didn't know how to respond to his about-face, or the fluctuations in his behavior. I tried calling him Dad. He said to call him Sir. I didn't know what motivated him when he began to say that I was *idiotic scum*, that I was *nothing*. When Sir gave names to two of his leather belts, Betsy and Eagle, perhaps he had decided to beat nothing until it became something again. I was made to read from the Bible before our sessions in the master bedroom. A fan blew weakly as his belts struck my limbs.

The verses I read were from Proverbs.

13:24: "He that spareth his rod hateth his son: But he that loveth him chasteneth him betimes."

Or 23:13–14: "Withhold not correction from the child: for if thou beatest him with the rod, he shall not die. Thou shalt beat him with the rod, and shalt deliver his soul from hell."

The lashings were unpredictable. Only Sir knew his reasons. What I thought to be my complete stillness in Sir's presence, he saw as disrespectful "gesturing"—an insolent flicker of my thumb, the rolling of an eye, a turn of the head too quick for his liking. I reviewed my actions constantly after the beatings and began corseting my movements. I don't remember many details about that time. I recall that being forced to remain in my room from sunrise to sunset some days made me silent and reflective. My carpeted bedroom was not an attic chamber, at least. There was direct, tantalizing sunlight. According to the unreliable schedule that Sir set, my door would open and my mother, with a torn face, would hand me a white saucer with two pieces of white bread, a slice of American cheese, and a smear of Miracle Whip.

I could rarely tell what my mother was thinking during that time. Because of the love I felt from her in the years before her marriage, and in the years since, that period exists as an anomaly to me. My mother should have helped me, and someone should have helped her. There was a monstrosity in our lives and neither of us could name it. My mother felt unable to throw me a lifebuoy very far because Sir would hear when it splashed in the water. He would watch *Smallville* in his living room recliner as my mother tended to the baby, my sister.

At ten years old, I meditated using *Our Daily Bread*, a devotional booklet with scriptures and short messages for every day of the year. The lessons come up blank for me now. I know there were many words. The words interrupted the blankness of walls. I was never more of a believer than when I was in that solitary state. Piety saved me from boredom. Reading was an excellent hobby because of the minimal movement it required. Only a quick flip of the page. I had epiphanies. I cannot say where I went but the skies were cloudless and the seas were calm. Sometimes I didn't want the door to open.

◇◇◇◇◇◇◇

I started to believe that severance from others was a precondition for self-reliance. I accepted that I was a parentless child. Sisterless, too, as

Sir would tell me when I returned from Promise Land the summer my sibling was born, in 2003. Sir showed me a picture someone had taken of the three of them at the hospital.

"You weren't there," he said.

He was not accusing me. He was cutting me out. I was not present. The boy who returned to Sir's house from Promise Land every summer was some kind of ghost that he had to exorcise again and again. I had no proof at the time, but I've learned since that both sides of my family were discussing my situation as though it were a distant war. People were all around me, but they were unhelpful shadows. In what Albert Cleage might have called my "prison house of loneliness," I began to feel a new kind of ambition. I wanted to test the perfectibility of man, of myself. Christ was perfect despite his suffering, I knew. And if the purpose of Christian life was to emulate the messiah, my own cuts and bruises must have been trying to tell me something.

I felt that I understood what my faith wanted from me, which was to look for mountaintops from within a lightless valley. So many people in my life had described beautiful images and a satisfying arc when speaking of the search for the Promised Land. As the first grandson of James and Heidi Staples, I was destined to be a young man firm in the faith, an ambassador of Christ. Material things would not matter to me, but I would attain an education that attained comfort. I could excel at silence and formality as well as my family had.

At church, Sir had become a well-regarded deacon who was complimented for his stepson's public confession of faith. I sputtered after the shock of my baptism at ten years old and was pleased by the applause. Darkly, I could see one thing: the parishioners did not know wheat from chaff. The piety of this man they admired was false. Or his was just a personal god, and we could all choose to worship different things.

◇◇◇◇◇◇◇

When my mother told me she was leaving Sir after four years, I closed my eyes. The promise of renewal washed over me. As the movers carried our furniture out of Sir's apartment, he closed my bedroom door, lifted me by the front of my shirt, and held me against the wall. I thought he might punch me. He said that I was a jackass. Not long after, my mother began visiting Sir's new home to see my sister. For some reason that I didn't understand, he had retained custody. Because I was young and my mother decided I should not be left alone at home, I sometimes accompanied her to the house, staying in the car. I chose to remain there with my seat belt on, ready for my mother to return. Sometimes I watched the sunset and fell asleep. Was my mother gone so long in that house to savor the time with my sister, or had she not fully left the orbit of Sir's manipulation? I wanted her to come back.

Sir came out one day. He woke me in the car to inform me that my father was in prison. He said this was to be expected. It was the first time I'd heard the news. I hadn't seen my father much during those years, and my mother had only recently learned he'd been incarcerated for more than a year at that point. I wished I hadn't heard it from Sir. When my mother and I drove away, I wept for what must have been many things. The final disappearance of a man whose laugh and smile I liked but only faintly knew; what seemed like another betrayal by my mother, even in our freedom; whatever pain and illness had caused Sir to gloat at a child's loss; and the relief that we were finally going home.

◇◇◇◇◇◇

My father and I exchanged letters and phone calls once I was free. I was happy to receive his manila envelopes and hear the robotic voice of a woman on the prison's automated message system. I took the calls from Granny and Papa's kitchen, after they had finished talking to him. My father and I coasted on the surface of things. There was no point getting him upset about what I'd experienced. He couldn't do anything about it. I worried that if he found out, he would sabotage himself whenever he was released by hurting Sir and going right back in.

My father rarely spoke about his life in prison. It was easier to discuss things like films I had seen. Enough time was passing that I could tell my father about a movie and its sequel. He kept telling me how he should have courted my mother the right way. I was proud to hear how much he was reading. He enjoyed learning about business and the law. One of his favorite books was the eighth edition of *Black's Law Dictionary.*

I didn't know how to ask at the time what he had done to go to prison. I had learned that it was easy for people, even those who loved me, to close a door in my face and say, "that is none of your business" or "why do you care so much about my past?" The partitions on both sides of my family only came down so much. The first time my father told me what he did, he shaded the truth with a lie. He said there was a mix-up after an armed robbery attempt and the police took him in because he looked like the culprit. I thought it sounded farcical, but I accepted it.

My occasional correspondence with my father felt less real than my mother's daily attendance to the architecture of our lives, and therefore more notable, much grander, and full of some potential epic sweep. I leaned into the pleasures of something intangible—not Dorian himself, but a kind of fantastical relationship that hovered between dream and reality. Separation took many forms and my father's imprisonment was only the most blatant. The courts were keeping him in longer than he expected, he said. My grandparents and I sometimes drove a couple of hours through Michigan farmland to see him. I took off my socks and emptied my pockets for the security check. My father smiled and always looked good in his blue-and-orange jumpsuit because he played ball and lifted weights. I ate plasticky cheeseburgers from the vending machine and watched the other men and the people who had come to see them. Mostly women.

I have forgotten our visiting room conversations. I mostly remember how my father would lead us in prayer before we left, the tightness of his grip for the last hug, and the tackily painted wall scenes against which another prisoner photographed us. The backdrops embarrassed me. One showed the bright greens of a woodland, mystical fauna, and a path pushing deeper into a pastel wonderland. I felt like we were clowns standing in front of tree branches that didn't bend and leaves that didn't wilt. Did the artist think we would find the crumpled Kodak picture years later and have difficulty remembering where we were when we took it?

My father frequently changed prisons. I thought this meant he was closer to release, which I suppose was true. I lost count of his transfers. He was once in Jackson State, which had been known as Southern Michigan Prison when Glanton Dowdell was there. One artist my father met inside sketched a portrait based on an elegant studio photo of Granny and Papa. It hung in Granny's living room for years when she first moved to Ohio after Papa died. For a long time, it was the only prison art I was thankful for.

⬦⬦⬦⬦⬦

In 2013, two years after Granny and Papa left Detroit once my grandfather got bone cancer, I was a first-year college student. One of my uncles, who was like a brother to Dorian, called me and said, "I have someone who would like to speak with you."

By then, I had stopped responding to my father's letters until they tapered off completely. Time and distance away from him bred apathy. My father and I had not built our love on a broad foundation. As I grew, it became harder to see the groundwork at all. I was becoming aware of the ways my life had been framed for me, in contradistinction to Detroit and its people, who everyone said was suffering. Detroit was a place where I would not need to stay for long. My mother and I moved into my grandparents' old house on Steel Street, where they had lived for more than forty years. I left for Princeton within two months of Detroit's declaration of bankruptcy.

The sound of my father's voice on the line frightened me. I was afraid for him. I didn't think I was the person he thought I was. I didn't know what I would be able to give him, and I was afraid of what he might ask. We had come to know each other remotely, as trifold pieces of paper and disembodied voices. Even in the years since his release, he has been something that mostly happens over the phone. We were stuck in a rut for many years. He made repeated requests for forgiveness. I could think of nothing to forgive him for. He hadn't harmed me, but he equated his absence with injury.

I could see then why one of my girlfriends in high school had kept encouraging me to read "Sonny's Blues," a story by James Baldwin. She was surprised to learn I'd never heard of him. I thought he was white like everyone else I'd been reading, another Jack London or Ernest Hemingway. Sonny, the narrator's brother, gets arrested for selling dope. When he goes to prison, the narrator confesses, "I didn't write Sonny or send him anything for a long time." Sonny writes his brother a letter that makes him "feel like a bastard," saying things like *You don't know how much I needed to hear from you.*

Sonny and his brother had seven years between them. That age gap, "like a chasm," was different from the time separating my father and me. I did feel older than him, though, in a way. I puzzled over his desire to become a motivational speaker for young black men, just as Sonny's brother doubted that he could become a jazz pianist like he wanted. It wasn't easy for us to let those who served their time get out of prison.

◇◇◇◇◇◇

In one of his new letters to me, my father describes prison as a half circle that did not fully close around him, leaving openings for the new. His freedom brought with it a frightening set of questions, and the neat parable of a man redeemed, which had once sounded so essential, became nothing more than a partial outline of what was to come. He began asking himself if there was anything after freedom, or if freedom was a short road that ended in a cliff. Would it be spoiled by his fear that he might not know what to do with it?

Dorian wanted repair. He wanted to unwind time and imagine a new world in which he and I lived in the same state, he had a relationship with his daughter, and his two children worked together to understand the conditions that shaped them. He wanted his son to write a memoir about his travels. He wanted to court my mother the right way, marry her, and give her the five children she had asked for. Hearing any mention of my parents' early dreams excited me. What else had my mother and father wanted? He had hoped to live with family in Tennessee. She had wanted to become an elementary school teacher. The earliest picture I've seen of the three of us, buried in a box in my mother's basement, was taken in front of a statue of a French explorer in Detroit. My father was eighteen, my mother was nineteen, and I was a few months away. I was happy looking at the photo, not because I could have imagined them together one day but because, at that time, where they stood was the only place they wanted to be.

After taking care of Granny in Columbus, Ohio, and spending some years among other relatives there, my father moved with his

girlfriend, a former high school classmate, to Texas in 2018. He had space there and a home of his own. He found his footing in work that finally felt stable. He proposed after a couple of years and she said yes. Instead of going back to a traditional church, my father began listening to speakers on YouTube. The internet came with none of the social pressures of being unknown in an unfamiliar place. The apocalyptic preaching and news my father watched described brutalities against blacks that he knew were plausible. He had an intimate awareness of other people's cruelty—like that of the prison guards who had denied him access to diabetes medicine and put him in solitary confinement.

Dorian did his own research so that he could share with others esoteric truths about a broken, depraved world. He listened to people talk about fascism, white supremacy in American Christianity, and the need for preparedness in case of a government-sponsored extermination plot against black people. "What if we are living in a scripted existence?" my father asked. "What if the things that are going on—with financial difficulties, hardships, loss of jobs, coronavirus—what if all of this is a plan?" In 2020, mainstream news stations and right-wing conspiracy channels on YouTube started to find common talking points, it seemed, fretting about the unraveling of American democracy. "We are at war," my father texted me. "The offense is crafty, lethal, hidden in sanctioned authority by the wicked."

I had a passport, my father reminded me, a way to flee if it became necessary. He was careful to distinguish the alarmism of others from his own pragmatic desire to take credible threats seriously. "Many people who are capable have left North America," he wrote. "If you ever leave I'd be interested in looking at alternatives."

Was it paranoia or wisdom that planted the idea in my father's mind that a race war was the probable end point of American society, patiently waiting for the right moment to break out? On the other side of any belief that better days were coming for black people and that white domination would cease, there was the expectation that whites who were losing power would put down the slaves to keep it. My father wanted to be prepared for any possibility, those most desired and those most feared. To conjure a vision of New Jerusalem, he had to also conjure the demons capable of setting it on fire.

◇◇◇◇◇◇◇

In 2020, my father introduced me to the videotaped sermons of Stephen Darby. Three years earlier, Darby, a husky, mutton-chopped Kentucky preacher, collapsed and died at the site of a Christian village retreat he was planning. Darby was never a big televangelist. He had maintained a small congregation that knew how to livestream. In the last years of his life, Darby endorsed popular lies about crisis actors participating in the Pulse nightclub and Sandy Hook Elementary shootings. He believed 9/11 was a hoax. He was an unabashed antisemite, a fact that my father demurely chastised. He conceded that Darby wasn't right about everything and could, at times, be a little extreme.

The pastor also spoke of the Last Days and the time of Noah. "The people were not aware of the impending doom of the flood until the *day* it started to rain," Darby said in one message. Dangers were everywhere. They included the lead contaminants in Flint's water, the expansion of cashless transactions ("a digital New World Order"), hyperinflation, and the inciters who would bring about a third world war, in which China and Russia clashed with the United States.

The Christianity that white people loved would do black people no good in the end times. "The problem is the Bible was not written by white people or for white people," Darby said. "Paul and them was black, everybody was black. The Bible is a book about a *black* people." The Book of Revelation said that the coming messiah would have white woolen hair, eyes as red as fire, a voice like rushing waters, and feet like fine, burned brass. He would be an earth-toned black man. "What's going to happen when the black Christ show up?" Darby asked. "I know that's hard for some of y'all to believe."

My father thought of Stephen Darby when I asked him to tell me about his vision of utopia. He pointed me to one of his most-watched sermons, on a place called Negroland. Darby spoke of a region that cartographers had charted at the end of the eighteenth century. The mapmaker Emanuel Bowen was believed to have been in London when he drafted *A new & accurate map of Negroland and the adjacent countries* (1771). Some said it was a region inhabited by more than 30 million blacks. Ancient geographers knew it by different names—Sudan, Ethiopia, Nigeria, Nigrita, Tekrour, Genewah. The Land of the Blacks stretched from the Atlantic to the southern portion of the Red Sea, bordered to the north by the Sahara Desert and the Berber states.

"I gotta mess with y'all slave Negro theology," Darby said. "I gotta destroy that Negro theology. [The black Christ is] coming for a *people* . . . They erased you. That's why you don't know Negroland . . . If they didn't erase [you], you would know Negroland is a place . . . These maps have been erased from history because this is how they hid who you are, who we are, and they cut our history off." Without a coherent history, Darby said, there was no coherent map for the future. Using small fragments of truth and many dangerous lies, Darby urged my father and others in his own enlightened black nation to realize that truth was a collage of competing perspectives.

◇◇◇◇◇◇

The assumption undergirding the beliefs of many black utopian movements is that false information about the nature of black people's humanity has been passed down for centuries to obscure our views of ourselves. Because reality has been distorted by the lie of black inferiority, some utopians have insisted that there are hidden stores of knowledge available to those who know where to look. The forces of hatred and alienation have made many black people into gnostics and mystics, those who declare that they have access to fundamental truths that others cannot see.

My father said that Darby was not a Hebrew Israelite. But like the Black Hebrew Israelites, Darby did boast of the chosenness of black people. Many contemporary Black Hebrew Israelite groups claim that they are descended from one of Israel's twelve lost tribes and are the "true" Jews, destined to find the Promised Land. Black Christian Nationalists, too, identified as God's special elect. They did not claim that they were Jewish people but rather that they best fulfilled the symbolic, liberatory promise of Israel—a small nation that would triumph over those it perceived as oppressors.

Those black utopians who did not say they were God's chosen people found other ways to assert their distinctiveness. Some devotees of the Nation of Islam believed themselves to be descendants of the original "Asiatic" black man who was the father of all civilizations and the first to walk the earth. Members of an offshoot of the NOI that was founded in 1964, known as the Five Percenters, believed that only a small number of people understood the truth that black men were synonymous with divinity, that they were themselves gods.

I have always distinguished my father's declaration about God being within every member of our family from the more insidious suggestion that we were gods. *I am not God*, he wrote, *but what I am saying is that I see God in us. God is in me.* It means that although we may not be able to control every aspect of our lives, we do have the ability to choose the names we are called by—the lenses through which we see ourselves.

My father answered Darby's call to emulate Daniel, the Jewish noble taken captive by King Nebuchadnezzar. An angel came to Daniel with news of an impending war. He was the only one who could see the vision of what terrible things were coming. He fell on his knees and the angel restored him, saying, *Be strong! Be strong!* The angel would show Daniel "what is inscribed in the true writings." Knowledge of oneself was a precondition for finding Negroland, and it was hard to know oneself in isolation. Able to breathe fresh air again, my father stretched his hand out for me to take it.

"I do hate that the world is a place of conflict and war," he texted me. "I hope that we overcome in the most apparent and triumphant way . . . Be at peace. Life does get better. I love you."

An Armful of Beautiful Roses

◇◇◇◇◇◇◇

Early in the pandemic, Rose Waldon told me stories about her modeling dreams. She went to the Shrine a few more times after the unveiling of the Black Madonna, but her heart was soon thereafter set on show business as requests from talent agents came in. The interest overwhelmed her. Now the mother of two—her second son was born in 1966—dreamed of New York City. The Black Madonna appeared in the pages of papers around the country and on the backs of postcards. Rose herself appeared in a 1970 special issue of *Ebony* about the rise of the black model. Her headshot in the magazine, alongside those of supermodels such as Madelyn Sanders and Donyale Luna, was the closest she would ever get to those fashion royals.

Hudson's department store in Detroit put Rose in her first print ads as a model for clothes and shoes. She found herself in a world of trade and fashion shows that took her between Detroit and New York City. Rose loved it. She narrated auto show recordings and posed beside cars on revolving stands. She appeared in health insurance documentaries and industrial films, showed off shoes, and crowned herself with Frank Olive and Mr. John hats. She modeled for stores like Henri Bendel, Jacobson's, and Winkelman's. The owner of the King's Row banquet and jazz lounge in Detroit invited her to emcee for artists such as Grant Green, Grover Washington, Jr., Natalie Cole, Billy Paul, and Esther Phillips.

It was almost unanimously agreed that Rose's features were remarkable. They were "so classic her face looks like a fine piece of sculpture suddenly come to life," a reporter wrote for the *Detroit Free Press* in 1969. "And if you are standing next to her when the shutter clicks, she will fade you right out of the picture. Those swept back cheekbones covered by that rich matt chocolate skin, the haughty chiseled nose softened by great moon-calf eyes, produce an effect extraordinarily vivid . . . She'll knock 'em dead when she has learned to make her body a boneless backdrop, to flow from one movement into another instead of striking poses."

In the early 1970s, Rose played bit parts in blaxploitation films such as *Cotton Comes to Harlem* and *Detroit 9000*. She was mugged the night before the New York City promotional tour for *Cotton* began, and she left the city to return to Detroit. She would try New York City once more, ten years later, striking out on her own, working as a cocktail waitress and struggling to find modeling gigs. She lodged for her first five years in the city at the Longacre Hotel on West Forty-seventh Street, near Times Square. Like the more famous Barbizon "Dollhouse" on Lexington Avenue, the Longacre was known as a hotel for women. Visiting men were supposed to wait in the lobby until called for (though Rose and her friends found ways to sneak some of the more handsome ones in). For

Rose, the Longacre was no settlement house, just a resting place for a woman in an unfamiliar city that had not been especially kind to her.

"When I went to places [for auditions]," Rose said, "they would tell me my derrière was too heavy. 'Lose some more [weight] and come back.' Oh boy, what a disappointment that was."

When Rose's older sister visited her from California for her birthday in the late 1980s, by which point she was living in Brooklyn, she made sure not to leave the city without Rose. The sisters left for Los Angeles, where Rose worked "a beautiful gig" for almost a year as a food service worker at the UCLA hospital, feeding seniors and children. Afterward, she clerked for various temp agencies. "I'm not good at anything," she told me. "Typing in high school? I was terrible!"

It was enough of a blessing for Rose to live with her sister close to the water. "I went on a pretty beach with my sister, with pretty white sand . . . A thing that looked like a shower was on it. And I said, 'Oh, you can wash the sand. I've never seen anything like this.'" In 1997, when her aunt in Detroit became ill with cancer, Rose moved her back to Memphis where she wanted to die. Then Rose returned to Detroit. Although she was baptized at a now-defunct church, she did not find a new spiritual home. As always, she spoke to God as she kept private devotionals. With two sons, a daughter, and a granddaughter who had received a scholarship to study biomedical sciences, Rose had everything she needed.

◇◇◇◇◇◇

Rose kept the portfolio from her modeling days and let me flip through it one afternoon on her couch in Detroit, telling me stories of how awful it was to work with the Ugandan model Princess Elizabeth of Toro on the set of *Cotton Comes to Harlem*—Rose found her rude and entitled—and showing me some of the love poetry she had been writing for years. One of her sons visited often, but she lived alone. She and her ailing ex-husband had divorced many years ago. A painting of Rose that Glanton Dowdell had made for her during their short time working together hung prominently on one of her foyer walls.

◇◇◇◇◇◇◇

It was hard to determine where most of Glanton's surviving paintings were in the world. His family had some, as did a black art collector in Philadelphia, and there were probably more in private collections throughout Sweden. In this one, Rose is pensive and looks almost downcast. Dressed in a colorful blouse, she turns slightly away from our gaze and fixates on something we can't see. Her skin is almost as dark as the pupilless eyes Glanton had also given the Madonna. It is a beautiful but not joyous image. Rose adored it.

She remembered those early, busy years in Detroit, in 1969, when she met the television producer Tony Brown, a friend of Rev. Cleage's and host of the popular interview program *Black Journal*. Brown ran a finishing school next door to Rose's hair salon. "He points to me to come to him," Rose said. "I said, *Now what does he want? I'm getting my hair done. I got things to do.*"

"I go up on the porch and he says, 'Well, I'm having a beauty contest with such and such, and the Most Promising Model is the title. You'll go to the schools, get some albums and a wardrobe."

"I said, 'How much are the tickets? Tell me more.'"

"He says, 'Five dollars a ticket.'"

"I said, 'Oh, that's not bad at all.' And he says, 'You have to sell at least twenty . . .' Oh man, I could sell those like hotcakes. And sure enough, I went back to family and friends, and they all bought the tickets. The time comes. Man, there are forty-nine—I'm excluding myself—gorgeous women. I said, 'Well, I'm going home.' Are you kidding me? All of these gorgeous girls? Get out. No way. Sure enough, as time progresses, they call the fifth runner-up. I'm up there still and my legs are shaking like you wouldn't believe. Oh, I'm trembling . . . We're all holding hands. Okay, it comes down to the fourth. I said, 'Well, I'm still here.' The third. I just knew that was gonna—you know, they'll get me now. That passed me up. And it came down to the winner and *aww*, I bawled like a baby. I did some crying. The flashing, the photographers all going crazy. Tony's right there beside me and I've got an armful of beautiful roses and the crown. And I said, 'Oh my God, I'm in seventh heaven! Somebody pinch me, please!' I think I cried all the way home. I couldn't believe it. Me?"

A Place Flowing with Milk and Honey

◇◇◇◇◇◇◇

In John Bunyan's seventeenth-century allegory *Pilgrim's Progress*, an abridged, illustrated version of which I read as a child, the land of Beulah lies on the rim of the Celestial City, separated from it by the River of Death. The pilgrim, Christian (who I loved for the funny, cumbersome boulder strapped to his back), sees in a dream near the end of his life "the country of Beulah, whose air was very sweet and pleasant," where all faithful travelers "solaced themselves . . . for a season" and "heard continually the singing of birds, and saw every day the flowers appear in the earth." The sun shone continuously in Bunyan's fable. Doubt, despair, and the Valley of the Shadow of Death were conquered. The holy city was just over there. Beulah Land's name comes from Isaiah 62:4. It is the land in which the exiled Israelites and Christ shall be married, the place to which they will return.

◇◇◇◇◇◇◇

In Abbeville County, South Carolina, a dirt road called Divine Lane juts off Highway 81. It snips through a curving, tree-lined tunnel that opens onto flat green. At the end of this half-mile path is the Jahi House. For four days in spring 2022, I stayed in this one-story, white-frame cottage. I was told that the Jahi House would be used for lodging when Shrine kids went there for the Alkebu-lan Academy summer camp a couple months later.

There were interruptions in the flat verdure of Beulah Land, wide fields dotted with clumped sedges. Small patches in the tufted grass had turned sallow. Trees to the north, in the direction of Lake Russell, were dark smudges against the sky. When I arrived, birdsong filled the air like chimes. I had called ahead from New York. Andrew Seegars, the Shrine bishop who managed the church's affairs in South Carolina, joked on the phone that he wouldn't be coming to rescue me if I encountered a black bear or boar mother on my own. There were plenty of curious coyotes around Beulah Land, too. The bishop was a city boy like me. His friends called him "JB," short for Judas Maccabeus, the Jewish priest who led the Maccabean revolt against Greek incursion. JB pulled up where I first stopped in front of the red-brick entryway that read *Beulah Land Farms*, a few hundred feet from Divine Lane.

"We're going to go across the street."

JB lived with his wife and daughter just up the way on Seegars Road, which took the family's surname. They were among the last Black Christian Nationalists who still lived on Beulah Land. I was advised to stick to paved trails or stay in my car if I didn't know the country. Beyond range of the utility pole light outside the Jahi House, the nights stayed black.

"We want you to have a nice stay," JB said. He was a big guy who had played football in school, once taught martial arts, and had been carrying a Bowie knife shoulder holster since he was a young man. His large, still eyes gave him the appearance of a patient bouncer. JB's administrative competence and reputation as a trusted confidant in the Shrine was a greater source of pride for him than his renown as an enforcer. In Detroit, he was in a friend group with other future Maccabees like Kimathi Nelson, boys who lived near one another and found their way to the Shrine in the early 1970s. Even back then, Jomo Ribbron, the food chemist who mentored this group of boys and led JB to the church, had spoken about the potential of an operation like the Beulah Land farm.

Within the Jahi House were stately wooden desks and a massive stone hearth. There were housewarming decals, as well as decorative floor vases filled with bamboo. Unpacked boxes betrayed a state of transition. Retro furniture shared space with upholstered chairs and table lamps that seemed to be from an earlier period. I browsed in the quiet. The house was less ghostly than I had imagined it would be. On one table, and then on a bookshelf, and in half-opened boxes in a library room, I found many books on the French Revolution. Some of the books in the Jahi House were too recent to have belonged to Cleage, but many were his.

The library in the Jahi House contained resources for living, vital practices. It offered a partial reading list for a potential student of black utopianism. The works were linked but did not always build on one another in obvious ways. It was possible to trace patterns, which I attempted to do:

> How do the masses destroy the old world that created gods and
>   kings? (see works on the French Revolution)
> Is a revolution to destroy the old world order of slavery possible?
>   (*John Brown*, W. E. B. Du Bois)
> If a white messiah failed, was it still possible? (*Citizen Toussaint*,
>   Ralph Korngold)
> What is the brutish world order that the modern masses want to
>   overturn? (*The Cultural Contradictions of Capitalism*, Daniel Bell)

What does the new world look like in its most desirable form? (*Pan-Africanism or Communism?*, George Padmore)

How are the spiritual masses who embrace Pan-Africanism to think about a utopian like Karl Marx? (*Communism and Christianism*, Bishop William Montgomery Brown)

What is a church that models itself according to the principles of biblical communism? (*The Underground Church*, ed. Malcolm Boyd)

Who leads the underground church? (*Small Groups: Some Sociological Perspectives*, Clovis R. Shepherd)

If this alternative church is indeed worth saving, what must be done to ensure the health of its members? (*Reality Therapy: A New Approach to Psychiatry*, William Glasser; *Meditation: A Practical Study*, Adelaide Gardner; *Prevention: The Magazine for Better Health*)

What is the greatest threat to the small groups that will transform our known, scripted world? (*The Culturally Deprived Child*, Frank Riessman)

How does one ensure that the black child is protected? (*Women in the Kibbutz*, Lionel Tiger and Joseph Shepher)

And if women are not content merely to produce the guarantors of the future? (*When God Was a Woman*, Merlin Stone)

Wouldn't declaring the blackness of God undo the world of the old kings, showing that we have misunderstood the foundations of all reality? (*The Consciousness of the Atom*, Alice Bailey)

Can we decide where to begin the world anew? In the lowest places? In the South Carolinian cradle of the Confederacy? In Detroit "Murder City"? (*The Death and Life of Great American Cities*, Jane Jacobs)

◇◇◇◇◇◇

Beulah Land is a ranch that has mostly been dormant since the Great Recession halted many of its operations. It measures just short of four thousand acres. Central Park could fit within its boundaries nearly five times over. Beulah Land's manager at the time of my visit, a Georgia-born farmer in his thirties named Ryan Pressley, believed that of the 28,700 farms in the United States owned by blacks (compared to the nearly 2 million owned by whites), the Shrine likely owned one of the largest. It dwarfed the better-known Clemmons Family Farm in Vermont, the Soul Fire Farm in Petersburgh, New York, and the Taylor-Stevenson century ranch in Houston. But if Beulah Land is one of the biggest rural tracts that African Americans own in the United States, it is also one of the most unproductive.

For a farm of its size and type—black-owned land that was acquired by outspoken participants in the twentieth century's black freedom movements—Beulah Land may have had only a handful of rivals. In the late 1960s, the Nation of Islam maintained several farms throughout the South collectively known as the Salaam Agricultural System. The organization owned more than 13,000 acres in total across Georgia and Alabama, though it eventually paused its agricultural endeavors for decades, until the 1990s, when it purchased a 1,600-acre plot in southwest Georgia. It was named Muhammad Farms. Muhammad Farms was supposed to provide dignified work, healthy food, affordable housing, and a place of retreat for black people. Though it did produce meats and vegetables that were distributed through some of the NOI's urban supermarkets and restaurants, the farm never flourished and much of its land was eventually sold.

In 1968, a former SNCC organizer and land reformer in Georgia named Charles Sherrod visited some of Israel's Jewish farming communities. He believed that the model of the *moshav ovdim* was more likely to be adopted by black American farmers than the kibbutz. The moshav was a cooperative settlement in which Jewish families pooled their resources to buy farm equipment and finance other large-scale projects. Unlike the kibbutz, whose tenants shared all property in common and distributed their income equally, families in moshavim kept private property, like leaseholds, and raised their own children.

Charles and his wife, Shirley, wanted to provide land and work opportunities for destitute black sharecroppers. In 1970, using the moshav as a model, the Sherrods helped establish the 5,700-acre Featherfield Farm in Georgia. Although the farm's founders planned to practice agriculture and build villages that would enable recreation, education, and more for hundreds of families, financing problems killed it. The nonprofit that supported the farm, New Communities, Inc., had gone into debt to make the initial purchase. Unless it could get access to federal subsidies, the farm's chances of survival were slim. Georgia's racist governor, Lester Maddox, blocked the government's attempts to fund the Sherrods' planned villages. By 1985, lacking the loans they needed to install infrastructure and pay off their debt, and after three years of drought, New Communities organizers lost their land and buildings.

Another black-led experimental community in the South, Soul City in Warren County, North Carolina, suffered a similar fate as New Communities. Conceived in 1969 by Jaramogi's friend Floyd McKissick, Jr., Soul City was meant to be an integrated community with tens of thousands of residents that primarily gave poor and unemployed black people avenues to economic prosperity. Its rural location—which included land that had once been worked by enslaved people—was motivated partly by McKissick's belief that by ameliorating black poverty in the countryside, which many people left to find jobs in the North, new planned communities could help stave off the crisis of black poverty in the cities. McKissick envisioned a town organized on egalitarian principles and replete with housing, shopping centers, churches and schools, factories and hospitals, hotels, parks, and even light rail and an airport. For the next ten years, as McKissick tried wrangling financial support from slow-moving federal government agencies and risk-averse corporations, national media coverage of Soul City was extensive. Although Soul City barely had any infrastructure built, some hailed it as a forward-looking plan for a black paradise in the South. Skeptics deemed it a regressive, separatist concept that undermined the gains of the Civil Rights Movement.

Multiple factors prevented Soul City from ever being completed. There was a national economic downturn that discouraged banks and businesses from investing in a struggling region like Warren County, the glacial pace of funding approvals in the Department of Housing and Urban Development (HUD), a devastating audit of Soul City ordered by the conservative Senator Jesse Helms, and, perhaps most consequential, negative media attention that portrayed Soul City as an exclusionary, all-black enterprise. The dream ended when HUD withdrew its funding for Soul City in 1979.

For any ambitious land-owning project for black people, Soul City and New Communities offered sobering lessons. Economic self-determination was the only practical and dignified way forward. Financial support from white-owned banks or government agencies could not be relied on. And wherever black people attempted to establish a large base of land, there would almost certainly be political resistance, public outcries, or misunderstandings that could stifle a project before it ever got off the ground.

◇◇◇◇◇◇◇

Albert Cleage was using the name "Beulah Land" as early as 1967 when, in an interview with the writer Studs Terkel, he vowed that black Americans were "gonna build the kind of world that we want, the Beulah Land" in "every black ghetto across the country." The Beulah Land Farm Project was officially given its name in 1981, almost fifteen years before anyone knew what or where it would be. The church sought a southern farm of roughly 5,000 acres. JB learned of the Beulah Land Farm Project during church service one day, as almost everyone else did. When his father hit the numbers in Detroit and came out flush, JB's mother asked her son if there was anything he wanted. He asked for a donation toward a farm that did not exist except in name, and which many Black Christian Nationalists doubted they would live to see.

After JB explained the purpose of the Beulah Land Farm Project to his mother, she made regular contributions for the rest of her life. Some longtime members of the Shrine gave thousands of dollars. A few of the younger Black Christian Nationalists switched their college majors to study agribusiness. Faith, in practice, looked like an annual pledge made at the Shrines in every region; yearly balls and galas; raffles and rummage sales; car washes; and, as always, digging around for spare change.

In 1971, the Shrine's agricultural, technical, and manufacturing (ATM) program was conceived so that the Black Christian Nationalists could one day grow and can their own food, train their own corps of construction, electrical, and plumbing specialists, and provide resources to meet whatever unforeseen needs might one day arise. Shrine members were asked to make their skills and interests known. Amateurs could be trained. Colleges in Michigan and some of the HBCUs had good programs in agronomy, aquaculture, and livestock economics. Nurses and doctors would be needed to run the medical clinic that Cleage talked about opening. To make brochures and bulletins, someone had to know graphic design and how to work a printing press. The children needed teachers and offices needed managers. It was time to get to work.

The Shrine's food co-op began in Detroit with the early morning produce runs of a couple in the church, Thomas and Letitia Sykes. The Sykes frequented Eastern Market, the largest farmers market in the city, and owned an eight-acre farm in Belleville, west of Detroit. They harvested fruits in the summers and gave them to Shrine members. People in the church were asked to package food on weekends so that they could sell five-dollar bags the next morning. The Sykes' Belleville farm, the produce sales at the Shrine, and the creation of the ATM program, as well as the example of Father Divine's affordable Harlem banquets during the Depression, were the currents beneath Cleage's attack on food retail supply chains in *Black Christian Nationalism*. "Your corner grocer sells inferior produce at exploitative prices," he wrote. "The store is just a small part of an international process that somehow puts a can of beans on the shelf of your corner store and makes Black people pay five cents more for it than white people pay. Who do you fight—the farmer? the canner? the wholesaler? the trucker?"

There were many obstacles to the "Nation's search for a Promised Land flowing with milk and honey, where every man can sit with dignity under his own vine and fig tree." One of the problems was that in black communities deprived of easy access to milk, honey, figs, and other fruits—many grocery stores began leaving Detroit in the 1970s—the allegorical delights of the Promised Land faded. Women and men were forced to consider how little food and how little land they truly had. Those who had anything "would degenerate and start fighting and exploiting each other and they would lose the Promised Land," Cleage wrote, "because they had identified with it geographically." Hunger might rip black communities apart so badly that there would be nowhere left on earth for them to care about.

Cleage dreamed of a national distribution network that would send food from black farms to inner cities throughout the country. He wrote, "We will be related through one co-operative economic movement which will enable us to distribute goods raised in the rural counties of the South on Black farms in northern urban centers where Black people are now dependent on white merchants for their produce; we will establish regional canneries and wholesalers to distribute the food that Black people grow." By the end of the 1980s, church leaders hoped to feed black families through BCN Community Service Outlets. Wherever it was, Beulah Land was expected to consist of a greenhouse, apiary, fish nursery, cattle ranch, dairy farm, smokehouse, cannery, KUA center, and medical and recreational facilities.

In 1972, a church-run farm in Georgia went on the market. The owners, facing financial difficulties and familiar with Cleage's work, asked him if he wanted to take over. Cleage's interest in the land was overshadowed by more immediate concerns, so he let the offer go. The Shrine had enough to do between its new ministerial training program, Alkebu-lan Academy, political lobbying efforts, and plans to open Shrines in other cities. Over the next twenty-five years, Cleage would find that such opportunities did not usually present themselves so easily.

◇◇◇◇◇◇◇

Of the individuals who were crucial in making Beulah Land a reality, Wesley Godfrey was the sole farmer. As a student at the Tuskegee Institute, when most others were gone for holidays and vacations, Godfrey watched after the animals. He ran the school's cattle and beef operation. His expertise in animal husbandry saved him from punishment when he and other students protested the lack of black history classes at Tuskegee in the late 1960s. The chief skill Godfrey would hone throughout his life was that of making himself indispensable.

In summer 1967, Godfrey was visiting his grandmother in Detroit. In the city, he could attend Shrine and UNIA meetings, get the best bean pies from the black Muslims at Temple No. 1, and hear Aretha Franklin sing. After the season of revolt in Detroit, he returned to Tuskegee with one of Aretha's albums and blasted Stevie Wonder's "Fingertips" in his hallway, becoming the hero of his dormitory. Godfrey's politics sometimes scared young women away. He had received his earliest education in race relations from his bedroom in Port Arthur, Texas, pressing his ear to the wall and eavesdropping on conversations in his mother's kitchen. At Tuskegee, he was not merely prepared to hear speakers such as H. Rap Brown, Julian Bond, Stokely Carmichael, and Dr. King—he possessed the energy and charisma to charm their kind. He led five student organizations, played baseball and football, and befriended Muhammad Ali after serving as grand marshal during his visits three years in a row.

Godfrey joined the Shrine when he moved to Michigan after college. He got involved with those in the church who were handing out bags of vegetables and fruit, eggs, sugar, and flour every Saturday at noon. Godfrey first learned of the Shrine's farm dream in 1973, years before the Beulah Land Farm Project had a name. He volunteered to assist the Shrine as a consultant. "We wanted a piece of ground in the South where we'd have more days of illumination, water resources, and timber resources on the property so there would be diversification," Godfrey told me. "Once the decision was made back in '75 to send a college cadre to Atlanta, proximity to Atlanta became germane for the farm so that it would be supported indirectly by the church."

The search for Beulah Land often led the Black Christian Nationalists to dead ends, from central California to the Rio Grande Valley, from Georgia to Mississippi. The locals were too leery about blacks, or the land wasn't quite right. Godfrey appraised properties and, in some instances, visited with locals alongside Jaramogi himself. In the case of Texarkana, Texas, a plot of land formerly owned by the *Bonanza* actor Dan Blocker was available. When Godfrey and Cleage showed up at the auction and organizers realized that black people of means were among the serious bidders, the event was shut down and rescheduled. In the late 1970s, Godfrey moved from Michigan to Shreveport, Louisiana, to work as a city planner. From Shreveport, for the next twenty years, he would continue making monthly surveying trips and writing reports for the Shrine.

◇◇◇◇◇◇◇

Thumbing through *The Wall Street Journal*, Godfrey came across a mention of the Trask family. In old age, the bearded patriarch Neil Webster Trask looked like Walt Whitman. He was one of the most renowned cattle ranchers in the country. Born in Wilmington, North Carolina, two years after the city's 1898 race massacre, he moved to Beaufort to start the South Carolina branch of his father's company, G. W. Trask & Sons, one of the largest truck farming operations in the Southeast. Early in the Depression, Trask purchased an island off the South Carolina coast that was populated with Hereford cattle, a breed unbothered by the state's hot pasturelands. He was especially drawn to hornless Herefords, cows as thick and russet colored as bison. Trask bred these with his native herd and searched the country for the finest soils, grasses, and Hereford pedigrees.

Because of his peerless, line-bred cattle, Trask amassed a significant enough fortune by the late 1930s to begin buying thousands of acres of depleted cotton farms in Abbeville County, in South Carolina's upcountry. He converted eroded cotton fields into some of the most productive pasturelands in the state. Trask's magical touch with cattle—his ability to raise thousands of cows that grew fat and fast on grass—earned him rare fame among ranchers. His 3,200-acre Pal-

metto Hereford Ranch in Calhoun Falls became one of the most acclaimed cattle farms in the United States.

Trask was obsessed with identifying an heir to carry on his legacy.
Well into his nineties, he considered his grandson James Wright to be
the most suitable candidate. Wright had been helping on the cattle
ranch since he was young. Confident that the ranch would one day
be his, Wright quit one family job for another, moving to the Palmetto
ranch. After Trask suffered a stroke in 1994, Wright spent much of his
time caring for him. Trask became furious when his grandson leased
deer hunting rights on some of the ranch's wooded areas and sold a
couple of his grandfather's favorite cows. He was so mad, in fact, that
a year before his death in 1997, he fired Wright as ranch manager,
changed his will to disinherit him, and demanded the return of his
former cattle, land, and equipment. Wright sued for breach of contract.
A court ruled in his favor after Trask died. The victory was short-lived.
The court battle's legal expenses were so high that Wright was forced
to sell all the cattle.

Through Godfrey, the Black Christian Nationalists learned about
the Palmetto ranch. Two years before Trask died, the church approached the family to buy its lakefront property. Trask's response was
"Niggers don't own the land, they work the land." It did not matter
to him that the church was offering to pay upfront with money it had
accumulated over nearly two decades. Only when Trask died and his
cattle were sold was an agreement reached to sell the deteriorating land.
The Shrine would effectively need to build it back up from scratch.

The sale was brokered by Ernest Cleage Martin, Jaramogi's nephew,
who had coincidentally been a psychiatrist in Abbeville County for
years. It would take four more years for the Shrine and the Trask-
Wrights to agree on a final price. In May 1999, the church acquired
its first 1,000 acres along a five-mile-long stretch. Later that year, in
October, it took possession of the remaining 2,000 acres outlined in
the deal. The Black Christian Nationalists purchased the property
using $10 million in cash. There was more land to come.

The World System

When the Shrine completed its purchase of Beulah Land, the farm immediately faced its first stress test. In January 1999, FEMA had issued an advisory statement urging emergency service agencies and the public to prepare for problems that might arise because of a computer glitch. Black Christian Nationalists had been on alert in light of recent news about the "Year 2000 Bug." There was a fear that, when the clock struck midnight on the first day of 2000, a coding oversight might cause computing systems to interpret the date incorrectly and start over, as it were, by turning to January 1, 1900. If this happened, some people predicted that disruptions in utility, manufacturing, and transportation lines could cause supply shocks around the world. Would thermostats, power supply equipment, and medical devices still work? What else might happen as a result?

The Shrine was preparing for Y2K before the Beulah Land purchase was complete. As early as April 1999, Maccabees were stocking ammunition, windup and shortwave radios, hand warmers, and night-vision binoculars. For Black Christian Nationalists in Detroit, the predictions of what might come to pass in the first hours, days, and months of the new millennium evoked memories of Devil's Night, the eve of Halloween. Devil's Night was an arsonist's holiday in the city. The 1980s and '90s had seen the worst of it. Hundreds of malevolent fires bloomed in the dark. The pictures made it look almost as though

Detroit's houses were self-immolating, and the rest of the world seemed to believe that as well. The incendiaries slipped away into the night.

Many people in the Shrine assumed that any night leading up to Y2K could turn into a Devil's Night, or a repeat of the chaos in 1967. Security would be on duty at all times at each of the Shrine's buildings in Detroit. One Maccabee wrote to another in September 1999: "I am amazed that so few black people are aware of the possibility of what might happen in the event of a breakdown of the support system . . . what groups might try to off us under the cover of the chaos of a social breakdown and what the government may try to do. I got maps of nuclear reactors, lists or [sic] military installations, white racists [sic] groups, and patriot and militia groups that might move on the black community." The Maccabee urged Black Christian Nationalists to monitor updates from grassroots information-sharing networks and y2knewswire.com. He said they should be wary of state defense forces, which were likely to have been infiltrated by "ultra right wing survivalists."

The Shrine's Y2K Preparedness Strategy and Implementation Plan, drafted in collaboration with survivalist consulting firms, was intended to help Black Christian Nationalists stay afloat until an "alternative societal structure for survival is in place." As Cleage had been saying for as long as he'd seen factory workers lose their jobs to automation, the new century called for specialized technical knowledge. Shrine members would need to stay ahead of sharp technological curves, including developments in the digital future which, the author of the Y2K plan wrote, "undergirts [sic] the World System."

The World System, a concept developed by sociologists in the 1970s, typically described a perspective that viewed modern world history as a story of unequal development between wealthy capitalist societies, poor societies on the peripheries, and the middle-class societies in between. For some black radicals in the 1970s and beyond, the World System loosely encapsulated a network of institutions that were believed to preserve the status quo and disadvantage the marginalized people who might be able to overthrow it—institutions like the military and police, the U.S. government, and the mainstream media. By the early 1980s, Jaramogi was describing the World System as one that "enslaves and exploits [black people] through the ruthless use of power to establish and maintain white supremacy." His black nation's "Struggle for Survival require[d] a recognition of the fact that we are outside of the System and we must build a System of our own."

If the Black Christian Nationalists' aversion to the World System sounded like unnecessarily paranoid thinking, which drove them into the countryside, the tragic example of MOVE, a communal religious movement in Philadelphia, showed that perhaps their preparations were justified. The beliefs of MOVE, founded in 1972 by the Korean War veteran John Africa, were based on a series of his teachings that stressed the need for new ways of thinking and of interacting with the physical world. These revolutions were meant to free individuals from a "reform world system," John Africa wrote, which included "all categories of thought that further abstracted [humanity] from the natural order of life." Some of MOVE's methods for rejecting the World System included eating raw and unprocessed foods, rejecting modern amenities such as medicine and electrical heat, supporting animal rights, and abstaining from alcohol and drugs. Although MOVE was based in Philadelphia, it was sometimes considered a back-to-the-land movement because of its members' radical environmentalist stances.

Though MOVE never had more than a few dozen members, the movement drew the ire of Philadelphia police, residents who lived near the various MOVE houses in the city, journalists, and others who viewed it as an extremist cult that intentionally provoked conflicts with authorities. After the baby of two MOVE members was killed during a clash with Philadelphia police in 1976, the movement's reliance on nonviolent resistance gave way to an embrace of armed self-defense. MOVE became increasingly insular. John Africa began to warn his followers that MOVE's conflicts with Philadelphia police would lead to an apocalyptic scenario that might very well destroy them.

After more than a decade of confrontations with the police, John

Africa's prophecies proved correct. On May 13, 1985, after a year of intensive planning within the Philadelphia police department, a raid was conducted on the MOVE commune on Osage Avenue. Arrest warrants had been issued for MOVE members charged with parole and firearms violations, contempt of court, and making threats against public officials. With hundreds of Philadelphia police surrounding the MOVE house, a ninety-minute shootout ensued. The children and some of the adults retreated to the basement, where they had prepared wet blankets in case the police attempted to drive them out with tear gas. As the morning progressed, police destroyed parts of the house with C-4 explosives, water cannons, and gunfire.

Later that afternoon, to destroy a shed atop the MOVE house where police feared gunmen lay in wait, a helicopter dropped a bomb on the compound. The explosion was felt from blocks away and fires spread rapidly from the obliterated MOVE commune to adjacent homes. Hours later, some MOVE members who tried to escape the hot, smoke-filled basement were shot at by the police. More than sixty houses were destroyed by the end of the day and, eventually, the remains of eleven MOVE members were recovered. Five were children. They died from bomb blasts and gunshot wounds, smoke inhalation and the fire itself.

Perhaps what it meant for black utopians to go "back to the land" was to separate themselves from the proven dangers of the World System in search of more decentralized, sustainable forms of living. The point was to disentangle oneself from the web of social forces that prevented black people from enriching their lives. Simplifying one's life did not necessarily entail going off the urban grid. Rather, in a society dominated by the World System, black people were compelled to find or create their own spaces that could exist as shrines, sacred places where they could feel protected from the System's menaces.

Black back-to-the-landers might purchase former slave plantations in the South and start their own projects on it. They could also build new forms of life within big cities, transforming vacant lots into gardens, practicing sustainable consumption, and creating food security networks that could connect various food sovereignty movements around the country.

◇◇◇◇◇◇◇

In the months leading up to Y2K, Shrine leaders thought it might be too dangerous to send its missionaries on reaching trips. If cars stopped working, how much would diesel generators cost? Fuel? Once the Shrine had Beulah Land, church leaders decided it had to be prepared as a refuge in case infrastructure in the cities crumbled. Early in 1999, the church conducted site studies on Beulah Land to determine where to erect a chapel, barns, equipment sheds, and office buildings. Temporary housing was set up for skilled laborers from all three Shrine regions to come to Beulah Land, where they worked for months. Fall was about to give way to winter.

In Detroit especially, Shrine members felt the clock ticking. Fears of "panic, hostile groups, or rioting" increased. What work was left for them to do? They would need to drain water from the pipes in their properties to keep them from freezing, install double-steel rackets on the Mother Shrine's doors, build six-foot fencing around the National Training Center, place bars on its first- and second-floor windows, assemble and test propane heaters, gather wood, and secure the art in the cultural center. In early December, the leaders of Shrine No. 1 decided to send the Alkebu-lan Academy youth and staff to Beulah Land by the middle of the month. The second wave of Beulah Land settlers would join them a week later. Although the church spent tens of thousands of dollars, it was becoming clear that the staggered departures would give the Shrine "less time to finish the Y2K preparation and to secure our institutions."

Beulah Land was, Godfrey told me, a "sanctuary during that window of time" when it was still unclear if madness would take over in cities when the lights went out. JB, who at the time was living in Atlanta, was made the administrator of Beulah Land to ensure its smooth operation. He arrived shortly after the children, joining the seventy-odd Black Christian Nationalists who would wait the year out in this improbable Elysium. Members shipped their belongings ahead of them before the first Beulah Land cadre in Detroit caravanned south. They stopped before Christmas to regroup and collect others in Atlanta. The scramble to gather on the farm was hectic enough that some of the adults initially forgot to purchase gifts for the children.

Andou Allen, who had been a minister in the Shrine since 1975, moved to Beulah Land with her son and daughter during this time. They would live there for the next four years. "This going to sound funny," she told me, "but for the most part, most of us at Beulah Land, they thought we was like the Zealots. Everybody thought, 'You got a good job. You quitting your job going to Beulah Land?' Most of us that went to Beulah Land in that initial group, we were highly educated. That's how we could do it. We all were skilled, but they thought we was missing out because we wasn't in the city wearing all the pretty clothes."

Plenty of Shrine city folk who knew nothing about farming were reluctant to move to South Carolina. Others rejected a rural lifestyle that, Andou said, reminded them "too much, I guess, of Reconstruction." Andou's own Alabama-born mother was initially concerned about her daughter and the children living in the wilderness. "They thought we might've been doing some Jim Jones stuff!" she said, laughing.

If reaching Beulah Land was a crowning achievement for the BCN movement, it was also a fault line that exposed what some perceived as distinct subgroups: those who were fully committed and those whose loyalty to the dream had limits. Some found it concerning and others found it funny that when January 1, 2000, arrived, the men in charge of putting backup generators on the farm hadn't yet installed them. Andou laughed. "We were glad nothing happened with 2000 K!"

◇◇◇◇◇◇

Although the Black Christian Nationalists made it to the new century, the fact that a Pan-African religious movement had chosen to build its earthly haven in the cradle and grave of the Confederacy portended complications. In the county seat of Abbeville, sixteen miles east of Beulah Land, was Secession Hill. There local citizens gathered in November 1860 to adopt South Carolina's ordinance to secede from the Union. It was the first state to do so. The Burt-Stark Mansion in Abbeville was where the Confederacy held its last war council in 1865, and where Jefferson Davis had to concede that the war was over.

Abbeville County's national reputation in the late 1990s and early 2000s cast it as a hotbed of antigovernment sentiment, a shelter for tax protestors, and a hub for white nationalist groups such as the League of the South, which opened its state office in Abbeville in 2001. In 2004, one journalist wrote, "There may be more antigovernment extremists in the vicinity of Abbeville than anywhere else in America." Two years later, the Southern Poverty Law Center listed South Carolina as the state with the third-largest number of active hate groups, behind California and Florida. From the moment Cleage and the Beulah Land settlers moved to the area, rumors had spread throughout Abbeville County that the old Palmetto ranch had been purchased by AK-47-wielding followers of Louis Farrakhan.

The farm's open-door approach toward curious white people in the area was a successful tactic. It turned out that one effective way for the Black Christian Nationalists to show they were no threat was to invite skeptics to church and get involved with nearby ministries. JB would be assigned to take courses at Erskine College, a private Christian institution in Due West, South Carolina, that turned out chaplains for the military. Avoiding certain topics was the basic strategy for a harmonious, even fraternal coexistence.

Cleage was slowing and stooping, but he was there, living full-time in a double-wide trailer on Beulah Land. In the first two months of the year, he presided over farm development meetings, assigned people to gather information on local politics, and reassigned Black Christian Nationalists who clearly were not fit for country living to go back to one of the cities. The groundwork was being laid for a revamped livestock operation. The church purchased poultry stock from magazines. Daily labors centered around pasture and forestry maintenance, security checks along the property's perimeter (the forests attracted hunters), reviewing collegiate animal programs for livestock sales, and seeing which students at these colleges had training in poultry science and fisheries.

In coordinating this beehive, Cleage was as prickly as ever and insistent upon his rules. Under most circumstances, he was not to be bothered until 3 p.m. at the earliest. Lord help those who brought him food that was hard to digest. JB did his best to help concerned Shrine members understand that, at eighty-eight years old, not even Rev. Cleage could be expected to be as vigorous as the rest of them.

Was he sick? Perhaps he should be seeing a doctor more.

JB shook his head. He knew about end-of-life care from his old job as an occupational therapist. Was it so difficult to see that their Jaramogi had no intention of leaving the land he had chosen to call his home?

A Model Community

◇◇◇◇◇◇◇

Ten years before Beulah Land was purchased, Jaramogi had pushed Kimathi Nelson toward seminary. St. Mary's Seminary in Houston, the oldest Catholic training institute in the South, denied Kimathi admission in part because of fears provoked by the recent excommunication of Father George Augustus Stallings. Stallings, a black priest in Washington, D.C., who was known for integrating African American cultural practices into the traditional Mass, had denounced the hierarchies and white leadership of the Catholic Church in 1990. In response, he broke off from the church of Rome and opened his own, the Imani Temple.

Kimathi's sterling academic record wasn't enough to clear suspicions about his motives. If a protégé of the firebrand Albert Cleage was going to attend Catholic seminary with no intention of becoming a Catholic priest, he must have been planning to use their theology against them, as Stallings had done. The priest in charge of St. Mary's academics was so embarrassed by his staff's decision that he gave Kimathi a stack of catalogs with other seminary options.

Jaramogi, who was living mostly in Houston at the time, swept them all aside and told Kimathi to apply to Harvard's and Yale's divinity schools. By now, Kimathi had been bringing Jaramogi dinner every day as his care needs increased. He brought his briefcase by Jaramogi's room one day and opened it to reveal two acceptance letters. Kimathi had rarely seen Jaramogi smile so widely. Jaramogi picked up the letter from Harvard.

"Let's just set this one over here. Tomorrow, you call Yale."

"Wait a minute," Kimathi said. "What about Harvard?"

"Oh, you want to go to Harvard? Then go to Harvard. Get the hell out of my house!"

When Kimathi brought Jaramogi his meal the next day, he walked silently into the room. Jaramogi asked if he knew why he had cussed him out the night before. Kimathi did not.

"If you're going into law or divinity, you go to Yale. I couldn't get in Yale School of Divinity. Martin Luther King couldn't get in Yale School of Divinity." And besides, Jaramogi said, "I don't like the kind of niggas that go to Harvard. They get big-headed and think that they're special."

Jaramogi's roughshod displays of love continued unabated for the next three years as Kimathi excelled in New Haven. He was offered a religious deanship at Yale and a preaching job at the church where the mayor and other local officials went. Jaramogi wanted to know if he would accept these lucrative opportunities. "Are you going to go off and make your portion with the white folks?" he asked. Kimathi didn't understand why he was being singled out for insults.

"There are some things going on that I don't like, and I trust you," Jaramogi said.

He was referring to a situation at Shrine No. 9 in Atlanta. For the last twenty years, most people in the church had assumed that the charismatic senior bishop of Shrine No. 9, Sondai Nyerere, was the obvious choice to replace Cleage as the next Holy Patriarch. Kimathi had played ball with Sondai in high school before joining the Shrine. While Sondai was a professor at Western Michigan University, he taught many future Black Christian Nationalists. Kimathi respected him as much as everyone else did. Few were aware that Sondai and Jaramogi hadn't exchanged more than pleasantries in years. No. 9 had become an island unto itself. There seemed to be, Jaramogi told Kimathi, a developing "cult of personality," the kind he always feared could take root in his movement.

It hadn't occurred to Kimathi that the order of succession was in flux. The church that had been preparing its people for an eternal struggle over the last half century did not know how to think about the inevitable arrival of a new leader. At a 1996 synod in Houston, Jaramogi announced a shake-up in the Shrine's leadership that discarded all previous notions of who the next Jaramogi would be. Sondai was transferred to Detroit. Mbiyu Chui, a community leader who was part of the original Atlanta expansion cadre in 1974, would be senior bishop in Houston. And Menelik Kimathi Nelson, next in line to succeed Cleage as Jaramogi, would oversee the Shrine in Atlanta.

During one of Jaramogi's final trips to Atlanta, he asked Kimathi a question: "Do you know what Hercules's job was?"

"Hercules?" Kimathi asked. "His job was cleaning the stables, wasn't it?"

"Yeah. He cleaned out the horse stables on Olympus. But there were so many horses that he couldn't keep it clean. What he did was, he went and bent the River Alpheus. He bent the river and the river flowed through the stables. Do you know what that means?"

"I'm not sure."

"He washed all the shit out of the stables. That's your job."

"I guess that'll keep you busy for a little while," Kimathi laughed.

"No, that'll keep you busy for a lifetime. Anybody trying to re-create the church that we've had in the past is doomed to failure. There's no road map for where we're going and you gotta have somebody at the helm."

Kimathi had made the mistake before of promising Jaramogi that in twenty years, even though the founder would be gone, the Shrine would look just as he had known it in the 1960s.

"If it is," Jaramogi said, "I'm going to come back here and kick your ass! It has to change. We're running on fumes. We built this church on this generation. This generation is getting old. You're going to have to decide some things that are going to be very upsetting. They're going to have to be done, but I trust that you will recognize it and have the courage to do it when the time comes."

◇◇◇◇◇◇◇

During the race to Beulah Land in December 1999, Kimathi drove from Atlanta to the airport in Greenville, South Carolina, to pick up Jaramogi and take him to the farm. They arrived at night. "He was like a little kid," Kimathi said. "Couldn't see anything because it was dark. He couldn't wait. He was not an early riser. He couldn't wait for the sun to come up." Kimathi had to return to Atlanta the next morning to preach. He and Jaramogi spoke on the phone every day. On one call, Jaramogi's voice sounded funny. Kimathi asked if he was all right.

"Nothing hurts. I don't have any problems that I know of."

"Well, you sound kind of funny. Is it okay if I come out there to check on you?"

"Sure, sure."

Kimathi found someone to preach for him, got in his car, and went right back to the farm. Jaramogi was okay. He and Kimathi spoke well into the night until finally Jaramogi said, "Okay, I'm headed that way," the cue that he was going to bed. Kimathi fell asleep on a couch.

The next morning, around the time Jaramogi was usually up, Kimathi didn't hear him. He didn't want to disturb him if he was tired. He knew that Jaramogi's temper could flare if someone bothered him too much. Kimathi had eventually convinced Jaramogi to let him help with prescriptions, groceries, and laying out his clothes, and so, around 11 o'clock in the morning, he took his chances and went into his bedroom. Jaramogi was on the floor.

"Jaramogi!"

"What?"

"What are you doing on the floor?"

"Well, I got up last night and was going to the restroom and on my way back, I fell. I couldn't get up. I was calling your name, but I could hear you snoring from here. I just figured I'd make myself comfortable."

Kimathi picked him up, sat him in his chair, and for yet another day until the sun started to fall, the two men spoke. Before he went to sleep, Jaramogi wanted Kimathi to know that he had always been one of the few people who noticed when he needed help.

"I don't have any good, big will and testament to give to you," Jaramogi said. "You know everything I know."

Albert Cleage had no big will and testament to give to anybody, no exorbitant riches reaped from his father's estate, the once-full coffers of his church, or the renown of his name. He had streamlined his life by devoting it to the idea that black people could prosper in innumerable ways. Now it was a Saturday in mid-February. Kimathi hugged Jaramogi, shook his hand, and drove back to Atlanta in time for church the next morning.

◇◇◇◇◇◇◇

On Sunday, February 20, 2000, when JB went into Jaramogi's trailer to see if he needed anything, the founder was in his bed. JB knew it was time to call an ambulance. Around 2 p.m., Albert Cleage, Jr., was declared dead. Those who loved him would later say he simply tired himself out. There was a chair across from his bed where JB sat as one of the other Shrine ministers led small batches of Beulah Land's children through the side door to see the founder one more time and pray over his body. This minister would cry, then faint, and, once restored, she would guide another group of children through. Ernest Cleage Martin, his wife, and one Shrine member put Jaramogi's Sunday suit on him before the coroner arrived.

Jaramogi left nothing behind on Beulah Land but a few pieces of art, some furniture, and miscellany like the books I perused in the Jahi House on dusty shelves and in dusty boxes. Today, some of his ashes rest in an urn on an altar in JB's sunroom, which he calls the Ancestor Room. The ashes were a gift from Jaramogi's sister Barbara. They are mingled with the ashes of Jomo Ribbron and the adored theologian Woodrow Smith, Jr., who trained the Shrine's first ministers in the 1970s and helped Ernest negotiate the terms for Beulah Land. The remainder of Jaramogi's ashes are on the altar of the Mother Shrine, where his funeral was held.

It was a Sunday of confusion and fear at each of the Shrines. There were tears, reflections, and celebrations of a singular life. Albert Cleage, Jr., was not a messiah, but a man, and this fact was what he hoped his flock would remember. In Atlanta, the senior bishop received the news after service. He was to become the Holy Patriarch, Jaramogi Menelik Kimathi. For a length of time that he wouldn't be able to recall, Kimathi sat down in the dark and stared at it.

◇◇◇◇◇◇

In the years after Jaramogi Abebe's passing, the fate of his black nation in the cities was unclear. But at Beulah Land, Black Christian Nationalists were newly inspired to raise money for roads, ponds, wells, electricity, fencing, an underground pipe system, and more buildings and livestock. In 2005, approximately 1,000 acres of land adjacent to the farm became available. The church learned from U.S. Representative Carolyn Cheeks Kilpatrick, a former Shrine member whose son was then Detroit's mayor, that the Department of Defense was considering purchasing the land. Sensing that this potential new neighbor could decrease the value of church property and bring with it other untold dangers—surveillance of their operations, perhaps—the Shrine took out a loan and swiftly bought the parcel. This expanded the Shrine's holdings to nearly 4,000 acres and put the church $2 million in debt.

Black Christian Nationalists were largely optimistic that Beulah Land would one day become profitable. The Shrine was meeting its monthly mortgage notes consistently until the Great Recession. When financial calamity struck, weekly contributions to the church dropped precipitously. Beulah Land normally made money through the sale of timber, hay, hunting, and land leases, and by receiving support from government programs. When the economic crisis froze housing construction, the ranch's readily abundant timber lost value. Drought affected the rearing of cattle. Beulah Land's broad ponds of catfish, bream, tilapia, and bass, as well as the pastures that Shrine members had cared for, began reverting to their wild state. Animals, vehicles, and farm equipment had to be sold to meet the mortgage. It was getting harder for Black Christian Nationalists to see Beulah Land becoming its own municipality or the "model independent Black community" that church leaders hoped it would become.

◇◇◇◇◇◇

Ryan Pressley, who managed Beulah Land for two and a half years, until the fall of 2023, first learned of the Shrine's ranch in 2011. His own conflicts with the USDA had begun during the middle of the recession, when he was a twenty-one-year-old trying to use his family's land as collateral for a farm of his own. When his land was unexpectedly devalued by USDA officials, Ryan fell into a years-long court battle with the agency. He filed twenty appeals. Ultimately, in 2014, Ryan lost the farm that had been in his family for more than one hundred years, the land on which his grandmother was born: $2.5 million in land value and $1.5 million in equity vanished. He compared the aftereffects on his emotional health to the PTSD black American soldiers have described upon returning home from wars.

Black farmers have had a contentious relationship with the USDA since the department was formed in the mid-nineteenth century. Officials have been accused of preventing black farmers from accessing resources such as loans, grants, and subsidies, which contributes to the crises of land loss and economic instability. After decades of complaints,

hundreds of black farmers in 1997 sued the USDA for its discriminatory practices throughout the 1980s and '90s. Thousands more joined
the class-action lawsuit known as *Pigford v. Glickman*, which the plaintiffs won in 1999.

The more than $1 billion settlement was the largest in civil rights
history. The most substantial individual payment—$12 million—
was awarded to New Communities, Inc., the grassroots organization
founded by Charles and Shirley Sherrod that had lost much of its land
in 1985. With some of this money, New Communities bought a 1,600-
acre tract near Albany, Georgia, in 2011. It was renamed Resora. Purifying rituals were held there for three years after the founders realized
they had purchased land on the former site of one of Georgia's largest
slave plantations. Today, flush with orange groves and cypress trees, a
pecan orchard, squash garden, apiary, and 85-acre lake, Resora is used
as an agritourism site, private event space, and vacation destination.

When Ryan and I met over Easter dinner at JB's house in 2022, he
had started anew with 600 acres of his own in Augusta, Georgia. His
land was rich with crops: lima beans, peas, tomatoes, and cantaloupes.
Ryan made time to assist other farmers with their own antidiscrimi-
nation complaints against the USDA. Nearly ten years after his first
contact with the Shrine, Ryan was approached in September 2020
about coming on as the farm manager. His work began the following spring, in April 2021. The month before Ryan started his new
job, the Biden administration pledged to devote billions of dollars in
debt relief to black farmers who had been discriminated against by
the USDA. These plans to alleviate the struggles of minority farmers
would later stall. Critics dismissed them as unlawfully discriminatory
against white farmers.

At JB's dinner table, Ryan told me that he was preparing to buy
cattle with the hope of reviving the ranch's livestock operation. Growing crops was part of his long-term vision. The rhythms of Ryan's days
were similar to what I'd heard about Beulah Land in its settlement
period. He woke early, checking on his own farms before driving north
to cut and harvest Beulah Land's hay, restore its fields, remove saplings,

handle farm status reports for the USDA, and, when necessary, deal with lumber thieves and trespassing hunters. Ryan had one other full-time employee working for him and would get more in the coming months to supplement seasonal migrant labor. My sense that Ryan's blueprint for the ranch's revival was familiar didn't lessen its allure. I believed in his plan because his land and his spirit had already been diminished once before. It was clear to me, at least that day, that he would not allow himself to lose either of these again.

◇◇◇◇◇◇

Since 2020, there have been numerous attempts—some of them successful—to establish intentional communities that prioritize the mental, physical, and spiritual health of people of color, black and Indigenous folk especially. In response to the movements for racial justice that followed George Floyd's murder, the Foundation for Intentional Community, the main advocacy organization for such communities in the United States, created a special council to offer financial support and legal help to founders of cooperative living spaces for people of color. Eco-villages, designed to encourage regenerative practices that benefit the land and its stewards in a time of climate crisis, are among the most advertised intentional communities on the FIC's website today.

From Colorado and Arkansas to North Carolina and Vermont, residents of predominantly black utopian eco-villages advocate for culturally centered spaces; intergenerational education in land stewardship; affordable housing; recourse to the environmental knowledge of ancestors; sovereignty over the production, distribution, and consumption of their community's food; trauma-informed therapies; psychological healing from racist aggressions; elder care; and refuge for trans, queer, and gender-expansive people, as well as women of color. These places arise on a half-acre of land or they are spread across dozens. The founders call them *farms*, *villages*, *communities*, and *cooperatives*. It seems that most could fit their full-time residents in an average-size classroom. Their members oppose a capitalist world order that extracts finite resources from the earth, and robs black people of their joy, health, labor, and time.

Beulah Land has been diminished as a community, but it is still a conduit for the hopes of Black Christian Nationalists who see it as the great manifestation of a shared dream for black autonomy on earth. If it is not viable as a vegetable farm or eco-village, perhaps it can be revived as a cattle operation or turned into a solar farm funded by the Department of Energy. If it will not permanently house a black nation, then maybe it can be used as a conference site for black professionals or a wellness retreat space, not unlike Resora.

My aunt Yolanda, a mental health counselor in Columbus, Ohio, had mentioned a similar dream of turning Promise Land into a retreat. Black people who could stop asking *How do we get land?* and start wondering *What's to be done with it now?* were lucky. Yolanda put it in simple terms: "God's not making any more land . . . Even if you don't have an immediate plan for it, why would you let land go?"

◇◇◇◇◇◇◇

When Beulah Land's settlers first arrived, some of them, in blue jeans and straw hats and green tees, squinted and laughed in the sun when they first saw the South Carolina countryside. They had claimed this unknown and potentially hostile place as their own. At first, there was nothing but fields and trees. Now it was theirs. Black Christian Nationalists who had read Elijah Muhammad's *How to Eat to Live* or Dick Gregory's *Natural Diet for Folks Who Eat: Cookin' with Mother Nature* could imagine that this land might be able to feed and harbor them, as well as other black people who may have had nowhere else to go. Those who had kept private gardens in their hometowns, missed the greenery of their childhood parks, or fantasized about visiting Martha's Vineyard whenever they wished now had claim to a place with room enough for tenfold gardens and tenfold parks.

The eye could not easily see Beulah Land's outer limits. If its size mattered at all, it was for this reason. It was important to feel that there was something much more expansive than oneself. I arrived long after the fish-processing plants, chicken coops, and Max the great black stallion had gone. I didn't see the trees that bore pears, oranges, plums, apples, and nuts. I did find fog over the land, though, and during my morning walks, I cut through the vapor. If it was possible to stroll through a prophecy amid fulfillment, not fully living and evidently not dead, I felt that this was it.

Shrines

◇◇◇◇◇◇◇

By the time Osakwe Ndegwa Jahi—Sok—was entering his third year at Eastern Michigan University in 2006, some Black Christian Nationalists believed the nineteen-year-old was already on the path to one day succeed Jaramogi Kimathi. Six years into his role as Holy Patriarch, Kimathi saw it too. Sok told him that he wanted to study construction and business administration so he could erect buildings for the black nation that its people could touch and see.

The boy was smooth. Sok had been a Black Christian Nationalist since birth. He showed a level of dedication to the church's evolving mission that convinced both his peers and his elders that Jaramogi

Abebe's vision still had a strong heartbeat. Sok was not a singer or a preacher, but his build, eyes, and smile were like Sam Cooke's. Among older church members, the young women who sometimes accompanied Sok to the Shrine became a running joke. He assured them that the women were not romances but friends he had brought to see this place he couldn't stop talking about.

For Sok, as for many of his young peers in the church, the purchase of Beulah Land was proof of concept for the Black Christian Nation's liberation project. It confirmed that heaven was a place on earth. Sok, born in 1987, was part of an early wave of American millennials who, by 2020, would be associated with a sharp decline in church attendance and formal religious affiliation. He was a suave, convincing poster child for the Shrine at a time when a growing number of young people were losing touch with the traditions of their parents and grandparents.

Some members of the Shrine glowed at the thought of Sok's eventual rise in the church and, perhaps, electoral politics. He wrote for *Black Slate Digest*, the publication of the Shrine-affiliated political lobbying group. He appeared on the Black Slate's FM radio program to argue why Kwame Kilpatrick, a rising Democratic star in Detroit who had grown up in the Mtoto House, should be the next mayor of Detroit. Kimathi saw that Sok was able to walk down the street with sinners on one side of him and saints on the other. His charisma was helpful for youth outreach and essential in maintaining cohesion among his peers who thought the Shrine was starting to look like any other Protestant church.

One of Cleage's granddaughters, Jilo, had married a man named Andre Tisdale. He had been taking care of himself since he was twelve years old. Andre had served with the Marines in Iraq and, when he returned from his tour, was drafted into the Maccabees. He was a sharpshooter on the gun range, a useful asset to the security force, but the war in Iraq left him disturbed. Sensing that Cleage did not trust Andre, Jilo had asked Kimathi to vouch on his behalf. When he tried, the reverend told him to stay out of his family's business.

"That nigga ain't no good," Cleage told Kimathi. "I know niggas. He ain't no good."

In 2006, as Fourth of July weekend celebrations ended in Detroit, Kimathi was preparing to send his daughter to a summer program at the University of Michigan. He escorted her to the parking lot of the National Training Center, where they saw Sok. Kimathi asked if he wanted a ride back to Eastern Michigan since his family was driving up that way anyways.

"Oh, no, thanks," he said. "I'll get a ride later."

If Sok had gone with them that day, Kimathi told me, "I would've had the leadership I needed for the next generation." Sok and Andre were friends even though Kimathi had warned Sok that the man was unpredictable. No one knew what provoked Andre to shoot Sok in the back that evening. He threw the young man's body into the Detroit River, where he was found five days later. Events moved too quickly for comprehension. Soon after the murder, Andre fired on a police officer. The police tracked him down and killed him in a shootout.

Paul Lee, a professor who studies Malcolm X's thought and is also sometimes called the Shrine's unofficial historian, knew Sok personally. He wrote after his death: "Looking into his eyes as he breathlessly laid out his plans, I doubted that I could conceive the world that [he] would build, but I trusted that it would be a better one. I retain that trust, but, like all of those who were blessed to know and love Sok, and young people like him who will never have the chance to 'build a new dream' because their promise was snuffed out by a 'decadent society,' I fear that it will take longer to realize."

◇◇◇◇◇◇◇

Sok's death sent shockwaves throughout every Shrine, becoming a symbol of the destabilizing transformations taking place within the Black Christian Nationalism movement, and of broader social crises that black communities faced in the new century. In Cleage's estimation, the golden age of black liberation movements was over by the mid-1970s, laid low by economic suffering, spiritual despair, the growing crack epidemic, and the related expansion of the War on Drugs in the 1980s. In the next decade, the 1994 Crime Bill was signed into law, transforming the carceral landscape and sending more black people than ever to prisons. The Crime Bill's support of more punishing minimum sentencing guidelines would, in fact, be the very shift my own father cited as one of the many threats against movements for black freedom in the twenty-first century.

Changes in the Shrine's liturgical practices had been the focus of discussions in the church since the early 1980s, as these issues were being felt in cities across the country. In the absence of an organized mass black movement, Cleage believed, something like the Afrocentric turn of the 1990s felt gauche and passé. Too many black people were merely putting on dashikis, reading black books, and sending their kids to black-centered schools, thinking those decisions were enough.

The Shrine's latest spiritual philosophy, KUA, was in some ways a rejection of Afrocentrism, or at least an acknowledgment that this mentality would not be enough to carry black people into the future. KUA took emphasis away from the material aspect of cultural signifiers—the "clothes you wear, the way you talk, the food, everything," Cleage said in a 1976 sermon—in favor of "soul force." Soul force, a concept rooted in Mahatma Gandhi's notion of satyagraha ("truth force") and popularized by Martin Luther King, Jr., in the late 1950s, was something more universal, less focused on the dead end of heritage worship. It pushed the black struggle away from the external world and toward an "inner being."

In the early 2000s, the Shrine's African naming ceremonies ceased. The Prayer of the Black Messiah reverted to the more recognizable Lord's Prayer, and the Sacrament of Commitment was restored to Holy Communion. The militaristic red-and-black uniforms went away. The BCN Creed, which Black Christian Nationalists had been reciting for decades at the start of worship every Sunday, was taken out of the morning services, although church members continued to say it in meetings and classes. Church leadership thought the creed might be too alienating for a new generation, too liable to be misunderstood as an out-of-touch obsession with the bygone era of Black Power. Part of the creed went: "I believe that the revolutionary Spirit of God embodied in the Black Messiah is born anew in each generation and that Black Christian Nationalists constitute the living remnant of God's chosen people in this day and are charged by Him with responsibility for the liberation of Black people . . ."

Jaramogi Abebe's death, the attainment of Beulah Land, and the gradual loss of churchgoers in the Shrine over the previous two decades swayed Kimathi to update the BCN belief system. It would be the most substantial shift since the introduction of KUA in the mid-1970s. Kimathi named it Best-Self Theology. It was a philosophy of self-improvement rooted in the same basic conditions that inspired KUA. The pretext for its creation was the evident failure, or incompleteness, of the last half century's social revolutions.

Like the Inward Light of the Quakers, or the Higher Self espoused by the actress and New Age mascot Shirley MacLaine, Best-Self Theology held that every person, no matter their race or background, had within them the "spark of divinity." Every soul was a field in need of constant cultivation. The theology embraced a "growth mindset" and restated the chief goal of religion as the maximization of one's own potential. It aimed "not to heal a sin-sick soul," Kimathi told me, or to destroy harmful social structures that white society created, "but to create an optimal human being." Best-Self Theology's sensitivity to the individual soul was a concession to the fact that Black Christian Nationalism, which sought spiritual and material development for blacks in a hostile world, would never succeed if it could not guarantee the well-being of its members. As Kimathi told me, Best-Self Theology evolved from one of the Shrine's longstanding tenets, which Black Christian Nationalists in the age of Black Power had expressed like this: "If we want a better world, we have to be better people."

◇◇◇◇◇◇

A small contingent of members were confounded by what they believed to be Black Christian Nationalism's philosophical shift. Under

Best-Self Theology, self-determination looked very much like self-help. Many people still found joy and necessary fellowship in their church. But those who left often did so because the Shrine of the new millennium did not seem to be the church they had joined. Black Christian Nationalism "was what it needed to be at the time it needed to be," Kimathi told me. "If it doesn't change with the times to become what it needs to be, it's going to die."

Monifa—Shelley McIntosh—was one of the people who believed that the practices, teachings, and commitments of Black Christian Nationalism were being altered beyond recognition. In their varying roles over the decades, Monifa and Kimathi sat at the feet of Cleage, first in Detroit and then in Houston. When the founder died, Kimathi enlisted a judge in the church to help him get the Shrine's financial records in order. Monifa had been helping Kimathi throughout the transition, but the Nation was shrinking at the same time it was becoming more complicated than ever to manage. Monifa was beginning to wonder whether there was a place here for her or others who shared her worries.

In 2001, the Shrine's missionary outreach trips ended. The missionaries were too old to solicit in front of stores upwards of twelve hours a day. They were too old to travel hundreds of miles in cramped cars and sleep in a single hotel room for days. Church leaders decided from then on to rely on weekly tithes and profits from Beulah Land to sustain the Shrine's finances. The church would also start selling some of its properties. In Houston, the Alkebu-lan Academy stopped operating in 2007, not long after Monifa left as its director. Within a few years, the other Mtoto Houses in Atlanta and Detroit closed as well.

By 2002, fewer than twenty paying residents still covered the maintenance and utility costs for one of the three apartment complexes where Atlanta Shrine members lived. The buildings, though mostly occupied, were a drain on the Shrine's treasury. Despite some church leaders' past assurances that selling the Shrine's properties wouldn't be necessary, the Atlanta properties were eventually sold, too, and proceeds from the sales were invested in Beulah Land.

The economic reality of the movement was changing as older Black Christian Nationalists died, depriving the Shrine of members who occupied its various communes full-time. These people had also been the missionaries who, when younger, dropped everything to travel around the country to raise money. As their numbers declined in the years leading up to the Great Recession, the balance sheets looked increasingly grim. The Shrine was losing bodies and money. Expansion was no longer an option. Skeptical members became upset, wondering to what good ends their tithes were being devoted. Was there anything productive coming out of Beulah Land, or would it be permanently stalled?

In the twenty-first century, what good were the Shrine's kibbutzim in rearing black children who may have wanted to explore the diverse and beautiful world beyond the intimate community? Did some of the older, more dogmatic Black Christian Nationalists wish to preserve the rituals they knew without giving their heirs an opportunity to improve upon the formula? "To see those institutions sold," Monifa said, "we began to ask ourselves, 'What do we show for our work? What do we show for our sacrifices, besides the seeds that we placed in our children?'"

The Shrine continues to play its part in the world. Once the Shrine's apartment complexes were sold, the church paid for a tenant relocation service to ensure that Black Christian Nationalists who needed housing found it. It has provided disaster relief for every major hurricane that has affected the Southwest since Hurricane Katrina. The Shrines in each of the three regions host frequent food giveaways, a custom the church has been engaged in for the last fifty years. The church's cultural center in Houston, a 40,000-square-foot space that was once a bowling alley, has served as an election site, a hub for community events, and a COVID-19 immunization center.

◇◇◇◇◇◇◇

Within five years of Jaramogi's passing, Monifa wrote two books that, for the first time since the publication of *Black Christian Nationalism* in 1972, outlined some of the Shrine's beliefs and communal practices so that they would not be completely forgotten. Her book *Genesis II: The Re-Creation of Black People* (2001) was based on the black theology sermons Jaramogi planned with her and other ministers in his Houston apartment. It was a warning about the ways that "the society of which we are part is on a collision course with disaster."

Working-class people were "doomed to extinction" (in Detroit, when the Great Recession came, Jaramogi's prophecy of black economic obsolescence seemed to be fulfilled). "We are blind to the reality that the new millennium holds for us," Monifa wrote, echoing Cleage's words, which included "disintegration of family, of a quality life, of social continuity, and the threat of our very survival. We are still excluded from the mainstream of America. Ecological dangers can no longer be dismissed as the cult fact of flower children who lived beyond their time. Nuclear and chemical contamination threaten the very existence of human life upon a planet where man has poisoned the air, the earth, and the fresh water supply."

When Monifa was writing this, new prisons were being built across the country. Unions were disappearing. Police brutality and gerrymandering persisted. Black preachers had lost their way by shouting the gospel of prosperity. "Even though we say we believe," Monifa wrote, "our belief is not strong enough to motivate us to work sacrificially to build a New World."

Monifa's 2005 book, *Mtoto House: Vision to Victory—Raising African American Children Communally*, memorialized the Mtoto Houses in the hope that they might be used as prototypes for future attempts to provide black children with moral and intellectual educations. In 2019, the year I first spoke to Monifa, the Shrine finalized its sale of the Abington apartment complex in Detroit. No one lived on the seventh floor anymore, where the first Mtoto House was located and where Cleage once resided. The small group of old Black Christian Nationalists who stayed as renters, with expenses covered by the Shrine, occupied one side of the building as the other side underwent renovations.

The website of the Abington Detroit, as the building is now called, advertises it as "modern luxury in a historic setting."

Monifa has not been a member of the Shrine since 2007, though she still identifies as a Black Christian Nationalist. She is close with current and other ex-members of the church. She has attended weddings, funerals, and an event that former Mtoto House children threw in her honor. When the despair of the pandemic struck her in 2020, and she realized that twenty years had passed since Jaramogi Abebe's death, Monifa spoke to him, even though he was gone. "That's the time I had to talk with God and say, 'You knew why I committed myself to this—and I committed everything to it,'" Monifa said. "'God, you know my heart.'"

Over the phone, I asked Monifa about George Floyd's murder soon after the protests began. What would Jaramogi have said about the global movement for racial justice or the violence that had killed Floyd, who had attended the same high school in Houston as some Shrine members had?

"If it was my child, I would've just fought like hell," she said. "He was our brother."

Monifa had recently listened again to the sermon Jaramogi gave on the morning the Detroit uprising began in 1967. Another video clip of the reverend speaking to an energetic crowd at the Mother Shrine about police brutality had started circulating on social media around this time as well. For Monifa, the Black Lives Matter movement was evidence that the revolutionary Holy Spirit was still operative. "[Jaramogi] mentioned that when black people are fed up and tired and know that this system is not only oppressing but killing us . . . it's a righteous uprising. At this juncture, African Americans are going to have to be self-sufficient in their own communities."

As she told me this, Monifa began to cry. She apologized for not speaking "programmatically," for having no firm plan to disarm the slave culture, which tended to be as adaptive and resistant as the urges that had always been necessary to counteract it. "How do we become self-sufficient? How do we slowly detach ourselves from dependence on this system?"

◇◇◇◇◇◇◇

Utopia is not a fiction set apart from history, but a method of shaping it. As joyful as it has been for me to speak with black people whose lives attest to this, I have also felt a chronic nausea, swerving between visions of an equitable future for all and their opposites—utopian dreams of an exclusionary future, in which the bodies, souls, and histories of non-whites are not only neglected but eradicated. There are other kinds of utopians who would kill my grandmother at prayer hour if they could. A four-hour drive from Beulah Land, in Charleston, South Carolina, the terrorist Dylann Roof, radicalized by his exposure to white nationalists online, murdered nine black churchgoers during Bible study at Mother Emanuel AME in 2015. Of the many mass shootings that have happened in the United States during my lifetime, Roof's crime is, for me, the most indelible. His idea of a better world was one emptied of blacks, whom he viewed as an invasive species that might be tamed in a race war. He saw himself as the necessary catalyst for a new, purifying phase of history.

Warnings of a coming race war and fear of a "great replacement" have reemerged as potent rhetorical devices. Today, under the banner of white Christian nationalism, an increasingly vocal and politically powerful minority are attempting to redefine what it means to be an American and punish those who do not meet these strict criteria. White Christian nationalism is a broad belief system which asserts that white Americans, particularly evangelical Protestant men, should reclaim their divinely ordained dominion over lesser races and minority groups, through violence if necessary. The January 6 insurrection was a long-awaited coming-out moment for many of them. The Capitol rioters, many of whom sympathized with the goals of white Christian nationalism, hadn't expected to walk so easily into their end-time vision of ethno-nationalist rule. Their revenge fantasies were a few broken doors away from fulfillment. What had once seemed unlikely was no longer speculative. The future was full of terrible possibilities.

On January 20, 2021, the day Joe Biden was sworn in as president, First Lady Jill Biden and the Republican senator Roy Blunt gave him an inauguration day gift at a reception: *Landscape with Rainbow* (1859), a pastoral painting by the black American artist Robert S. Duncanson. The image is Arcadian. It depicts a couple roaming through cattle-rich pastureland. They are dwarfed by the scale of an indigo sky, a placid body of water behind them, and a rainbow whose arc is so great that the viewer can only see its end point. Senator Blunt, who had been under siege with his colleagues in the Capitol two weeks earlier, described the image as "this classic 'America as a paradise' painting . . . For [Duncanson], a black artist, painting this painting that's so much like an American utopia on the verge of a war that we would fight over slavery makes all of that even more interesting." Despite Duncanson's status as a black man in a slaveholding country, Blunt said, "obviously [he] was optimistic, even in 1859, about America."

President Biden had promised in his inaugural address that "the dream of justice for all will be deferred no longer." Like Blunt, his public cheeriness belied the severity of dark trends that were erupting into public life. In one of his first acts as president, Biden dissolved the 1776 Commission, which Donald Trump had established as a presidential advisory committee the previous fall. Two days before the inauguration, the Commission published its 1776 Report, a propaganda document that took an apologist stance toward slavery in the United States, pined for the glorious years when pioneers cleared America's "untamed wilderness," and called for a "rediscovery of our shared identity rooted in our founding principles." The report also invoked the American Civil War. Unlike Senator Blunt, however, who meant to dispel the notion that violence was inevitable, the report's authors seemed to anticipate further conflict. They wrote that contemporary political divisions were reminiscent of "those between the Confederate and Union forces [. . .] They amount to a dispute over not only the history of our country but also its present purpose and future direction."

They were correct that we are now at a crossroads. We are witnessing a clash of utopian perspectives on what the United States ought to be. Like Albert Cleage's Black Christian Nationalists, white Christian nationalists hope for a world that will soon be wholly transformed. Many believe that they are God's chosen people, and they are mainly concerned with protecting the integrity of their spiritual nation. They fabricate grand narratives of a romantic past for their race, and they interpret social upheavals as preludes to an apocalypse that will reorganize the distribution of social, political, and economic power. But the liberation theology that the Black Christian Nationalists embodied is, in many ways, the antithesis of white Christian nationalism. White Christian nationalists understand the dispossession and diminishment of blacks—and many others—as a task prescribed by God, not a notion anathema to Him. They would limit our collective sense of who will thrive in the future, whereas those who have been touched by Cleage's message of black dignity wish to expand what it means to create a beloved community today.

In her *GQ* profile of Roof, Rachel Kaadzi Ghansah wrote that what the killer "didn't understand when he walked into that church was the genius of black America's survival and the nature of our overcoming." He knew nothing of the ways black people had used "their fugitivity, their grief, their history for good." Cleage likely would have agreed. The true radicalism of his movement, the Black Madonna, and the Black Messiah was their insistence that the classical myths undergirding our nation's history are just that—tales that, though powerful, are not settled. The nature of myths is that they are open to elaboration by anyone who believes they can tell a better and more enduring story.

The Cumberland

◇◇◇◇◇◇

When I was a child, my grandfather Ruffus drove me down a country path in Promise Land that led to a quiet glade. It was a cemetery. The tree canopy turned whatever sunlight slipped through a dark blue. More than the silence of this place or Papa's sudden solemnity, I was unsettled by something unknown. My grandfather could not account for everyone who was buried here. Some of the graves belonged to family on his mother's side, but most of the dates and names on the headstones had worn away. We were there to tend the grave sites. It would have taken more people and time to properly restore these grounds.

As we cleared brush, Papa said he wanted me to take care of the cemetery after he died. He paced the graveyard slowly, looking much like he did when walking the tilled rows of his garden in Detroit. He believed that by tending the lands that fed us in life and housed us in death, we committed ourselves to a relationship with it as fruitful as any we might have with another person. He was the first to suggest to me that the places we so easily call our own have not been guaranteed to us but are earned through continual care. Long before Detroit meant anything to me beyond my grandparents' home, Papa sometimes took me to a neglected playground nearby to pick up scattered trash. Once I had done my share, I would scale the park's geodesic dome and linger atop it like a spider, wondering how I would get back down. Papa took these outings more seriously. He was imagining the community that might arise where once there had only been garbage and weeds. And at some point, other children did come.

In Detroit, I had always been surrounded by people who, on vastly different scales, honed their ability to find life in discarded places. In backyard gardens, apartment communes, churches, and other shrines, new principles for what a community and one's own life could be were constantly being articulated. The Shrine of the Black Madonna did not reflect the world in its totality. The Black Christian Nationalists' many social projects did not, for instance, address issues specifically affecting black trans and queer people during the worst years of the AIDS epidemic. These communities have been central to present-day currents in black utopian thought, which generally embrace perspectives that are less bound to hierarchy and patriarchy than those found in the Shrine.

But for many people, the church accomplished something that few other institutions of its time had done: it made clear that black Americans belonged in a long, global struggle for the commons. Black Christian Nationalism was a hidden chapter in the book of historical movements toward a world less structured around exploitation and greed, and more attuned to the sacrosanct nature of black lives. The movement imagined black futures where others saw only hellfire. It was, at least for a time, the face of a mighty tendency.

◇◇◇◇◇◇◇

Papa's answer to people who asked where he was from was "the place where everyone's trying to go." After learning of the pain that migrated from Papa's neck to his shoulders and chest in spring 2010, his doctor cleared him to return home again for the Promise Land Festival that June. He spent three weeks there under the care of my grandmother, aunt, and uncle before returning to Detroit. The tumor soon found on his chest was the size of a baseball. My aunt Yolanda immersed herself in his care. She kept a blog to track her father's healing journey.

Sunday, August 8, 2010: "The first thing Daddy did was go out to his garden. He had been concerned about the lack of water . . . But all was well in his collard green, cucumber, tomato, and squash land."

On August 12, Papa watched me cut his lawn. I saw that he was thinning. The hospital bed in the den of his house was an intruder. It rearranged the order of our lives. Auntie wanted to get Papa a jigsaw puzzle of the Promise Land School to help him pass the time. He wasn't interested. He watched *Bonanza* and CNN, ate pork skins, and listened to commentaries by the preacher Kenneth Hagin. Yolanda and my uncle Harry often drove up from Columbus to visit. Shortly after Papa's diagnosis, he and Granny moved to Promise Land. Papa did not leave Detroit without first making sure the city knew that he loved it as much as he loved where he was about to go next. He kept checking the house for belongings, going in and out, down to the basement and coming back up again. Yolanda was telling him they had to go. He snapped at her. He never did that. He said goodbye to his garden.

Once they arrived in Promise Land, his pains briefly eased. "When we hit his land and got to his home," Yolanda told me, "Dad walked that whole area. I mean, he just walked and looked at his flowers and looked at the grass. It was like he had not experienced some excruciating pain just hours before. That place was magic for him."

My mother and I had seen him around Easter at a family gathering for Papa in Columbus. The last time I saw him, he was dancing the Cupid Shuffle, dipping his shoulders and rising again. When he sat to rest, he looked around at all of us who had come. Back in Promise Land, Papa asked for Yolanda whenever she left for Ohio to reset and check on her children. She always returned. Eventually, Papa stopped eating. My family could no longer get him to the hospital in Nashville and arranged for hospice care. They listened to the nurse and they listened to the Holy Spirit.

One July Sunday, the Spirit told Yolanda that by the time Harry came that day, her father would be gone. A few members of the family milled in the house and outside. Granny and Yolanda carefully monitored who was allowed into the master bedroom, where Papa rested. He was on morphine. Yolanda heard his shallow breathing. She told her mother, who was searching for something in her dresser drawer, that she needed to come over immediately. They watched over and put their hands on him. His breathing calmed at the familiar voices. My grandfather died on the grounds he hoped those of us who were left would tend.

◇◇◇◇◇◇

Driving past Granny and Papa's old house in Detroit years later, I watched young black boys around a hoop on the street miss their shots and try again. They paused and parted as my mother and I rolled by. We remarked on cosmetic changes. A truck was in the driveway of the Steel Street house and blocking my view of the side door. I used to run through that door whenever my basketball bounced off the hoop mounted on the garage and rattled the wasp's nest hanging in the tree. Although these things were not there anymore, I saw the afterimages of a porch cover and bushes, a peach tree in the backyard, tomato and pepper plants in the old garden, a girlfriend's sundress over the grass.

Shortly after the pandemic began, I joined a virtual coffee hour after one of the Shrine's online services to introduce myself. One man said to me, "Welcome home, brother." I don't know if he was in Detroit, Atlanta, Houston, or somewhere else. Church was no place at all, and I tried to recall the verse about holy places and the body of Christ not requiring a physical presence. Cleage had written something to that effect: "The Promised Land is a state of being in which people achieve the kind of existence God intended men to have."

I did wonder. Many of us—my family and people of the Shrine—

had been in Detroit together and were unknown to one another. Who would we have been had we broken bread together? All of us were told that the good church leads to a city, and that this city would lift the church towards perfection. The city, whether earthbound or celestial, was a beautiful place that we ran to meet.

Today, Granny says "God will handle it" when asked what may happen to her and Papa's home in Promise Land when she is gone. Her surrender to heaven implies a request. She is asking God to work through her children and grandchildren. The only way for Him to do that was if we did not stop looking for Him. In the years since Papa's death, those of us who have lost touch with the religion of our grandmother have expanded the meaning of God. It is a name that means: returning to a place we thought behind us, a state we once believed to be in the untouchable above.

Rest

◇◇◇◇◇◇◇

Cheza is Kiswahili for "play," or what Monifa described to me as "a brief pause in the struggle." In the Shrine, Cheza was a party, once held at least three times a year around holidays, celebrating the renewal of communal love. This, too, had a purpose. Jaramogi Abebe knew that if he was going to direct his young people away from slave pleasures, like excessive drinking at bars, they would need structured time and space for recreation. In the Shrine's fellowship halls, the training groups had their own tables with refreshments. There was a year in the mid-1980s when Monifa was in charge of decorations. She bought strobe lights, hats, horns, and table centerpieces.

Jaramogi sat at his own table sipping Johnnie Walker Red as members of the church went up and spoke with him. Dancers did the Funky Chicken and breakdanced in a *Soul Train* line. The song that put a little tap in Jaramogi's foot was George Benson's "This Masquerade."

Minutes before midnight on New Year's Eve, Monifa joined a circle of more than one hundred people that formed to recite the Cheza pledge:

"I believe in the healing powers of the revolutionary BCN group process."

"I pledge to bring a black counterculture into being by expressing a wider and deeper love and respect for my brothers and sisters in my everyday life."

"I feel the love and power of the group passing through my hands and strengthening both heart and mind for the struggle in which we are joined."

"I can sense the communal oneness which binds us together in a sacred brotherhood."

"May God and the Black Nation be my witness."

"I exist to take Black Christian Nationalism to black people everywhere!"

They kept hollering *I exist!* and the DJ put on a song. "Lean on Me" or "We've Been Blessed." Every person in the circle received the right hand of fellowship, and if for some reason you were on the outside, they hugged and lifted you until you were pulled in.

Notes

Introduction: Utopia in Black

5　*returning to the past*: Joe P. L. Davidson, "The Sociology of Utopia, Modern Temporality and Black Visions of Liberation," *Sociology* 57, no. 4 (2022): 827–42: "The African American experience is defined by a dialectic of hope and disappointment, whereby 'divine' events . . . that promise 'the end of all doubt' are accompanied by a feeling that the catastrophes of the past will never be eclipsed."

7　*abolishing cops or prisons was wise*: See Angela Y. Davis, *Are Prisons Obsolete?* (New York: Seven Stories Press, 2003); Zoé Samudzi and William C. Anderson, *As Black as Resistance: Finding the Conditions for Liberation* (Chico, CA: AK Press, 2018); Derecka Purnell, *Becoming Abolitionists: Police, Protests, and the Pursuit of Freedom* (New York: Astra House, 2021); Andrea Ritchie, *Practicing New Worlds: Abolition and Emergent Strategies* (Chico, CA: AK Press, 2023). See also Derrick Darby, *A Realistic Blacktopia: Why We Must Unite to Fight* (New York: Oxford University Press, 2022); Cedric G. Johnson, *The Panthers Can't Save Us Now: Debating Left Politics and Black Lives Matter* (New York: Verso Books, 2022); Walter Mosley, *Folding the Red into the Black: Developing a Viable Untopia for Human Survival in the 21st Century* (New York: OR Books, 2016).

7　*the new world*: Nathalie Jonas, "Fire and Futurity: Riot, Its Object, and Queer Potentiality in the George Floyd Uprising," *Liminalities: A Journal of Performance Studies* 18, no. 4 (2022). See also Cedric G. Johnson, *After Black Lives Matter: Policing and Anti-Capitalist Struggle* (New York: Verso, 2023); Tikkun Bambara, "George Floyd and What Black Utopian Thinking Can Offer Us," *Mn Artists*, May 29, 2020, mnartists.walkerart.org/george-floyd-what-black-utopian-thinking-can-offer-us; Ashon Crawley, "Otherwise Movements," *The New Inquiry*, January 19, 2015, thenewinquiry.com/otherwise-movements/.

7　*possibilities inherent in black social life*: See Alex Zamalin, *Black Utopia: The History of an Idea from Black Nationalism to Afrofuturism* (New York: Columbia University Press, 2019); Jayna Brown, *Black Utopias: Speculative Life and the Music of Other Worlds* (Durham: Duke University Press, 2021); Richard A. Jones, "The Politics of Black Utopia," in *Postmodern Racial Dialectics: Philosophy Beyond the Pale* (New York: University Press of America, 2015), 71–108.

7–8　*our daily lives blur*: William Paris, "Crisis Consciousness, Utopian Consciousness, and the Struggle for Racial Justice," *Puncta: Journal of Critical Phenomenology* 5, no. 4 (2022): 144–66.

10　Black Priest, White Church: Lawrence Lucas, *Black Priest, White Church: Catholics and Racism* (New York: Random House, 1970).

11 *a black realist*: Betty DeRamus, "A Man of Controversy Achieves 'Black Realism,'" *Detroit Free Press*, December 26, 1972.

11 *maroons who lived in the swamplands*: See also Timothy J. Lockley, ed., *Maroon Communities in South Carolina: A Documentary Record* (Columbia: University of South Carolina Press, 2009); Sylviane A. Diouf, *Slavery's Exiles: The Story of the American Maroons* (New York: New York University Press, 2014).

12 *wasn't convinced that Christianity was the only lens*: C. Eric Lincoln and Lawrence H. Mamiya, *The Black Church in the African American Experience* (Durham: Duke University Press, 1990). For the lectures on the black church that Cleage delivered at the Princeton Theological Seminary in spring 1969, see "The Black Church (part 1)," *Michigan Chronicle*, November 22, 1969; "The Black Church (part 2)," *Michigan Chronicle*, November 29, 1969; "The Black Church (part 3)," *Michigan Chronicle*, December 6, 1969; "The Black Church (part 4)," *Michigan Chronicle*, December 13, 1969.

12 *an apocalyptic movement*: Charles L. Krysinski, "Black Theology and the End of Time" (PhD diss., University of California Santa Cruz, 2022).

12 *Justice was understood as a power balance*: Arrigo Colombo, "The New Sense of Utopia: The Construction of a Society Based on Justice," *Utopian Studies* 11, no. 2 (2000), 181–97.

12 *"communal child-rearing structure"*: Velma Maia Thomas, "The Black Madonna and the Role of Women," in *Albert Cleage Jr. and the Black Madonna and Child*, ed. Jawanza Eric Clark (New York: Palgrave Macmillan, 2016), 117–34.

12 *first led the Detroit Mtoto House*: Shelley McIntosh, *Mtoto House: Vision to Victory—Raising African American Children Communally* (Lanham, MD: Hamilton Books, 2005).

13 *American dystopia, black despair, and the dead end of progress*: Heidi Ewing and Rachel Grady, *Detropia* (New York: Loki Films, 2012); Mark Binelli, *Detroit City Is the Place to Be: The Afterlife of an American Metropolis* (New York: Metropolitan Books, 2012); Dora Apel, *Beautiful Terrible Ruins: Detroit and the Anxiety of Decline* (New Brunswick: Rutgers University Press, 2015); Sara Safransky, *The City After Property: Abandonment and Repair in Postindustrial Detroit* (Durham: Duke University Press, 2023); Kate Wells, "Detroit Was Always Made of Wheels: Confronting Ruin Porn in Its Hometown," in *Ruin Porn and the Obsession with Decay*, ed. Siobhan Lyons (New York: Palgrave Macmillan, 2018), 13–29; Eli Rosenberg, "Motown or Ghostown? Ruin Porn in Detroit," *The Atlantic*, January 20, 2011.

13 *utopia and the people who seek it*: For an alternative map of black people's lives in a misunderstood American city, see Sarah M. Broom's *The Yellow House: A Memoir* (New York: Grove Press, 2019).

Promise Land

21 *one of the oldest known settlements*: Josh Arntz, "Black Community Played Key Role in Charlotte's Heritage," *Dickson Herald*, February 23, 2011.

22 *Black Towns & Settlements: Foundation for the Future*: Next Leadership Development, "Black Towns & Settlements: Foundation for the Future," February 2022, storymaps.arcgis.com /stories/f33c40b9ae044f878db0fe7a4b912fb2. See also Sebastian N. Page, *Black Resettlement and the American Civil War* (Cambridge, UK: Cambridge University Press, 2021).

22 *blacktowns and settlements that existed throughout North America*: Danielle M. Purifoy and Louise Seamster, "Creative Extraction: Black Towns in White Space," *Society and Space* 39, no. 1 (2021): 47–66; Amy Hart, "'Owned and Controlled by Negroes': Allensworth and the Study of Subnational Space," *Communal Societies* 38, no. 1 (2018): 59–79; Lawrence B. de Graaf, "Recognition, Racism, and Reflections on the Writing of Western Black History," *Pacific Historical Review* 44, no. 1 (1975): 22–51; Mikal Brotnov Eckstrom and Richard Edwards, "Staking Their Claim: DeWitty and Black Homesteaders in Nebraska," *Great Plains Quarterly* 38, no. 3 (2018): 295–317; Thomas Knight, *Sunset on Utopian Dreams: An Experiment of Black Separatism on the American Frontier* (Lanham, MD: University Press of America, 1977).

23   *"forged a settlement based on economic security"*: Elizabeth Raul Bethel, *Promiseland: A Century of Life in a Negro Community* (Philadelphia: Temple University Press, 1981), 5.

25   *tail end of the Great Migration*: See Isabel Wilkerson, *The Warmth of Other Suns: The Epic Story of America's Great Migration* (New York: Vintage Books, 2010); Ira Berlin, *The Making of African America: The Four Great Migrations* (New York: Penguin Books, 2010).

26   *"Charlotte's 'little Harlem'"*: "Colored Picnic to Be on August 18," *The Leaf-Chronicle*, August 18, 1939.

26   *mines and metals*: Robert B. Gordon, *American Iron, 1607–1900* (Baltimore: Johns Hopkins University Press, 1996); Anne Kelly Knowles, *Mastering Iron: The Struggle to Modernize an American Industry, 1800–1868* (Chicago: University of Chicago Press, 2013); Samuel D. Smith et al., "A Cultural Resource Survey of Tennessee's Western Highland Rim Iron Industry, 1790s–1930s" (Tennessee Department of Conservation, Division of Archaeology, Research Series No. 8, 1988).

27   *fueling the purchase of slaves to work them*: Samuel C. Williams, "Early Iron Works in the Tennessee Country," *Tennessee Historical Quarterly* 6, no. 1 (1947): 39–46.

27   *who most of the miners and smelters would be*: See Lester C. Lamon, *Blacks in Tennessee, 1791–1970* (Knoxville: University of Tennessee Press, 1981); Anita S. Goodstein, "Black History on the Nashville Frontier, 1780–1810," *Tennessee Historical Quarterly* 38, no. 4 (1979): 401–20.

27   *"father of Tennessee"*: For accounts of James Robertson's role in the opening and development of the Tennessee frontier, see Harriette Simpson Arnow, *Seedtime on the Cumberland* (Lexington: University Press of Kentucky, 1960); Harriette Simpson Arnow, *Flowering of the Cumberland* (1963; repr., Lincoln: Bison Books, 1996); Margaret Burr DesChamps, "Early Days in the Cumberland Country," *Tennessee Historical Quarterly* 6, no. 3 (1947): 195–229; Anita S. Goodstein, "Leadership on the Nashville Frontier, 1780–1800," *Tennessee Historical Quarterly* 35, no. 2 (1976): 175–98.

27   *one quarter of slaves in Dickson County*: Robert E. Corlew, "Some Aspects of Slavery in Dickson County," *Tennessee Historical Quarterly* 10, no. 3 (September 1951): 224–48; Robert E. Corlew, "Some Aspects of Slavery in Dickson County (Continued)," *Tennessee Historical Quarterly* 10, no. 4 (December 1951): 344–65. Tennessee's iron age coincided with a boom in American utopian communities, the majority of which excluded blacks. For more, see John Egerton, *Visions of Utopia: Nashoba, Rugby, Ruskin, and the "New Communities" in Tennessee's Past* (Knoxville: University of Tennessee Press, 1977); Gail Bederman, "Revisiting Nashoba: Slavery, Utopia, and Frances Wright in America, 1818–1826," *American Literary History* 17, no. 3 (2005): 438–59; Christopher Clark, *The Communitarian Moment: The Radical Challenge of the Northampton Association* (Ithaca: Cornell University Press, 1995); Sean Griffin, "Antislavery Utopias: Communitarian Labor Reform and the Abolitionist Movement," *Journal of the Civil War Era* 8, no. 2 (2018): 243–68; Carl J. Guarneri, "Two Utopian Socialist Plans for Emancipation in Antebellum Louisiana," *Louisiana History: The Journal of the Louisiana Historical Association* 24, no. 1 (1983): 5–24.

27   *The months it took to yield whole tons*: Charles B. Dew, "Disciplining Slave Ironworkers in the Antebellum South: Coercion, Conciliation, and Accommodation," *The American Historical Review* 79, no. 2 (1974): 393–418; Michael Thomas Gavin, "From Bands of Iron to Promise Land: The African-American Contribution to Middle Tennessee's Antebellum Iron Industry," *Tennessee Historical Quarterly* 64, no. 1 (2005): 24–42; "Furnaces and Forges," *Tennessee Historical Magazine* 9, no. 3 (1925): 190–92; Anne Kelly Knowles, "Labor, Race, and Technology in the Confederate Iron Industry," *Technology and Culture* 42, no. 1 (2001): 1–26.

27   *charcoal would burn at the proper speed*: Justin L. Hart et al., "Legacy of Charcoaling in a Western Highland Rim Forest in Tennessee," *The American Midland Naturalist* 159, no. 1 (2008): 238–50.

A Church and a One-Room School

29   *The Nesbitt brothers had been born into bondage*: See Maria C. Brent and Joseph E. Brent, *Ready to Die for Liberty: Tennessee's United States Colored Troops in the Civil War* (Nashville: Tennessee Wars Commission, 2013).

29   *in defiance of the Fugitive Slave Act*: Richard J. M. Blackett, "Resistance to Slavery in Middle Tennessee," *Tennessee Historical Quarterly* 76, no. 4 (2017): 300–41.

29   *Union encampments that sprouted*: Amy Murrell Taylor, *Embattled Freedom: Journeys Through the Civil War's Slave Refugee Camps* (Chapel Hill: University of North Carolina Press, 2018); Patricia C. Click, *Time Full of Trial: The Roanoke Island Freedmen's Colony, 1862–1867* (Chapel Hill: University of North Carolina Press, 2001); Janet Sharp Hermann, *The Pursuit of a Dream* (New York: Oxford University Press, 1999); Stephen Joseph Ross, "Freed Soil, Freed Labor, Freed Men: John Eaton and the Davis Bend Experiment," *The Journal of Southern History* 44, no. 2 (1978): 213–32; Neil Canady et al., "Race and Local Knowledge: New Evidence from the Southern Homestead Act," *The Review of Black Political Economy* 42 (2015): 399–413; Angela S. Jaillet, "The People of Pandenarium: The Living Landscape of a Freed African American Settlement" (master's thesis, Indiana University of Pennsylvania, 2011).

30   *shantytowns and bottomlands fell to ruin*: Lisa Goff, *Shantytown, USA: Forgotten Landscapes of the Working Poor* (Cambridge, MA: Harvard University Press, 2016).

30   *Negro or freedom colonies*: Barbara Arneil, *Domestic Colonies: The Turn Inward to Colony* (New York: Oxford University Press, 2017). See also William Lynwood Montell, *The Saga of Coe Ridge: A Study in Oral History* (Knoxville: University of Tennessee Press, 1981).

32   *"I'll make me a world"*: James Weldon Johnson, "The Creation," in *God's Trombones: Seven Negro Sermons in Verse* (New York: Viking Books, 1927).

33   *standardized public education for whites and blacks*: David Tyack and Robert Lowe, "The Constitutional Moment: Reconstruction and Black Education in the South," *American Journal of Education* 94, no. 2 (1986): 236–56.

33   *the Jim Crow system*: Margaret A. Burnham, *By Hands Now Known: Jim Crow's Legal Executioners* (New York: W. W. Norton, 2022).

34   *aura of total harmony*: See introduction of Sylvia Edmondson-Holt, *Between the Pews: More Than a Sabbath Day's Journey from the Promise Land* (New York: Xlibris, 2016).

34   *much of the remaining acreage owned by black people*: Roy W. Copeland, "Heir Property in the African American Community: From Promised Lands to Problem Lands," *Professional Agricultural Workers Journal* 2, no. 2 (2015); Avanthi Cole, "For the 'Wealthy and Legally Savvy': The Weaknesses of the Uniform Partition of Heirs Property Act as Applied to Low-Income Black Heirs Property Owners," *Columbia Journal of Race and Law* 11, no. 2 (2021): 343–72.

35   *black land loss over the last hundred years*: Charles Nesbitt, "Rural Acreage in Promise Land, Tennessee: A Case Study," in *The Black Rural Landowner: Endangered Species: Social, Political, and Economic Implications*, ed. Leo McGee and Robert Boone (Nashville: Tennessee State University, 1976), 28–40.

35   *land which has been in their families or communities*: Valerie Grim, "African American Landlords in the Rural South, 1870–1950: A Profile," *Agricultural History* 72, no. 2 (1998): 399–416; Janet K. Wadley and Everett S. Lee, "The Disappearance of the Black Farmer," *Phylon* 35, no. 3 (1974): 276–83.

35   *an earthly inheritance for black communities*: Michael L. Lanza, *Agrarianism and Reconstruction Politics: The Southern Homestead Act* (Baton Rouge: Louisiana State University Press, 1999); Bruce J. Reynolds, "Black Farmers in America, 1865–2000: The Pursuit of Independent Farming and the Role of Cooperatives" (United States Department of Agriculture Rural Business-Cooperative Service, RBS Research Report 194, 2002).

The Promised Land That Wasn't

40   *no single narrative about black utopia*: I have chosen to focus on post–Civil War utopian projects and communities, but earlier examples abound: Vickie Cimprich, "Free and Freed Shak-

ers and Affiliates of African Descent at Pleasant Hill, Kentucky," *The Register of the Kentucky Historical Society* 111, no. 4 (2013): 489–523; Theodore Hershberg, "Free Blacks in Antebellum Philadelphia: A Study of Ex-Slaves, Freeborn, and Socioeconomic Decline," *Journal of Social History* 5, no. 2 (winter 1971–1972): 183–209; Mary Gehman, *The Free People of Color of New Orleans: An Introduction* (Donaldsonville, LA: Dville Press, 1994); Melvin Patrick Ely, *Israel on the Appomattox: A Southern Experiment in Black Freedom from the 1790s Through the Civil War* (New York: Vintage Books, 2004); Jon Sensbach, *Separate Canaan: The Making of an Afro-Moravian World in North Carolina, 1763–1840* (Chapel Hill: University of North Carolina Press, 1998).

40 *the Oklahoma Territory*: Daniel Littlefield, Jr., and Lonnie E. Underhill, "Black Dreams and 'Free' Homes: The Oklahoma Territory, 1891–1894," *Phylon* 34, no. 4 (1973): 342–57.

41 *Promise Landers would not do until a few decades later*: Louis M. Kyriakoudes, "Southern Black Rural-Urban Migration in the Era of the Great Migration: Nashville and Middle Tennessee, 1890–1930," *Agricultural History* 72, no. 2 (1998): 341–51.

41 *emanated from shared concerns*: W. E. B. Du Bois, *Black Reconstruction in America: An Essay Toward a History of the Part Which Black Folk Played in the Attempt to Reconstruct Democracy in America, 1860–1880* (New York: Harcourt, Brace, 1935); Thulani Davis, *The Emancipation Circuit: Black Activism Forging a Culture of Freedom* (Durham: Duke University Press, 2022). See also Cheryl Janifer LaRoche, *Free Black Communities and the Underground Railroad: The Geography of Resistance* (Champaign: University of Illinois Press, 2013); Eric Foner, *Gateway to Freedom: The Hidden History of the Underground Railroad* (New York: W. W. Norton, 2015).

42 *colored people's conventions*: Gabrielle Foreman, *The Colored Conventions Movement: Black Organizing in the Nineteenth Century* (Chapel Hill: University of North Carolina Press, 2021); Shawn C. Comminey, "National Black Conventions and the Quest for African American Freedom and Progress, 1847–1867," *International Social Science Review* 91, no. 1 (2015): 1–18.

42 *white "pale riders"*: Kidada E. Williams, *I Saw Death Coming: A History of Terror and Survival in the War Against Reconstruction* (New York: Bloomsbury, 2023).

42 *first mass relocation of African Americans*: Nell Irvin Painter, *Exodusters: Black Migration to Kansas After Reconstruction* (New York: Alfred A. Knopf, 1977). See also Richard Edwards, Jacob K. Friefeld, and Mikal Brotnov Eckstrom, "'Canaan on the Prairie': New Evidence on the Number of African American Homesteaders in the Great Plains," *Great Plains Quarterly* 39, no. 3 (2019): 223–41.

42 *nationalized education system for black children*: Mary Niall Mitchell, *Raising Freedom's Child: Black Children and Visions of the Future after Slavery* (New York: New York University Press, 2008).

42 *Colored People Cooperative Land and Emigrant Association*: Selena Sanderfer, "Tennessee's Black Postwar Emigration Movements, 1866–1880," *Tennessee Historical Quarterly* 73, no. 4 (2014): 254–79.

42 *Freedom and the Nation*: Thelma Jennings, "Tennessee and the Nashville Conventions of 1850," *Tennessee Historical Quarterly* 30, no. 1 (1971): 70–82. See also Matt Sandler, *The Black Romantic Revolution: Abolitionist Poets at the End of Slavery* (New York: Verso Books, 2020).

42 *It could not be allowed to*: Edward J. Blum, "'To Doubt This Would Be to Doubt God': Reconstruction and the Decline of Providential Confidence," in *Apocalypse and the Millennium in the American Civil War Era*, ed. Ben Wright and Zachary W. Dresser (Baton Rouge: Louisiana State University Press, 2013).

42 *the Eastern States*: Kristin Cleage, "E is for 'Eastern States,'" *Finding Eliza* (blog), April 5, 2014, findingeliza.com/archives/16764.

43 *"I know nothing about you people"*: Kristin Cleage, "Dr. Albert Buford Cleage & Pearl Doris Reed Cleage: Their Families—Pearl Reed Cleage," 1993, Box 45, Folder 11, Pearl Cleage Papers, Emory University, Atlanta, GA.

44 *a decorated member of the literary society*: "Prescott Medal Contest at Knoxville College," *Knoxville Sentinel*, June 13, 1903.

44   *literary, classical, and scientific education for black people*: See Richard Sears, *A Utopian Experiment in Kentucky: Integration and Social Equality at Berea, 1866–1904* (Westport, CT: Greenwood Press, 1996); Paul David Phillips, "Education of Blacks in Tennessee During Reconstruction, 1865–1870," *Tennessee Historical Quarterly* 46, no. 2 (1987): 98–109.

44   *employed in state educational institutions*: Cynthia Griggs, "The Plight of Black Educators in Postwar Tennessee, 1865–1920," *Journal of Negro History* 64 (1979): 355–64; Cynthia Griggs Fleming, "The Effect of Higher Education on Black Tennesseans after the Civil War," *Phylon* 44 (1983): 209–16.

44   *"War, Hell, and Slavery"*: W. E. B. Du Bois, "Of the Meaning of Progress," in *The Souls of Black Folk* (Chicago: A. C. McClurg, 1903).

45   *"where does the greatest success await"*: Kristin Cleage, "Q is for Questions," *Finding Eliza*, April 19, 2014.

45   *the Appalachian Exposition*: The definitive account of the exposition can be found in W. M. Goodman, ed., *The First Exposition of Conservation and Its Builders: An Official History of the National Conservation Exposition, Held at Knoxville, Tenn., in 1913 and of Its Forerunners, the Appalachian Expositions of 1910–11, Embracing a Review of the Conservation Movement in the United States from Its Inception to the Present Time* (Knoxville: Knoxville Lithographing Co., 1914). See also "A New Knoxville," *Art and Progress* 2, no. 1 (1910): 23–24; "Appalachian Exposition 'Dee-lights' Roosevelt," *Knoxville Sentinel*, October 8, 1910; Robert Douglas Lukens, "Portraits of Progress in New South Appalachia: Three Expositions in Knoxville, Tennessee, 1910–1913" (master's thesis, University of Tennessee, Knoxville, 1996); "Scope of the Appalachian Exposition," *Journal and Tribune*, September 1, 1910.

45   *Inspired by previous world's fairs*: Courtney L. Novosat, "Spectacular Struggles: Utopian Whiteness, Black Resistance, and the National Imaginary in Nineteenth-Century America" (PhD diss., West Virginia University, 2016).

45   *a world coming of age*: "Architectural Achievements of Appalachian Exposition," *Knoxville Sentinel*, September 6, 1910.

46   *Colored People's Day*: "Knoxville Negro Day Tuesday at Exposition," *Knoxville Sentinel*, October 3, 1910; "Knoxville Negro Day," *Knoxville Sentinel*, October 4, 1910; "10,000 Negroes See Exposition Upon Negro Day," *Knoxville Sentinel*, September 27, 1910; "Robert Clay Made Address to Negroes," *Journal and Tribune*, September 17, 1910.

46   *the contained world of the Negro Building*: "Negroes and Their Building," *Journal and Tribune*, August 28, 1910.

47   *black people who had moved to Kalamazoo*: Carson Jeanne Leftwich, "Survival Strategies of Black Kalamazooans: Migration, Kinship Networks and Work in a Midwestern Village, 1860–1900" (master's thesis, Western Michigan University, 1997).

47   *hailed as world wonders*: Conrad Kickert, *Dream City: Creation, Destruction, and Reinvention in Downtown Detroit* (Cambridge, MA: MIT Press, 2019).

47   *newly arrived migrants from the South*: "New Hospital Staff Named: Sisters of Charity (Colored) Will Open Institution Today," *Indianapolis Star*, June 17, 1911.

48   *practitioner of race work*: Jerome H. Schiele and M. Sebrena Jackson, "The Atlanta School of Social Work and the Professionalization of 'Race Work,'" *Phylon* 57, no. 2 (2020): 21–40.

48   *political support from the Ku Klux Klan*: "Where Did Reading Hide His KKK Gown?" *United Automobile Worker*, October 18, 1937.

49   *point other members of his race to jobs*: "Mrs. Carrie Riley Appointed Inspector of Beauty Shops," *Detroit Tribune*, November 16, 1935.

49   *Sigma Gamma Rho debutante balls*: "Noted Violinist Appears Before Large Audience," *Detroit Tribune*, October 11, 1941.

49   *friends from Knoxville College*: "Mr. and Mrs. J. Beck and Miss Chairs Feted by Friends," *Detroit Tribune*, August 29, 1936.

49   *the New Negro ethos*: Henry Louis Gates, Jr., "Reframing Race: Enter the New Negro," in *Stony the Road: Reconstruction, White Supremacy, and the Rise of Jim Crow* (New York: Penguin

Press, 2019), 235–46; Alain Locke, *The New Negro: Voices of the Harlem Renaissance* (New York: Albert & Charles Boni, 1925).

49 *good home environments*: "West Side Human Relation Council Looks to Mothers," *Detroit Tribune*, February 26, 1938.

49 *Michigan's "Black Eden"*: For accounts of black people's relationships with resorts, recreational spaces, and leisure experiences—generally underacknowledged aspects of black utopian visions—see Victoria W. Wolcott, *Race, Riots, and Roller Coasters: The Struggle Over Segregated Recreation in America* (Philadelphia: University of Pennsylvania Press, 2012); Cherene Sherrard-Johnson, *Dorothy West's Paradise: A Biography of Class and Color* (New Brunswick: Rutgers University Press, 2012); Ronald J. Stephens, "Garveyism in Idlewild, 1927 to 1936," *Journal of Black Studies* 34, no. 4 (2004): 462–88; Mark S. Foster, "In the Face of 'Jim Crow': Prosperous Blacks and Vacations, Travel and Outdoor Leisure, 1890–1945," *The Journal of Negro History* 84, no. 2 (1999): 130–49; Myra B. Young Armstead, "Revisiting Hotels and Other Lodgings: American Tourist Spaces through the Lens of Black Pleasure-Travelers, 1880–1950," *The Journal of Decorative and Propaganda Arts* 25 (2005): 136–59; John Fraser Hart, "A Rural Retreat for Northern Negroes," *Geographical Review* 50, no. 2 (1960): 147–68.

51 *a leader in the Social Gospel tradition*: "Rev. Horace White Asks Lifting of Racial Barriers," *Detroit Free Press*, December 30, 1945; Matthew Pehl, "'Apostles of Fascism,' 'Communist Clergy,' and the UAW: Political Ideology and Working-Class Religion in Detroit, 1919–1945," *The Journal of American History* 99, no. 2 (2012): 440–65; Alfred Cassey, "Christian Church Must Fight for Justice, Says Rev. Horace White," *Detroit Tribune*, October 7, 1939.

51 *the City on a Hill that its architects wanted it to be*: Daniel M. Bluestone, "Detroit's City Beautiful and the Problem of Commerce," *Journal of the Society of Architectural Historians* 47, no. 3 (1988): 245–62.

51 *Albert Jr. passed a civil service exam*: "Pass Civil Service Examination Here," *Detroit Tribune*, July 16, 1938.

51 *Detroit's overburdened welfare department*: "32,000 on Dole; 16,000 Seek It," *Detroit Free Press*, February 5, 1938; "Engel Submits Welfare Audit," *Detroit Free Press*, May 7, 1938; "Mayor Orders Relief Speedup," *Detroit Free Press*, December 22, 1938; "City Hall Backs State Relief Act," *Detroit Free Press*, October 18, 1938.

51 *supplementary welfare stations*: "Firemen to Aid in Relief Crisis," *Detroit Free Press*, February 3, 1938.

51 *laid-off autoworkers*: "Who's on Relief in Detroit? Weekly Report Shows Facts," *Detroit Free Press*, May 8, 1938; "WPA to Restudy Its Layoff Orders," *Detroit Free Press*, May 21, 1939.

51 *welfare department had been disgraced*: "Mayor Pushes Welfare Probe," *Detroit Free Press*, March 16, 1938.

51 *dole chiselers*: "115 Convictions Are Obtained, Restitution of $42,000 Is Ordered," *Detroit Free Press*, October 9, 1938; "Ex-McCrea Aide Held in Fraud Case," *Detroit Free Press*, December 22, 1938; "Reading Tells Advisers to Widen Study," *Detroit Free Press*, March 6, 1938.

51 *acute crisis for the poor in Detroit*: "$1,000,000 Cut in Relief Is Hit," *Detroit Free Press*, March 11, 1938; "Welfare Crisis Believed Near," *Detroit Free Press*, March 24, 1939; Leo M. Donovan, "The City Hall," *Detroit Free Press*, July 31, 1938; "Reading Shifts WPA Cash for Welfare Crisis," *Detroit Free Press*, Feb. 22, 1938.

52 *the kingdom of God on earth*: Cleage owned Frederick C. Grant's *The Gospel of the Kingdom* (New York: Scribner, 1940). He underlined part of this passage: "We may suspect, then, that the Gospel of the Kingdom really had a social or possibly even a political reference from the start: we should expect to find that it was a Kingdom to be established here upon earth, not a transcendent state of bliss in the after-world."

52 *active church youth organizations*: "Plymouth Establishes New Group," *Detroit Tribune*, February 28, 1942; "Youths Hear Much Talk About Fascism and War at Four-Day Allied Conference," *Detroit Tribune*, April 30, 1938; "Negroes Study the Ford Strike," *Detroit Free Press*, April 7, 1941.

Black Bottom

53 *experiences and aspirations of the disinherited*: There is a substantial body of literature on black liberation theology. See Lilian Calles Berger, *The World Come of Age: An Intellectual History of Liberation Theology* (New York: Oxford University Press, 2018); Dwight N. Hopkins, *Black Theology: Essays on Global Perspectives* (Maryknoll, NY: Orbis Books, 2017); James J. Gardiner and J. Deotis Roberts, Sr., eds., *Quest for a Black Theology* (Minneapolis: Fortress Press, 2010); Dwight N. Hopkins, *Heart and Head: Black Theology—Past, Present, and Future* (New York: Palgrave Macmillan, 2002); Gayraud S. Wilmore, *Black Religion and Black Radicalism: An Interpretation of the Religious History of African Americans* (New York: Doubleday Books, 1970); Major J. Jones, *Christian Ethics for Black Theology: The Politics of Liberation* (Nashville: Abingdon Press, 1974); Darren Webb, "Christian Hope and the Politics of Utopia," *Utopian Studies* 19, no. 1 (2008): 113–44; Anthony Pinn, "Jesus and Justice: An Outline of Liberation Theology within Black Churches," *CrossCurrents* 57, no. 2 (2007): 218–26; Tom Moylan, "Mission Impossible?: Liberation Theology and Utopian Praxis," *Utopian Studies*, no. 3 (1991): 20–30; Rosemary Reuther, "Black Theology and Black Church," *Religious Education* 64, no. 5 (1969): 347–51; Weldon Merrial McWilliams IV, "'To Proclaim Liberty to the Captives': The Pan-African Orthodox Christian Church and Its Relationship to Black Theology" (PhD diss., Temple University, 2010); Thomas A. Johnson, "Black Religion Seeks Own Theology," *New York Times*, January 30, 1971. For more on black religious nationalism, see Tracey E. Hucks, *Yoruba Traditions and African American Religious Nationalism* (Albuquerque: University of New Mexico Press, 2012).

54 *Black Bottom neighborhood*: Jeremy Williams, "The Rise and Fall of Black Bottom" (master's thesis, Prescott College, 2011); Jeremy Williams, *Detroit: The Black Bottom Community* (Mount Pleasant, SC: Arcadia Publishing, 2009); Darlene C. Conley, "Driven and Pursued: Black Migrant Detroit—An Analysis of the Neighborhoods Black Bottom and Paradise Valley, 1916–1968" (master's thesis, Morgan State University, 2016).

55 *an unfinished memoir*: Glanton Dowdell's untitled, unpublished manuscript was shared with me by one of his daughters, Anna Simoni. My recreation of Glanton's childhood years wouldn't have been possible without this remarkable account.

59 *when the Depression came*: E. Franklin Frazier, "Some Effects of the Depression on the Negro in Northern Cities," *Science & Society* 2, no. 4 (1938): 489–99.

60 *the River Rouge factory*: Elizabeth Esch, *The Color Line and the Assembly Line: Managing Race in the Ford Empire* (Oakland: University of California Press, 2018); Charles Williams, "The Racial Politics of Progressive Americanism: New Deal Liberalism and the Subordination of Black Workers in the UAW," *Studies in American Political Development* 19, no. 1 (2005): 75–97; Joyce Shaw Peterson, "Black Automobile Workers in Detroit, 1910–1930," *The Journal of Negro History* 64, no. 3 (1979): 177–90.

61 *Harlem's Liberty Hall in 1924*: "Black Church Head Talks 'Black' God from White Ritual," *New York Age*, August 9, 1924. See also E. David Cronon, *Black Moses: The Story of Marcus Garvey and the Universal Negro Improvement Association* (Madison: University of Wisconsin Press, 1955).

61 *"why should not the Negro believe that he resembles God?"*: Melbourne S. Cummings, "The Rhetoric of Bishop Henry McNeal Turner," *Journal of Black Studies* 12, no. 4 (1982): 457–67. For more on Bishop Turner, see Wilson Jeremiah Moses, *The Golden Age of Black Nationalism, 1850–1925* (New York: University of Oxford Press, 1978); Tunde Adeleke, *UnAfrican Americans: Nineteenth-Century Black Nationalists and the Civilizing Mission* (Lexington: University Press of Kentucky, 1998).

No One Starved in California

64 *Blacks in the train yard's tent city*: Nathaniel Mills, *Ragged Revolutionaries: The Lumpenproletariat and African American Marxism in Depression-Era Literature* (Amherst: University of Massachusetts Press, 2017).

64 *pamphlets of smiling field workers*: Carey McWilliams, "California Pastoral," *The Antioch Review* 2, no. 1 (1942): 103–21; Clarke A. Chambers, *California Farm Organizations: A Historical Study of the Grange, the Farm Bureau, and the Associated Farmers, 1929–1941* (1952; repr., Berkeley: University of California Press, 2022); Nelson A. Pichardo, "The Power Elite and Elite-Driven Countermovements: The Associated Farmers of California During the 1930s," *Sociological Forum* 10, no. 1 (1995): 21–49.

68 *the National Negro Congress*: Lawrence S. Wittner, "National Negro Congress: A Reassessment," *American Quarterly* 22, no. 4 (1970): 883–901; John Baxter Streater, Jr., "The National Negro Congress, 1936–1947" (PhD diss., University of Cincinnati, 1981).

69 *Communist sympathies*: Robin D. G. Kelley, *Hammer and Hoe: Alabama Communists During the Great Depression* (Chapel Hill: University of North Carolina Press, 1990).

69 *separate nation within the United States*: Harry Haywood, *Negro Liberation* (Chicago: Liberator Press, 1948); Gwendolyn Midlo Hall, ed., *A Black Communist in the Freedom Struggle: The Life of Harry Haywood* (Minneapolis: University of Minnesota Press, 2012).

69 *Boys' Vocational School*: Vickki Dozier, "Lansing's Reform School for Boys," *Lansing State Journal*, November 14, 2018; Michigan Department of Social Welfare, *State of Michigan Statutory Provisions Governing Boys' Vocational School, Girls' Vocational School [and] Michigan Children's Institute* (Lansing: Michigan Department of Social Welfare, 1948); "'Crime School' Charge Held Unfair to Institution for Boys," *Detroit Free Press*, March 24, 1940; James M. Haswell, "'Crime School' Relief Offered," *Detroit Free Press*, May 18, 1940; "State Judges Renew Reform School Pleas," *The Herald-Press*, February 12, 1941.

70 *Among the boys were white supremacists*: Salaina Catalano, "When It Happened Here: Michigan and Transnational Development of American Fascism, 1920–1945," *Michigan Historical Review* 46, no. 1 (2020): 29–67.

The Kingdoms of God

72 *multiracial in nature*: See Victoria W. Wolcott, *Living in the Future: Utopianism and the Long Civil Rights Movement* (Chicago: University of Chicago Press, 2022); Louis Venters, *No Jim Crow Church: The Origins of South Carolina's Bahá'í Community* (Gainesville: University Press of Florida, 2015); Erik S. Gellman and Jarod Roll, *The Gospel of the Working Class: Labor's Southern Prophets in New Deal America* (Champaign: University of Illinois Press, 2011); Tracy Elaine K'Meyer, *Interracialism and Christian Community in the Postwar South: The Story of Koinonia Farm* (Charlottesville: University of Virginia Press, 1997); Hoda M. Zaki, "From Montgomery to Tahrir Square: The Transnational Journeys of Nonviolence and Utopia," *Utopian Studies* 26, no. 1 (2015): 203–19; Francis Shor, "Utopian Aspirations in the Black Freedom Movement: SNCC and the Struggle for Civil Rights, 1960–1965," *Utopian Studies* 15, no. 2 (2004): 173–89.

72 *Christians, socialists, and those who identified as both*: Carl J. Guarneri, "The Associationists: Forging a Christian Socialism in Antebellum America," *Church History* 52, no. 1 (1983): 36–49; Gordon K. Lewis, "The Ideas of the Christian Socialists of 1848," *The Western Political Quarterly* 4, no. 3 (1951): 397–429; John C. Cort, *Christian Socialism: An Informal History* (Maryknoll, NY: Orbis Books, 1988); Patrick W. Carey, "Christian Socialism in the Early Brownson," *Records of the American Catholic Historical Society of Philadelphia* 99, no. 1/4 (March-December 1988): 17–27, 29–39; Robert Hunt Ferguson, *Remaking the Rural South: Interracialism, Christian Socialism, and Cooperative Farming in Jim Crow Mississippi* (Athens: University of Georgia Press, 2018). Ferguson explicitly links liberation theology with Christian socialism. Describing the activists associated with the Delta and Providence cooperative farms in Mississippi during the 1930s, he writes that their work was "informed by socialist ideology, a commitment to interracialism, and an early form of Liberation Theology rooted in Christian Socialism—a kind of 'practical' Christianity pioneered most notably by Reinhold Niebuhr and meant to put the teachings of Jesus into practice building a more socially just world."

72   *Reverend Horace White*: White's influence in Detroit receives extensive treatment in Angela Dillard, *Faith in the City: Preaching Radical Social Change in Detroit* (Ann Arbor: University of Michigan Press, 2007). Dillard's excellent book provided the most detailed study of Cleage's political theology and intellectual influences to that point.

73   *serving as a student pastor*: Kristin Cleage, "St. John's Church Elects Rev Albert Cleage Pastor," *Finding Eliza*, February 11, 2012.

73   *liberal bastion with abolitionist roots*: Gary J. Kornblith and Carol Lasser, *Elusive Utopia: The Struggle for Racial Equality in Oberlin, Ohio* (Baton Rouge: University of Louisiana Press, 2018); James Oliver Horton, "Black Education at Oberlin College: A Controversial Commitment," *The Journal of Negro Education* 54, no. 4 (1985): 477–99.

73   *"inner equality in ability and character"*: W. E. Bigglestone, "Oberlin College and the Negro Student, 1865–1940," *The Journal of Negro History* 56, no. 3 (1971): 198–219.

74   *prized his own intuition*: Given his intellectual influences and his experiences pastoring at a historic New England church, one might call Cleage a modern Transcendentalist. See Peter Wirzbicki, *Fighting for the Higher Law: Black and White Transcendentalists Against Slavery* (Philadelphia: University of Pennsylvania Press, 2021). See also Philip F. Gura, *Man's Better Angels: Romantic Reformers and the Coming of the Civil War* (Cambridge: Harvard University Press, 2017); Lydia Willsky, "The (Un)Plain Bible: New Religious Movements and Alternative Scriptures in Nineteenth-Century America," *Nova Religio: The Journal of Alternative and Emergent Religions* 17, no. 4 (2014): 13–36.

74   *Harry Ward's writing*: Doug Rossinow, "The Radicalization of the Social Gospel: Harry F. Ward and the Search for a New Social Order, 1898–1936," *Religion and American Culture: A Journal of Interpretation* 15, no. 1 (2005): 63–106.

74   *human history and human nature*: See Thomas S. Kepler, ed., *Contemporary Religious Thought: An Anthology* (Nashville: Abingdon-Cokesbury Press, 1941). Cleage had this book, which he annotated heavily, at Oberlin in 1942.

75   *a life that honored the collective good*: See Robin W. Lovin, *Reinhold Niebuhr and Christian Realism* (Cambridge, UK: Cambridge University Press, 1995). See also Reinhold Niebuhr, *Moral Man and Immoral Society: A Study in Ethics and Politics* (New York: Scribner, 1932).

75   *problem that demanded creative solutions*: Dennis N. Voskuil, "American Protestant Neo-Orthodoxy and Its Search for Realism (1925–1939)," *Ultimate Reality and Meaning* 8, no. 4 (1985): 277–87; Dennis N. Voskuil, "The Reformed Roots of American Neo-Orthodoxy," *Reformed Review: A Theological Journal of Western Theological Seminary* 39, no. 3 (1986): 271–80.

76   *lauded in the black press*: "Brevities," *Detroit Tribune*, November 5, 1938; "Social Sixteen Club," *Detroit Tribune*, December 4, 1937.

76   *founding trustee of Plymouth Congregational*: Kristin Cleage, "Plymouth Congregational Church," *Finding Eliza*, September 16, 2010.

76   *"policy of segregation and oppression"*: "Thunder on the Social Front," *Detroit Tribune*, January 29, 1944.

76   *"fog is too heavy or something"*: Kristin Cleage, "Christmas Day 1944—Part 3," *Finding Eliza*, December 21, 2011.

76   *One of Albert's former sociology teachers*: This was Charles Johnson, one of the most renowned black sociologists of the twentieth century. For more on Johnson's involvement with Cleage, see Walter Earl Fluker, ed., *The Papers of Howard Washington Thurman (Vol. 3): The Bold Adventure, September 1943–May 1949* (Columbia: University of South Carolina Press, 2015), 22–23.

76   *interim black co-pastor*: "Detroit Pastor to California Church," *Michigan Chronicle*, February 5, 1944.

76   *theologian and Christian socialist*: Peter Eisenstadt, *Against the Hounds of Hell: A Life of Howard Thurman* (Charlottesville: University of Virginia Press, 2021); Howard Thurman, *With Head and Heart: The Autobiography of Howard Thurman* (New York: Harcourt Brace Jovanovich, 1979).

76   *meeting with Mahatma Gandhi*: Quinton Dixie and Peter Eisenstadt, *Visions of a Better World: Howard Thurman's Pilgrimage to India and the Origins of African American Nonviolence* (Boston: Beacon Press, 2014).

77   *the interracial church movement*: Howard Thurman, *Footprints of a Dream: The Story of the Church for the Fellowship of All Peoples* (New York: Harper, 1959).

77   *"in many ways quite immature"*: Alfred G. Fisk letter to Howard Thurman, December 28, 1943, in *The Papers of Howard Washington Thurman*, 22.

78   *"isolated areas of living"*: Albert Cleage, Jr., "'Fellowship Church: Adventure in Interracial Understanding': Critical Analysis of First Six Months of San Francisco's Interracial Fellowship Church—Co-Pastored by One White and One Negro Minister," in *The Papers of Howard Washington Thurman*, 93.

78   *In Los Angeles*: Kristin Cleage, "Well, we is in Los Angeles . . . ," *Finding Eliza*, October 26, 2019; Kristin Cleage, "Christmas Day 1944—Part 2," *Finding Eliza*, December 21, 2011; Kristin Cleage, "Christmas Day 1944—Part 1," *Finding Eliza*, December 21, 2011; Kristin Cleage, "My Parents Smoking—1944 & 1952," *Finding Eliza*, May 2, 2013.

79   *"old New England Elite outfits"*: Kristin Cleage, "Guess we must be writing too often . . . ," *Finding Eliza*, January 30, 2012.

79   *"a more Christian world"*: Cleage, "Adventure in Interracial Understanding," 91

79   *not yet a black nationalist*: John H. Bracey, Jr., August Meier, and Elliot Rudwick, eds., *Black Nationalism in America* (Indianapolis: Bobbs-Merrill, 1970). This is an essential anthology covering the origins of black nationalism.

80   *The church Albert inherited*: National Register of Historic Places, "St. John's Congregational Church & Parsonage/Parish Home for Working Girls Registration Form," United States Department of the Interior, National Park Service, June 28, 2016. See also Imani Kazini, "Black Springfield: A Historical Study," *Contributions in Black Studies: A Journal of African and Afro-American Studies* 1 (1977): 5–14.

80   *restore St. John's*: "Springfield Pastor Takes Detroit Post," *Transcript-Telegram*, April 13, 1951.

80   *slavery-era plantation churches*: See Albert J. Raboteau, *Slave Religion: The "Invisible Institution" in the Antebellum South* (New York: Oxford University Press, 1978).

80   *suspicions of Communist influence*: In 1956, the progressive white Methodist minister Ralph Lord Roy, who would one day be a Freedom Rider in Albany, sheepishly wrote to Cleage asking whether he was a Communist. Roy was a representative for the Fund for the Republic, a project of the Ford Foundation that sought to promote free thought, pluralism, and minority rights in the United States. The reason for Roy's telegram was that Cleage's signature had been spotted on the Stockholm Peace Appeal, a global call for nuclear disarmament that first circulated in 1950, the year the United States intervened in the Korean War. W. E. B. Du Bois and Paul Robeson were among the black American signatories. The World Peace Council, which circulated the appeal, was accused by the federal government of being a Soviet front. Cleage replied to Roy that he had received the appeal while he lived in Springfield, though he never signed it. Still, he didn't disagree with the appeal's objective. "The use of atomic weapons must be banned if civilization is to continue!" he wrote to Roy. "I have never accepted the idea that 'truth' and 'goodness' automatically become 'evil' if they are supported by either Russian Communists or American Communists." Cleage said he did not sign the appeal because he did not want to be put under surveillance.

81   *Te Deum and Gloria Patri*: "St. Mark's Community Church Mother's Day Bulletin," May 11, 1952, Box 6, St. Mark's Presbyterian/Independent/Congregational Church, 1952–1954, Albert B. Cleage Jr. Papers, Bentley Historical Library, University of Michigan, Ann Arbor, MI.

81   *speakers such as Paul Robeson*: Martin Duberman, *Paul Robeson: A Biography* (New York: Alfred A. Knopf, 1988).

81   *thousands of new NAACP members*: "Devise New Methods to Get NAACP Members," *Detroit Tribune*, March 21, 1953; "Detroit NAACP Membership Drive Over Top," *Detroit Tribune*, May 30, 1953.

81 *followed him out*: "Church Members Quit in Squabble: Protest Dismissal," *Chicago Defender*, March 28, 1953.
82 *opened its auditorium for their use*: Lowell Locke, "Lolly Pop Society," *Detroit Tribune*, February 21, 1953.

Southeast Corner of My Cell

83 *Working under a false name*: The following account of Glanton's years leading up to his arrest in 1948 comes from a profile of Glanton in the Swedish publication *Ny i Sverige* [*New in Sweden*] 5, no. 4 (Stockholm: National Immigration Board, October 1976).
84 *little use anymore for talk of class revolt*: Erik S. Gellman, *Death Blow to Jim Crow: The National Negro Congress and the Rise of Militant Civil Rights* (Chapel Hill: University of North Carolina Press, 2014).
84 *one of the most powerful labor unions*: August Meier and Elliott Rudwick, *Black Detroit and the Rise of the UAW* (New York: Oxford University Press, 1979); Beth Tompkins Bates, *The Making of Black Detroit in the Age of Henry Ford* (Chapel Hill: University of North Carolina Press, 2012).
85 *the Art Institute of Chicago*: The Art Institute of Chicago had accepted black students since its inception in 1879. See Julia R. Myers, *Harold Neal and Detroit African American Artists: 1945 Through the Black Arts Movement* (Ypsilanti: Eastern Michigan University Art Galleries, 2020); Maggie Taft and Robert Cozzolino, eds., *Art in Chicago: A History from the Fire to Now* (Chicago: University of Chicago Press, 2018); Wadsworth A. Jarrell, *AFRICOBRA: Experimental Art Toward a School of Thought* (Durham: Duke University Press, 2020).
85 *never identify with any specific school*: See Lynne Cooke, ed., *Boundary Trouble in American Vanguard Art, 1920–2020* (New Haven: Yale University Press, 2022).
85 *fled the state*: "Glanton Dowdell Suspect Sought," *Detroit Tribune*, June 5, 1948.
86 *shot at the boss, killing him*: *Ny i Sverige*, October 1976.
86 *most certainly dead*: "Gunshot Fatal," *Detroit Free Press*, May 25, 1948.
86 *"John Singleton"*: "Sentences of Two in Assault Suspended," *Baltimore Evening Sun*, September 7, 1948.
86 *State Prison of Southern Michigan*: For a breakdown of Glanton's various run-ins with the law, see "Riots, Civil and Criminal Disorders: Hearings Before the Permanent Subcommittee on Investigations of the Committee on Government Operations, 90th Cong. (1968), 2nd sess." (Washington, D.C.: U.S. Government Printing Office, 1968).
86 *Glanton's time in prison was brutal*: For an account of a prison strike that Glanton led, see Betty DeRamus, "Glanton Dowdell: Artist, Drop-Out, Ex-Con, Leader," *Michigan Chronicle*, September 9, 1967.
86 *"long johns your only clothes"*: *Ny i Sverige*, October 1976.
86 *Department of Individual Treatment*: Robert L. Michaeu, "Prison Inmates Write, Paint Way to Freedom," *Battle Creek Enquirer*, February 23, 1958.
87 *"I sketch to overcome my depression"*: "Convict's Paintings Called 'Outstanding,'" *Battle Creek Enquirer*, October 7, 1956.
87 *an honorable mention*: "Local Artists Win Prizes at Exhibition in Detroit," *Lansing State Journal*, November 17, 1955.
87 *one-man shows*: Ken McCormick, "Convict Artist Ponders Loss of a Fortune," *Detroit Free Press*, September 4, 1956.
87 *They did not even need a canvas*: See Janie Paul, *Making Art in Prison: Survival and Resistance* (Los Angeles: Hat & Beard Press, 2023). See also Lisa M. Corrigan, *Prison Power: How Prison Influenced the Movement for Black Liberation* (Jackson: University Press of Mississippi, 2016).
88 *"further the evolutionary process"*: Joe Strickland, "Glanton Dowdell . . . Artist and Ten-Year Prisoner!" *Pittsburgh Courier*, December 12, 1959.
88 *depicting the life of the Negro in America*: "Inmate Painter Plans to Depict Life of Negro," *Lansing State Journal*, November 17, 1957.

Imperium in Imperio

93   *a public nuisance*: "No More Hoses in Street: Sweet Daddy Found Guilty as Nuisance," *Detroit Free Press*, July 27, 1957; James Sullivan, "Worshipers Are Tagged 'Nuisance': Sweet Daddy Grace Called to Court," *Detroit Free Press*, July 18, 1957.

93   *loudspeakers mounted on sound trucks*: "Religious Service 'Too Boisterous,'" *The News-Palladium*, July 18, 1957.

94   *lined with crimson silk*: "Sweet Daddy's Battle Against Sinners Ends," *Detroit Free Press*, January 13, 1960.

94   *under a sombrero*: John Driver, "Sweet Daddy's Debut Is No 'Spectacular,'" *Detroit Free Press*, April 26, 1956.

94   *believed he was God on earth*: Many people have written about the significance of Father Divine and the International Peace Mission Movement. See Jill Watts, *God, Harlem U.S.A.: The Father Divine Story* (Berkeley: University of California Press, 1992). In the 1930s and '40s, Father Divine's movement was the subject of psychological studies that described it as psychosis-inducing and cultlike. For example, Hadley Cantril and Muzafer Sherif, "The Kingdom of Father Divine," *Journal of Abnormal and Social Psychology* 33 (1938): 147–67; James A. Brussel, "Father Divine: Holy Precipitator of Psychoses," *The American Journal of Psychiatry* 92, no. 1 (1935): 215–23; Lauretta Bender and Zuleika Yarrell, "Psychoses Among Followers of Father Divine," *The Journal of Nervous and Mental Disease* 87, no. 4 (1938): 418–49. For more on this central figure of the black utopian tradition, see R. Marie Griffith, "Body Salvation: New Thought, Father Divine, and the Feast of Material Pleasures," *Religion and American Culture: A Journal of Interpretation* 11, no. 2 (2001): 119–53; Robert Weisbrot, *Father Divine and the Struggle for Racial Equality* (Champaign: University of Illinois Press, 1983); Keith V. Erickson, "Black Messiah: The Father Divine Peace Mission Movement," *Quarterly Journal of Speech* 63, no. 4 (1977): 428–38; F. Blair Mayne, "Beliefs and Practices of the Cult of Father Divine," *The Journal of Educational Psychology* 10, no. 5 (1937): 296–306; Kenneth E. Burnham, *God Comes to America: Father Divine and the Peace Mission Movement* (Boston: Lambeth Press, 1979).

95   *he called them his "heavens"*: Carleton Mabee, *Promised Land: Father Divine's Interracial Communities in Ulster County, New York* (Fleischmanns, NY: Purple Mountain Press, 2008).

95   *moved into a château*: "Sweet Daddy Buys the Prophet's Castle," *Detroit Free Press*, April 11, 1956. Sweet Daddy Grace, Prophet Jones, and Father Divine are often mentioned in the same breath. See also C. Eric Lincoln and Lawrence H. Mamiya, *Daddy Jones and Father Divine: The Cult as Political Religion* (Nashville: Abingdon-Cokesbury, 1979).

95   *Temple No. 1*: Historic Designation Advisory Board of the Detroit City Council, "The Proposed Masjid Wali Muhammad/Temple No. 1 Historic District (Originally known as Workmen's Circle): Final Report," February 19, 2013.

95   *NOI had gained notoriety*: See Clifton E. Marsh, *From Black Muslims to Muslims: The Transition from Separatism to Islam, 1930–1980* (Metuchen, NJ: Scarecrow Press, 1984); Edward E. Curtis IV, *Islam in Black America: Identity, Liberation, and Difference in African-American Islamic Thought* (Albany: State University of New York Press, 2002).

95   *"voodooism"*: "Pastors Decry Growth of Cult Practices Here," *Detroit Free Press*, November 28, 1932; "New Human Sacrifice with a Boy as Victim Is Averted by Inquiry," *Detroit Free Press*, November 26, 1932; "Voodoo University Raided by Police; 13 Cultists Seized," *Detroit Free Press*, April 17, 1934. See also Danielle N. Boaz, "The Voodoo Cult of Detroit: Race, Human Sacrifice, and the Nation of Islam from the 1930s to the 1970s," *The Journal of Interreligious Studies* 23 (2018): 17–30; Jacob S. Dorman, *The Princess and the Prophet: The Secret History of Magic, Race, and Moorish Muslims in America* (Boston: Beacon Press, 2020); Les Payne and Tamara Payne, *The Dead Are Arising: The Life of Malcolm X* (New York: Liveright, 2020), 254–55.

95   *a redevelopment project*: Richard R. Leclair, "A Case Study of the Gratiot Redevelopment Project" (master's thesis, Wayne State University, 1955); Robert L. Goodspeed, "Urban Renewal

in Postwar Detroit: The Gratiot Area Redevelopment Project: A Case Study" (undergraduate thesis, University of Michigan, 2004).

95 *Paradise Valley*: Jeremy Peters, "Cultural and Social Mecca: Entrepreneurial Action and Venue Agglomeration in Detroit's Paradise Valley and Black Bottom Neighborhoods," *Artivate* 9, no. 1 (2020): 20–41.

95 *Twelfth Street corridor*: For a history of this neighborhood, see Robert Conot, "The Crossroads of the City," in *American Odyssey: A History of a Great City* (Detroit: Wayne State University Press, 1986), 435–40. This monumental book also discusses Albert Cleage's leadership within Detroit's black nationalist cohort, 527–43.

96 *"mesmerized the Ghetto"*: Albert Cleage, Jr., "Eulogy for the Black Church," 1984, Box 3, Poetry: Holy Crusade Words of Inspiration: Poems of Jaramogi, 1984, Albert B. Cleage Jr. Papers.

96 *"wraps himself with the 'right people'"*: Albert Cleage, Jr., "The Negro in Detroit," 1961, Box 6, Preliminary Self-Study #2 1961, Albert B. Cleage Jr. Papers.

96 *new location for his church*: Horace White, letter to Edward Wilcox, December 31, 1954, Box 6, Preliminary Self-Study #2 1961, Albert B. Cleage Jr. Papers.

97 *Congregational communion*: For more on black people's relationship with the Congregational church and Central's search for a permanent location, see Melanee C. Harvey, "'Upon This Rock': Architectural, Material, and Visual Histories of Two Black Protestant Churches, 1881– 1969" (PhD diss., Boston University, 2017), 269–73.

97 *one of the first white utopian communities*: Heike Paul, "Pilgrims and Puritans and the Myth of the Promised Land," in *The Myths That Made America: An Introduction to American Studies* (Bielefeld, Germany: Transcript Verlag, 2014), 137–96.

97 *Central Congregational was ready to be filled*: "Central Congregational Holds First Services in New Edifice," *Detroit Tribune*, September 28, 1957.

97 *raking leaves, cleaning basements, and holding bake sales*: "Tribune's Neighborhood of the Week," *Detroit Tribune*, October 29, 1955.

97 *their work in the community*: "Central Congregational Church Youth Fellowship Yearbook," 1956, Box 11, Central Congregational Church publications, Albert B. Cleage Jr. Papers.

98 *elsewhere in the world for inspiration*: See Brenda Gayle Plummer, "A New Era" in *Rising Wind: Black Americans and U.S. Foreign Affairs, 1935–1960* (Chapel Hill: University of North Carolina Press, 1996), 257–98; Brenda Gayle Plummer, "'Freedom's Struggle Crosses Oceans and Mountains,'" in *In Search of Power: African Americans in the Era of Decolonization, 1956–1974* (Cambridge, UK: Cambridge University Press, 2013), 97–129.

99 *"unfilled hopes and unfilled threats"*: John F. Kennedy, "Acceptance of the Democratic Nomination for President" (speech, Democratic National Convention, Los Angeles, July 15, 1960), John F. Kennedy Presidential Library and Museum, jfklibrary.org/learn/about-jfk/historic -speeches/acceptance-of-democratic-nomination-for-president.

99 *some kind of spontaneous protest*: Albert Cleage, Jr., "Who Killed Cock Robin?" *The Illustrated News*, November 13, 1961.

99 *a lithographic printing shop*: Kristin Cleage, "Cleage Printers," *Finding Eliza*, August 1, 2012.

100 *a spate of violence against blacks*: "NAACP Probes Shooting," *The Illustrated News*, November 20, 1961; "'GOAL' Takes New Tack," *The Illustrated News*, November 13, 1961.

100 *terrible conditions at their schools*: For example, see "Letter Box: Teacher Supports Fight for Better Schools," *The Illustrated News*, January 8, 1962; "What's Wrong With Our Schools?" *The Illustrated News*, February 12, 1962; "Teacher Continues Northwestern Expose," *The Illustrated News*, February 19, 1962.

100 *the term* New Negro: Albert Cleage, "Struggle for Negro Equality," *The Illustrated News*, April 29, 1963.

101 *nonviolent tactics*: Tom Moylan, "'To Live Consciously Is to Sow the Whirlwind': Reflections on the Utopian Standpoint of Nonviolence," *Utopian Studies* 26, no. 1 (2015): 184–202.

101 *"a moral and spiritual superiority which is invincible"*: Cleage, "Struggle for Negro Equality."

101 *the era of automation*: Albert Cleage, Jr., "Crisis and Survival," *Michigan Chronicle*, June 1, 1968. See also Charles Denby, *Indignant Heart: A Black Worker's Journal* (Detroit: Wayne State University Press, 1952); Heather Ann Thompson, *Whose Detroit?: Politics, Labor, and Race in a Modern American City* (Ithaca: Cornell University Press, 2001).

101 *against school millage increases*: "Detroit School Millage, Bond Issue Defeated," *Detroit Tribune*, April 6, 1963.

102 *drew loud outcries*: "Rev. Cleage, Horace Sheffield Debate Millage," *Michigan Chronicle*, March 30, 1963.

102 *pastor of the New Bethel Baptist Church*: Nick Salvatore, *Singing in a Strange Land: C. L. Franklin, the Black Church, and the Transformation of America* (New York: Little, Brown, 2005).

102 *in the North as well*: Jeanne F. Theoharis and Komozi Woodard, eds., *Freedom North: Black Freedom Struggles Outside the South, 1940–1980* (New York: Palgrave Macmillan, 2003).

102 *"palace revolution"*: Albert Cleage, Jr., "Freedom March," *The Illustrated News*, June 10, 1963.

102 *"Detroit NAACP is a class organization"*: Ibid.

103 *When June 23 came*: "King, Cavanagh to Head March Down Woodward," *Detroit Free Press*, June 23, 1963; John Mueller and John Diebel, "Marchers Agree: 'It's a Great Day to be Walking,'" *Detroit Free Press*, June 24, 1963; "Road Beyond the End of the Freedom March," *Detroit Free Press*, June 25, 1963; Johnnie M. Holt, "What Kind of a Day Was It?" *Detroit Tribune*, July 6, 1963.

103 *"without even striking a blow"*: Albert Cleage, Jr., *Black Christian Nationalism: New Directions for the Black Church* (New York: William Morrow, 1972), xix.

103 *black business owners*: "Leaders Plan to Picket A&P," *Detroit Tribune*, June 22, 1963; "Marchers Call for Freedom," *Michigan Daily*, June 25, 1963.

103 *largest civil rights demonstration*: Martin Luther King, Jr., letter to Reverend C. L. Franklin, July 10, 1963, Martin Luther King, Jr., 1963, in C. L. Franklin Papers, 1957–1991, Bentley Historical Library, University of Michigan, Ann Arbor, Michigan.

103 *a philanthropic fund*: "Whites Move to Buy Control of Negro Civil Rights Fight," *The National Observer*, repr. *The Illustrated News*, July 8, 1963.

104 *last version of the man*: Albert Cleage, Jr., "Dr. King Did Teach Us," *Michigan Chronicle*, April 13, 1968; Albert Cleage, Jr., "A New Leadership Technique: Symbolic Protest," *The Illustrated News*, August 19, 1963.

104 *Freedom Now Party*: For more on the Freedom Now Party, see George Breitman, "How a Minority Can Change Society," *International Socialist Review* 25, no. 2 (1964): 34–41; Van Gosse, "The Black Freedom Struggle: From 'We Shall Overcome' to 'Freedom Now!'" in *Rethinking the New Left: An Interpretive History* (New York: Palgrave Macmillan, 2005), 31–52.

104 *"a clean break with the cold-war liberals"*: William Worthy, "A Call to Action: Freedom Now Party," *The Illustrated News*, September 2, 1963.

104 *the 1964 elections*: See also Richard Pyle, "'Freedom Now' Group Organizing," *The Herald-Palladium*, May 9, 1964; "CORE Meeting Disavows 'Freedom Now' Party Idea," *Battle Creek Enquirer*, May 4, 1964.

105 *"the people they were 'leading'"*: Albert Cleage, Jr., "Prelude to Revolution," *The Illustrated News*, November 25, 1963.

105 *unpalatable Marcus Garvey type*: Peniel E. Joseph, *Waiting 'til the Midnight Hour* (New York: Henry Holt, 2006), 87; "Rev. Cleage Quits Civil Rights Unit," *Detroit Free Press*, October 29, 1963.

106 *feel-good Walk to Freedom*: "Martin L. King Repudiates All Negro Party," *Ironwood Daily Globe*, November 2, 1964; "King Rips Negro Party," *Detroit Free Press*, October 31, 1964.

106 *"white clowns and black clowns"*: Malcolm X, "Message to the Grassroots," in *Malcolm X Speaks: Selected Speeches and Statements*, ed. George Breitman (New York: Grove Press, 1990), 3–17.

106 *borderless and black*: Ibid.

106 *message to the grassroots conference*: See Grace Lee Boggs, *Living for Change: An Autobiography* (Minneapolis: University of Minnesota Press, 1998), 128–30. For more on the importance of this speech, see also Garrett Felber, "'Harlem Is the Black World': The Organization of Afro-American Unity at the Grassroots," *The Journal of African American History* 100, no. 2 (2015): 199–225; Kwame Kalimara et al., "Witnesses to Struggle: Reflections on Oppression and Resistance in the USA," *Prabuddha: Journal of Social Equality* 2 (2018): 17–25.
106 *Christ dies on the cross*: Cleage, "Prelude to Revolution."

A Strategy of Chaos

110 *the pro-black* Illustrated News: There were other protests to *The Illustrated News*. See "Negro Paper Hit for Racism," *Fort Worth Star-Telegram*, August 4, 1962. For the church's stance on white attendance, see: "Code of Conduct," n.d., Box 10, Heritage Committee, Albert B. Cleage Jr. Papers: "White people attending services—The Nation is incorporated under the laws of the State of Michigan. The state laws forbids [*sic*] discrimination. Thus whites have a legal right to attend our services and we always have advance notice when they do." White people did occasionally attend services at Central Congregational (later, the Shrine), but in my conversations with former and current members, no one could recall a white member of the church. The only specific reference I could find to a white member of Central, who attended in the early 1960s, is in the *Detroit Free Press* reporter Hiley Ward's short biography of Albert Cleage, *Prophet of the Black Nation* (Philadelphia: Pilgrim Press, 1969). Her name was Lorene Smith Jandy. She may have been the last regularly attending white member of Cleage's church. The pastor reportedly said something abrasive, in reference to Jandy's presence, that caused her and some black parishioners to leave the church for good.
110 *this group left the church*: Alta Harrison, "A History of the Shrine of the Black Madonna with a Focus on the Development of Printed, Audio, and Visual Media," n.d., Box 4, History, Albert B. Cleage Jr. Papers.
110 *fair housing debates*: Sidney Fine, "Michigan and Housing Discrimination, 1949–1968," *Michigan Historical Review* 23, no. 2 (1997): 81–114.
110 *"every white home"*: Albert Cleage, Jr., "An All Black Party," October 11, 1963 (speech), repr., *Illustrated News*, February 17, 1964.
110 *"separate Negro communities"*: Albert Cleage, Jr., "The Next Step: Unite or Perish (part 3)," *Illustrated News*, January 13, 1964. For more on racial tensions amid Detroit's housing crises, see Michelle Wilde Anderson, *The Fight to Save the Town: Reimagining Discarded America* (New York: Avid Reader Press, 2022); Kevin Boyle, *Arc of Justice: A Saga of Race, Civil Rights, and Murder in the Jazz Age* (New York: Henry Holt, 2004); Thomas J. Sugrue, *The Origins of the Urban Crisis: Race and Inequality in Postwar Detroit* (Princeton: Princeton University Press, 1996); Richard Rothstein, *The Color of Law: A Forgotten History of How Our Government Segregated America* (New York: Liveright, 2017); Gerald C. Van Dusen, *Detroit's Birwood Wall: Hatred and Healing in the West Eight Mile Community* (Charleston, SC: History Press, 2019); Gerald C. Van Dusen, *Detroit's Sojourner Truth Housing Riot of 1942: Prelude to the Race Riot of 1943* (Charleston, SC: History Press, 2020).
111 *integration would never happen*: Albert Cleage, Jr., "Cleage Sees New Slavery; Calls for Organization," *Michigan Chronicle*, January 7, 1967.
111 *"sense of self-regard"*: Albert Cleage, Jr., "The Next Step (part 3)."
111 *distorting effects of self-hate*: See John H. Smith, "Nietzsche's 'Will to Power': Politics Beyond (Hegelian) Recognition," *New German Critique* 73 (1998): 133–63.
111 *"a program of complete disorder"*: Frantz Fanon, *The Wretched of the Earth*, trans. Constance Farrington (New York: Grove Press, 1963). See also Charles Athanasopoulos, "'A Program of Complete Disorder': The Black Iconoclasm Within Fanonian Thought," *Lateral: Journal of the Cultural Studies Association* 10, no. 1 (2021).
112 *Violence in self-defense*: Albert Cleage, Jr., "A Sense of Urgency," *Michigan Chronicle*, September 16, 1967.

113   *force concessions from Democrats*: "Negro Party Puts Strength to Test," *New York Times*, October 4, 1964.

113   *a few thousand votes*: Boggs, *Living for Change*, 134. See also "New Freedom Now Party Blanked But Not Broken," *Detroit Free Press*, November 5, 1964.

113   *simultaneous campaigns*: Roberta Mackey, "School Race Yields Surprise," *Detroit Free Press*, August 4, 1966; "Judge Rules Race for 2 Jobs Is OK," *Detroit Free Press*, June 18, 1966; "Primary Loser Urges Support Only for Negroes," *Detroit Free Press*, September 28, 1965.

113   *He wanted to win*: "Cleage Knocks Council, Police," *Michigan Chronicle*, July 17, 1965.

113   *It would be impractical*: Albert Cleage, Jr., "Are We Really Serious About Electing Blacks?" *Michigan Chronicle*, August 16, 1969.

114   *first black-owned bookstore*: National Register of Historic Places, "Vaughn's Book Store," United States Department of the Interior, National Park Service, February 28, 2023. See also "Black Literature Was a Vital Part of the Movement," *Michigan Chronicle*, February 15, 1968.

114   *Forum '66*: "Forum 66 Heritage Committee," 1966, Box 1, Folder 15, Edward Vaughn Papers, Walter P. Reuther Library, Wayne State University, Detroit, MI.

115   *Revolutionary Action Movement*: For more on RAM's relationship with Detroit activists, see Peniel E. Joseph, "Black Studies, Student Activism, and the Black Power Movement," in *The Black Power Movement: Rethinking the Civil Rights–Black Power Era*, ed. Peniel E. Joseph (New York: Routledge, 2006), 251–78; Muhammad Ahmad, *We Will Return in the Whirlwind: Black Radical Organizations, 1960–1975* (Chicago: Charles H. Kerr, 2007); Maxwell C. Stanford, "Revolutionary Action Movement (RAM): A Case Study of an Urban Revolutionary Movement in Western Capitalist Society" (master's thesis, Atlanta University, 1986).

115   *LeRoi Jones*: "Jones, Poussaint Are Among Speakers in Black Madonna Series," *Michigan Chronicle*, May 10, 1969.

115   *John Oliver Killens*: Albert Cleage, Jr., "We Are God's Chosen People," in *The Black Messiah* (New York: Sheed & Ward, 1968), 53: "John O. Killens . . . says the white folks took a black man and made a Nigger out of him. They robbed him of his dignity."

116   *the black nationalist turn in the 1960s*: For another perspective on the Black Arts Conference, see Melba Joyce Boyd, *Wrestling with the Muse: Dudley Randall and the Broadside Press* (New York: Columbia University Press, 2003), 126–27, 151. For more on the Black Arts Movement, see Jarrell, *AFRICOBRA*; Robert C. Maynard, "Negro Cultural Identity Is Black Nationalist Aim," *The Record*, October 2, 1967.

116   *Carmichael came back*: John Sinclair, "Stokely in Detroit: Who's Afraid of Black Power?" *Fifth Estate* 1, no. 16 (1966).

116   *Black Star Co-operative*: "By-Laws Cooperative Services, Inc.," n.d., Box 5, Cooperative Services, Inc., Albert B. Cleage Jr. Papers. See also Jessica Gordon Nembhard, *Collective Courage: A History of African American Cooperative Economic Thought and Practice* (University Park: Pennsylvania State University Press, 2014).

117   *Central's cultural committee*: Edward Vaughn, "Heritage Committee Report 1967," 1967, Box 10, Annual Report, 1967, Albert B. Cleage Jr. Papers; Edward Vaughn, "Welcome to the Black Nation!: A Guide for Members of Central United Church of Christ, the Shrine of the Black Madonna," 1968, Box 6, History, Draft, 1968, Albert B. Cleage Jr. Papers.

117   *dominant imagery of the past*: Edward Vaughn, "The Heritage Committee," 1966, Box 4, Annual Report, 1966, Albert B. Cleage Jr. Papers.

117   *DaVinci, and Angelo,*: Harold G. Lawrence, "Black Madonna," *Negro Digest* (June 1962): 52.

118   *Leslie and Glanton married*: Leslie Pursche, interview by author, September 2020.

"You Were Beautiful When Your Apparition Formed"

119   *the Navy or the nunnery*: Rose Waldon, interview by author, spring 2021.

121   *portrait study in charcoal*: For an extensive discussion of the art historical importance of Glanton Dowdell's Madonna mural, and a key document on Glanton himself, see Harvey, "'Upon This Rock.'"

122 *"hummed, chattered, and laughed"*: Dowdell, unpublished memoir.

123 *a divine archetype*: Courtney Hall Lee, *Black Madonna: A Womanist Look at Mary of Nazareth* (Eugene, OR: Wipf & Stock, 2017).

123 *glints of recognition*: Albert Cleage owned a copy of the American Methodist minister Halford E. Luccock's *Unfinished Business: Short Diversions on More than 100 Religious Themes* (New York: Harper & Brothers, 1956). Cleage annotated some sections, including the chapter "Image Making and Breaking," which begins: "One of the most powerful forces that act on every one of us is the image of ourselves that we carry around with us inside of our heads in our imaginations [. . .] The chief handicap that many people have is not a poor brain, but the wrong pictures of themselves, which come to dominate them [. . .] One of the biggest things Jesus did for men was to break up negative images they had of themselves and substitute positive images. He was both an image-breaker and an image-maker."

123 *various mythic traditions*: Robin Coste Lewis, *Voyage of the Sable Venus* (New York: Alfred A. Knopf, 2015).

123 *mystery of the Black Madonna's color*: Monique Scheer, "From Majesty to Mystery: Change in the Meanings of Black Madonnas from the Sixteenth to Nineteenth Centuries," *American Historical Review* 107, no. 5 (2002): 1412–40; Elina Gertsman, "The Lives and Afterlives of Shrine Madonnas," *California Italian Studies* 6, no. 1 (2016); Cassandra Walker, "The Role of Popular Piety in the Development of Black Madonna Iconography" (master's thesis, Georgetown University, 2011).

124 *best embodied the Aquarian age*: See Melanie Rose Landman, "An Investigation into the Phenomenon of the Black Madonna" (PhD diss., University of Roehampton, 2012); Ean Begg, *The Cult of the Black Virgin* (Wilmette, IL: Chiron Publications, 1985).

124 *an enemy of capitalism*: Anna Fedele, "'Black' Madonna Versus 'White' Madonna: Gendered Power Strategies in Alternative Pilgrimages to Marian Shrines," in *Gender and Power in Contemporary Spirituality: Ethnographic Approaches*, ed. Anna Fedele and Kim Knibbe (New York: Routledge, 2013), 96–114; Timothy Charles Murphy, "The Influence of Socialism in Black and Womanist Theologies: Capitalism's Relationship as Source, Sin, and Salvation," *Black Theology: An International Journal* 10, no. 1 (2012): 28–48.

124 *a humiliating failure*: Betty DeRamus, "'Keep the Faith' Strike Splits Community," *Michigan Chronicle*, January 28, 1967.

124 *"only a minority of his own people"*: Richard M. Woodruff, "Conyers Tops Cleage," *Detroit Free Press*, March 12, 1967.

124 *what of her son?*: Alex Poinsett, "Quest for Black Christ," *Ebony*, March 1969.

125 *the life of Jesus*: Philip F. Gura, *American Transcendentalism: A History* (New York: Hill and Wang, 2007), 21–45.

125 *son of the biblical Noah*: David M. Goldenberg, *The Curse of Ham: Race and Slavery in Early Judaism, Christianity, and Islam* (Princeton: Princeton University Press, 2003); Gay L. Byron, *Symbolic Blackness and Ethnic Difference in Early Christian Literature* (London: Routledge, 2002).

125 *Countee Cullen and Langston Hughes*: Countee Cullen, "The Black Christ," in *The Black Christ and Other Poems* (New York: Harper & Brothers, 1929); Langston Hughes "Christ in Alabama," *Contempo: A Review of Books and Personalities* 1, no. 4 (1931).

125 *Du Bois*: See Phil Maciak, "The Double Life of Superimposition: W. E. B. Du Bois's Black Christ Cycle," in *The Disappearing Christ: Secularism in the Silent Era* (New York: Columbia University Press, 2019), 134–75.

125 *the southern Levant*: Albert Cleage, Jr., "Our Glorious Past," *Michigan Chronicle*, September 13, 1969.

125 *a mixed-race Middle Easterner*: Colin Kidd, *The Forging of Races: Race and Scripture in the Protestant Atlantic World, 1600–2000* (Cambridge: Cambridge University Press, 2006), 258–59.

126 *nearly escalated into a riot*: Policing and Social Justice HistoryLab/U-M Carceral State Project,

"The Kercheval Incident, Detroit 1966: The Police Department's Illegal War on Black Power Activists," May 2021, storymaps.arcgis.com/stories/d626e10a71f44968ad7ce4ca0bd85ed8; Betty DeRamus, "Solitary Soldiers Can't Win the Battle," *Michigan Chronicle*, April 8, 1967.

126 *"weary earth mother"*: Ellen Goodman, "Black Madonna Stirs Empathy of Negroes," *Detroit Free Press*, March 25, 1967.

127 *"we despised ourselves"*: Cleage, *The Black Messiah*, 85. The exact language from Cleage's spoken sermon differs slightly from what is reproduced here on the page.

127 *"the good of black people"*: Ward, *Prophet of the Black Nation*, xvi.

127 *"we can hear the voice of God"*: Cleage, *The Black Messiah*, 6.

A New Faith

128 *fighting had broken out*: Cleage, *The Black Messiah*, 117.

128 *"Little boys who are nasty"*: Ibid.

129 *a rebellion*: Sidney Fine, *Violence in the Model City: The Cavanagh Administration, Race Relations, and the Detroit Riot of 1967* (1989, repr., East Lansing: Michigan State University Press, 2007); Max Arthur Herman, *Summer of Rage: An Oral History of the 1967 Newark and Detroit Riots* (New York: Peter Lang, 2017); Joel Stone, ed., *Detroit 1967: Origins, Impacts, Legacies* (Detroit: Wayne State University Press, 2017).

129 *thirty-four deaths*: Dominic J. Capeci, Jr., and Martha Wilkerson, *Layered Violence: The Detroit Riots of 1943* (1991, repr., Jackson: University of Mississippi Press, 2009); Alfred McClung Lee and Norman Draymond Humphrey, *Race Riot* (New York: Dryden Press, 1943).

129 *what a new and better world might look like*: On the utopian potential of urban rebellions, see Tikkun Bambara, "Daunte Wright: A Billion Clusters of Rebellion and Starlight," *Mn Artists*, April 19, 2021, mnartists.walkerart.org/daunte-wright-a-billion-clusters-of-rebellion-and-starlight; Tikkun Bambara, "Poly-fugitivity: Utopian Relations in Dystopian Structures," *Mn Artists*, January 15, 2021, mnartists.walkerart.org/poly-fugitivity-utopian-relations-in-dystopian-structures.

129 *"artifacts of their own haunted fate"*: Coleman Young and Lonnie Wheeler, *Hard Stuff: The Autobiography of Mayor Coleman Young* (Detroit: Wayne State University, 1994), 172.

129 *an unfounded conspiracy*: Boggs, *Living for Change*, 138. For more on Vaughn's legacy, see Danton Wilson, "Way of Life for Vaughn," *Michigan Chronicle*, December 11, 1982.

131 *"we won't tolerate anymore"*: Following the deaths of three black teenagers at the Algiers Motel in Detroit during the rebellion, at the hands of three rogue police officers, a "people's tribunal" was held at the Shrine of the Black Madonna. Among the jurors were the novelist John Killens, the Detroit resident Rosa Parks, and other local activists. The three cops suffered no legal consequences for their actions. At the conclusion of the mock trial at Cleage's church, which received wide media coverage, all three officers (as well as one black security guard) were found guilty. The events surrounding the Algiers Motel murders and the People's Tribunal at the Shrine have become central to the mythos of the rebellion. See John Hersey, *The Algiers Motel Incident* (New York: Alfred A. Knopf, 1968), 345–52; Jeanne Theoharis, *The Rebellious Life of Mrs. Rosa Parks* (Boston: Beacon Press, 2013), 197–99; Albert Cleage, "Tribunal Proves Now Fear is Gone," *Michigan Chronicle*, September 9, 1967.

131 *he vowed to rebuild*: For more on New Detroit, see Matthew Birkhold, "Theory and Practice: Organic Intellectuals and Revolutionary Ideas in Detroit's Black Power Movement, 1954–1972" (PhD diss., Binghamton University, 2016); Joel Mason Batterman, "A Metropolitan Dilemma: Regional Planning, Governance and Power in Detroit, 1945–1995" (PhD diss., University of Michigan, 2021), 103–105.

131 *Citywide Citizens Action Committee*: Albert Cleage, Jr., "Report to the Annual Meeting," *CCAC News*, January 22, 1969, Box 5, Citywide Citizen's Action Committee, 1967–1968,"Albert B. Cleage Jr. Papers; Albert Cleage, Jr., "Days of Decision (part 2): The White Man's Choice," *Michigan Chronicle*, October 7, 1967; Albert Cleage, Jr., "Unite or Perish," *Michigan Chronicle*, August 26, 1967.

131 *"a separate Negro state"*: Gary Blonston, "How Detroit's Militants Are Changing," *Detroit Free Press*, October 1, 1967. See also Albert Cleage, Jr., "'We Must Unite': Strong Efforts Made to Avoid Fragmentation," *Michigan Chronicle*, August 26, 1967.

132 *Rev. Cleage was the ringleader*: For more on Cleage's reputation, see Joseph, *Waiting 'til the Midnight Hour*, 54–63, 73–76; Albert J. Dunmore, "Events Impacting Black Detroit Since 1960," *Michigan Chronicle*, February 15, 1986.

132 *emigrationist seeking the western shores of Africa*: For histories of black emigration movements, see Edwin S. Redkey, *Black Exodus: Black Nationalist and Back-to-Africa Movements, 1890–1910* (New Haven: Yale University Press, 1969); Chris Dixon, *African Americans and Haiti: Emigration and Black Nationalism in the Nineteenth Century* (New York: Praeger, 2000); James Ciment, *Another America: The Story of Liberia and the Former Slaves Who Ruled It* (New York: Hill & Wang, 2013); Leslie M. Alexander, "Black Utopia: Haiti and Black Transnational Consciousness in the Early Nineteenth Century," *The William and Mary Quarterly* 78, no. 2 (2021): 215–22.

132 *the moderates*: "New Group to Contribute to the Dialogue in Detroit," *Detroit Free Press*, August 25, 1967; William Serrin, "Negro Plan Puts Committee on Spot," *Detroit Free Press*, December 31, 1967; Roger Allaway, "2 Negro Factions May Divide Funds," *Detroit Free Press*, January 5, 1968.

132 *a repeat of summer '67 in summer '68*: "Negroes Told to Be Ready for Rioting This Summer," *Journal Herald*, April 2, 1968; "Kennedy Entry Seen Cooling Summer," *News Journal*, March 16, 1968.

132 *the drastic move*: John Lottier, "Turning Off with Bob McBridge," *Michigan Daily*, January 26, 1968.

133 *in a private meeting*: Karl Gregory, "Dr. Karl Gregory," interview by Tobi Voigt, Detroit Historical Society Oral and Written History Archive, September 1, 2015, detroit1967 .detroithistorical.org/items/show/249.

133 *"What happened in Detroit"*: "Detroit Moving on Race Problem but Negroes Question Direction," *Newsday* (Suffolk Edition), February 20, 1968.

133 *"more important than anything"*: Gene Schroeder, "Black Nationalist Leaders' Move in Detroit May Set Pattern," *Battle Creek Enquirer*, January 10, 1968.

133 *three hundred ministers*: "Statement by National Committee of Negro Churchmen," *New York Times*, July 31, 1966.

133 *an imminent confederation*: "The Black Christian Nationalist Movement," 1967, Box 4, Annual Report, 1967, Albert B. Cleage Jr. Papers. For a short history of BCN's formation and a criticism of the black church, see Albert Cleage, Jr., "The Black Christian Nationalist Movement," *Michigan Chronicle*, January 11, 1969.

134 *"competent leadership"*: Albert Cleage, Jr., letter to Reverend Charles Cobb, December 3, 1967, Box 1, Correspondence, 1967, Albert B. Cleage Jr. Papers.

134 *his black theology*: Ann-Mary Currier, "Christ Black, Convention Told," *Boston Globe*, November 9, 1968.

134 *a bomb threat*: "Schools Closed in Inkster," *Lansing State Journal*, November 9, 1967; "Bomb Hoax Routs 600 in Meeting," *Detroit Free Press*, November 11, 1967; Kathy Colton, "Expulsion of Students Weighed," *Detroit Free Press*, November 16, 1967; "Two Schools Closed After Students Riot," *Detroit Free Press*, November 10, 1967; "Police Quell Outbreak at School," *Detroit Free Press*, November 9, 1967.

134 *"a scale model of Central Church"*: William H. Colquitt, "Mission Report—Temple of the Black Messiah," December 30, 1967, Box 10, Annual Report, 1967, Albert B. Cleage Jr. Papers.

New Afrika

139 *a provisional government*: "Black Power Separatists Form Republic of New Africa," *Holland Evening Sentinel*, April 2, 1968.

139 *Black Belt of the South*: See Edward C. Onaci, *Free the Land: The Republic of New Afrika and the Pursuit of a Black Nation-State* (Chapel Hill: University of North Carolina Press, 2020).

Utopian plans that would have relocated African Americans within the United States abound in American history, not all of them conceived by black people. In 1986, a fringe white supremacist group called the Aryan Nations created a map for a territory they called New America, which would have encompassed California, Nevada, Wyoming, Oregon, Washington, Idaho, Montana, British Columbia, and other locations throughout the United States and Canada. In New America, much of the middle section of the country would have been given over to the Nation of Islam. A vast part of the East Coast would comprise the so-called land of ZOG (Zionist Occupation Government). See Michael Barkun, "Racist Apocalypse: Millennialism on the Far Right," *American Studies* 31, no. 2 (1990): 121–40.

139   *Republic of New Afrika*: "Black Government Parley Called," *Michigan Chronicle*, March 23, 1968.

140   *"an independent nation"*: Malcolm X, "Message to the Grassroots."

140   *geographical interpretation of black separatism*: Ward, *Prophet of the Black Nation*, 18–20, 191–92. See also Dan Berger, "'The Malcolm X Doctrine': The Republic of New Afrika and National Liberation on U.S. Soil," in *Freedom on My Mind: The Columbia Documentary History of the African American Experience*, ed. Manning Marable, John McMillian, and Nishani Frazier (New York: Columbia University Press, 2003), 46–55. For an explicit definition of Cleage's concept of a nation-within-a-nation, see Albert Cleage, Jr., "Black Power Is the Answer—Not the Problem (part 1)," *Michigan Chronicle*, July 6, 1968. On visions of black freedom beyond the nation-state, see William C. Anderson, *The Nation on No Map: Black Anarchism and Abolition* (Chico, CA: AK Press, 2021).

140   *branch secretary for the Communist Party USA*: Henry Jacob, "How Queen Mother Moore Constructed Black Communities and Identity," *EUREKA: Social and Humanities* 1 (2022): 74–80.

140   *RNA's planned colony*: "'Black Government' Group Wants 5 Southern States," *Oakland Tribune*, March 31, 1968. Imari Obadele, in 1975, would compare the RNA to the "scattered colonies of freedmen all across the Union-occupied Confederacy," including Davis Bend. See also Imari Abubakari Obadele I, "National Black Elections Held by Republic of New Africa," *The Black Scholar* 7, no. 2 (1975): 27–30, 35–38.

140   *"to build a New Society"*: Southern Conference Educational Fund, "Mississippi . . . Old and New," 1972, Box 86, Folder 13, Clarie Collins Harvey Papers, Amistad Research Center, New Orleans, LA.

140   *to claim legitimacy*: Imari Abubakari Obadele, "People's Revolt Against Poverty: An Appeal and Challenge," *The Black Scholar* 9, no. 8/9 (1978): 35–39.

141   *"chemical warfare"*: Obadele, "National Black Elections," 37.

141   *Black Belt–bound exodus*: Paul Karolczyk, "Subjugated Territory: The New Afrikan Independence Movement and the Space of Black Power" (PhD diss., Louisiana State University and Agricultural and Mechanical College, 2014).

141   *headlines across the country*: James T. Anderson, "The Republic of New Africa: Genesis," *Boston Globe*, April 26, 1970.

141   *ended with a shootout*: Imari Abubakari Obadele, "The Struggle of the Republic of New Africa," *The Black Scholar* 5, no. 9 (1974): 32–41.

141   *The arrest of eleven RNA members*: Imari Abubakari Obadele, "Open Letter to U.S. President Jimmy Carter from RNA President Imari Abubakari Obadele I," *The Black Scholar* 10, no. 2 (1978): 53–67.

142   *systematically targeted and arrested*: For a detailed account of the persecution of RNA associates, see Chokwe Lumumba, "Short History of the U.S. War on the R.N.A.," *The Black Scholar* 12, no. 1 (1981): 72–81; Danton Wilson, "In 1970s, Stories Were on Militant Black Groups and Police Activities," *Michigan Chronicle*, September 27, 1986.

142   *"the land of the Beast"*: Imari Abubakari Obadele, letter to Albert Cleage, Jr., from Hinds County Jail, October 11, 1971, Box 1, Correspondence, 1971, Albert B. Cleage Jr. Papers.

142   *New Afrikans were also in the Shrine*: "Seek to Raise Bail for RNA President," *Michigan*

Chronicle, January 15, 1972. Imara Hyman, a former member of the Black Christian Nationalist and New Afrikan movements, told me this: "There were some people at Highland Park Community College who were members of the RNA. They would pass out literature. I went to a few meetings and at that point I really didn't have a clear focus, but the idea of black people being independent and totally autonomous inside of this country touched my heart more so than anything else. It seemed like the best thing for us to do because we were in perpetual struggle in this country to be looked at as human beings and be treated in an equitable manner. [. . .] We had a little office on Linwood, and we would come to meetings. They were organizing meetings in terms of how to set up a government. What were the important things in terms of running a country? [We were] sitting there like we were going to run a country very soon, talking about the things that were needed. Running a country would not be glamorous or fun. It would be hard work, it would be nasty, it would be dirty. I remember specifically somebody talking about, you know, you have to have a sewer system."

142   *fund the legal defense*: "Free on Bail, RNA Prexy Praises Detroit Support," *Michigan Chronicle*, April 21, 1973.

142   *open-minded approaches to religion*: Onaci, *Free the Land*, 119–25, 153–57.

143   *"cooperative economics"*: Yusufu Sonebeyatta and Joseph F. Brooks, "Ujamaa for Land and Power," *The Black Scholar* 3, no. 2 (1971): 13–20.

143   *Eugene McCarthy's presidential bid*: Daniel Okrent, "Eugene, Oh Eugene, Where to Now?" *Michigan Daily*, July 30, 1968; "Say Nationalists: 'We Are Not for McCarthy,'" *Michigan Chronicle*, August 3, 1968; Albert Cleage, Jr., "Law and Order," *Michigan Chronicle*, September 14, 1968.

143   *James Forman's 1969 Black Manifesto*: Albert Cleage, Jr., "Black Preachers Speak from Oakland (parts 1 and 2)," *Michigan Chronicle*, January 3 and 10, 1970; Albert Cleage, Jr., "How Liberal Is the White Church? (parts 1, 2 and 3)," January 31, February 14, and February 21, 1970; "RNA Blasts 'Idiocy' of Forman Reparation Plan," *Michigan Chronicle*, May 10, 1969. See also Keith Dye, "The Black Manifesto for Reparations in Detroit: Challenge and Response, 1969," *Michigan Historical Review* 35, no. 2 (2009): 53–83; John B. Coburn, "Blacks and the Church," *New York Times*, March 15, 1970; Thomas A. Johnson, "Black Press Reparations Demands," *New York Times*, June 10, 1970; Duke L. Kwon and Gregory Thompson, *Reparations: A Christian Call for Repentance and Repair* (Grand Rapids, MI: Baker Publishing Group, 2021); Michael T. Martin and Marilyn Yaquinto, eds., *Redress for Historical Injustices in the United States: On Reparations for Slavery, Jim Crow, and Their Legacies* (Durham: Duke University Press, 2007); Katrina Forrester, "Reparations, History and the Origins of Global Justice," in *Empire, Race and Global Justice* (Cambridge: Cambridge University Press, 2019), 22–51.

143   *black capitalist mindset*: Karl Gregory, interview by Tobi Voigt.

Politisk Asyl åt Glanton Dowdell!

148   *a target on his back*: Aretha Watkins, "Black Activist Target of Assassins' Bullets," *Michigan Chronicle*, December 9, 1967.

148   *the world of illegal gambling*: The following account comes from Aktionsenheten för politisk asyl åt glanton Dowdell, *Politisk asyl åt Glanton Dowdell* [Action Committee for Political Asylum for Glanton Dowdell, *Political Asylum for Glanton Dowdell*], 1971. All translations in this book from Swedish are courtesy of Kira Josefsson (kirajosefsson.com).

149   *one of the white men*: "Dowdell Charges Frame-Up," *Michigan Chronicle*, March 16, 1968.

149   *becoming untenable*: Ahmad A. Rahman, "Marching Blind: The Rise and Fall of the Black Panther Party in Detroit," in *Liberated Territory: Untold Local Perspectives on the Black Panther Party*, ed. Yohuru Williams and Jama Lazerow (Durham: Duke University Press, 2008), 181–231; Akinyele Omowale Umoja, "Repression Breeds Resistance: The Black Liberation Army and the Radical Legacy of the Black Panther Party," *New Political Science* 21, no. 2 (1999): 131–55.

149 *"street workers"*: Vaughn, interview by author.

150 *"a cultural regression"*: "Glanton Dowdell: The Fight Against Drugs," *Aftonbladet*, March 21, 1971, reprinted in *Political Asylum for Glanton Dowdell!*

151 *"not yet ready for that"*: Dowdell, unpublished memoir.

151 *"his creative ingenuity"*: Glanton Dowdell, "Comments on Chess," *Weekly Progress*, September 16, 1960.

151 *"the underworld or the underground"*: Albert Dunmore and C. C. Douglas, "'Underworld or Underground?' Detroit Cops Ask in 3 Slayings," *New Pittsburgh Courier*, May 18, 1968. See also "Gangland Murders Under FBI Probe," *Baltimore Afro-American*, May 7, 1968.

151 *protection from the authorities*: Federal Bureau of Investigation (FBI), redacted communication on black nationalist activity in Detroit, May 3, 1968, U.S. Department of Justice, Communications Section, Washington, D.C.

151 *drugs were affecting the city*: "The Fight Against Drugs," *Aftonbladet*.

151 *clippings about the uprising*: Tryggve Hedtjärn, emails to the author, September 5 and 28, 2020.

152 *for a Swedish audience*: Göran Olsson, *The Black Power Mixtape, 1967–1975* (New York: IFC Films, 2001), Amazon Prime Video. The connections between left-sympathizing Swedes and African American liberation movements are profound. During my research, I became acquainted with the Swedish filmmaker Mats Hjelm (matshjelm.se). His father, Lars, was, like Mats himself, a documentary filmmaker. Lars came to Detroit in 1967 to document the Rebellion. His footage of rallies, speeches by Black Power leaders such as Albert Cleage, and civilian confrontations with the police would later be used in various films and installations that Mats made, including *White Flight* (1997) and *Black Nation* (Herrlander Pictures, 2008). *Black Nation* was Mats's first film about the Shrine of the Black Madonna. His second film about the church, *A Pan-African Mission* (Herrlander Pictures, 2022), documents the Shrine's complicated effort to establish a satellite church in Monrovia, Liberia, in the years after Detroit's declaration of bankruptcy. The film is a fascinating snapshot of the relationship between African Americans, U.S. imperialism, and the trope of African redemption. See also Michele Mitchell, "'The Black Man's Burden': African Americans, Imperialism, and Notions of Racial Manhood, 1890–1910," *International Review of Social History* 44, no. 7 (1999): 77–99.

152 *soldiers who found refuge in Sweden*: Seymour M. Hersh, "Deserters Find Sweden a Home," *New York Times*, October 9, 1972; Barnaby J. Feder, "Deserters in Sweden: An Odd Little 'V.F.W. Post,'" *New York Times*, June 17, 1985.

153 *state welfare systems*: Devin Joshi and Neha Navlakha, "Social Democracy in Sweden," *Economic and Political Weekly* 45, no. 47 (2010): 73–80.

153 *Swedish Committee for Vietnam*: See Carl-Gustaf Scott, *Swedish Social Democracy and the Vietnam War* (Huddinge, Sweden: Södertörn University, 2017).

153 *minorities in the country*: See Martin Ericsson, "What Happened to 'Race' in Race Biology?: The Swedish State Institute for Race Biology, 1936–1960," *Scandinavian Journal of History* 46, no. 1 (2020): 125–48. For views on racial issues in contemporary Sweden, see Tiro Sanandaji, "Swedes and Immigration: End of Homogeneity?" *Fondation pour L'Innovation Politique*, August 2018, fondapol.org/en/study/swedes/; Mathilda Åkerlund, "The Sweden Paradox: US Far-Right Fantasies of a Dystopian Utopia," *Journal of Ethnic and Migration Studies* (2023): 1–20.

153 *one historian asked in 1972*: Robert G. Weisbord, "Scandinavia: A Racial Utopia?" *Journal of Black Studies* 2, no. 4 (1972): 471–88. See also Dominic Hinde, *A Utopia Like Any Other: Inside the Swedish Model* (Edinburgh: Luath Press, 2016). For a general history of Scandinavia's mythological (and racialist) allure, see Bernd Brunner, *Extreme North: A Cultural History* (New York: W. W. Norton, 2022).

153 *relocated to Sweden*: A *Dagens Nyheter* article dated October 21, 1978, describes Glanton Dowdell as one of several black artists who fled the United States starting in the 1950s and

ended up in Sweden. Other examples included Jerry Harris, George Murphy, Alfred Hicks, and Clifford Jackson.

153   *committees to support Black Panthers*: Dennis Levitt and Linda Gage, "Black Panthers Meet in Copenhagen," *Los Angeles Free Press*, April 2, 1971.

153   *black ex-soldiers*: The case of Joseph Parra was a well-known example. See "Sweden Expels U.S. Military Deserter," *Tampa Tribune*, November 26, 1970; "Sweden Deports GI Deserter on Drug Charge; 14 Others to Go," *Philadelphia Inquirer*, November 26, 1970; George Varcoe, "Tough Policy on U.S. Deserter," *Kansas City Times*, November 30, 1970.

154   *hanging from gallows*: "Fleeing Negro Leader Seeks Asylum in Sweden," *Dagens Nyheter*, April 11, 1970.

154   *FBI and CIA on alert*: Frank K. Rafalko, *MH/Chaos: The CIA's Campaign Against the Radical New Left and the Black Panthers* (Annapolis: Naval Institute Press, 2011), 138–40.

154   *a prosecutor in Detroit*: "Secret Agent Tapped to Bring Dowdell Home," *Dagens Nyheter*, April 3, 1971.

154   *Glanton's bid for asylum*: Action Committee for Political Asylum, *Political Asylum for Glanton Dowdell*. See also the Black Caucuses Association for International Black Appeal, "A Profile of Glanton Dowdell (at Home and Abroad)," 1971.

154   *Hans Göran Franck*: "Negro Leader Detained in Stockholm," *Dagens Nyheter*, March 16, 1971.

154   *global abolition of the death penalty*: Hans Göran Franck, *The Barbaric Punishment: Abolishing the Death Penalty* (Leiden, Netherlands: Martinus Nijhoff Publishers, 2003).

155   *"he knows his fate"*: "Fleeing Negro Leader," *Dagens Nyheter*.

155   *in touch with his family*: Aretha Watkins, "Son of Exiled Artist Birthday Wish: 'To Be with My Father Again,'" *Michigan Chronicle*, March 6, 1971.

155   *autoworker militancy*: On the League of Revolutionary Black Workers, see Dan Georgakas and Marvin Surkin, *Detroit: I Do Mind Dying: A Study in Urban Revolution* (New York: St. Martin's Press, 1975). See also Mark Jay and Philip Conklin, *A People's History of Detroit* (Durham: Duke University Press, 2020); Michael Hamlin with Michele Gibbs, *A Black Revolutionary's Life in Labor: Black Workers Power in Detroit* (Detroit: Against the Tide Books, 2013); Walda Katz-Fishman and Jerome Scott, "Race, Class, and Revolution in the Twenty-First Century: Lessons from the League of Revolutionary Black Workers," in *The Oxford Handbook of Karl Marx*, ed. Matt Vidal et al. (New York: Oxford University Press, 2018), 441–462; Birkhold, "Theory and Practice"; Luke S. Tripp, "Black Working Class Radicalism in Detroit, 1960–1970," *Ethnic and Women's Studies Working Papers* 7 (1994); Quinn Evans, Ruth E. Mills, Saundra Little, "The Civil Rights Movement and the African American Experience in 20th Century Detroit, Michigan: Part 1: Historic Context," Survey Report for Michigan State Historic Preservation Office, April 2021.

155   *the League's grassroots support*: Ahmad, *We Will Return in the Whirlwind*, 260.

155   *invisible glue that kept the League together*: John Bracey, Jr., email to author, May 12, 2021.

156   *Swedish Prosecution Authority*: "Detroit Militant Asks for Political Asylum in Sweden," *Traverse City Record-Eagle*, May 6, 1970; "Supreme Court to Determine Extradition of Negro Leader," *Dagens Nyheter*, March 17, 1971.

156   *a cause célèbre*: John Sundholm, "History Is, Media Studies Is," *European Journal of Media Studies* 10, no. 2 (2021): 93–97; "On Television Today: Detroit's Auto Plants—the New Plantations," *Dagens Nyheter*, March 23, 1971.

156   Reject US Government Pressure: "Swedes Demand Asylum for Glanton," *The Inner-City Voice* 2, no. 6 (1970); "Demonstrators Demand: Give Dowdell Asylum!" *Dagens Nyheter*, March 22, 1971.

156   *Joe Hill*: Bo Widerberg, dir., *Joe Hill* (New York: Paramount Pictures, 1971). In his Sergel's Square speech, Glanton said the following: "Sweden has an uncorrupted justice system. You might think that because there are certain similarities between the two countries, the United States' legal system resembles Sweden's. You might be inclined to think that cases like Bobby Seale, Angela Davis, Sacco and Vanzetti, and Joe Hill are exceptions to the rule. They are not.

These represent the hard reality of how things unfold as a rule, breaking through the varnish of propaganda [. . .] Workers of all nations, no matter their race or nationality, will triumph over the powers of tyranny and greed. Of this, I am convinced. Once that happens there will be no more Joe Hill, Sacco, Vanzetti, no more Bobby Seale or Angela Davis, no more miscarriages of justice against representatives of the people's wishes, known or unknown."

156 *a protest in Finland*: "Finnish Demonstrations in the Dowdell Case," *Dagens Nyheter*, March 23, 1971.

156 *"revolutionary terminology"*: Action Committee for Political Asylum, *Political Asylum for Glanton Dowdell*.

157 *Sweden's zero-tolerance policy*: On the punishing zero-tolerance policies and visions of a "drug-free" society in Sweden, see Leif Lenke and Börje Olsson, "Sweden: Zero Tolerance Wins the Argument?" in *European Drug Policies and Enforcement*, ed. Nicholas Dorn, Jørgen Jepsen, and Ernesto Savona (New York: Palgrave Macmillan, 1996), 106–18; Tham Henrik, "Law and Order as a Leftist Project?: The Case of Sweden," *Punishment & Society* 3, no. 3 (2001): 409–26; Johan Nordgren, Torkel Richert, and Anke Stallwitz, "Police Officers' Attitudes and Practices Toward Harm Reduction Services in Sweden: A Qualitative Study," *International Journal of Drug Policy* 104 (2022); Leif Lenke and Börje Olsson, "Swedish Drug Policy in the Twenty-First Century: A Policy Model Going Astray," *The ANNALS of the American Academy of Political and Social Science*, 582, no. 1 (2002): 64–79.

157 *"the emotional response of the Scandinavian"*: Ernest Dunbar, *The Black Expatriates: A Study of American Negroes in Exile* (London: Gollancz, 1968), 197. See also Johny Pitts, *Afropean: Notes from Black Europe* (London: Allen Lane, 2019), 207–43; Tamara J. Walker, *Beyond the Shores: A History of African Americans Abroad* (New York: Crown, 2023), 188, 300.

158 *"The Internationale"*: "'We Support Dowdell!'" *Dagens Nyheter*, April 5, 1971.

159 *a sympathetic ear*: "Mount Support Drive Here: Reveal Dowdell in Sweden Seeking Political Asylum," *Michigan Chronicle*, April 25, 1970; "Glanton Dowdell: The Case of a Black, Auto-workers Organizer," *The Next Step*, March 24, 1971.

159 *The event was a hit*: "Benefit to Aid Exiled Black Activist, Family," *Michigan Chronicle*, January 30, 1971; "Plans 'Go' for IBA Benefit," *Michigan Chronicle*, February 6, 1971; "Weighing Fate of Glanton Dowdell," *Michigan Chronicle*, April 3, 1971.

159 *insufficient evidence*: "Sweden Grants Dowdell 'Humanitarian' Asylum," *Michigan Chronicle*, July 4, 1970; "Prosecutor General Denies US Extradition Request," *Dagens Nyheter*, June 5, 1971.

160 *row house south of Stockholm*: "Dowdell Can Stay," *Dagens Nyheter*, June 17, 1971.

160 *her American citizenship*: "Black Women's Struggle Different from White Women's," *Dagens Nyheter*, Sep. 1, 1970.

160 *"an increasingly harsh fascist state"*: "Dowdell Can Stay," *Dagens Nyheter*.

161 *"to yell, to laugh, to cry"*: Profile of Glanton Dowdell, *New in Sweden*.

163 allemansrätten: Annika Dahlberg, Rick Rohde and Klas Sandell, "National Parks and Environmental Justice: Comparing Access Rights and Ideological Legacies in Three Countries," *Conservation & Society* 8, no. 3 (2010): 209–24.

The Valley of Dry Bones

168 *controversial desegregation proposal*: "7 Decentralization Plans of School Board Detailed," *Detroit Free Press*, March 4, 1970; William Grant, "School Decentralization's Moment of Truth," *Detroit Free Press*, March 8, 1970; William Grant, "Schools Get Race Balance," *Detroit Free Press*, April 8, 1970.

168 *"plan of hope"*: "Police Block Student Clash," *Detroit Free Press*, April 9, 1970.

168 *April fool's joke*: Hiley H. Ward, "Blacks Join Move to Recall Board," *Detroit Free Press*, May 9, 1970.

168 *whites did not want to integrate*: Edward Shanahan and William Schmidt, "750 Whites Rap School Changes," *Detroit Free Press*, April 8, 1970.

169 *"super school" district*: William Grant, "Detroit Widens School Plan," *Detroit Free Press*, March 1, 1972; William Grant, "Super Unit Urged for Metro Schools," *Detroit Free Press*, August 1, 1972.

169 *force school integration*: Michael Gray Savage, "The Metropolitan Moment: Municipal Boundaries, Segregation, and Civil Rights Possibilities in the American North" (PhD diss., University of Toronto, 2018).

169 *"blacktowns" of modern times*: Frank L. Keegan, *Blacktown, U.S.A.* (New York: Little, Brown, 1971). See also Ward, *Prophet of the Black Nation*, 29–31.

169 *high schools had transformed*: Joyce A. Baugh, *The Detroit School Busing Case:* Milliken v. Bradley *and the Controversy over Desegregation* (Lawrence: University Press of Kansas, 2011), 78.

169 *racially explosive battlegrounds*: William Schmidt and William Serrin, "Klan Chief, 5 Others Freed on Bond in Bus Bombing," *Detroit Free Press*, September 11, 1971; Jim Crutchfield, "Denby High Strife Ends, 14 Arrested," *Detroit Free Press*, March 11, 1976; Tom Nugent, "Cooley Shut Early by Unrest," *Detroit Free Press*, April 17, 1970; William Grant, "New Detroit Gives $88,500 for Anti-Racism Course," *Detroit Free Press*, June 4, 1971.

169 *onto an athletic field*: "Police Block Student Clash," *Detroit Free Press*.

169 *more than triple*: Baugh, *The Detroit School Busing Case*, 79. See also Michelle Adams, "418 U.S. 717 Supreme Court of the United States [*Milliken v. Bradley*]," in *Critical Race Judgments: Rewritten U.S. Court Opinions on Race and the Law*, ed. Bennett Capers et al. (Cambridge, UK: Cambridge University Press, 2022), 217–34; Michelle Adams, "Racial Inclusion, Exclusion and Segregation in Constitutional Law," *Constitutional Commentary* 28, no. 1 (2012): 1–35.

170 *were bused there*: For Cleage's remarks on busing, see "Rev. Cleage Tells You About Negro Separatism: Black Men in Search of a New Reality," *Detroit Free Press*, September 1, 1968.

170 *In March 1971*: Much of my account of the violence at Osborn High is drawn from my interviews with Kimathi Nelson and Marvin Roby.

170 *Ocean Hill–Brownsville school district*: Jerald E. Podair, *The Strike That Changed New York: Blacks, Whites, and the Ocean Hill–Brownsville Crisis* (New Haven: Yale University Press, 2002). See also "Black Teacher's Workshop," 1968, Box 4, Annual Report, 1968, Albert B. Cleage Jr. Papers; William Grant, "Who Will Control Detroit's Schools?" *Detroit Free Press*, November 17, 1968. Cleage writes more about Ocean Hill–Brownsville and community control of schools in "Anti-Semitism and the Revolution," *Michigan Chronicle*, January 25, 1969; Albert Cleage, Jr., "Black Parents Must Control Black Schools," *Michigan Chronicle*, March 15, 1969; Albert Cleage, Jr., "We Must Develop a Plan for Our Schools (part 2)," *Michigan Chronicle*, November 30, 1968; Albert Cleage, Jr., "What Is Community Control of Schools?" *Michigan Chronicle*, November 23, 1968.

170 *rename Osborn after some black martyr*: In "400 Years of Waiting Is Too Long!" (*Michigan Chronicle*, March 22, 1969), Cleage praises students at McMichael Junior High and Northwestern High in Detroit for trying (though ultimately failing) to rename their schools after Malcolm X. See also Albert Cleage, Jr., "Black and Beautiful," *Michigan Chronicle*, April 5, 1969.

171 *toward them*: Howard Kohn, "Racial Violence Closes Osborn High," *Detroit Free Press*, March 19, 1971. On disturbances at Cooley, Mackenzie, Kettering, and Romulus high schools, see "Sit-In Closes Northwestern," *Detroit Free Press*, March 20, 1971; Tim Holland, "Patrols Planned at Osborn as Board Delays Reopening," *Detroit Free Press*, March 22, 1971.

171 *citizens' clubs*: Jim Neubacher, "School Unrest Led Mother to Push Attack on Busing," *Detroit Free Press*, August 29, 1971; Maryanne Conheim, "Campaign Hits Busing in Pontiac," *Detroit Free Press*, August 14, 1971.

171 *another urban war*: Carol Schmidt, "Right Wing Extremists Building Well-Armed Suburban Power Base," *Michigan Chronicle*, September 23, 1967. See also Andrew Mollison, "Detroit's White Backlash: The Enemy Is Known as They," *Detroit Free Press*, September 28, 1967;

"Author Foresees Second Civil War: Police vs. Black Militants," *New York Amsterdam News*, February 17, 1968.

173   *inner-city parochial schools*: "6 Schools to Close," *Detroit Free Press*, August 10, 1968; Mary Ann Weston, "Harassed Catholic Schools Look for New Answers," *Detroit Free Press*, November 10, 1968; Mary Ann Weston and Robert Kraus, "Dwindling Parishes Multiply Schools' Woes," *Detroit Free Press*, November 11, 1968. For more on Detroit's parish school closures, see Jeffrey C. Bridger and David R. Maines, "Narrative Structures and the Catholic Church Closings in Detroit," *Qualitative Sociology* 21 (1998): 319–40. See also Nancy M. Davis, "Finding Voice: Revisiting Race and American Catholicism in Detroit," *American Catholic Studies* 114, no. 3 (2003): 39–58.

173   *theological revolution*: On Vatican II and the Black Power movement, see M. Shawn Copeland, "A Cadre of Women Religious Committed to Black Liberation: The National Black Sisters' Conference," *U.S. Catholic Historian* 14, no. 1 (1996): 123–44; Nancy M. Davis, "A Lutta Continua: Black Catholic Activism in Detroit, Michigan in the 1970s," *U.S. Catholic Historian* 26, no. 3 (2008): 15–32; Karen J. Johnson, "Beyond Parish Boundaries: Black Catholics and the Quest for Racial Justice," *Religion and American Culture: A Journal of Interpretation* 25, no. 2 (2015): 264–300; Myja R. Thibault, "Rock in a Hard Place: Black Catholics in the Era of Vatican II—A Case Study," *American Catholic Studies* 120, no. 3 (2009): 1–20; Matthew J. Cressler, "Black Power, Vatican II, and the Emergence of Black Catholic Liturgies," *U.S. Catholic Historian* 32, no. 4 (2014): 99–119; James H. Cone, "Black Liberation Theology and Black Catholics: A Critical Conversation," *Theological Studies* 61, no. 4 (2000): 731–47; Jamie T. Phelps, O.P., "Communion Ecclesiology and Black Liberation Theology," *Theological Studies* 61, no. 4 (2000): 672–99; Joseph P. Chinnici, "Ecumenism, Civil Rights, and the Second Vatican Council: The American Experience," *U.S. Catholic Historian* 30, no. 3 (2012): 21–49; Mary E. McGann and Eva Marie Lumas, "The Emergence of African American Catholic Worship," *U.S. Catholic Historian* 19, no. 2 (2001): 27–65.

173   *first black Catholic clergy caucus*: "Negro Priests Set Pre-Meeting Caucus," *The Amarillo Globe-Times*, April 15, 1968; Hiley H. Ward, "Detroiters to Spark U.S. Black Caucus," *Detroit Free Press*, October 26, 1968. See also Cyprian Davis, *The History of Black Catholics in the United States* (New York: Crossroad/Continuum, 1990); Stephen J. Ochs, *Desegregating the Altar: The Josephites and the Struggle for Black Priests, 1871–1960* (Baton Rouge: Louisiana State University Press, 1990); David J. Endres, ed., *Black Catholic Studies Reader: History and Theology* (Washington, D.C.: Catholic University of America Press, 2021); Diana L. Hayes and Cyprian Davis, eds., *Taking Down Our Harps: Black Catholics in the United States* (Maryknoll, NY: Orbis Books, 1998); Albert Raboteau, "Minority Within a Minority: The History of Black Catholics in America," in *A Fire in the Bones: Reflections on African-American Religious History* (Boston: Beacon Press, 1995), 117–37; Matthew J. Cressler, *Authentically Black and Truly Catholic: The Rise of Black Catholicism in the Great Migration* (New York: NYU Press, 2017); M. Shawn Copeland, ed., *Uncommon Faithfulness: The Black Catholic Experience* (Maryknoll, NY: Orbis Books, 2009).

173   *"they are your oppressors"*: Albert Cleage, Jr., "'Separatism' Necessary for Black Power," *Michigan Chronicle*, January 18, 1969.

174   *"gives us power"*: Albert Cleage, Jr., "Black Leadership in the Urban Crisis," April 1968, Box 5, Catholic Clergy Conference on the Interracial Apostolate, 1968, Albert B. Cleage Jr. Papers.

174   *"the rebellious 60s"*: Gary Blonston, "Cleage's 'Black Messiah': Surprising New Theology," *Detroit Free Press*, November 17, 1968.

175   *"integration of the Son of God"*: Clayton Rand, "Spinal Column," *The Dixie Guide*, December 1, 1968.

175   *Hartford Memorial Baptist Church*: For more on Reverend Charles Hill and his church, see Dillard, *Faith in the City*, 25–62; Sidney Fine, *Expanding the Frontiers of Civil Rights: Michigan, 1948–1968* (Detroit: Wayne State University Press, 2017).

175   *Donnie's school syllabi*: For more on the Black Teachers' Workshop, the Black Community Educators Conference, and the Inner City Parents Council—all of which Cleage was involved with—see Birkhold, "Theory and Practice"; Cleage, "Black Church, White School," in *The Black Messiah*, 227–40; "Community Control of Schools Has Developed as the Major School Issue of 1969," June 17, 1969, Box 5, Black Nation News, 1969–1977, Albert B. Cleage Jr. Papers; "Sikukuu: Festival Africaine," May 1968, Box 5, Black Teachers Workshop, Albert B. Cleage Jr. Papers; John Webster, "Black Teachers Workshop Newsletter," February 3, 1968, Box 5, Education, 1968, Albert B. Cleage Jr. Papers; "Teachers Form Group to 'Liberate' Students," *Michigan Chronicle*, February 7, 1970.

175   *put the Ribbrons to use*: Silvia Williams, "Action Group VII," January 25, 1970, Box 4, Annual Report, 1969, Albert B. Cleage Jr. Papers; Emma Ribbron, "Action Group VII," January 31, 1971, Box 4, Annual Report, 1970, Albert B. Cleage Jr. Papers.

175   *"no-no chart"*: Joan Newby, "Secondary Unit Lesson Plan," June 27, 1970, Box 10, School of Black Studies, 1970, Albert B. Cleage Jr. Papers.

176   *"miseducation of Black youngsters"*: "Shrine of the Black Madonna Newsletter," July 6, 1970, Box 5, Black Nation News, 1969–1977, Albert B. Cleage Jr. Papers.

176   *hottest place to go*: "Shrine of the Black Madonna Newsletter," August 17, 1970, Box 5, "Black Nation News, 1969–1977," Albert B. Cleage Jr. Papers.

176   *Cultural Center and Bookstore*: Albert Cleage, Jr., ed., "The Economic Development Corporation of Central Congregational Church," Box 5, Economic Development Corporation, 1967–1969, Albert B. Cleage Jr. Papers.

176   *fabrics by the yard*: Marji Kunz, "Cartoon Look . . . from a Detroiter," *Detroit Free Press*, March 9, 1973; "Clash Over the Afro Look Is Strong Among Blacks," *Detroit Free Press*, September 22, 1968.

177   *the Big Four*: "Arthur Carter III," in *Untold Tales, Unsung Heroes: An Oral History of Detroit's African American Community, 1918–1967*, ed. Elaine Latzman Moon (Detroit: Wayne State University Press, 1994), 264; Michael Graham, "The Life and Times of Rotation Slim, Detroit's Savviest Old Time Copper," *Detroit Free Press*, October 29, 1972; William Serrin, "How Police View Negroes," *Detroit Free Press*, February 23, 1969; Brian Flanigan and Jack Kresnak, "Detroit Police: The Long March from 1976," *Detroit Free Press*, November 25, 1979; Jack Kresnak, "Hart-Bannon Team Alters Police Work," *Detroit Free Press*, October 25, 1976; Michael Graham, "The Big Four Is on the Streets and, Baby, They Got Their Eyes on You," *Detroit Free Press*, September 5, 1971.

178   *the Top*: Lloyd Hogan, "Research Center Shows How Blacks Are Isolated," *Chicago Daily Defender*, November 27, 1968; Anderson, "The Republic of New Africa: Genesis"; Black People's Topographical Research Center, n.d., Box 57, Freedom House, Inc., records, M016, Northeastern University Archives and Special Collections, Northeastern University, Boston, MA.

178   *The ghetto reservation*: Robert Blauner, "Internal Colonialism and Ghetto Revolt," *Social Problems* 16, no. 4 (1969): 393–408; Nicholas Guyatt, "'An Impossible Idea?': The Curious Career of Internal Colonization," *Journal of the Civil War Era* 4, no. 2 (2014): 234–63. For Cleage's use of the word "colony" see Kathy Morgan, "'Black Power' Defender Demands Ghetto Control," *Michigan Daily*, November 3, 1967.

178   black folk on the maps of the world: See Ruth Wilson Gilmore, *Abolition Geography: Essays Towards Liberation* (New York: Verso Books, 2022); Brian D. Goldstein, "'The Search for New Forms': Black Power and the Making of the Postmodern City," in *Public Space/Contested Space: Imagination and Occupation*; ed. Kevin D. Murphy and Sally O'Driscoll (New York: Routledge, 2021), 45–77.

179   *a similar story to tell*: Nadine Brown, "Detroit Cops Blitz Blacks," *Michigan Chronicle*, December 23, 1972.

179   *the orientation center*: "The Chanza Process," n.d., Box 10, Procedures, policies, etc., Albert B. Cleage Jr. Papers.

Letter VII: The Art Shop

180   pro-Black inner visions: Kimberly Thigpen-Cockrel, "Shrine Still for Everyone as It Turns 21," *Michigan Chronicle*, March 6, 1991.

Time Rituals

182   *a New Black World*: Kevin Quashie, *Black Aliveness, or A Poetics of Being* (Durham: Duke University Press, 2021): "What would it mean to consider black aliveness, especially given how readily—and literally—blackness is indexed to death? To behold such aliveness, we have to imagine a black world . . . we have to imagine a black world so as to surpass the everywhere and everyway of black death." See also Philip Butler, ed., *Critical Black Futures: Speculative Theories and Explorations* (New York: Palgrave Macmillan, 2021); adrienne maree brown, *Emergent Strategy: Shaping Change, Changing Worlds* (Chico, CA: AK Press, 2017); Ruha Benjamin, *Imagination: A Manifesto* (New York: W. W. Norton, 2024); Sydney Halliburton, "Envisioning Utopia: The Aesthetics of Black Futurity" (master's thesis, DePaul University, 2019); Reynaldo Anderson and Clinton R. Fluker, eds., *The Black Speculative Arts Movement: Black Futurity, Art+Design* (New York: Lexington Books, 2019).

183   *utopian cooperative movements*: Bernard E. Harcourt, *Cooperation: A Political, Economic, and Social Theory* (New York: Columbia University Press, 2023), 75–88; Chris Jennings, *Paradise Now: The Story of American Utopianism* (New York: Random House, 2016).

183   *Rochdale Equitable Pioneers' Society*: See Cooperative Services, Inc., "By-Laws: Cooperative Services, Inc.," n.d., Box 5, Cooperative Services, Inc., Albert B. Cleage Jr. Papers: "The purpose of this cooperative shall be to promote the economic welfare of its members by utilizing their united funds and their united efforts for the purchase, distribution and production of commodities of quality and for the performance of services, with the business being run in accordance with the Rochdale Principles listed below: 1. One vote for each member. No proxy voting. 2. Overcharges to be returned to patrons in proportion to patronage. 3. Open membership. 4. Political, religious, and social neutrality. 5. Cash trading. No credit. 6. Ethical merchandising. 7. Adequate records and open accounting. 8. Fair labor policy. 9. Adequate education program and budget. 10. Association with other cooperatives for purposes of mutual aid." For Rochdale's influence on black cooperatives, see Gordon-Nembhard, *Collective Courage*; Jessica Gordon-Nembhard and Ajowa Nzinga Ifateyo, "African American Social and Solidarity Economy and Distributive Justice," in *Encyclopedia of the Social and Solidarity Economy: A Collective Work of the United Nations Inter-Agency Task Force on SSE (UNTFSSE)*, ed. Ilcheong Yi et al. (Cheltenham, UK: Edward Elgar Publishing, 2023); John Hope II, "Rochdale Cooperation Among Negroes," *Phylon* 1, no. 1 (1940): 39–52; Sam H. Franklin, Jr., "The Delta Cooperative Farm: Hillhouse, Mississippi," n.d., A. Eugene Cox Papers, 1953–1968 (in Small Manuscripts 1976), Archives and Special Collections, University of Mississippi Libraries, Oxford, MS; Johanna Bockman, "Home Rule from Below: The Cooperative Movement in Washington, D.C.," in *Capital Dilemma: Growth and Inequality in Washington, DC*, ed. Derek Hyra and Sibiyha Prince (New York: Routledge, 2016), 66–85; Samuel Lloyd Myers, "Consumers' Cooperation: A Plan for the Negro" (master's thesis, Boston University, 1942); Joshua L. Carreiro, "Consumers' Cooperation in Early Twentieth Century America: An Analysis of Race, Class and Consumption" (PhD diss., University of Massachusetts Amherst, 2015). Also Mary Hilson, Silke Neunsinger, and Greg Patmore, eds., *A Global History of Consumer Co-operation Since 1850: Movements and Business* (Leiden: Brill, 2017); David J. Thompson, *Weavers of Dreams: Founders of the Modern Co-Operative Movement* (Davis, CA: Center for Cooperatives, University of California, 1994).

183   *Ashanti and Black Star Co-operatives*: See Box 4, Ashanti Co-op/Black Star Co-op Supermarket, 1968–1969, Albert B. Cleage Jr. Papers.

183   *real estate for cooperative businesses*: Hiley H. Ward, "Cleage's New Denomination Seeks to Buy 3 Buildings," *Detroit Free Press*, August 19, 1972.

183 *the church's cooperative enterprises*: Jill Crabtree, "Building Co-Op Power: Militant Life Style for Urban and Campus Ghetto," *Michigan Daily*, November 15, 1968. See also "Black Ministers Urge Power for Blacks," *New York Amsterdam News*, July 12, 1969; Albert Cleage, Jr., "Black Power Is the Answer, Not the Problem (part 3)," *Michigan Chronicle*, July 20, 1968; Albert Cleage, Jr., "Ghetto Economics (An Analysis of the Detroit Position) [parts 1–5]," *Michigan Chronicle*, September 20 and October 4, 11, 18, and 25, 1969.

183 *storehouses and survival centers*: For one of Cleage's references to survival centers, see Albert Cleage, Jr., "Organize for Defense and Community Survival," *Michigan Chronicle*, March 2, 1968.

184 *Black Star Co-op Supermarket and the Black Star Gas Station*: Edward Vaughn, Norman Burton, and William Flowers, report on the Black Star Supermarket, December 2, 1968, Box 10, Black Star Market, 1968, Albert B. Cleage Jr. Papers; "Seventeenth Annual Meeting: Operation '69," January 25, 1970, Box 4, Annual Report, 1969, Albert B. Cleage Jr. Papers.

184 *"buy black" ethos*: Robert E. Weems, Jr., and Lewis A. Randolph, "The National Response to Richard M. Nixon's Black Capitalism Initiative: The Success of Domestic Détente," *Journal of Black Studies* 32, no. 1 (2001): 66–83.

184 *"counterstructures"*: Cleage, *Black Christian Nationalism*, 17.

185 *"group process"*: Mwalimu Akinyele, "Nationbuilding: Power," 1972, Box 6, Layout Booklet, 1972, Albert B. Cleage Jr. Papers.

185 *"time ritual"*: "The BCN Message and Mission: Revolutionary Transformation," in *BCN: National Convention (April 1–6, 1975, Atlanta, GA)* souvenir booklet (June 1991).

185 *"total environmental experiences"*: Ibid.

185 *the meaning of time*: Rasheedah Phillips, *Black Quantum Futurism: Theory and Practice, Vol. 1* (Philadelphia: The AfroFuturist Affair, 2015); Mina Kim, "What Does 'Utopia' Mean to You?" KQED, September 7, 2023; Jenny Odell, *How to Do Nothing: Resisting the Attention Economy* (New York: Melville House, 2019).

185 *In what other ways might this time have been used*: Tricia Hersey, *Rest Is Resistance: A Manifesto* (New York: Little, Brown Spark, 2022); Javon Johnson, "Black Joy in the Time of Ferguson," *QED: A Journal in GLBTQ Worldmaking* 2, no. 2 (2015): 177–83.

185 *predictable whir of the assembly lines*: On choosing to be out of step with oppressive rhythms and time structures, in the context of the Detroit-born genre of techno music, see DeForrest Brown, Jr., *Assembling a Black Counter Culture* (New York: Primary Information, 2022).

186 *bombed out, burned down, and razed*: Jovan Scott Lewis, *Violent Utopia: Dispossession and Black Restoration in Tulsa* (Durham: Duke University Press, 2022).

186 *Cleage's interpretation of black separatism*: Albert Cleage, Jr., "Being Together Gives Us Power," *Michigan Chronicle*, May 11, 1968. See also Raymond L. Hall, ed., *Black Separatism and Social Reality: Rhetoric and Reason* (Oxford, UK: Pergamon Press, 1977); C. Chinwoke Mbadinuju, "Black Separatism," *Current History* 67, no. 399 (1974): 206–13, 233.

186 *carefully designed intentional communities*: B. F. Skinner, *Walden Two* (New York: Macmillan, 1948). Skinner's influence is also noted in Lyman Tower Sargent, "Five Hundred Years of Thomas More's *Utopia* and Utopianism," *Utopian Studies* 27, no. 2 (2016): 184–92; Annette M. Magid, "Thomas More in America," *Utopian Studies* 27, no. 3 (2016): 521–28; Petteri Pietikaine, "Dynamic Psychology, Utopia, and Escape from History: The Case of C. G. Jung," *Utopian Studies* 12, no. 1 (2001): 41–55.

186 operant conditioning: "BCN Ideology, Draft #4," February 12, 1981, Box 5, Communalism Rituals, 1982, Albert B. Cleage Jr. Papers; Albert Cleage, Jr., "Transforming Community: Genesis II—The Recreation of Man," May 6, 1984, Box 2, Sermons, 1981–1990, Albert B. Cleage Jr. Papers.

187 *"total institutions"*: Erving Goffman, "On The Characteristics of Total Institutions," in *Asylums: Essays on the Social Situation of Mental Patients and Other Inmates* (New York: Doubleday, 1961). See also Christie Davies, "Goffman's Concept of the Total Institution: Criticisms and Revisions," *Human Studies* 12, no. 1/2 (1989): 77–95.

187   *"total pattern of life"*: Albert Cleage, Jr., "Report to the Detroit Association," 1961, Box 6, Preliminary Self-Study #2, 1961, Albert B. Cleage Jr. Papers.

187   *"most beautiful community in the world"*: On the paradisal aspects of the ghetto, see Saidiya Hartman, *Wayward Lives, Beautiful Experiments* (New York: W. W. Norton, 2019); Lance Freeman, *A Haven and a Hell: The Ghetto in Black America* (New York: Columbia University Press, 2019). See also: Adrian Shirk, "Utopia, the Bronx," in *Heaven Is a Place on Earth: Searching for an American Utopia* (New York: Counterpoint Press, 2022), 21–24.

Formation

188   *Formation*: This group portrait is based largely on interviews I conducted in 2020 and 2021 with current and former Shrine members, including Adisa Jones, Diallo Brown, Gail Carr, Hanifah Hightower, Imara Hyman, Marvin Roby, Kenyatta Holmes, Mama Isoke, Migozo Taylor, Nilaja Stewart, Nomsa N'Hau, Pat Brown, Rosa Boyd, and others. A complete list of Shrine associates that I spoke with can be found in the acknowledgments.

189   *"Black Protestant Reformation"*: Cleage, *Black Christian Nationalism*, 184. See also Eddie Anthony Robinson, "Rediscovering the Protestant Reformation in African American Worship" (PhD diss., Liberty University, 2023).

189   *Detroit's Northern High*: Dara R. Walker, "Black Power, Education, and Youth Politics in Detroit, 1966–1973" (PhD diss., Rutgers University, 2018), 1–4; Albert Cleage, Jr., letter to the Detroit Board of Education and Superintendent Norman Drachler, March 6, 1968, Box 5, Education, 1968, Albert B. Cleage Jr. Papers.

190   *painted black in front of a Catholic seminary*: Leslie Woodcock Tentler, *Seasons of Grace: A History of the Catholic Archdiocese of Detroit* (Detroit: Wayne State University Press, 1990).

190   *Night Call or Voice of the Black Nation*: "Cleage Philosophy Told: Militant Black Power Leader Here Friday," *Battle Creek Enquirer*, March 20, 1968.

190   *"in terms of one experience"*: Cleage, *Black Christian Nationalism*, xvii.

191   *a plantation religion based on falsehoods*: When he was preaching in Springfield, Cleage procured a copy of Gunnar Myrdal's *An American Dilemma: The Negro Problem and Modern Democracy* (New York: Harper & Brothers, 1944). Cleage annotated Myrdal's chapter "The Negro Church." He drew attention to passages such as: "But there was a new factor, which increased the possibility of the Negro church to serve as a power agency for Negroes; the white preachers and the white observer in the Negro church disappeared"; "In practically all rural areas, and in many of the urban ones, the preacher stood out as the acknowledged local leader of the Negroes. His function became to transmit the whites' wishes to the Negroes and to beg the whites for favors for his people. He became—in our terminology—the typical accommodating Negro leader. To this degree the Negro church perpetuated the traditions of slavery"; "But on the whole even the Northern Negro church has remained a conservative institution with its interests directed upon other-worldly matters and has largely ignored the practical problems of the Negroes' fate in this world."

192   *their prison cells*: Box 10, "Letters from Inmates, 1967–1972," Albert B. Cleage Jr. Papers.

192   *asked to come to Detroit*: Oba Diallo, "BCN Ministerial Training Group," 1972, Box 4, Annual Report, 1971, Albert B. Cleage Jr. Papers.

193   *"Black Theology for the Black Church"*: Albert Cleage, Jr., letter to Alice Mayhew, February 17, 1970, Box 10, Second Book Correspondence, 1970, Albert B. Cleage Jr. Papers.

193   *our Black Brothers and Sisters*: Jaramogi Abebe Agyeman, "Minister's Report," 1972, Box 4, Annual Report, 1971, Albert B. Cleage Jr. Papers.

193   *a "Black communal society"*: Cleage, *Black Christian Nationalism*, 16.

193   *a real collective*: Albert Cleage, Jr., "Operation '69," January 25, 1970, Box 4, Annual Report, 1969, Albert B. Cleage Jr. Papers.

194   *international headquarters in Kingston, Jamaica*: Ibid.

194   *a democratic socialist became prime minister*: Michael Kaufman, "Democracy and Social Transformation in Jamaica," *Social and Economic Studies* 37, no. 3 (1988): 45–73. Michael Manley,

the aforementioned prime minister, spoke at the Shrine in the 1980s. See "Ex-Jamaican Leader Speaks Here June 21," *Michigan Chronicle*, June 13, 1981.

194   *"church-centered Black Counter institutions"*: "The BCN Training Program," January 12, 1973, Box 4, College Cadre, 1973, Albert B. Cleage Jr. Papers.

194   *Shrine on Long Island, New York . . . the one in Harlem*: See "Black Madonna Festival," *New York Amsterdam News*, May 23, 1970; "Shrine Says It'll Serve Harlem Needs," *New York Amsterdam News*, August 1, 1970; "Vandals Desecrate Church," *New York Amsterdam News*, August 16, 1969.

195   *the Third Covenant*: Shelley McIntosh, *I Give You a Mustard Seed*, 2020, unpublished manuscript, courtesy of the author.

195   *Holy Order of Nehemiah*: Ibid.

195   *Muslim Girls' Training and General Civilizational Class*: See E. U. Essien-Udom, *Black Nationalism: A Search for Identity in America* (Chicago: University of Chicago Press, 1962); Hakim M. Rashid, "The Sister Clara Muhammad Schools: Pioneers in the Development of Islamic Education in America," *The Journal of Negro Education* 61, no. 2 (1992): 178–85.

195   *they promised to abolish it*: Ashley D. Farmer, *Remaking Black Power: How Black Women Transformed an Era* (Chapel Hill: University of North Carolina Press, 2017); Kimberly Springer, *Living for the Revolution: Black Feminist Organizations, 1968–1980* (Durham, NC: Duke University Press, 2005); Jeanne Theoharis, Komozi Woodard, and Dayo F. Gore, eds., *Want to Start a Revolution?: Radical Women in the Black Freedom Struggle* (New York: New York University Press, 2009); Keisha N. Blain, *Set the World on Fire: Black Nationalist Women and the Global Struggle for Freedom* (Philadelphia: University of Pennsylvania Press, 2018); Jacquelyn Grant, *White Women's Christ and Black Women's Jesus: Feminist Christology and Womanist Response* (Atlanta: Scholars Press, 1989); Delores S. Williams, *Sisters in the Wilderness: The Challenge of Womanist God-Talk* (Maryknoll, NY: Orbis Books, 1993).

196   *trials of Nzinga*: See Linda M. Heywood, *Njinga of Angola: Africa's Warrior Queen* (Cambridge, MA: Harvard University Press, 2017).

196   *money for the Shrine's projects*: "Black Fashion Show Aiding Cultural Center," *New York Amsterdam News*, February 6, 1971.

197   *items they loved wearing*: Marji Kunz, "Bold African Prints and Bone Jewels," *Detroit Free Press*, April 21, 1972.

197   *Operation Kodi began*: "Action Group V," January 10, 1971, Box 4, Action Group #5, Albert B. Cleage Jr. Papers.

197   *"go to the gas ovens"*: "Action Group V Minutes," December 13, 1971, Box 4, Action Group #5, Albert B. Cleage Jr. Papers.

197   *labor stoppage in Lordstown, Ohio*: "The White Projection, Draft 1," 1973, Box 4, Annual Meeting, 1973, Albert B. Cleage Jr. Papers; Dan Kaufman, "The End of the Line," *New York Times Magazine*, May 1, 2019; Bennett Kremen, "Lordstown—Searching for a Better Way of Work," *New York Times*, September 9, 1973; Alexandra Orchard, "The 1972 Lordstown Strike," Walter P. Reuther Library, August 12, 2013, reuther.wayne.edu/node/10756.

197   *Workplace unrest in the country*: Melvyn Dubofsky, "Labor Unrest in the United States, 1906–90," *Review (Fernand Braudel Center)* 18, no. 1 (1995): 125–35; Aaron Brenner, Robert Brenner, and Cal Winslow, eds., *Rebel Rank and File: Labor Militancy and Revolt from Below During the Long 1970s* (New York: Verso Books, 2010).

198   *language of black extermination*: Albert Cleage, Jr., "'Genocide Acts' in U.S. Draw Rev. Cleage Attack," *Michigan Chronicle*, November 28, 1970.

198   *National Training Center and Residence Hall*: Box 5, Training Center and Residence Hall, 1970–1975, Albert B. Cleage Jr. Papers.

198   *700 Seward Street*: National Register of Historic Places, "Shrine of the Black Madonna of the Pan African Orthodox Christian Church Registration Form," United States Department of the Interior, National Park Service, December 22, 2020.

198   *the Abington, north of the city center*: "Vacant Detroit Building Had Illustrious Past as Hotel," *Detroit Free Press*, October 29, 2016.

198   *their first commune*: "Tax Exemption for Church Hit," *Detroit Free Press*, March 30, 1973.

199   *conscientious objector status*: Box 10, Draft Information—Selective Service, etc., 1969–1975, Albert B. Cleage Jr. Papers.

199   *black antiwar activists*: Amanda L. Higgins, "'Instruments of Righteousness': The Intersections of Black Power and Anti–Vietnam War Activism in the United States, 1964–1972" (PhD diss., University of Kentucky, 2013); Marcus S. Cox, "'Keep Our Black Warriors Out of the Draft': The Vietnam Antiwar Movement at Southern University, 1968–1973," *The Journal of Educational Foundations* 20, no. 1/2 (2006): 123–44.

199   *teach-ins*: "Teach-In Critics Attack U.S. Society, Viet War," *Michigan Daily*, October 5, 1967.

199   *surveilled by federal authorities*: Cleage had also been surveilled by state authorities. See "Albert Cleage, Background Profile Created by Michigan State Police, 1967," July 28, 1967, Box 44, Folder 3, Pearl Cleage Papers, Emory University, Atlanta, GA.

199   *a plaintiff in* Laird v. Tatum: Ralph Michael Stein, "*Laird v. Tatum*: The Supreme Court and a First Amendment Challenge to Military Surveillance of Lawful Civilian Political Activity," *Hofstra Law Review* (1973): 244–75; Staff of the Subcommittee on Constitutional Rights, *Army Surveillance of Civilians: A Documentary Analysis* (Washington, D.C.: U.S. Government Printing Office, 1972).

199   *exercise of free speech*: "Supreme Court Is Urged to Cut Off Test of Army Surveillance," *Vernon Daily Record*, March 27, 1972.

199   *white hippie communes*: Timothy Miller, *The 60s Communes: Hippies and Beyond* (Syracuse, NY: Syracuse University Press, 1999); Donald E. Pitzer, ed., *America's Communal Utopias* (Chapel Hill: University of North Carolina Press, 1997); Harry Quintana and Charles Jones, "Black Commune in Focus," *Perspecta* 12 (1969): 39–42.

200   *"each family has its own apartment"*: Jaramogi Abebe Agyeman, "Minister's Report," 1972, Box 4, Annual Report, 1971, Albert B. Cleage Jr. Papers: "In '72, we will move into our first BCN Communal Housing Project [. . .] The 'Group Process' will be much more effective when we do not have to scatter to different sections of the city and live with people who are not involved in the Black Liberation Struggle. Communes are basic to our effort to build a communal way of life."

200   *a network of caves near the Dead Sea*: John J. Collins, *The Dead Sea Scrolls: A Biography* (Princeton: Princeton University Press, 2012).

200   *the Essenes*: Anne Meurois-Givaudan and Daniel Meurois-Givaudan, *The Way of the Essenes: Christ's Hidden Life Remembered* (Rochester, VT: Destiny Books, 1993); Mary Ann Beavis, "Christian Origins, Egalitarianism, and Utopia," *Journal of Feminist Studies in Religion* 23, no. 2 (2007): 27–49; Andrew R. Krause, "Community, Alterity, and Space in the Qumran Covenant Curses," *Dead Sea Discoveries* 25, no. 2 (2018): 217–37; J. Duncan and M. Derrett, "Gemistus Plethon, the Essenes, and More's Utopia," *Bibliothèque d'Humanisme et Renaissance* 27, no. 3 (1965): 579–606; Doron Mendels, "Hellenistic Utopia and the Essenes," *The Harvard Theological Review* 72, no. 3/4 (1979): 207–22; John J. Collins, "Models of Utopia in the Biblical Tradition," in *A Wise and Discerning Mind: Essays in Honor of Burke O. Long*, ed. Saul M. Olyan and Robert C. Culley (Providence, RI: Brown Judaic Studies, 2000), 51–67; Paul M. Sweezy, "Origins of Present Day Socialism," *Science & Society* 12, no. 1 (1948): 65–81; Jacob Neusner, "Qumran and Jerusalem: Two Jewish Roads to Utopia," *Journal of Bible and Religion* 27, no. 4 (1959): 284–90; Bill Metcalf, "Utopian Struggle: Preconceptions and Realities of Intentional Communities," *RCC Perspectives* 8 (2012): 21–30. For the influence of the Essenes on other black utopian projects, see Andrew S. Chancey, "'A Demonstration Plot for the Kingdom of God': The Establishment and Early Years of Koinonia Farm," *The Georgia Historical Quarterly* 75, no. 2 (1991): 321–53; Hans A. Baer and Merrill Singer, "Toward a

Typology of Black Sectarianism as a Response to Racial Stratification," *Anthropological Quarterly* 54, no. 1 (1981): 1–14.

200   *"trying to get close to God"*: Albert Cleage, Jr., "Prelude to a New Era: KUA," July 16, 1978, Box 1, Sermons, 1978, Albert B. Cleage Jr. Papers. See also Cleage, *Black Christian Nationalism*, 219–21.

201   *hoped-for crucible of a better future*: "A 'Black Nation' Is Achieved," *Detroit Free Press*, December 26, 1972.

Messiahs

202   *on the fringes of public approval*: "U.S. Black Theology Called Racist," *National Catholic Reporter*, July 28, 1978; "The NBEA: Striving to Be Both Black and Biblical," *Christianity Today*, June 27, 1980.

202   *religious believers*: For Cleage's broader impact on religion, see Elizabeth Pérez, "Space, Time, and Ache," in *Religion in the Kitchen: Cooking, Talking, and the Making of Black Atlantic Traditions* (New York: New York University Press, 2016), 25–52; "A Bridge Too Far?: Benjamin Chavis," *New York Times*, June 12, 1994; "Black Churchmen Organize Caucus," *New York Times*, November 9, 1970.

202   *one straw poll*: "Guess Who Wins the Name Game?" *Detroit Free Press*, October 16, 1977.

203   *Henry Louis Gates, Jr.'s popular book*: Henry Louis Gates, Jr., *The Black Church: This Is Our Story, This Is Our Song* (New York: Penguin Press, 2021).

203   *he appeared as a guest speaker*: James Cone, *Said I Wasn't Gonna Tell Nobody* (Maryknoll, NY: Orbis Books, 2018). Cone participated in various events at the Shrine, including the 1969 John Webster Forum and the First Annual BCN Convention in 1970.

203   *God's relationship to blackness*: Anthony G. Reddie, *Introducing James H. Cone: A Personal Exploration* (London: SCM Press, 2022), 62–67.

203   *reasons that the church isn't more widely known*: Raphael G. Warnock, *The Divided Mind of the Black Church: Theology, Piety, and Public Witness* (New York: New York University Press, 2013), 104–107.

203   *preacher and mystic Thomas Müntzer*: Eugene Genovese, "Religious Foundations of the Black Nation," in *African American Religious Thought: An Anthology*, ed. Cornel West and Eddie Glaude, Jr. (Louisville: Westminster John Knox Press, 2003), 305–306.

203   *his role in the German Peasants' War of 1525*: Müntzer is discussed at length in Karl Mannheim, *Ideology and Utopia: An Introduction to the Sociology of Knowledge*, trans. Louis Wirth and Edward Shils (New York: Harcourt, Brace, 1936); Ernst Bloch, *The Principle of Hope*, trans. Neville Plaice, Stephen Plaice, and Paul Knight (Cambridge, MA: MIT Press, 1986); Ruth Levitas, *The Concept of Utopia* (1990; repr., Bern, Switzerland: Peter Lang, 2010); Friedrich Engels, *The Peasant War in Germany*, trans. Moissaye J. Olgin (New York: International Publishers, 1926); Tom Scott, *Thomas Müntzer: Theology and Revolution in the German Reformation* (London: Macmillan, 1989).

204   *new religious movements*: Merrill Singer, "The Social Context of Conversion to a Black Religious Sect," *Review of Religious Research* 30, no. 2 (1988): 177–92. See also Joseph L. Tucker, *The Other Black Church: Alternative Christian Movements and the Struggle for Black Freedom* (New York: Lexington Books/Fortress Academic, 2020), 9, 101–42.

204   *within the bounds of the existing social order*: Anita J. Mixon, "Women Speaking in and for Institutions: A Rhetorical History of the Politics of Respectability in Black Chicago, 1919–1939" (PhD diss., University of Illinois at Urbana-Champaign, 2017); Sherman Roosevelt Tribble, "Images of a Preacher: A Study of the Reverend Joseph Harrison Jackson, Former President of the National Baptist Convention, U.S.A., Inc." (PhD diss., Northwestern University, 1990); Sandy Dwayne Martin, "Uncle Tom, Pragmatist, or Visionary?: An Assessment of the Reverend Dr. Joseph Harrison Jackson and Civil Rights," in *Black Conservatism: Essays in Intellectual and Political History*, ed. Peter Eisenstadt (1999), 169–200; Wallace Best, "'The Right Achieved and the Wrong Way Conquered': J. H. Jackson, Martin Luther King, Jr., and

the Conflict over Civil Rights," *Religion and American Culture: A Journal of Interpretation* 16, no. 2 (2006): 195–226.

204 *an all-powerful patriarch*: Ann Walton Sieber, "Ghetto Utopia" *CITE* 36 (winter 1996): 32–35.

205 *Fauset wrote of "black cults"*: Arthur Huff Fauset, *Black Gods of the Metropolis* (Philadelphia: University of Pennsylvania Press, 1944). See also Edward E. Curtis IV and Danielle Brune Sigler, eds., *The New Black Gods: Arthur Huff Fauset and the Study of African American Religions* (Bloomington: Indiana University Press, 2009).

205 *"islands of moral unity"*: Joseph R. Washington, Jr., *Black Sects and Cults* (Garden City, NY: Doubleday, 1967). Washington also mentions Cleage in *Black and White Power Subreption* (Boston: Beacon Press, 1969): "The new perspective of what it means to be black in the crisis of our time has taken an extraordinarily interesting direction within one congregation. The Reverend Mr. Al Cleage, Jr., Minister of the Central United Church of Christ in Detroit, has been deeply influenced by Black Power [. . .] Mr. Cleage had declared himself a black nationalist Christian minister. In so doing, he removed the images of Jesus as a blue-eyed white in his church as well as expressions of the white Madonna and replaced them with a black Jesus and a black Madonna. We are told that the response was immediate and overwhelming; the average attendance of fifty increased to nine hundred in a few short weeks [. . .] A good deal of what he says and does has been finely worked out in earlier contexts by non-Christian blacks who were nationalists. He is not to be ignored—because he is trying to find a way to express black consciousness in a Christian context, for which we have few if any historical precedents."

205 *three white brides*: "Three Pairs Repeat Vows at Joint Altar Ceremony," *Ukiah Daily Journal*, June 11, 1969.

206 *Jewell wrote a short letter to Albert Cleage*: The following letters can be found in Box 1, Correspondence, 1969, Albert B. Cleage Jr. Papers.

206 *Jones, a white man, had been styling*: Jeff Guinn, *The Road to Jonestown: Jim Jones and Peoples Temple* (New York: Simon & Schuster, 2017); Tim Reiterman with John Jacobs, *Raven: The Untold Story of the Rev. Jim Jones and His People* (New York: E. P. Dutton, 1982).

207 *"To act against evil. To do good"*: Mary R. Sawyer, "The Church in Peoples Temple," in *Peoples Temple and Black Religion in America*, ed. Rebecca Moore, Anthony B. Pinn, and Mary R. Sawyer (Bloomington: Indiana University Press, 2004), 166–93.

207 *his wife, Marceline, singing*: Shena McAuliffe, "Marceline Wanted a Bigger Adventure," *True Story* 26 (2021), creativenonfiction.org/writing/marceline-wanted-a-bigger-adventure/.

207 *abusive practices at the Peoples Temple*: For Kinsolving's published and unpublished articles on Peoples Temple, see "Lester Kinsolving Series on Peoples Temple," Jonestown Institute, originally posted on February 17, 2013, jonestown.sdsu.edu/?page_id=14081.

207 *"white-hating minister"*: Lester Kinsolving, "Black Caucus Denounced," *Kilgore News Herald*, October 22, 1972. Across the 1970s, the Shrine was occasionally described in the media as a bigoted religious sect. See George Stanley, "Group Trades Laughs for Largess: Beneath Is Goal of Black Superiority," *Capital Times*, May 26, 1979.

207 *"a Utopian community"*: Lester Kinsolving, "The Prophet Who Raises the Dead," *San Francisco Examiner*, September 17, 1972. See also Adam Morris, "Jim Jones," in *American Messiahs: False Prophets of a Damned Nation* (New York: W. W. Norton, 2019), 269–79.

207 *compound in rural Guyana*: "Sixty Ex-Mendocino Residents at Colony," *Press Democrat*, November 20, 1978; Julia Scheeres, *A Thousand Lives: The Untold Story of Hope, Deception, and Survival at Jonestown* (New York: Free Press, 2011); Morgan Shipley, "Apocalyptic Redemption and Utopian Resignation: How Visions of Dystopia Made Community Impossible in Jonestown," *Communal Societies* 38, no. 2 (2018), 135–62; Rebecca Moore and Fielding McGhee III, eds., *New Religious Movements, Mass Suicide, and Peoples Temple: Scholarly Perspectives on a Tragedy* (New York: Edwin Mellen Press, 1989).

208 *"personality cults"*: Albert Cleage, Jr., "Organization Called Key to the Black Revolution (part 1)," *Michigan Chronicle*, December 2, 1967.

209 *like the persecuted Israelites*: Cleage, "We Are God's Chosen People," in *The Black Messiah*, 48–59.

209 *utopian prophets*: Wilson Jeremiah Moses, *Black Messiahs and Uncle Toms: Social and Literary Manipulations of a Religious Myth*, rev. ed. (University Park, PA: Penn State University Press, 1993); Miriam Kupka Berger, "The Worldview of Prophets and Utopians: A Study in Contrasts," *Conversations: The Journal of the Institute for Jewish Ideas and Ideals* 26, jewishideas.org /article/worldview-prophets-and-utopians-study-contrasts; Nicholas Campion, *The New Age in the Modern West: Counterculture, Utopia and Prophecy from the Late Eighteenth Century to the Present Day* (New York: Bloomsbury, 2015); Agata Bielik-Robson, "The Messiah and the Great Architect: On the Difference Between the Messianic and the Utopian," *Utopian Studies* 29, no. 2 (2018): 133–58.

The Science of Becoming What You Already Are

212 *an eleven-year-old girl*: Shelley McIntosh, *A Principal's Tale: Life in 31 Days* (Murrells Inlet, SC: Covenant Books, 2018), 7.

213 *her four children*: Shelley McIntosh, *Memoir of a Black Christian Nationalist: Seeds of Liberation* (Columbus, OH: J. Merrill Publishing, 2021), 12.

214 *"security from the cradle to the grave"*: Dara Mathis, "A Blueprint for Black Liberation," *The Atlantic*, January 10, 2023, theatlantic.com/ideas/archive/2023/01/black-christian-nationalism -liberation-movement-detroit-commune/672682/.

215 reaching: Box 9, Missionary Outreach Interdepartmental Communications, 1978, Albert B. Cleage Jr. Papers; Box 9, Securing Trips, 1979, Albert B. Cleage Jr. Papers; Box 9, MOR Minutes, 1978, Albert B. Cleage Jr. Papers; "Ritual for Out of Town Outreachers," n.d., Box 10, Procedures, policies, etc., Albert B. Cleage Jr. Papers.

215 *Shrine's communal budget*: Box 9, 1978, Communal Budget Listing, Albert B. Cleage Jr. Papers; Box 9, 1979, Communal Budget, Albert B. Cleage Jr. Papers.

215 *Acts 2:44–45*: See Eugene McCarraher, *The Enchantments of Mammon: How Capitalism Became the Religion of Modernity* (Cambridge, MA: Harvard University Press, 2019), 25–27; Ariel Hessayon, "Early Modern Communism: The Diggers and Community of Goods," *Journal for the Study of Radicalism* 3, no. 2 (2009): 1–49; Janet R. White, "The Bethel Colony: Intersections of Culture and Built Form in a Bible Communist Utopia," *Utopian Studies* 28, no. 1 (2017): 1–44; Cardinal Aswad Walker, "Princes Shall Come Out of Egypt: A Theological Comparison of Marcus Garvey and Reverend Albert B. Cleage Jr.," *Journal of Black Studies* 39, no. 2 (2008): 194–251. Walker writes: "Cleage also found scriptures in the Synoptic Gospels that speak to communal salvation. Acts 2:1–4, which describes the Holy Spirit coming upon the group of disciples in the upper room, is viewed as how God can transform a group of seekers [. . .] It is through this process of people divesting themselves of the obsession with self for the good of others that they are saved."

216 *there were those who chose to leave*: Susan Morse, "Despite Religion, 2 Kids Go to Mom," *Detroit Free Press*, November 18, 1976.

216 *one of the various Shrine outposts*: Gene Yarnell, "Second Black Madonna Shrine Opens Oct. 15," *Detroit Free Press*, October 14, 1972.

216 *churches in Kalamazoo and Flint*: See "Kalamazoo Cadre," Box 4, Central Congregational Church Administrative, Executive Committee, 1967–1971, Albert B. Cleage Jr. Papers.

216 *cities throughout the Midwest and Northeast*: Summary of the BCN movement's plans for expansion, 1968, Box 6, History, Draft 1968, Albert B. Cleage Jr. Papers. There were plans to open Shrines in Cleveland, Pittsburgh, and Chicago, among other locations. See also Thomas A. Johnson, "New Role Urged for Black Church," *New York Times*, April 6, 1970.

217 *"make other churches change"*: Ward, *Prophet of the Black Nation*, 209.

217 *Tuskegee Airman, labor organizer, and state senator*: Wilber C. Rich, *Coleman Young and Detroit Politics: From Social Activist to Power Broker* (Detroit: Wayne State University Press, 1989).

217   *one of Jaramogi's occasional confidants*: See Aaron Robertson, "Attack the Block: Redefining Policing in Detroit," *The Point*, June 14, 2020; Luetishia Blake, letter to state representative Rosetta Ferguson on behalf of the Concerned Parents and Citizens Club, February 12, 1971, Box 10, Black Teacher's Caucus, 1970, Albert B. Cleage Jr. Papers.

217   *Young's campaign*: Danton Wilson, "How the Black Slate Became a Political Power in Detroit," *Michigan Chronicle*, November 3, 1984.

217   *work in Young's administration*: Saeed Sanders, "The Black Slate's Dilemma," *Michigan Chronicle*, August 14, 1996.

217   *Maynard Jackson*: Box 4, 1975, Third Biennial Convention, 1975, Albert B. Cleage Jr. Papers.

218   *"a separate communal black state"*: Chuck Bell, "BCN Pursues Separatism," *Atlanta Constitution*, April 3, 1975. For more on the Atlanta Shrine, see Joe E. Green, "Shrine Funded on the Street Now Prospering in West End with Gospel of Black Pride," *Atlanta Constitution*, August 27, 1978; Joe E. Green, "Black Women Play Crucial Role in the Shrine," *Atlanta Constitution*, August 27, 1978; Thonnia Lee, "Shrine of the Black Madonna Fosters Spiritual, Economic Advancement," *Atlanta Constitution*, March 31, 1990; Mark Barnette, "Shrine Moves into Politics" *Atlanta Constitution*, August 20, 1981; Lisa Marie Butler, "Atlanta's Shrine Related to Detroit Church," *Atlanta Constitution*, August 20, 1981; Beverly Barnes, "Shrine Classes Help Students Prepare for Technological Future," *Atlanta Constitution*, November 10, 1983; Pat Burson, "Shrine a Symbol of Hope for Blacks," *Atlanta Constitution*, October 1, 1987; Connie Green, "West End, City's Oldest Neighborhood, a Blend of Diverse Cultures," *Atlanta Constitution*, August 12, 1987. For a personal account of the Atlanta Shrine, see Dadisi Mwende Netifnet, *Upward Road: The Autobiography of Poet Dadisi Mwende Netifnet* (Atlanta: Go To Publish, 2019).

218   *any semblance of a united front*: James Kirkpatrick Davis, *Spying on America: The FBI's Domestic Counter-Intelligence Program* (Westport, CT: Praeger, 1992); Brian Shih and Yohuru Williams, eds., *The Black Panthers: Portraits from an Unfinished Revolution* (New York: Bold Type Books, 2016); Peniel E. Joseph, ed., *The Black Power Movement: Rethinking the Civil Rights–Black Power Era* (New York: Routledge, 2006); Michelle Alexander, *The New Jim Crow: Mass Incarceration in the Age of Colorblindness* (New York: New Press, 2010); James Forman, Jr., *Locking Up Our Own: Crime and Punishment in Black America* (New York: Farrar, Straus and Giroux, 2017).

218   *"urban enclaves"*: BCN: *National Convention* booklet.

219   *probationary hearing*: Box 9, 1978, "Disciplinary Action," Albert B. Cleage Jr. Papers.

219   *Shrine No. 10*: Harrison, "A History of the Shrine," 24.

220   *Pan-African Orthodox Christian Church*: "Articles of Association: Constitution and By-Laws of the Pan African Orthodox Christian Church," July 3, 1978, Box 4, Articles of Association: Pan-African Orthodox Christian Church, 1978, Albert B. Cleage Jr. Papers.

220   *transitions to independence*: Cleage spoke of black liberation efforts in Africa as early as 1970. See Albert Cleage, Jr., "Churchmen Speak Out on S. Africa (parts 1 and 2)," *Michigan Chronicle*, January 17 and 24, 1970.

220   *on the American front*: W. Kim Heron, "'Look for Me in the Whirlwind': Marcus Garvey's Call for Unity Stirred Black Souls Here, Abroad," *Detroit Free Press*, February 2, 1986; "Spokesman to Discuss Angola," *Michigan Chronicle*, February 28, 1976; Larry Plump, "Tanzania Ambassador: Colonial Rule Must Go," *Michigan Chronicle*, July 19, 1975; Hilary Sapire, "Liberation Movements, Exile, and International Solidarity: An Introduction," *Journal of Southern African Studies* 35, no. 2 (2009): 271–86. For more on the Shrine's extensive support of South African independence efforts, read about the work of the Shrine member Akua Badu Watkins ("'We Aren't Making the Same Mistakes,'" *Detroit Free Press*, February 2, 1986); "Apartheid Exile to Speak Here Sunday," *Michigan Chronicle*, September 17, 1983.

220   *Guerrilla war wasn't likely anymore*: Elizabeth Hinton, *America on Fire: The Untold History of Police Violence and Black Rebellion Since the 1960s* (New York: Liveright, 2021).

220   *"transformation rather than revolution"*: D. Kimathi Nelson, "The Theological Journey of Albert B. Cleage Jr.: Reflections from Jaramogi's Protégé and Successor," in *Albert Cleage Jr. and the Black Madonna and Child*, 33. See also Stephen A. Kent, "Political Frustration and Religious Conversions," in *From Slogans to Mantras: Social Protest and Religious Conversion in the Late Vietnam War Era* (Syracuse: Syracuse University Press, 2001), 25–43.

221   *"Seekers in every generation"*: Albert Cleage, Jr., "Kutafuta," in "Holy Crusade Words of Inspiration."

221   *"the birds, the trees"*: McIntosh, *I Give You a Mustard Seed*.

221   *Egypt and India had rich spiritual traditions*: See Wilson Jeremiah Moses, *Afrotopia: The Roots of African American Popular History* (Cambridge, UK: Cambridge University Press, 1998).

222   *the standard model of particle physics*: Jawanza Eric Clark, "Nothing Is More Sacred Than the Liberation of Black People: Albert Cleage's Method as Unfulfilled Theological Paradigm Shift," in *Albert Cleage Jr. and the Black Madonna and Child*, 54. See also David Kaiser, *How the Hippies Saved Physics: Science, Counterculture, and the Quantum Revival* (New York: W. W. Norton, 2012); John Polkinghorne, *Quantum Physics & Theology: An Unexpected Kinship* (London: Society for Promoting Christian Knowledge, 2007); Jeff Carreira, *The Spiritual Implications of Quantum Physics: Reflections on the Nature of Science, Reality and Paradigm Shifts* (Philadelphia: Emergence Education, 2023); Diarmuid O'Murchu, *Quantum Theology: Spiritual Implications of the New Physics* (Spring Valley, NY: Crossroad, 1997); David Kaiser and W. Patrick McCray, eds., *Groovy Science: Knowledge, Innovation, and American Counterculture* (Chicago: University of Chicago Press, 2016).

222   *revelations from beyond the known world*: See Wouter J. Hanegraaff, *New Age Religion and Western Culture: Esotericism in the Mirror of Secular Thought* (Albany: State University of New York Press, 1997); Wouter J. Hanegraaff, *Western Esotericism: A Guide for the Perplexed* (New York: Bloomsbury Academic, 2013); Walker, "Princes Shall Come Out of Egypt," 220: "Cleage asserted that the mystics and priests of ancient Africa and other non-Western cultures that came to know the nature of God through direct religious experience discerned that beyond the boundaries of the rational mind, there exist a wholeness and unity of existence stemming from the reality of God. Moreover, this theology was the theology of the African Mystery System and served as foundational thought for the 'Christianity' of Jesus, Buddhism, Hinduism, and Taoism."

222   *"creative intelligence of God"*: Cleage, "Transforming Community: Genesis II."

222   *the Science of Creative Intelligence*: Lee Fergusson and Anna Bonshek, eds., *The Unmanifest Canvas: Maharishi Mahesh Yogi on the Arts, Creativity, and Perception, 1970–2006* (Fairfield, IA: Maharishi University of Management Press, 2014); Jack Forem, *Transcendental Meditation: Maharishi Mahesh Yogi and the Science of Creative Intelligence* (New York: Dutton, 1973); Constance Holden, "Maharishi International University: 'Science of Creative Intelligence,'" *Science* 187, no. 4182 (1975): 1176–80; Geoffrey A. Wells, Lee Fergusson, and Anna Bonshek, "The Foundations of Maharishi's Science of Creative Intelligence: An Introduction," *Journal of Maharishi Vedic Research Institute* 15 (2021): 79–133.

222   *"as thought, as conscience"*: Henry Sloane Coffin, *Joy in Believing: The Message of the Book of Job* (New York: Charles Scribner's Sons, 1916).

223   *the Transforming Community*: Albert Cleage, Jr., "The Church as a Transforming Community: Conversion #2," November 5, 1978, Box 1, Sermons, 1978, Albert B. Cleage Jr. Papers; Albert Cleage, Jr., "The Church as a Transforming Community: Response to the Holy Spirit," November 12, 1978, Box 1, Sermons, 1978, Albert B. Cleage Jr. Papers.

223   *George Ivanovitch Gurdjieff*: See Jacob Needleman and George Baker, eds., *Gurdjieff: Essays and Reflections on the Man and His Teaching* (New York: Continuum, 1998); Anna Neima, "The Forest Philosophers of Fontainebleau," in *The Utopians: Six Attempts to Build the Perfect Society* (London: Picador, 2021), 125–62.

223   *"Human Potential Movement"*: *The Orange Book: The Meditation Techniques of Bhagwan Shree Rajneesh* is cited in the Cleage papers (see Monifa Dara Omowale, "Confession Sermonette,"

October 19, 1992, Box 6, KUA Small Group Devotionals, 1992, Albert B. Cleage Jr. Papers). See also Nick Totton, *Psychotherapy and Politics* (London: Sage Publications, 2000); Gordon Spence, "Further Development of Evidence-Based Coaching: Lessons from the Rise and Fall of the Human Potential Movement," *Australian Psychologist* 42, no. 4 (2007): 255–65; Lewis F. Carter, "The 'New Renunciates' of the Bhagwan Shree Rajneesh: Observations and Identification of Problems of Interpreting New Religious Movements," *Journal for the Scientific Study of Religion* 26, no. 2 (1987): 148–72.

223 the *"science of becoming what you already are"*: Albert Cleage, Jr., "The Black Dilemma: KUA," March 25, 1979, Box 2, Sermons, 1979, Albert B. Cleage Jr. Papers; Cleage, "Prelude to a New Era."

224 *"The church must have therapies"*: Nelson, "Reflections from Jaramogi's Protégé," 28.

224 *New Age phenomenon of the 1970s and '80s*: See Kenneth L. Woodward, "Getting Your Mind Together," *Newsweek*, September 6, 1976. For the roots of New Ageism in black religion, see Hans A. Baer, "The Father Hurley Sect: The Untold Story of a Black God's Kingdom," in *The Black Spiritual Movement: A Religious Response to Racism* (Knoxville: University of Tennessee Press, 1984), 82–109. See also John Patrick Deveney, *Paschal Beverly Randolph: A Nineteenth-Century Black American Spiritualist, Rosicrucian, and Sex Magician* (Albany: State University of New York Press, 1996); Vaughn A. Booker, "'God's Spirit Lives in Me': Metaphysical Theology in Charleszetta 'Mother' Waddles' Urban Mission to the Poor," *Nova Religio* 22, no. 1 (2018): 5–33; Stephen C. Finley, "The Afro-Theosophics of Robert T. Browne: Preliminary Thoughts on Theory and Method in the Study of Religion," *Journal of the American Academy of Religion* 89, no. 4 (2021): 1199–1207; James A. Santucci, "The Notion of Race in Theosophy," *Nova Religio* 11, no. 3 (2008): 37–63.

Black Kibbutzniks

226 *social needs of black children*: William Grant, "Cleage's Protégé a Surprise Leader for School Post," *Detroit Free Press*, September 14, 1977; Bianca A. Suárez, "The Rise of Educational Consciousness: Racial and Class Politics of the Detroit Public Schools, 1943–1974" (PhD diss., University of California, Berkeley, 2018); Kefentse K. Chike, "From Black Power to the New Millennium: The Evolution of African Centered Education in Detroit, Michigan, 1970–2000" (PhD diss., Michigan State University, 2011).

226 *principals and superintendents*: Cleage also criticized administrators in "Administrators: Being Black Isn't Enough," *Michigan Chronicle*, April 6, 1968; "Black Administrators Must Put Kids First," *Michigan Chronicle*, November 11, 1967; "Individuals Are Weak, the Nation Is Strong," *Michigan Chronicle*, October 28, 1967; "Open Letter to Dr. Drachler and the Board of Education," *Michigan Chronicle*, March 1, 1969.

226 *"free the child"*: Barbara Martin, "The Afram River and Freedom School—1964," *Finding Eliza*, originally published in *Now! News of Detroit and the World*, findingeliza.com/archives /9966.

228 *"catch their psychological sickness"*: Cleage, *Black Christian Nationalism*, 212.

228 *"so that our children can enter in"*: Cleage, *The Black Messiah*, 277–78.

229 *Soviet preschools*: See also Rodney Barfield, "Lenin's Utopianism: State and Revolution," *Slavic Review* 30, no. 1 (1971): 45–56.

229 the *"Sovietization" of preschool education*: Olivia B. Waxman, "The U.S. Almost Had Universal Childcare 50 Years Ago. The Same Attacks Might Kill It Today," *TIME*, December 9, 2021; Nancy L. Cohen, "Why America Never Had Universal Child Care," *New Republic*, April 24, 2013. See also Kristen R. Ghodsee, *Everyday Utopia: What 2,000 Years of Wild Experiments Can Teach Us About the Good Life* (New York: Simon & Schuster, 2023).

229 *"Soviet experiments with raising children in institutions"*: Bruno Bettelheim, *Children of the Dream* (New York: Macmillan, 1969). See also George P. Jan, "Mass Education in the Chinese Communes," *Asian Survey* 4, no. 10 (1964): 1102–14; John W. Bennett, "Communes and Communitarianism," *Theory and Society* 2, no. 1 (1975): 63–94; Shakhar Rahav, "How Shall

We Live?: Chinese Communal Experiments after the Great War in Global Context," *Journal of World History* 26, no. 3 (2016): 521–48.

230   *enfant terrible of child psychology*: David Dempsey, "Bruno Bettelheim Is Dr. No," *New York Times*, January 11, 1970; Terrence des Pres, "The Bettelheim Problem," *Social Research* 46, no. 4 (1979): 619–47; Daniel Goleman, "Bruno Bettelheim Dies at 86; Psychoanalyst of Vast Impact," *New York Times*, March 14, 1990.

230   *The collective farms of Israel's kibbutzim*: See Henry Near, *Where Community Happens: The Kibbutz and the Philosophy of Communalism* (Bern, Switzerland: Peter Lang AG, 2011); Dov Darom, "Utopia and Reality: Some Contradictions and Challenges in Kibbutz Education," *Communal Societies* 8 (1988): 67–76; John R. Snarey, "Becoming a Kibbutz Founder: An Ethnographic Study of the First All-American Kibbutz in Israel," *Jewish Social Studies* 46, no. 2 (1984): 103–30; Stephen Charles Mott, "The Kibbutz's Adjustment to Industrialization and Ideological Decline: Alternatives for Economic Organization," *Journal of Religious Ethics* 19, no. 1 (1991): 151–73; Eliezer Ben-Rafael and Sasha Weitman, "The Reconstitution of the Family in the Kibbutz," *European Journal of Sociology* 25, no. 1 (1984): 1–27; Erich Schanze, "The Israeli Kibbutz as a Socialist Model: Comment," *Journal of Institutional and Theoretical Economics* 148, no. 1 (1992): 190–94.

231   *a black utopian settlement inspired by the kibbutz*: Martin Gelman, "Adat Beyt Moshe—The Colored House of Moses: A Study of the Contemporary Negro Religious Community and Its Leader" (PhD diss., University of Pennsylvania, 1965). See also Emma Mai Ewing, "Black Jews Find a Haven in State," *New York Times*, April 9, 1978; "Kibbutz-Like New Jersey Community Is Home to Black Jewish Congregation," *Washington Post*, March 2, 1979; Sophie Panzer, "Rabbi Abel Respes Spent Lifetime Urging Jews of Color to Discover Their Roots," *Jewish Exponent*, February 17, 2021.

231   *their spiritual homeland*: On the Black Hebrews of Dimona, Israel, see Janice Wendi Fernheimer, "The Rhetoric of Black Jewish Identity Construction in America and Israel: 1964–1972" (PhD diss., University of Texas, Austin, 2006); Morris Lounds, *Israel's Black Hebrews: Black Americans in Search of Identity* (Washington, D.C.: University Press of America, 1981); Martina Könighofer, *The New Ship of Zion: Dynamic Diaspora Dimensions of the African Hebrew Israelites of Jerusalem* (Münster, Germany: LIT Verlag, 2008); Michael T. Miller, "Black Judaism(s) and the Hebrew Israelites," *Religion Compass* 13, no. 11 (2019).

231   *amid Israel's conflicts with Arab countries*: Michael Fischbach, *Black Power and Palestine: Transnational Countries of Color* (Redwood City, CA: Stanford University Press, 2018).

231   *a similar kibbutz tour in 1966*: Ibid., 79.

231   *a delegation of black journalists*: Dick Edwards, "Kibbutzim—Togetherness (Black Man in Israel)," *New York Amsterdam News*, February 7, 1970; "Black Columnist Back from Israel Reports Favorable Impression," *Jewish Telegraphic Agency*, January 27, 1970.

232   *depopulated and razed Arab villages*: Noga Kadman, *Erased from Space and Consciousness: Israel and the Depopulated Palestinian Villages of 1948* (Bloomington: Indiana University Press, 2015).

232   *white Jews with European ancestry*: Albert Cleage, Jr., "The Crisis in the Middle East: Whose Side Is God On?," 1967, Box 4, Church Policy, Albert B. Cleage Jr. Papers.

232   *"the Palestinian people's struggle for national liberation"*: Committee of Black Americans for Truth About the Middle East, "An Appeal by Black Americans Against United States Support for the Zionist Government of Israel," *New York Times*, November 1, 1970. See also Annalisa Jabaily, "1967: How Estrangement and Alliances Between Blacks, Jews, and Arabs Shaped a Generation of Civil Rights Family Values," *Minnesota Journal of Law & Inequality* 23, no. 1 (2005): 197–237.

233   *living arrangements for children*: Sharone L. Maital and Marc H. Bornstein, "The Ecology of Collaborative Child Rearing: A Systems Approach to Child Care on the Kibbutz," *Ethos* 31, no. 2 (2003): 274–306; Mordechai Benyakar, Rina A. Kretsch, and Merav Gurevitch, "The Disintegrative Factor in Therapeutic Groups as Illuminated by Kibbutz Life," *Group* 21, no.

1 (1997): 47–59; Christopher Warhurst, "High Society in a Worker's Society: Work, Community and Kibbutz," *Sociology* 30, no. 1 (1996).

233 *"how do you develop children to sustain Israel?"*: For more on the relationship between African American youth and the kibbutzim, see Donna Britt, "Pretense Is Pulled Away on a Kibbutz," *Washington Post*, April 30, 1993; Vincent Singleton, dir., *Taking Israel: A Journey of African American Students* (Xenia, OH: Ammak Productions, 2016); Madeleine Ali, dir., *Black to the Promised Land* (Midbar Films, 1991); Erin J. Aubry, "Latino, Black Students to Try Life on Israeli Kibbutz," *Los Angeles Times*, March 26, 1994; Tom Hundley, "Cha Residents Search for Insight—in a Kibbutz," *Chicago Tribune*, October 22, 1991; Jackie Headapohl, "African American Students Take in All Sides of Israel," *Detroit Jewish News*, July 19, 2017.

233 *the houseparent crooned*: Cardinal Monifa Imarogbe, "History of the Youth Program," n.d., Box 4, Alkebu-lan Academy and Nursery, Albert B. Cleage Jr. Papers.

234 *inferior educations*: Danton Wilson, "A Grassroots Effort to Change Community," *Michigan Chronicle*, October 22, 1983.

235 *kinship clans of the kibbutzim*: Ben-Rafael and Weitman, "The Reconstitution of the Family," 5.

235 hevruta: Near, *Where Community Happens*, 17.

235 hovat hagshama: Ibid., 7.

Letter IV: Prodigal Son

241 the destruction of others: João Helion Costa Vargas, *Never Meant to Survive: Genocide and Utopia in Black Diaspora Communities* (New York: Rowman & Littlefield, 2008), x, xii: "Anti-Black genocide generates the imperatives of liberation and revolution [. . .] If We were never meant to survive, then We must destroy the conditions under which this statement continues to be true and invent alternative realities."

The Prison Letters of Dorian Robertson Are Missing

247 *The residents of Meadow Villages*: Margo Jefferson, *Negroland: A Memoir* (New York: Vintage, 2016). This book was one of the many starting points for my own: "In Negroland we thought of ourselves as the Third Race, poised between the masses of Negroes and all classes of Caucasians. Like the Third Eye, the Third Race possessed a wisdom, intuition, and enlightened knowledge the other two races lacked. Its members had education, ambition, sophistication, and standardized verbal dexterity."

252 *the crumpled Kodak picture*: Nicole Fleetwood, "Posing in Prison: Family Photographs, Practices of Belonging, and Carceral Landscapes," in *Marking Time: Art in the Age of Mass Incarceration* (Cambridge, MA: Harvard University Press, 2020), 231–54.

253 I needed to hear from you: James Baldwin, "Sonny's Blues," in *Going to Meet the Man* (New York: Dial Press, 1965).

255 *government-sponsored extermination plot*: My father read books including Jason Stanley, *How Fascism Works: The Politics of Us and Them* (New York: Random House, 2018), and Robert P. Jones, *White Too Long: The Legacy of White Supremacy in American Christianity* (New York: Simon & Schuster, 2020). His worries about a federal scheme to kill black people were stoked by Dr. Ray Hagins, of the Afrikan Village and Cultural Center in St. Louis, Missouri, who has spoken about the King Alfred Plan. For more on the fictional origins of the King Alfred Plan, see Robert E. Fleming, "The Nightmare Level of 'The Man Who Cried I Am,'" *Contemporary Literature* 14, no. 2 (1973): 186–96; Richard Hancuff, "Pan-African Pessimism: The Man Who Cried I Am and the Limits of Black Nationalism," in *Surveillance, Race, Culture*, ed. Susan Flynn and Antonia Mackay (New York: Palgrave Macmillan, 2018), 246–65; John M. Reilly, "Thinking History in The Man Who Cried I Am," *Black American Literature Forum* 21, no. 1/2 (1987): 25–42; "The King Alfred Plan & Concentration Camps," *Alternative Considerations of Jonestown & Peoples Temple*, August 20, 2014, jonestown.sdsu.edu/?page_id=60990; Merve Emre, "How a Fictional Racist Plot Made the Headlines and Revealed an American Truth" *Newyorker.com*, December 31, 2017. See also Maxine L. Montgomery, *The*

Apocalypse in African-American Fiction (Gainesville: University Press of Florida, 1996); Frank Wilderson III, *Afropessimism* (New York: W. W. Norton, 2019); Andrew Santana Kaplan, "Notes Toward (Inhabiting) the Black Messianic in Afro-Pessimism's Apocalyptic Thought," *The Comparatist* 43 (2019): 68–89.

256 *a place called Negroland*: Stephen Darby, "Negroland," YouTube video, 1:11:21, November 16, 2015.

257 *truths that others cannot see*: Stephen Finley, Margarita Guillory, and Hugh Page, Jr., eds., *Esotericism in African American Religious Experience* (Leiden: Brill, 2015).

257 *the chosenness of black people*: See "Extremist Sects Within the Black Hebrew Israelite Movement," *American Defamation League*, August 7, 2020.

257 *the "true" Jews*: Jacob S. Dorman, *Chosen People: The Rise of American Black Israelite Religions* (New York: Oxford University Press, 2013); Fran Markowitz, "Israel as Africa, Africa as Israel: 'Divine Geography' in the Personal Narratives and Community Identity of the Black Hebrew Israelites," *Anthropological Quarterly* 69, no. 4 (1996): 193–205; Alan James, "Cult-Induced Renunciation of United States Citizenship: The Involuntary Expatriation of Black Hebrews," *San Diego Law Review* 28, no. 3 (1991): 645–69; Howard Brotz, *The Black Jews of Harlem: Negro Nationalism and the Dilemmas of Negro Leadership* (New York: The Free Press of Glencoe, 1964).

258 *original "Asiatic" black man*: Marjorie Corbman, "The Creation of the Devil and the End of the White Man's Rule: The Theological Influence of the Nation of Islam on Early Black Theology," *Religions* 11, no. 6 (2020).

258 *they were themselves gods*: R. Drew Smith, "Black Religious Nationalism and the Politics of Transcendence," *Journal of the American Academy of Religion* 66, no. 3 (1998): 533–47; Biko Gray, "The Traumatic Mysticism of Othered Others: Blackness, Islam, and Esotericism in the Five Percenters," *Correspondences* 7, no. 1 (2019): 201–37.

An Armful of Beautiful Roses

259 *the rise of the black model*: "Have Black Models Really Made It?" *Ebony*, May 1970. See also Alex Vadukul, "'We Fascinated Them': Shailah Edmonds on a Golden Era of Black Models," *New York Times*, June 14, 2020.

260 *"She'll knock 'em dead"*: Jennifer Jarratt, "Rose Waldon, Model," *Detroit Free Press*, January 19, 1969.

261 *the Longacre was no settlement house*: Anne-Marie Schiro, "For Women, Safe Places to Stay," *New York Times*, November 7, 1982; "Roomers with View," *Daily News*, August 10, 1984.

A Place Flowing with Milk and Honey

266 *the French Revolution*: Cleage greatly admired the enlightened rebels and architects of the French Revolution. He also took inspiration from one particular Frenchman, the philosopher and abolitionist C. F. Volney, author of *The Ruins, or, A Survey of the Revolutions of Empires* (London: printed for J. Johnson, 1792). *The Ruins* was a touchstone for freethinkers, rationalists, and other nonconformists throughout the eighteenth and nineteenth centuries. In it, Volney analyzes world religions, the decline of ancient civilizations, and the corruption of the Christian church, among other subjects. For some late-twentieth-century Pan-Africanists, the text has been most significant for Volney's discussion of ancient Ethiopia. He attributes to this "black" nation significant civilizational contributions: "'The Ethiopians,' says Lucian, 'were the first who invented the science of the stars, and gave names to the planets, not at random and without meaning, but descriptive of the qualities which they conceived them to possess; and it was from them that this art passed, still in an imperfect state, to the Egyptians.' It would be easy to multiply citations upon this subject; from all which it follows, that we have the strongest reasons to believe that the country neighboring to the tropic was the cradle of the sciences, and of consequence that the first learned nation was a nation of Blacks; for it is incontrovertible, that, by the term Ethiopians, the ancients meant to represent a

people of black complexion, thick lips, and woolly hair. I am therefore inclined to believe, that the inhabitants of Lower Egypt were originally a foreign colony imported from Syria and Arabia, a medley of different tribes of savages, originally shepherds and fishermen, who, by degrees formed themselves into a nation, and who, by nature and descent, were enemies of the Thebans, by whom they were no doubt despised and treated as barbarians. I have suggested the same ideas in my *Travels into Syria*, founded upon the black complexion of the Sphinx."

268 *28,700 farms*: U.S. Department of Agriculture, National Agricultural Statistics Service, *2022 Census of Agriculture*, February 13, 2024, https://nass.usda.gov/Publications/AgCensus/2022 /index.php#full_report..

268 *much of its land was eventually sold*: Priscilla McCutcheon, "'Returning Home to Our Rightful Place': The Nation of Islam and Muhammad Farms," *Geoforum* 49 (2013): 61–70.

268 *the model of the* moshav ovdim: Robert Swann and Shimon Gottschalk, "Planning a Rural New Town in Southwest Georgia," Schumacher Center for New Economics, October 1970; John Emmeus Davis, "Origins and Evolution of the Community Land Trust in the United States" (Cambridge, MA: Lincoln Institute of Land Policy, 2010).

269 *Soul City*: Thomas Healy, *Soul City: Race, Equality, and the Lost Dream of an American Utopia* (New York: Metropolitan Books, 2021). See also Makaveli Gresham, "Two Black Utopias of the United States: Self Determination and Survival" (undergraduate thesis, Portland State University, 2020).

269 *black poverty in the cities*: See also Sidney Walton, Jr., "Geographic Proposals for Black Economic Liberation," *The Black Scholar* 3, no. 6 (1972): 38–48.

270 *"every black ghetto across the country"*: Albert Cleage, Jr., "Reverend Albert B. Cleage Jr. Discusses His Book 'The Black Messiah,'" interview by Studs Terkel, WFMT, 1967, studs terkel.wfmt.com/programs/reverend-albert-b-cleage-jr-discusses-his-book-black-messiah?t =NaN%2CNaN&a=%2C.

271 *agricultural, technical, and manufacturing*: Albert Cleage, Jr., "End of an Era: We Are the Messianic Hope of the Twentieth Century," December 25, 1977, Box 1, Sermons, 1977, Albert B. Cleage Jr. Papers.

271 *"the wholesaler? the trucker?"*: Cleage, *Black Christian Nationalism*, 49.

272 *"identified with it geographically"*: Ibid., 203.

272 *"distribute the food that Black people grow"*: Ibid., 231.

274 *South Carolina's upcountry*: For more on South Carolina's important role in the cotton industry, see Sven Beckert, *Empire of Cotton: A Global History* (New York: Vintage, 2015), 100–105, 280–92. See also Willie Lee Rose, *Rehearsal for Reconstruction: The Port Royal Experiment* (New York: Bobbs-Merrill, 1964).

275 *one of the most acclaimed cattle farms*: Orville K. Sweet, *Birth of a Breed: The History of Polled Herefords—America's First Beef Breed* (Kansas City, MO: Lowell Press, 1975); "Neil Trask Sees Bright Future for Beef Cattle Industry in This State," *Beaufort Gazette*, July 5, 1946; "Trask Will Join Cattle Group's Shrine," *Index-Journal*, November 12, 1975.

275 *The court battle's legal expenses*: *Wright v. Trask*, 329 S.C. 170, 495 S.E.2d 222m (1997).

275 *"Niggers don't own the land, they work the land"*: D. Kimathi Nelson, interview with author.

275 *the church acquired its first 1,000 acres*: "Church to Buy Land for Farm Community," *The Atlanta Voice*, June 5, 1999.

The World System

276 *The Shrine was preparing for Y2K*: Bruce Kratofil and Keith Burbank, "The Impact of the Y2K Bug," *Business Economics* 34, no. 1 (1999): 39–43; Andrea Hoplight Tapia, "Y2K: Apocalyptic Opportunism," *Enculturation* 3, no. 1 (2000).

277 *slipped away into the night*: Cleage's concerns about the anti-black violence that Y2K might precipitate stemmed from more than just Devil's Night or the 1967 rebellion. In the struggles of Cleage's friend Charles Koen, leader of the United Front of Cairo, Illinois, and briefly the

"secretary of political action" for the Black Christian Nationalist movement, the reverend glimpsed one possible outcome for urban blacks if they should ever find themselves trapped in a city terrorized by police and white vigilantes. As executive director of the United Front in 1969 and 1970, Koen led a multiyear boycott of white businesses in Cairo that refused to hire blacks. In 1967, the death of a nineteen-year-old black soldier on leave, Robert Hunt, who had supposedly killed himself in a jail cell following his arrest for disorderly conduct, tipped the segregated town into years of violence. The situation in Cairo reminded many black people around the country of the discontent that had led to the Montgomery bus boycott, and the efforts of groups such as the United Front gained support even as the situation there was devolving into a siege. At the 1970 Black Christian Nationalist convention, Koen appeared at the Shrine to give "reports from the Cairo battlefront." That fall, the Shrine launched a monthlong fundraising drive to aid blacks in Cairo, which the *Michigan Chronicle* described as the "racial battleground of the north." Teenagers in the BCN student movement solicited cash and sold "Save Cairo" buttons, as well as recordings of Koen's speeches. By the time of the Shrine's "Save Cairo" rally that November, Cairo had long since become the site of open racial warfare. A white vigilante group known as the White Hats, the formation of which had prompted the creation of the United Front, was ordered to disband by the Illinois state assembly to no avail. Houses were bombed, sending black people onto the streets. Memories of the 1909 lynching of Will "Froggy" James, a black man convicted of raping and murdering a white shop clerk in Cairo, resurfaced. The former riverside boom town that had once been a stop along the Underground Railroad was gutted as businesses failed and the city's population shrank. See "Cairo Violence Intensifies, Local Aid Drive Continues," *Michigan Chronicle*, December 19, 1970; "Slate Drive to Aid Cairo Blacks," *Michigan Chronicle*, October 24, 1970. For an account of the devastating violence in Cairo, see Hinton, "The Vigilantes," in *America on Fire*, 70–93.

277   *"what groups might try to off us"*: Shrine member letter to Major Kay, September 10, 1999, Box 8, Y2K, Albert B. Cleage Jr. Papers.

277   *"undergirts [sic] the World System"*: "BCN National Training Center Y2K Preparedness Strategy and Implementation Plan," 1999, Box 8, Y2K, Albert B. Cleage Jr. Papers.

277   *a network of institutions*: Christopher Chase-Dunn and Richard Rubinson, "Toward a Structural Perspective on the World-System," *Politics & Society* 7, no. 4 (1977): 453–76; Andre Gunder Frank and Barry K. Gills, eds., *The World System: Five Hundred Years or Five Thousand?* (Abingdon, UK: Routledge, 1994); George E. Marcus, "Ethnography in/of the World System: The Emergence of Multi-Sited Ethnography," *Annual Review of Anthropology* 24 (1995): 95–117; Cedric Robinson, "C. L. R. James and the World-System," *Race & Class* 34, no. 2 (1992): 49–62; Yousuf Al-Bulushi, "Thinking Racial Capitalism and Black Radicalism from Africa: An Intellectual Geography of Cedric Robinson's World-System," *Geoforum* 132 (2022): 252–62.

278   *"we must build a System of our own"*: "BCN Ideology, Draft #4," February 12, 1981, Box 5, Rituals, Communalism Rituals, 1982, Albert B. Cleage Jr. Papers.

278   *MOVE's methods for rejecting the world system*: Richard Kent Evans, *MOVE: An American Religion* (New York: Oxford University Press, 2020). For more on MOVE, see Morgan Shipley and Jack Taylor, "Life as Eutopia: MOVE's Natural Revolution as a Response to America's Dystopian Reality," *Utopian Studies* 30, no. 1 (2019): 25–44; Robin Wagner-Pacifici, *Discourse and Destruction: The City of Philadelphia Versus MOVE* (Chicago: University of Chicago Press, 1994); Michael Boyette and Randi Boyette, *Let It Burn: MOVE, the Philadelphia Police Department, and the Confrontation That Changed a City* (San Diego: Quadrant Books, 1989); Onyekachi Joi Ekeogu, "'MOVE People Are Used to This': The MOVE Organization, Media Representations, and Resistance During pre-MOVE-Philadelphia Conflict Years" (master's thesis, Arizona State University, 2014).

278   *radical environmentalist stances*: Gillian Moise, "MOVEing Beyond Anti-State to Anti-Civ: Black Lives Matter and the MOVE Organization Through the Critical Environmental Justice

Lens," *Environmental Justice* 15, no. 1 (2022): 58–64; Anthony T. Fiscella, "Forgotten Pioneers in Degrowth: John Africa and the MOVE Organization," *Journal of Political Ecology* 29, no. 1 (2022): 405–29.

279 *spaces that could exist as shrines*: Tina Campt, "Constellations of Freedom: Assembly, Reflection, and Repose," in *In Search of African American Space: Redressing Racism*, ed. Jeffrey Hogrefe et al. (Baden, Switzerland: Lars Müller Publishers, 2020), 12–18.

279 *purchase former slave plantations*: See Sydney Nathans, *A Mind to Stay: White Plantation, Black Homeland* (Cambridge, MA: Harvard University Press, 2017).

280 *food sovereignty movements*: Dona Brown, *Back to the Land: The Enduring Dream of Self-Sufficiency in Modern America* (Madison: University of Wisconsin Press, 2011); Monica M. White, *Freedom Farmers: Agricultural Resistance and the Black Freedom Movement* (Chapel Hill: University of North Carolina Press, 2018); Hanna Garth and Ashanté M. Reese, eds., *Black Food Matters: Racial Justice in the Wake of Food Justice* (Minneapolis: University of Minnesota Press, 2020); Leah Penniman, *Farming While Black: Soul Fire Farm's Practical Guide to Liberation on the Land* (White River Junction, VT: Chelsea Green Publishing, 2018); Jade Aguilar, "Food Choices and Voluntary Simplicity in Intentional Communities: What's Race and Class Got to Do with It?" *Utopian Studies* 26, no. 1 (2015): 79–100.

280 *"less time to finish the Y2K preparation"*: Letter about Y2K from Command Council, December 10, 1999, Box 8, Church Leaders, Kokayi Enharo (Carl Ware) files, Albert B. Cleage Jr. Papers.

281 *forgot to purchase gifts for the children*: Andou Allen, interview with author.

281 *"some Jim Jones stuff!"*: The Nahziryah Monastic Community, sometimes referred to as "the Purple People," is a black communal group whose isolation was prompted, in part, by fears about Y2K. Abusive practices within the Nahziryah community have been documented in recent years. See Jacqueline Froelich, "Reclusive Ozarks Commune Operates Under Veil of Violence," National Public Radio, KUAF, February 26, 2018; "Refugees from an Ozarks Cult Detail Abuse," *Arkansas Times*, April 1, 2019; Margarita Simon Guillory and Aundrea Matthews, "Portraying Portraits: The Intersectionality of Self, Art, and the Lacanian Gaze in the Nahziryah Monastic Community," in *Esotericism in African American Religious Experience*, 262–76; Thomas Michael Kersen, *Where Misfits Fit: Counterculture and Influence in the Ozarks* (Jackson: University Press of Mississippi, 2021), 87–102.

282 *a hub for white nationalist groups*: Vic MacDonald, "Abbeville County Getting Attention for Wrong Reasons," *Index-Journal*, June 17, 2006.

282 *"antigovernment extremists"*: Bob Moser, "'Patriot' Shootout in Abbeville, S.C., Raises Questions About the Town's Extremist Past," *Intelligence Report*, April 20, 2004.

282 *fraternal coexistence*: Andrew Seegars, interview with author.

A Model Community

284 *the Imani Temple*: Laura Parker, "Breakaway Priest Discusses His Rift with Roman Catholic Church," *Detroit Free Press*, August 6, 1995; Glen Elsasser, "Renegade Priest: African-Catholic Church Alive and Kicking," *Detroit Free Press*, March 24, 1995.

290 *sold to meet the mortgage*: "The Beulah Land Story: The National Farm Project of the Shrine of the Black Madonna of the Pan African Orthodox Christian Church," n.d., *The Year of Restoration*, theyearofrestoration.org/the-beulah-land-storyhtml.

290 *"model independent Black community"*: "National Board of Pastor's Beulah Land Survey," n.d., *The Year of Restoration*, theyearofrestoration.org/beulah-land.

290 *land loss and economic instability*: Phyliss Craig-Taylor, "African-American Farmers and the Fight for Survival: The Continuing Examination for Insights into the Historical Genesis of this Dilemma," *North Carolina Central Law Review* 26, no. 1 (2003): 21–37; Nadra Nittle, "Black-Owned Farms Are Holding on by a Thread," *Eater*, February 23, 2021, eater.com /22291510/black-farmers-fighting-for-farmland-discrimination-in-agriculture; Pete Daniels, *Dispossession: Discrimination Against African American Farmers in the Age of Jim Crow* (Chapel

Hill: University of North Carolina Press, 2015); Nathan Rosenberg and Bryce Wilson Stucki, "How USDA Distorted Data to Conceal Decades of Discrimination Against Black Farmers," *The Counter*, June 26, 2019; Thomas W. Mitchell, "Destabilizing the Normalization of Rural Black Land Loss: A Critical Role for Legal Empiricism," *Wisconsin Law Review* 557 (2005): 557–615.

291   Pigford v. Glickman: Dorceta E. Taylor, "Black Farmers in the USA and Michigan: Longevity, Empowerment, and Food Sovereignty," *Journal of African American Studies* 22 (2018): 49–76.

291   *Resora*: Shirley Sherrod, "The Struggle for the Land: A Story from America's Black Belt," *Nonprofit Quarterly*, February 18, 2020, nonprofitquarterly.org/the-struggle-for-the-land-a -story-from-americas-black-belt/; Shirley Sherrod, "Civil Rights History Project Interview," interviewed by Joseph Mosnier on behalf of the Southern Oral History Program, September 15, 2011, loc.gov/item/2015669149/; Ligaya Figueras, "Agritourism Trail Spotlights Black Farms in Georgia," *The Macon Telegraph*, June 21, 2022.

291   *discriminatory against white farmers*: Alan Rappeport and Ana Swanson, "Biden Adminis-tration Ramps Up Debt Relief Program to Help Black Farmers," *New York Times*, March 25, 2021; Alan Rappeport, "Climate and Tax Bill Rewrites Embattled Black Farmer Relief Program," *New York Times*, August 12, 2022.

292   *lose either of these again*: Priscilla McCutcheon, "'Peace Be Still': Rediscovering My Spirit Through Agrarian Fieldwork," *Antipode: A Radical Journal of Geography*, 2019; Priscilla Mc-Cutcheon, "Prophetic Black Ecologies: Liberatory Agriculture on Beulah Land Farms," *Black Perspectives*, July 27, 2020; "Growing Black Food on Sacred Land: Using Black Liberation Theology to Imagine an Alternative Black Agrarian Future," *Environment and Planning D: Society and Space* 39, no. 5 (2021): 887–905.

292   *a special council*: BIPOC Intentional Community Council, www.bipocicc.org/.

292   *oppose a capitalist world order*: See the examples of Tender Care Farm (Boulder, CO), est. 2022; Stellar Roots Cooperative (Amherst, VA), est. 2020; Sovereign Earth Works (Wash-ington, DC), est. 2021; Sankofa Village (Little Rock, AR), est. 2022; MoonSeed Collective (Louisa County, VA); Grandmothers Village Project (Randolph, MA); SUSU commUNITY (Newfane, VT), est. 2020. See also Danielle M. Purifoy and Jade Wilson, "'To Live and Thrive on New Earths,'" *Southern Cultures* 26, no. 4 (2020): 78–89.

293   *a solar farm*: D. Kimathi Nelson, interview with author.

Shrines

296   *formal religious affiliation*: Pew Research Center, "In U.S., Decline of Christianity Contin-ues at Rapid Pace," *Pew Research Center*, October 17, 2019; Jeffrey M. Jones, "U.S. Church Membership Falls Below Majority for First Time," *Pew Research Center*, March 29, 2021; Pew Research Center, "Modeling the Future of Religion in America," *Pew Research Center*, September 13, 2022.

296   *Sok's eventual rise in the church*: Akindele Akinyemi, "Brother Osakwe," *Akindele Unleashed*, July 16, 2006, onedetroitnetwork.blogspot.com/2006/07/brother-osakwe-by-akindele -akinyemi.html.

298   *"soul force"*: Albert Cleage, Jr., "The Revolutionary Mysticism of Jesus," October 1, 1978, Box 1, Sermons, 1978, Albert B. Cleage Jr. Papers. See also V. Geetha, ed., *Soul Force: Gandhi's Writings on Peace* (Chennai, India: Tara Books, 2004); Martin Luther King, Jr., letter to Chester Bowles, October 28, 1957, Group 628, Box 142, Chester Bowles Collection, Yale University, Beinecke Rare Book and Manuscript Library, New Haven, CT.

303   *"If it was my child"*: Alexis Pauline Gumbs, China Martens, and Mai'a Williams, eds., *Revo-lutionary Mothering: Love on the Front Lines* (Binghamton, NY: PM Press, 2016).

303   *revolutionary Holy Spirit*: Kelly Brown Douglas, *Resurrection Hope: A Future Where Black Lives Matter* (Maryknoll, NY: Orbis Books, 2021); Kelly Brown Douglas, *Stand Your Ground: Black Bodies and the Justice of God* (Maryknoll, NY: Orbis Books, 2015).

303 *disarm the slave culture*: Keeanga-Yamahtta Taylor, *From #BlackLivesMatter to Black Liberation* (Chicago: Haymarket Books, 2016).

304 *purifying phase of history*: Rachel Kaadzi Ghansah, "A Most American Terrorist: The Making of Dylann Roof," *GQ*, August 21, 2017.

304 *through violence if necessary*: See Philip S. Gorski and Samuel L. Perry, *The Flag and the Cross: White Christian Nationalism and the Threat to American Democracy* (New York: Oxford University Press, 2022); Public Religion Research Institute and Brookings Institution, "A Christian Nation?: Understanding the Threat of Christian Nationalism to American Democracy and Culture: Findings from the 2023 PRRI/Brookings Christian Nationalism Survey," February 8, 2023; Gregory A. Smith, Michael Rotolo, and Patricia Tevington, "45% of Americans Say U.S. Should Be a Christian Nation," Pew Research Center, October 27, 2022; Kevin J. Burke, Mary Juzwik, and Esther Prins, "White Christian Nationalism: What Is It, and Why Does It Matter for Educational Research?" *Educational Researcher* 52, no. 5 (2023): 286–95; Adam Russell Taylor, "Do We Dare to Disciple People Out of Christian Nationalism?" *Sojourners*, October 13, 2022; Bob Smietana, "Who Are the Christian Nationalists? A Taxonomy for the Post-Jan. 6 World," Pulitzer Center, January 6, 2023. For contrasts between Black Christian Nationalism and the far-right Christian Identity movement, see Craig R. Prentiss, "Coloring Jesus: Racial Calculus and the Search for Identity in Twentieth-Century America," *Nova Religio: The Journal of Alternative and Emergent Religions* 11, no. 3 (2008): 64–82.

304 *sympathized with the goals of white Christian nationalism*: Baptist Joint Committee for Religious Liberty/Freedom From Religion Foundation, "Christian Nationalism and the January 6, 2021, Insurrection," February 9, 2022, bjconline.org/jan6report/.

305 *"rooted in our founding principles"*: The President's Advisory 1776 Commission, "The 1776 Report," January 18, 2021, trumpwhitehouse.archives.gov/briefings-statements/1776 -commission-takes-historic-scholarly-step-restore-understanding-greatness-american -founding/?utm_source=link.

306 *preludes to an apocalypse*: See Francisco G. Mendoza III, "The End of the World According to Q," *PANDION: The Osprey Journal of Research and Ideas* 2, no. 1 (2021): 1–15.

306 *the Black Christian Nationalists embodied*: For more on the concept of embodied or lived theology, consult the resources of the Project on Lived Theology (livedtheology.org). See also Kelly Brown Douglas and Liz Theoharis, "In This Kairos Time, Will We Embody Church?" *Sojourners*, March 26, 2020; Stacy Johnson, "Teaching a Living Theology," *Sojourners*, November–December 1998.

The Cumberland

308 *garbage and weeds*: Ruha Benjamin, *Viral Justice: How We Grow the World We Want* (Princeton: Princeton University Press, 2022).

308 *present-day currents in black utopian thought*: Pamela Lightsey, "He Is Black and We Are Queer: The Legacy of the Black Messiah for Black LGBTQ Christians," in *Albert Cleage Jr. and the Black Madonna and Child*, 251–68; Ashon Crawley, *Blackpentecostal Breath: The Aesthetics of Possibility* (New York: Fordham University Press, 2016); Ashon Crawley and Roberto Sirvent, eds., *Spirituality and Abolition* (Philadelphia: Common Notions, 2023); Maya Bhardwaj, "Embodying Transnational Queer Black and Brown Utopia in Alternative QTPOC Nightlife Spaces," *Agenda* 36, no. 3 (2022): 122–37; Shaka McGlotten, "Ordinary Intersections: Speculations on Difference, Justice, and Utopia in Black Queer Life," *Transforming Anthropology* 20, no. 1 (2012): 45–66; Kimberly Drew and Jenna Wortham, eds., *Black Futures* (New York: One World, 2020); José Esteban Muñoz, "Cruising the Toilet: LeRoi Jones/Amiri Baraka, Radical Black Traditions, and Queer Futurity," in *Cruising Utopia: The Then and Now of Queer Futurity* (New York: New York University Press, 2009); adrienne maree brown, *Pleasure Activism: The Politics of Feeling Good* (Chico, CA: AK Press, 2019); Shira Hassan, *Saving Our Own Lives: A Liberatory Practice of Harm Reduction* (Chicago: Haymarket Books, 2022).

308   *global struggle for the commons*: Elandria Williams and Mabrouka M'Barek, "From Self-Determination to Community-Determination: Black-Led Commons in the United States," in *Cities of Dignity: Urban Transformations Around the World*, ed. Mabrouka M'Barek et al. (Brussels: Rosa-Luxemburg-Stiftung, 2020), 132–79.

308   *sacrosanct nature of black lives*: Dori J. Maynard, "Shrine's Madonna Stands as Symbol of Black Power, Struggle," *Detroit Free Press*, June 3, 1990.

310   *"the kind of existence God intended men to have"*: For an alternative quotation, see Albert Cleage, Jr., "Self-Determination and Accountability," *Michigan Chronicle*, January 13, 1968: "We know that the Promised Land isn't any certain place. It is a state of mind. It is a determination."

Acknowledgments

Although this book had many starting points, it is impossible to imagine it absent the stewardship of my friends and editors at *The Point* magazine. My thanks to Jon Baskin and Rachel Wiseman for shepherding my early essays on Black Christian Nationalism ("It Was More Than a Notion") and the Maccabees ("Attack the Block") in 2020. Then-contributing editors Carina del Valle Schorske, Robert L. Kehoe III, and Jesse McCarthy asked valuable, clarifying questions. My August 2021 conversation with *Point* contributor Elisa Gonzales and *Plough* magazine editor Phil Christman (the event was titled "Seeing Each Other's Souls: Integration, Justice, and the Christian Imagination") helped me work through rudimentary thoughts on interracialism, integration, and the contemporary Christian church.

To this day, I am stunned by how swiftly my agent, Julia Eagleton, contacted me after the *Point* essays were published. Thank goodness she asked what my writing goals were, incentivizing me to think of some. Julia's sharp editorial suggestions broadened my sense of what this book could be.

Julia steered this project to my dream publisher, Farrar, Straus and Giroux. My editors, Alex Star, Ian Van Wye, and Julia Ringo, were exceedingly patient and smart. In the United Kingdom, I found a supportive partner in Chatto and Windus. Thank you to Greg Clowes, who brought my project there, publishing director Clara Farmer, and editor Kaiya Shang. I'm grateful to the art, publicity, and marketing teams at these houses, and for the spectacular advocacy of my publicist, Whitney Peeling.

Thanks to the Robert B. Silvers Foundation for supporting my research on Beulah Land, and to the Lewis Center for the Arts at Princeton University for the Mary MacKall Gwinn Hodder Fund grant. Those pandemic-era Hodder Fund grants were awarded to encourage early-career artists to keep going in a difficult time.

At Stanford University, the manuscript workshop through the McCoy Family Center for Ethics in Society was an invaluable experience at a late stage in my editing process. Thanks to the brilliant graduate students, professors, and administrators who devoted so much care to my work: Michelle Wilde Anderson, James Campbell, Valerie Soon, Jackie Hwang, Marci Kwon, Mark Greif, Destin Jenkins, Collin Anthony Chen, Christian Greer, Benoit Monin, Rob Reich, Wendy Salkin, Alexis Wells-Oghoghomeh, Joan Berry, and Ashlyn Jaeger.

In the fall of 2021, when I was finally able to access archives in person, the first place I visited was the Bentley Historical Library (University of Michigan) in Ann Arbor, Michigan. I would like to thank Diana Bachman, Sarah McLusky, and Caitlin Moriarty for making it so easy to browse the Albert B. Cleage Jr. Papers. At the Walter P. Reuther Library at Wayne State University, Kristen Chinery kindly assisted me with the Edward Vaughn Papers. I'd like to thank Kathy Shoemaker, the reference coordinator for the Stuart A. Rose Manuscript, Archives, and Rare Book Library at Emory University, for facilitating my access to the Pearl Cleage Papers. The graduate student Richard Parnell photographed documents that unlocked some of the Cleage family history for me.

Some of the most important conversations I had for this book were with people who probably don't know how much they meant to it. I am thinking of the former League of Revolutionary Black Workers member Charles Simmons, the filmmaker Mats Hjelm, the historians Nishani Frazier and Paul Tennassee, and the founders of *The Fifth*

Estate—Harvey Ovshinsky, Peter Werbe, and Frank Joyce. All these people enriched my understanding of left internationalism and coalition building in the 1960s and '70s.

Kristin Cleage's *Finding Eliza* blog is unquestionably the most comprehensive and accessible source on the Cleage family history. This would have been a very different book without it.

My thanks to Kira Josefsson for her crucial translations of the Swedish pamphlet for Glanton Dowdell's political asylum campaign, as well as news articles from *Dagens Nyheter*. Kira's brother Linus generously visited the Lund University Library to scan pages from one of two copies of *Political Asylum for Glanton Dowdell* available in the Swedish library system.

Without Glanton's family members—Stacy McIntyre, Lindiwe Richardson, Leslie Pursche, Anna Simoni, and Kimberly Dowdell—I wouldn't have had much of a story to tell about him. Stacy, Lindiwe, and Leslie's stories about their lives in Sweden anchored Glanton's life in the beautifully mundane, making him a little less of a mythic folk hero. Stacy, an artist herself, provided the striking paintings included throughout the book (except for her father's self-portrait, *Southeast Corner of My Cell*). I'd like to thank Glanton's daughter Anna Simoni for passing along her father's memoir and connecting me with the late Tryggve Hedtjärn, who eagerly shared the details of his relationship with Glanton.

I'm grateful to the labor historian David Goldberg for sharing essential documents related to Glanton and the Collingwood Apartments murders, as well as back issues of *The Illustrated News*.

My thanks to each of my early readers for their insights and suggestions: Lyman Tower Sargent—whose contributions to the field of utopian studies are immeasurable—and my friends Zachary Fine, Brianna Zimmerman, Claire Ashmead, and Molly Montgomery. Their feedback transformed this book in radical ways. They encouraged me to stop hiding in history so much and offer a little more of myself.

It took a nation to write this book. I was constantly surprised by the stories my relatives told me. Thank you to the Robertsons (Bettie,

Dorian, Birdie, Hubert, Ethel, Natalie), Harry and Yolanda Zellars, Serina Gilbert, and James Staples.

My mother, Cindy Staples, has been the backbone of my endeavors from the beginning. Her unquestioning support of my aspirations enabled me to pursue a life in the arts without shame.

I would like to believe that the spirit of every friend and member of the Shrine I spoke to made this story what it is. Thank you to: Mbiyu Chui, Wesley Godfrey, Sandra Ramsey, Malaika Jabali, Masai May, Nan Moore, Linda Patton, Sentwali Oslohouah, Malik Ware, Italo Johnson, Sharifa Jones, Pat Brown, Terry Collins, Talibah Garnett, Adesola Holmes, Mary Blackmon, Kefentse Chike, Kenya Rivers, Malika Jackson, Makini Jackson, Jamar Walker, Diana Stewart, Kandia Milton, Roger Short, Lumumba Seegars, Zuberi Chui-Moore, Kambui Chui-Moore, Nomsa N'Hau, Migozo Taylor, Isoke Nimmons, Diallo Brown, Andrew Seegars, Amina Seegars, Ryan Pressley, Djenaba Akida, Pamela Wise, Wendell Harrison, Velma Thomas, Hanifah Hightower, Mona Morenike, Marvin Roby, Gail Carr, Melanie Roby, James Ribbron, Imara Hyman, Kenyatta Holmes, Lutalo Sanifu, Rosa Boyd, Nyasha Chui-Smith, Adisa Jones, Onitara Nelson, Anika Sala, Andou Allen, Ifetayo Brown, Rukiya Johnson, the late Barbara Rose-Collins, Rose Waldon, Edward Vaughn, Demosthene Kimathi Nelson, and Shelley McIntosh.

Index

ghettoes, 51, 52, 68, 96, 159, 178, 187, 218, 230, 270
Gilbert, Serina Kay, 20–23, 30, 33, 34
Ginzburg, Ralph, 114
Giovanni, Nikki, 177
Glasser, William, 267
God, ix, 3, 32, 52, 53, 54, 60, 61, 67, 74–75, 92, 107–108, 125, 185, 203, 240–42, 257–58, 306, 310, 311; chosen people of, 209, 258, 299, 306; as creative energy field, 222–24; see also Christ
Godfrey, Wesley, 272–75, 280
God's Trombones (Johnson), 32
Goffman, Erving, 187
GQ, 306
Grace, Charles Manuel "Sweet Daddy," 93–96, 206
Great Depression, 49–51, 59, 72, 80, 84, 94–95, 149–50, 183, 271, 274
Great Migration, 25, 54, 72, 73
Great Recession, 267, 290, 300, 302
Great Society, 177
Green, Grant, 260
Gregory, Dick, 293
Grimmett, Tamika, 181
Group on Advanced Leadership (GOAL), 100, 113, 226
group process, 185, 193
Guinea-Bissau, 220
Gurdjieff, George, 223, 224

Hagin, Kenneth, 309
Haiti, 98, 227
Ham, 125
Hampton, Fred, 155
Harlem, 61, 95, 113, 194, 271; Renaissance, 100–101, 125
Hartford Memorial Baptist Church, 175
Hartman, Saidiya, 17
Harvard University, 285
Hate That Hate Produced, The, 129
Haydon, Eustace, 74
Haywood, Harry, 69, 140
Head of an African American Woman (Artis), 122
Hedtjärn, Tryggve, 151–52, 154
Helms, Jesse, 270
Henry, Milton, see Obadele, Gaidi

Henry, Richard, see Obadele, Imari
Hercules, 286
Highland Park Community College, 336n
Hill, Joe, 156
Hilliard, Asa, III, 177
Hiroshima bombing, 79
Histadrut, 231
Hitler, Adolf, 186
Hjelm, Lars, 337n
Hjelm, Mats, 337n
Hoffer, Eric, 186, 187
Holland, Sue, 223
Holy Order of Nehemiah, 195
Holy Order of Nzinga, 195–96, 216
Hosea, 96
House Un-American Activities Committee, 100, 217
housing, 110, 129, 132, 174, 178, 184
Housing and Urban Development, Department of (HUD), 270
Houston, TX, 11, 194, 219–20, 286, 301
Howard University, 20–21, 76
How to Eat to Live (Muhammad), 293
Huddleston, Ollie, 33
Hudson, J. L., Jr., 131, 132
Hughes, Langston, 125
Human Genome Project, 21
Hunt, Robert, 358n
Hunter, W. L., 125
hurricanes, 301
Hyman, Imara, 336n

Idlewild, MI, 49–50
Ijames, Judy, 207
Illustrated News, The, 99–104, 110, 111, 113, 114, 175, 226
Imani Temple, 284
Imarogbe, Monifa, see McIntosh, Shelley Monifa
India, 76, 221
Indianapolis Star, 45
individualism, 186, 192
Industrial Workers of the World, 156
Inkster, MI, 134
integration, 72, 73, 79, 101, 110, 111, 185; interracial church movement, 72, 77, 79; of schools, 23, 104, 111, 168–72, 174–75, 189

Dickson, 24–27; education system in, 33, 42, 44; Free Hill, 22; Nashville, 24, 25, 27; Promise Land, *see* Promise Land, TN
Tennessee Historical Commission, 17
Terkel, Studs, 270
Texas, 6, 274; Houston, 11, 194, 219–20, 286, 301
Texas Rangers, 219
Third Covenant, 195
Thoreau, Henry David, 74
Thurman, Howard, 76–79, 207
Tiger, Lionel, 267
Tillich, Paul, 74
time, 185, 228
Tisdale, Andre, 296, 297
Tisdale, Jilo, 296
Tittle, Ernest Fremont, 74
total institutions, 187, 201
totalitarianism, 186
trans and queer people, 292, 308
Transcendentalists, 74
"Transformation" (Agyeman), 243–44
Trask, Neil Webster, 274–75
True Believer, The (Hoffer), 186, 187
Trump, Donald, 305
Turner, Henry McNeal, 61
Tuskegee Institute, 272–73

Underground Church, The (Boyd, ed.), 267
Underground Railroad, 157, 358n
Undiscovered Self, The (Jung), 124
unions, 7, 50–52, 60, 65, 66, 69, 72, 78, 84, 131, 302
Union Theological Seminary, 203
United Auto Workers (UAW), 51, 84, 131
United Church of Christ, 10, 133–34
United House of Prayer, 93–94
United Nations, 140
United War Veterans for Defense of the U.S. Constitution, 171
Universal Negro Improvement Association (UNIA), 94, 183, 195, 273
University of Houston, 228
University of Mississippi, 101
University of Southern California, 78
Urban League, 47, 50, 100
USDA (U.S. Department of Agriculture), 35, 290–92

utopias, 8–9, 55, 72, 97, 183, 203, 209, 256, 304–306; Acts verses and, 215; compromises and, 113; fascist, 186; Jones and, 207; kibbutzim and, 13, 230–31; time and, 185; white supremacist, 335n; *see also* black utopianism

Vanleer, Essie, 21
Vanleer, Washington, 17, 23, 29
Van Peebles, Melvin, 177
Vaughn, Edward, 113–18; bookstore of, 114, 116, 130, 175; Detroit rebellion and, 129, 130; Dowdell and, 149, 150; Shrine cooperative enterprises led by, 183
Vietnam, Democratic Republic of, 153
Vietnam War, 128, 246; deserters from, 152–53, 156, 157; opposition to, 199
Virgil (factory worker), 59–60, 65, 69
Voice of the Black Nation, 190
Volney, C. F., 356n

Walden Two (Skinner), 186
Waldon, Bernard, 121
Waldon, Bernard "Barney," Jr., 121
Waldon, Rose Brooks, 119–23, 259–62
Walk to Freedom, 102–103, 106
Wallace, George, 110
Wall Street Journal, The, 274
Ward, Harry, 74
Ward, Hiley, 142
War in America (Obadele), 143
Warnock, Raphael, 203
Washington, Booker T., 46, 204
Washington, Grover, Jr., 260
Washington, Joseph R., Jr., 205, 349n
Watts Rebellion, 128
Wayward Lives, Beautiful Experiments (Hartman), 17
Weaver, Kitty, 229
welfare, 51
Wells, H. G., 96
West Side Human Relations Council, 49
Wheeler School, 44
When God Was a Woman (Stone), 267

Permissions Acknowledgments

Grateful acknowledgment is made for permission to reprint the following previously published and unpublished material:

Excerpts from *The Papers of Howard Washington Thurman, Vol. 3: The Bold Adventure*, edited by Walter Earl Fluker, courtesy of the University of South Carolina Press.

Excerpts from the *Finding Eliza* blog (https://findingeliza.com/) courtesy of Kristin Cleage.

Excerpts of archival materials from the Albert B. Cleage Jr. Papers courtesy of Kristin Cleage.

Translations from the Swedish of text from *Politisk asyl åt Glanton Dowdell* (Political Asylum for Glanton Dowdell) political pamphlet and *Dagens Nyheter* news articles courtesy of Kira Josefsson.

Excerpt from *American Histories*, by John Edgar Wideman, copyright © 2018 by John Edgar Wideman, reprinted with the permission of Scribner, an imprint of Simon & Schuster LLC. All rights reserved.

Excerpts from *Prophet of the Black Nation*, by Hiley H. Ward, courtesy of The Pilgrim Press. .

Excerpt from *The Black Expatriates*, by Ernest Dunbar, copyright © 1968 by Ernest Dunbar. Used by permission of Dutton, an imprint of Penguin Publishing Group, a division of Penguin Random House LLC. All rights reserved.

Illustration Credits

Pages 3, 5, 19, 40, 93, 119, 147, 188, 212, 259, 264, 295, and 312: Paintings by Stacy McIntyre, courtesy of the artist.

Pages 53, 56, 67, and 162: Photographs courtesy of Stacy McIntyre and Lindiwe Richardson.

Page 83: *Southeast Corner of My Cell*, by Glanton Dowdell, courtesy of Donnell Walker.

Pages 168 and 182: Photographs from the Albert B. Cleage Jr. Papers, courtesy of Kristin Cleage.

Pages 243 and 254: Photographs from the author's family collection, courtesy of Cindy Staples.

Pages 262 and 307: Photographs by the author.

Page 284: Photograph courtesy of Onitara Nelson.

A Note About the Author

Aaron Robertson is a writer, an editor, and a translator of Italian literature. His translation of Igiaba Scego's *Beyond Babylon* was short-listed for the 2020 PEN Translation Prize and the National Translation Award, and in 2021 he received a National Endowment for the Arts grant. He has contributed to two anthologies: *Violent Phenomena: 21 Essays on Translation* and *The Heart of a Stranger: An Anthology of Exile Literature.* His work has appeared in *The New York Times, The Nation, Foreign Policy, n+1, The Point, Literary Hub,* and elsewhere. He lives in Brooklyn, New York.